# Buddhist Moral Philosophy

The first book of its kind, *Buddhist Moral Philosophy: An Introduction* introduces the reader to contemporary philosophical interpretations and analyses of Buddhist ethics. It begins with a survey of traditional Buddhist ethical thought and practice, mainly in the Pali Canon and early Mahāyāna schools, and an account of the emergence of Buddhist moral philosophy as a distinct discipline in the modern world. It then examines recent debates about karma, rebirth and nirvana, well-being, normative ethics, moral objectivity, moral psychology, and the issue of freedom, responsibility and determinism. The book also introduces the reader to philosophical discussions of topics in socially engaged Buddhism such as human rights, war and peace, and environmental ethics.

**Christopher W. Gowans** is Professor of Philosophy at Fordham University.

D1568258

# Buddhist Moral Philosophy

## An Introduction

Christopher W. Gowans

Routledge
Taylor & Francis Group

NEW YORK AND LONDON

First published 2015
by Routledge
711 Third Avenue, New York, NY 10017

and by Routledge
2 Park Square, Milton Park, Abingdon, Oxon, OX14 4RN

*Routledge is an imprint of the Taylor & Francis Group, an informa business*

*Library of Congress Cataloging-in-Publication Data*

Library of Congress Control Number: 2014942959

ISBN: 978-0-415-89066-3 (hbk)
ISBN: 978-0-415-89067-0 (pbk)
ISBN: 978-1-315-76607-2 (ebk)

Typeset in Times New Roman
by Apex CoVantage, LLC

For

Hannah Sophie Gowans

and

Gabrielle Ji Xiang Gowans

# Contents

# Abbreviations

*AN The Numerical Discourses of the Buddha: A Translation of the Aṅguttara Nikāya,* translated by Bhikkhu Bodhi, Boston: Wisdom Publications, 2012.

*BCA* Śāntideva, *The Bodhicaryāvatāra,* translated by Kate Crosby and Andrew Skilton, Oxford: Oxford University Press, 1995.

*DN The Long Discourses of the Buddha: A Translation of the Dīgha Nikāya,* translated by Maurice Walshe, Boston: Wisdom Publications, 1987.

*MN The Middle Length Discourses of the Buddha: A New Translation of the Majjhima Nikāya,* translated by Bhikkhu Ñāṇamoli and Bhikkhu Bodhi, Boston: Wisdom Publications, 1995.

*SN The Connected Discourses of the Buddha: A New Translation of the Saṃyutta Nikāya,* 2 volumes, translated by Bhikkhu Bodhi, Boston: Wisdom Publications, 2000.

*Vism.* Buddhaghosa, *The Path of Purification (Visuddhimagga),* translated by Bhikkhu Ñāṇamoli, Seattle: Buddhist Publication Society Pariyatta Editions, 1999.

# Introduction

Buddhist moral philosophy is a contemporary inquiry rooted in some very ancient texts. Traditional Buddhist thought and practice in India and elsewhere was centrally concerned with ethics, with how we should live our lives. It was also, in its more intellectual manifestations, centrally concerned with philosophy. But philosophical reflection in traditional Buddhist texts was oriented primarily toward metaphysical and epistemological themes. It is widely acknowledged that there is little that could be considered explicit and systematic moral philosophy in these texts. The traditional Buddhist work that perhaps comes closest to being a work in moral philosophy is Śāntideva's *Bodhicaryāvatāra.* This text is certainly concerned with ethics, and in its chapter on wisdom it contains detailed philosophical analyses pertaining to what Mahāyāna Buddhists call emptiness. But it is nonetheless a very different kind of text than canonical works of moral philosophy in the Western tradition such as Aristotle's *Nicomachean Ethics,* Immanuel Kant's *Groundwork of the Metaphysics of Morals* and John Stuart Mill's *Utilitarianism.* The *Bodhicaryāvatāra* is an inspirational work about cultivating the awakening mind *(bodhicitta)* and about the ethical, meditative and intellectual training of a Bodhisattva. It includes praise for the awakening mind, confessions of faults and resolutions to persist in the training. At most, it contains occasional discussions that might be construed as excursions into moral philosophy, but it does not have a unified argumentative structure centered primarily on themes in moral philosophy such as we find in Aristotle, Kant and Mill.

Nonetheless, in recent decades a number of scholars have examined traditional Buddhist works from the perspective of moral philosophy as it is commonly understood in the Western world. In some cases, they have developed interpretations of these works, often arguing that they are implicitly committed to some position or another in moral philosophy. In other cases, they have tried to construct a defensible position in moral philosophy by reference to these traditional Buddhist works. Sometimes they have tried to do both. Whatever may be said about the extent of moral philosophy in traditional Buddhist texts, there is no question that there is now a flourishing genre of scholarship engaged in these enterprises that may reasonably be called Buddhist moral philosophy. This book is an introduction to this scholarship.

We should not simply assume that Buddhist moral philosophy, so understood, is a cogent and worthwhile endeavor. Whether it is, and if it is to what extent and in what respects, are issues readers of this volume will want to consider. Buddhist thought and practice, in virtually all its manifestations, is animated by a fundamental concern: human life is permeated by suffering, and to overcome this and attain ultimate liberation we need to realize our selflessness or (in Mahāyāna Buddhism) the emptiness of all things. This soteriological project is foreign to the main concerns of moral philosophers in the Western world. Why should we suppose that these concerns are relevant to the Buddhist quest for liberation? An optimistic response might envision these two enterprises as partly overlapping circles, as in a Venn diagram: despite significant differences, there is enough common ground to generate a reasonable expectation that something valuable will come from examining Buddhist thought through the perspectives of Western moral philosophy. However, a more pessimistic response may call forth a rather different image: any such examination is, in the end, basically a futile effort to fit square pegs into round holes. In this view, it is a counterproductive exercise in frustration to attempt to understand the Buddhist liberation project by translating it into the categories of Western moral philosophy. Readers may feel the force of both responses at different points in the chapters that follow. In any case, reflection on the nature and value of Buddhist moral philosophy is—or should be—part of the inquiry.

The book is governed by several presuppositions. First, much (though certainly not all) of the work in Buddhist moral philosophy has focused on the Indian or South Asian Buddhist traditions from the earliest texts of the Pali Canon up through Mahāyāna figures and texts such as Śāntideva and the *Bodhicaryāvatāra*—a rich and diverse period of over a thousand years in the early development of Buddhist thought and practice. We will be primarily, though not exclusively, concerned with these traditions. Second, much (though again certainly not all) of this work is oriented toward the mainstream understanding of moral philosophy in the English-speaking world, in what is often called analytic philosophy, and its assumptions about which questions, perspectives, categories and the like are important. We will also mostly conform to this orientation. Finally, Buddhist moral philosophy is fundamen- #3 tally an interpretation and analysis of ideas, outlooks, arguments and the like as they are represented in texts in the Buddhist traditions. Though these texts are very much oriented toward practice (for example, toward following the path to enlightenment), to a large extent the immediate focus of Buddhist moral philosophy is the textual representation of practice rather than the actual lives of Buddhists whether past or present. For the most part, we will not be discussing how Buddhists live or have lived. We will be discussing intellectual reflections pertaining to how they should live. Each of these presuppositions might be regarded as a limitation: a more comprehensive approach could emphasize other Buddhist traditions, additional philosophical perspectives and a broader range of sources and concerns than texts. Such an approach could certainly be valuable. However, a book of this kind would be a much longer book, or a much less detailed one, than the present work. Moreover, though these presuppositions might be considered limitations, there are advantages to remaining within them: to a large extent, the scholarship represented in this book has a unity of focus, perspective and method that would be difficult to convey in the context of a more ambitious endeavor.

The book has three parts. The first part contains two introductory chapters summarizing the teaching of the Buddha and subsequent developments in Buddhist traditions, primarily in India, that are relevant to the main themes of the book. Readers already familiar with this history may wish to skip these chapters. The next two chapters examine the nature of Buddhist moral philosophy and consider some skeptical concerns that many Western scholars working in this discipline have regarding karma, rebirth, nirvana and related topics. These chapters situate Buddhist moral philosophy within the broader perspectives of Buddhist modernism. The second part of the book consists of a series of chapters on the main theoretical areas of Buddhist moral philosophy in its current state of development: well-being, normative ethics, moral objectivity, moral psychology and the problem of free will and determinism. The last part of the book concerns what is usually called applied or practical ethics. The discussion of these topics in Buddhist moral philosophy is often closely related to a contemporary movement called socially engaged Buddhism (this is one context in which somewhat more attention is paid to the lives of Buddhists). This movement is introduced and examined in the opening chapter, followed by chapters on human rights, violence, war and peace and environmental ethics. Though other topics in Buddhist applied ethics have received attention, such as bioethics and economic justice, the issues considered here are especially important and have been central areas of debate in Buddhist moral philosophy. All the chapters in the book consider both interpretive and philosophical questions, but there are variations in the relative emphasis given to these. Basic categories of Western moral philosophy are employed in most of the chapters of Parts 2 and 3, but there are differences in the ways in which, and extent to which, these categories organize the discussions. At the beginning of each of these chapters, there is usually a brief overview of the topic of the chapter as understood in Western moral philosophy. Persons already knowledgeable about these discussions may wish to skip these overviews.

The main purpose of the book is to introduce readers to the debates in Buddhist moral philosophy: it is not to defend specific positions in these debates. It is obvious that complete neutrality in presenting these debates is not possible—and there is certainly no claim to have attained this here. Various arguments, replies, rejoinders and the like are introduced in order to provide a sense of the shape of these debates, not as a way to defend a specific resolution of them. To the extent that these presentations express a point of view, it is that of a critic pointing out philosophical difficulties that need to be addressed. Such a critical stance is characteristic of much work in Buddhist moral philosophy and, as I will suggest in Chapter 3, it does reflect an approach common in some forms of Buddhist modernism. But this is different than arguing for the correct conclusion with respect to the interpretative and philosophical issues themselves.

The main languages of Indian Buddhism are Pali and Sanskrit. Pali is the language of a set of texts called the Pali Canon that the Theravāda tradition regards as authoritative. Sanskrit is the main language of Indian Mahāyāna Buddhism (though some of these texts now exist only in Tibetan or Chinese translations). The vocabulary of the two languages is sometimes similar. Transliterations of key Pali and Sanskrit terms are introduced as appropriate (when similar Pali and Sanskrit words are both listed, the Pali word comes first). There are three words based on transliterations of the Sanskrit term that have become common in English: dharma, karma and nirvana. These words appear in their English form in all contexts, including translations, even though the Pali version of the words is somewhat different (respectively *dhamma, kamma* and *nibbāna*). A uniform policy is more sensible because the words are common in English, and in some contexts it is unhelpful or confusing to switch between the Pali and Sanskrit spellings.

Page references employ standardized pagination where this is commonly used (the *Nikāyas* and *Dhammapada* in the Pali Canon, Buddhaghosa, Nāgārjuna and Śāntideva in the Buddhist sources, and Aristotle and Kant in the Western philosophers). Otherwise references are to pages in the editions cited.

# PART 1

# Buddhist Ethical Thought and Buddhist Moral Philosophy

# CHAPTER 1

# The Teaching of the Buddha

The purpose of this chapter is to provide an overview of the teaching of the Buddha. The next chapter will give a summary of the development of this teaching in the centuries immediately after his death and in subsequent centuries during the rise of Mahāyāna Buddhism (primarily, though not exclusively, in India). Together these two chapters will establish a context for a more detailed examination of Buddhist ethics and Buddhist moral philosophy. Readers already familiar with this context may wish to skip these chapters.

## Our Knowledge of the Buddha's Teaching

The Buddha lived in India nearly 2,500 years ago. He wrote nothing, and our knowledge of his teaching (*dhamma/dharma*) derives primarily from a large body of texts that are thought to be based on and to preserve this teaching. According to the Theravāda tradition (the form of Buddhism that prevails today in Sri Lanka and parts of Southeast Asia), shortly after the Buddha died a large group of his enlightened disciples met for a group recitation of what he said during the 45 years that he taught. This was the beginning of an organized oral tradition in which the memory of Buddha's teaching was passed down by his followers from generation to generation. After quite some time, perhaps close to four centuries, this oral tradition was put in the written form that is the source of the texts we have today.

One group of these texts is entitled the *Vinaya Piṭaka:* it contains the rules regulating the monastic community established by the Buddha, and it is one source for our understanding of the ethical aspects of his teaching. A second group of the texts is called the *Sutta Piṭaka:* most of the five *Nikāyas* that make up this group purport to represent the conversations and discourses in which the Buddha (or his disciples) explained his thought. It is our main source for comprehending his original teaching. A third and final group of texts is entitled the *Abhidhamma Piṭaka:* in comparison with the texts in the first two groups, these texts offer a more analytical, abstract and systematic account of the Buddha's teaching. They are widely believed to have been developed primarily in the centuries after the life of the Buddha (and so are a much more indirect and interpretive representation of his thought). This group will be discussed in the next chapter. The three groups together are known as the "three baskets" *(Tipiṭaka/Tripiṭaka).* The best-known and most complete version of the three baskets is in Pali, a language related to Sanskrit that is thought to be close to, but not identical with, the language the Buddha spoke (there are also renditions of many of these texts in Chinese and Tibetan). The Pali version, commonly referred to as the Pali Canon, is considered authoritative by Theravāda Buddhism. It has been translated into English almost in its entirety and is the primary basis for this chapter (especially the *Sutta Piṭaka*).

The genealogy of the Pali Canon raises obvious concerns about its accuracy as an account of what the Buddha actually taught. Since it is the product of a long oral tradition lasting nearly four centuries, it is natural to wonder whether it includes mistakes or even more or less conscious changes (additions, subtractions or modifications) to what the Buddha said. This concern is aggravated by the fact that during this period there were numerous schools (18 according to one tradition) that sometimes differed in their interpretation of the Buddha's thought. The Theravāda school that is the source of the Pali Canon and the ancestor of contemporary Theravāda Buddhism was but one of these. Though consistency across different renditions of these texts may provide some reassurance, these different versions may have common sources that are themselves problematic. To a very large extent, there is no way to know in detail with any certainty how accurate the Pali Canon is as a representation of the Buddha's teaching.

However, it is the teaching of the Buddha as depicted in these texts that has been historically influential—certainly in the Theravāda tradition, and in overall substance in other traditions as well. What the world has regarded, and continues to regard, as the Buddha's original teaching is basically the ensemble of ideas and practices put forward in these texts. Moreover, though there is scholarly disagreement about what can be known about the Buddha's ideas, it is widely thought that there was a single person who came to be called the Buddha and who is the source of the ideas in these texts at least in broad outline. In any case, for the most part there is little reason to think that there is a better source for understanding the teaching of the Buddha than the Pali Canon (for discussion of the development of the Pali Canon, see Gethin 1998: ch. 2).

*700 – 400 ish BCE*

## The Life of the Buddha

One entrée into the teaching of the Buddha is the traditional representation of his life. Buddhist traditions as well as contemporary scholars generally agree that the Buddha lived in the vicinity of the Ganges River basin in the northeastern area of present-day India. However, there is disagreement about exactly when he lived. The dates assigned by different traditions range from the seventh to the fourth centuries BCE, but today most Western scholars think that the Buddha probably died close to 400 BCE. Hence, *400s BCE* he probably lived most of his life in the fifth century BCE (and so about the same time as Socrates). In any case, it was a very long time ago, and we can have little confidence about any specific details of the Buddha's life. Nonetheless, there is a traditional understanding of his life that is mostly rooted in the Pali Canon and presumably is a product of the same oral tradition that produced the texts of this Canon. If we set aside the virtually unanswerable question of the historical accuracy of this account, there is much that we can learn from it about what, traditionally, the Buddha is supposed to have taught. The representation of his life is itself a partial statement of his thought (for an account of the life and thought of the Buddha, see Carrithers 1983).

The man who became the Buddha, Siddhattha Gotama (Siddhārtha Gautama), is said to have been born near the present-day border of India and Nepal, in a park named Lumbinī, and to have been raised in nearby Kapilavatthu (Kapilavastu). (Strictly speaking, Gotama is said to have been *reborn*, and more complete accounts refer to his previous lives leading up to this one.) His father was a rather well-off and powerful leader of the Sakka (Śākya) tribe. Gotama probably grew up in comparative good fortune by the standards of the day. At age 16 he married a woman named Yaśodharā, and when he was 29 he and Yaśodharā had a son named Rāhula. At this point in his life, Gotama may well have possessed what for many people, then and now, have been regarded as largely sufficient for happiness: a measure of prosperity, reputation and power as well as a beautiful spouse, a son and even, we are told, good looks. However, when Gotama was born, it was foretold that he would become either a great political leader or a great spiritual leader. His father hoped he would follow the political path and so he protected his son from troublesome features of life that might lead him in a spiritual direction. But this protection could not last forever. One day, not long after the birth of his son, Gotama went out and saw a very old man: he discovered that human beings age and decline over time. On another occasion he went out and saw someone who was very sick: he realized that human beings are subject to illness. On a third outing he saw a funeral procession: he found out that human beings eventually die. The three-part realization of aging, illness and death, as inevitable features of human life, greatly disturbed Gotama. He left his wife and child and set out on a quest to understand and overcome such suffering.

The quest was to last six years. At first Gotama studied with two figures rooted in traditional Brahminism. He quickly mastered their respective meditation systems and realized their highest states of concentration, but he was dissatisfied with the value of these states. He then spent considerable time with five *samaṇas (śramaṇas),* spiritual seekers who had abandoned Brahminism and the household life that was at the center of its concerns, and who lived lives of extraordinary asceticism and meditation in search of true understanding and happiness. Once again Gotama proved extremely proficient in their spiritual disciplines, but he concluded that the rigors of the most extreme asceticism imaginable did not bring him the wisdom and relief from suffering that he sought. So he took some nourishment and set off on his own. After a period of reflection and meditation, he achieved three forms of knowledge. First, he saw the specific details of his own past lives. Second, he grasped the nature of karma *(kamma/karma)* and rebirth, that morally good actions bring about greater happiness for the person who performs them and morally bad actions bring about greater unhappiness for this person, both in the person's current life and throughout the series of lives, past and future, that all human beings undergo. Third, he understood the Four Noble Truths that explain the nature, origin, cessation and way leading to the cessation of suffering. He was now a Buddha, an enlightened or awakened being, someone who had discovered and attained nirvana *(nibbāna/nirvāṇa).* This meant that he had overcome suffering in this life and would escape the cycle of rebirth, with its inevitable suffering, in the future.

An interesting feature of the traditional story is that, immediately after his enlightenment, the Buddha was momentarily perplexed about what to do and needed some guidance. He realized that what he had learned is rather difficult to understand and he observed that the people of his time were quite preoccupied with the pleasures of the senses. So he thought it would be pointless, indeed "wearying and troublesome," to try to teach them. But then the Brahmā Sahampati appeared and convinced the Buddha that some persons would understand his teaching. And so, we are told, the Buddha decided to teach what he had discovered "out of compassion for beings" (*MN* I 168–9). This episode may be interpreted in different ways. But it is striking that, though the Buddha is often presented as an extraordinary being, more godlike than human (especially in Mahāyāna Buddhism), here, in this account of a pivotal moment in his life, he appears all too human—uncertain, a bit anxious, in need of help—even though he is enlightened, and as enlightened, has the compassion to devote the remaining 45 years of his life to enabling others to attain enlightenment themselves.

The Buddha first taught the Four Noble Truths to the *samaṇas* he had lived with earlier when he was seeking enlightenment. At first they were wary of him: had he not betrayed them by abandoning their ascetic ways for what they perceived as a life of luxury? The Fourth Noble Truth, the way to the cessation of suffering known as the Eightfold Path, was presented as a response to this concern. It was said to be a "middle way" (*majjhimā paṭipadā*) between the sensuous lives of most people and the ascetic lives of the *samaṇas*. As will be seen, by most standards, the Eightfold Path is still pretty ascetic, and in any case this was enough to convince the *samaṇas*. They became the Buddha's first disciples and the first under his tutelage to attain enlightenment—persons who are called *Arahants (Arhats)*.

This was the beginning of the monastic order established by the Buddha, the *Sangha*, a group of male disciples called "bhikkhus" who had forsaken an ordinary life of work and family for a disciplined and celibate life supported by alms and devoted to the pursuit of enlightenment. Some years later the Buddha established a parallel community of female disciples called "bhikkhunīs." Another striking feature of the traditional story is that he had to be talked into this by his attendant Ānanda and his step-mother Mahāpajāpatī: only after three pleas did the Buddha agree that women could attain enlightenment as well as men and so should have their own monastic order (there is more about this in Chapter 12). The Buddha also had male and female lay followers, known as *upāsakas* and *upāsikās,* who lived ordinary non-celibate lives of work and family, but in certain ways embraced values of the Buddha and provided support for the *Sangha*. However, though he addressed all of these groups of people, much of his teaching in the *Sutta Piṭaka* seems to be directed primarily to an audience of male monastics. In this connection, it is worth noting that the Buddha did not return to his wife Yaśodharā and son Rāhula (though Rāhula later became one of his followers). He did not think the "household life" was a suitable environment for seeking enlightenment, and as the leader of the monastics pursuing enlightenment he evidently did not think it was a suitable environment for himself. To a large extent, early Buddhism is centrally a monastic tradition.

At age 80, according to the traditional account, the Buddha became ill (perhaps from food poisoning) and died. Though he was enlightened and hence had in some sense overcome suffering, he nonetheless grew old, got sick and died—the three features of human life that had disturbed him so much that he began his quest for enlightenment more than 50 years earlier. Since he was enlightened, the Buddha was not to be reborn into another such life. However, *in this life* overcoming suffering evidently meant, not the elimination of these features, but a change in attitude toward them. As he was dying, he said to Ānanda: "Whatever is born, become, compounded is liable to decay—that it should not decay is impossible. And that has been renounced, given up, rejected, abandoned, forsaken" (*DN* II 118). He also left these instructions for the bhikkhus: "You should live as islands unto yourselves, being your own refuge, with no one else as your refuge, with the Dharma as an island, with the Dharma as your refuge, with no other refuge" (*DN* II 100). He appointed no successor, leaving behind only this rather sparse advice to take refuge in oneself and the Buddha's teaching. Summing up these points, his final words were, "all conditioned things are of a nature to decay—strive on untiringly" (*DN* II 156).

The Buddha's life, as represented in the tradition, is most plausibly regarded, less as a factual record of events, and more as a statement of the Buddha's teaching. From this point of view, there are several lessons that we might take away from his life. First, the things that people commonly suppose will bring them happiness are not sufficient for happiness. The Buddha had most of these things: he was married and had a son, he was in a position of some prestige, power and wealth, he was good looking and so forth. But all of this was overshadowed by the realization that all human beings, including ourselves and those we love, will decline with age, become ill and eventually die. We are "of a nature to decay." By itself, this might seem a rather depressing lesson, and so it appeared to the Buddha at first. However, what the remainder of his life is supposed to teach is that there is a way, somehow, to overcome this pessimistic perspective. Whatever this way is, it is clear that it involves a basic reorientation in our attitudes to those things we thought would bring us happiness. As will be seen, a key to this reorientation is overcoming craving (*taṇhā/trṣnā*), and attachment or possessiveness (*upādāna*), with respect to these things. The Buddha's later life might give the impression that this basically requires a monastic life, and one of the challenges for ascertaining the relevance of Buddhism in the world today is determining whether this impression is correct.

## Karma and Rebirth

We are now in a position to look more closely at the teaching of the Buddha. The place to begin is with karma and rebirth, two doctrines that are distinct but very closely related in the Buddha's thought (for an overview of these doctrines in early Buddhism, see McDermott 1980). It is noteworthy that two of the three things the Buddha discovered when he was enlightened involved these doctrines: the nature of karma and rebirth as well as the details of his own past lives. In contemporary philosophical discussions of Buddhism in the West, there has been a debate about whether karma and rebirth, at least as traditionally understood, are unimportant, problematic, or dispensable features of Buddhism (see Chapter 4). However, there can be no question that for the Buddha, and for the early Buddhist tradition, they were fundamental features of his ethical thought. The third thing he discovered upon his enlightenment, the Four Noble Truths, take karma and rebirth for granted and explain how to attain liberation from the cycle of rebirth.

The concepts of karma and rebirth were already features of Brahmanism, the main religious tradition in India when the Buddha lived, but they were understood differently. For the Brahmanic tradition, the correct performance of ritual determined the quality of a person's rebirth. The Buddha's innovation was to diminish the importance of ritual (though it has hardly disappeared from Buddhist traditions) and to emphasize the importance of the morality of our actions. The Jains had a similar position. This is one of the primary ways in which morality is central to the Buddha's thought. For the Buddha, our measure of happiness or unhappiness in this and future lives is determined by how morally good or bad our actions are. Hence, his position is partly similar to, and partly critical of, the Brahmanic viewpoint (for discussion of this background, see Gombrich 2009: chs. 3–4).

Karma and rebirth are not manifestations of a cosmic justice in which a divine being similar to the God of the monotheistic religions distributes rewards and punishments. The Buddha did not recognize such a God and he did not think of karma as a form of desert. There is no suggestion that morally good people deserve to be happy and morally bad people deserve to be unhappy. Rather, karma and rebirth are regarded as natural causal processes in the world. A fundamental feature of the Buddha's thought, arguably the centerpiece of his metaphysics, is that all things (except for nirvana) are causally conditioned or dependently arisen (translations of *paṭicca samuppāda/pratītya-samutpāda*). Karma and rebirth are among the most important respects in which this is true. It is better to think of the principle of karma as similar to causal principles of biology, such as that describing photosynthesis, than as the work of a divine being in the universe. A frequent metaphor for karma in Buddhists texts is a biological metaphor, that our actions are similar to seeds that will bear fruit in the future:

> Whatever sort of seed is sown,
> That is the sort of fruit one reaps:
> The doer of good reaps good;
> The doer of evil reaps evil.
> By you, dear, has the seed been sown;
> Thus you will experience the fruit.
> (*SN* 1 227)

Of course, both doctrines—divine justice in the future, and karma and rebirth—might function in motivationally similar ways to promote morally good actions and discourage morally bad ones. Karma and rebirth are certainly invoked in Buddhism for this purpose (and gruesome depictions of the horrors that await those who are immoral rival traditional portrayals of hell in Christianity).

Moreover, though the doctrines of karma and rebirth are not a matter of divine justice, they clearly state that the universe is morally ordered. In the Pali Canon, this order is associated with a cosmology in which there are 31 planes of existence of sentient (or potentially sentient) beings arranged hierarchically from lower to higher levels of happiness (non-sentient beings are not included). At the top are four immaterial or formless planes followed by 22 planes occupied by a wide variety of gods *(devas)*. Though beings in all of these higher planes are happier than human beings, they are still part of the cycle of rebirth that involves suffering. Human beings are located immediately below the gods and above various animals, ghosts and other denizens of the four planes of the lower world. In this middle space, human beings suffer enough to be motivated to seek enlightenment, but not nearly as much as the creatures below us. Depending on the moral quality of our lives, each of us could be reborn as another human being, with a greater or lesser measure of happiness, or perhaps as a god or some kind of animal. The same is true of beings at each level: from life to life, we are all circulating through the various planes of existence, with more or less happiness, but always with some degree of suffering. This process of rebirth governed by karma is called "perpetual wandering" *(saṃsāra)*. There is no

*Moral actions* ← bodily — Killing / verbal — Lying / mental — Desiring

claim that it has a beginning or a purpose. This is simply the basic circumstance in which we find ourselves. But we can be liberated from it by attaining enlightenment, and so never again being reborn, just as the Buddha did.

The basic causal principle that regulates rebirth is the principle of karma, an account of the consequences of a being's actions for that being (the term 'karma' means action). There are three elements of this principle: first, our actions are morally good or bad; second, our lives may be characterized in terms of happiness and unhappiness; and third, most importantly, there is a specific causal relationship such that a person's morally good actions produce happiness for that person and a person's morally bad actions produce unhappiness for that person. The first two elements are not very controversial. But the third is, and this element is the primary respect in which the Buddha taught that we live in a morally ordered universe: there is a *causal* relationship between a person's morality and that person's happiness. As usually understood, the order of explanation in this relationship is that morally good actions bring about some happiness for the person performing them because they are morally good. They are not morally good because they bring about this happiness (however, there is discussion of this difference in Chapter 6). On this understanding, there must be some specification of morally good and bad actions that is independent of the causal fact that they generate happiness and unhappiness for the person. *[NB in margin]*

In fact, as we will see, there are many specifications and classifications of morally good and bad actions, and other states such as character traits, in the Buddha's teaching (the Pali Canon has an extraordinary number of lists, perhaps because originally it was communicated orally). Many examples of these actions are rather obvious and are common features of the Buddha's moral teaching. Most often people are told to abstain from morally bad actions such as killing, stealing and lying. However, sometimes Buddhist moral values are expressed in more positive terms. For instance, we are urged to be compassionate, loving and generous. One common classification divides morally relevant actions into the categories of bodily, verbal and mental actions. For example, killing is a bodily action, lying is a verbal action, and being covetous is a mental action.

The English expressions 'morally good' and 'morally bad' do not have precise equivalents in traditional Buddhist texts. However, two pairs of contrasting terms cover similar semantic territory, but with distinctive connotations that are not ordinarily implied by the English expressions. The first is the distinction between *puñña/puṇya* and *apuñña/apuṇya* actions. To say that an action is *puñña* is to say that it is purifying or meritorious, and so will bring about a positive outcome for the person performing it. To say that an action is *apuñña* is to say the opposite: it is impure and will

*Actions are morally good v bad*
*Our lives are happy v not*
*Good actions bring joy n bad bring unhappiness*

lead to a negative outcome for the person performing it. The second pair of terms, and the more important pair in Buddhist morality, is the distinction between *kusala/kuśala* and *akusala/akuśala* actions. An action that is *kusala* is an action that is wholesome and healthy as well as skillful (it is often translated as wholesome or skillful). An action that is *akusala* is the opposite. It has been argued that in early Buddhism *puñña* is used primarily in reference to actions that will have better consequences within the cycle of rebirth on account of karma, while *kusala* is employed mainly in contexts referring to actions that promote enlightenment and hence an escape from the cycle of rebirth (for discussion of this claim, see Vélez de Cea 2004: 130–1).

One of the most important moral motifs in Buddhism is the claim that there are three roots of *akusala* actions, namely greed *(lobha)*, hatred *(dosa/dveṣa)* and delusion *(moha)*, and likewise three roots of *kusala* actions, namely the contrasting states of non-greed, non-hatred and non-delusion. The contrasting states could also be depicted in more positive terms as generosity *(dāna)*, loving-kindness *(mettā/maitrī)* or compassion *(karuṇā)*, and wisdom *(paññā/prajñā)*. The emphasis on the roots of *akusala* and *kusala* actions brings out an important feature of the Buddhist understanding of karma. The moral quality of actions crucially depends on the extent to which they are manifestations of good or bad moral character. It is the mental state of the agent, his or her intention and motivation, which matter most. In a well-known passage, the Buddha says that: "It is volition *(cetanā)*, bhikkhus, that I call karma. For having willed, one acts by body, speech, or mind" (*AN* III 415). The term '*cetanā*' has been translated in different ways, but is perhaps best thought of as intention or intending (for discussion of this, see Chapter 10). This passage brings out the importance of mental states for the moral quality of actions, even though read literally it may overstate the case (what the person does and its consequences also matter).

The second element of the principle of karma, the characterization of our lives in terms of happiness or unhappiness, is usually presented in terms we are likely to find familiar. Actions that are morally good are said to bring about a variety of goods, in this life and in future lives, which are commonly thought to contribute to happiness. These goods include such things as physical health, peace of mind, long life, good reputation, influence, confidence, wealth, beauty and wisdom. Actions that are morally bad bring about contrary conditions such as disease, anxiety, short life, bad reputation, lack of influence, diffidence, poverty, ugliness and ignorance or delusion (for example, see *MN* III 202–6 and *AN* II 202–5). Another form of karmic effect is the influence of morally good and bad actions on the

*Generosity*
*Compassion/loving-Kindness*
*Wisdom*

*Greed*
*Hatred*
*Delusion*

growth of a person's moral character. For instance, generous actions can lead to more generous actions and eventually to the development of the virtue of generosity. The same is true of contraries of these: greedy actions can promote development of the vice of greed. Since virtues are often presented as aspects of happiness, and vices as aspects of unhappiness, the principle of karma plays a role in the Buddhist understanding of moral development.

The final element in this principle, the causal relationship between morality and happiness, is the crucial one. In the *Cūḷakammavibhanga Sutta*, a student asked the Buddha to state "the cause and condition" of various forms of unhappiness and happiness (referred to as being in "inferior or superior" states). In his well-known response, he said:

> Student, beings are owners of their actions, heirs of their actions; they originate from their actions, are bound to their actions, have their actions as their refuge. It is action that distinguishes beings as inferior and superior.

(*MN* III 203)

The basic causal principle is conceptually straightforward, but it was acknowledged that there are many complexities in its actual operation. A prominent example is that generosity has more beneficial effects when its recipients have greater virtue or are more spiritually advanced. Giving to the *Sangha* is especially propitious. Some forms of meditation such as the meditation on the "divine abode" of loving-kindness also have positive effects (there is more about this later). The effects of good and bad actions can take place at any time in the future. The assumption seems to be that this is rather open ended: they might be soon, later in this life, or else in some future life. There is also variation in the kinds of effects of our actions. But a common theme is that there is a connection between the moral quality of an action and its effect. For example, my killing another person may result in my being short-lived in a future life.

The Buddha presented the doctrines of karma and rebirth as if they were evident. He did not offer philosophical arguments for them, and he did not refer to ordinary empirical evidence as a basis for accepting them (however, philosophical arguments were developed in later Buddhist traditions; see Arnold 2008). The Buddha apparently found his own enlightenment experience, and other experiences, to be sufficient evidence (see *MN* I 22–3 and 74–7). Moreover, it seems that his report of his experience was enough for his followers as well, though they may have believed that they found confirmation of it in their own meditative experiences. Nonetheless, the Buddha did realize that there were persons who rejected the doctrines of karma and rebirth, and he and his disciples sometimes engaged critics of these doctrines.

In one exchange reported in the *Pāyāsi Sutta* (see *DN* II 316–57), Prince Pāyāsi gave several reasons for denying these doctrines, specifically rebirth, and the Buddha's disciple Kumāra-Kassapa responded to these. For instance, Pāyāsi asked people to report back to him after they had died if they experienced some form of life after death. But no one reported back. Kassapa had an explanation: if they had gone to a woeful place, they would not have been permitted to report back, and if they had gone to happy place, they would not have wanted to return. Again, Pāyāsi said (foreshadowing contemporary naturalist objections) that there is no reason to think that the soul *(jīvaṁ)* leaves the body after death: for instance, we do not see it leave, and the body does not weigh less after death than before death. Kassapa found these concerns foolish and unreasonable. He also suggested that we should not assume that something is unreal simply because we are unaware of it, just as a blind person should not assume that there are no light and dark objects just because he cannot see them. In any case, Kassapa said, there are persons who have seen the phenomenon of rebirth in meditative experiences.

An obvious objection to the doctrine of karma is that there appear to be people who commit serious moral wrongs and yet manage to live out their lives with considerable happiness. The Buddha's response to this kind of objection was to appeal to future lives. If someone has "killed living beings," the Buddha said, "he will experience the result of that either here and now, or in his next rebirth, or in some subsequent existence" (*MN* III 214). This response suggests that the plausibility of the doctrine of karma depends on the plausibility of the doctrine of rebirth. Ordinary experience does not establish, and arguably refutes, any close connection *within this life* between morality and happiness such as the Buddha asserted. Only an appeal to other lives in the cycle of rebirth, past or future, could establish this connection. But ordinary experience has no access to these lives, as Kassapa in the earlier text seemed to grant. There will be more discussion of these issues in Chapter 4.

## The Four Noble Truths

The doctrines of karma and rebirth are fundamental to the Buddha's teaching. But they are, in effect, only half of his teaching and, from his perspective, the less important half. The more important half has two aspects. First, whatever a person's level of happiness within the cycle of rebirth, the entire cycle is in some fundamental sense problematic. However, second, it is possible for us to attain a kind of wisdom that allows us, in some way, to escape the cycle of rebirth and to attain a state of great bliss—nirvana—that involves much greater happiness than any happiness that can be achieved within the cycle. This is the Buddha's doctrine of liberation. It has parallels in many other Indian traditions, such as the schools of Vedānta, in which it is supposed that we can attain liberation *(mokṣa)* from a troublesome cycle of rebirth. Nonetheless, the Buddha's doctrine of liberation is distinctive in a number of respects, especially in its reliance on the metaphysics of no-self that is at the heart of Buddhist wisdom. This doctrine is the subject of the Four Noble Truths, the third and final feature of the Buddha's enlightenment experience, and the best-known summary of his most important teaching (for an account of the Four Noble Truths, see Harvey 1990: ch. 3).

The Four Noble Truths describe the nature, origin, cessation and way leading to the cessation of the suffering that the Buddha thought permeated the cycle of rebirth. He taught these truths solely to make it possible for people to gain liberation from this suffering. His aim was preeminently practical. For this reason, he was often compared to a physician and his teaching was regarded as akin to a medical diagnosis (for example, see *MN* I 510–12 and II 260). In a well-known story in the *Cūḷamālunkya Sutta,* a man was wounded by a poison arrow and, before he would allow a doctor to treat him, the man demanded that the doctor first answer a number of questions such as what the name of the person who shot him is. The Buddha commented that, for the practical purpose of healing the wound, the man had no need to have these questions answered. Similarly, the Buddha said, he was not going to take a position on some philosophical questions that Mālunkyāputta had put to him (for example, about the eternity and infinity of the world). He did not take a position on these questions because doing so would not promote enlightenment and the end of suffering. Rather, the Buddha said, he taught the Four Noble Truths precisely because doing so would promote enlightenment and the end of suffering (see *MN* I 426–32). These truths are sometimes portrayed as similar to a medical treatment. For example, the great fifth century CE Theravāda commentator Buddhaghosa said, "the truth of suffering is like a disease, the truth of origin is like the cause of the disease, the truth of cessation is like the cure of the disease, and the truth of the path is like the medicine" (*Vism.* XVI 87; for discussion of the medical analogy in Buddhism, see Burton 2010 and Gowans 2010).

The First Noble Truth states that the lives of all beings in the cycle of rebirth, and hence all human beings, are characterized by suffering, no matter where they are situated in the hierarchy of happiness. This is why the cycle of rebirth is fundamentally problematic. The key term here is *dukkha/duḥkha,* most commonly translated into English as suffering, but perhaps better understood as unsatisfactoriness (though to save syllables the standard translation as suffering will be employed in this book). The Buddha did not think that unenlightened human beings are always miserable. After all, various levels of happiness are available to us. Nonetheless, something is always amiss in our lives irrespective of our degree of happiness. As we have seen, suffering is especially associated with aging, illness and death. But there are other, more general, specifications. Suffering is said to involve unpleasant experiences and failing to get what we want. In a very general characterization, we are told that, "what is impermanent is suffering" (*SN* IV 1). The impermanence of all things is one of the most central features of the Buddha's teaching. It is easy to see the relationship to suffering: when we have what we want or find pleasing, we fear losing it, and when we have escaped what we do not want or find displeasing, we are anxious that we will not escape it for long. However, though the Buddha emphasized these familiar concerns, what is most important for suffering is not just what happens to us, but our attitude to what happens (there is more discussion of suffering in Chapter 5).

This point is brought out in the Second Noble Truth, according to which suffering originates in craving, the standard English translation of *taṇhā/ tṛṣṇā*. The suggestion is that suffering is rooted in a class of desires that are powerful, insistent and nearly impossible to satisfy. In Buddhist thought, craving is closely related to greed, lust *(rāga)*, attachment and hatred. In some texts, it appears to be claimed that all desires bring about suffering. If this were the case, then an enlightened person, someone who has overcome suffering, would have no desires at all. This is a possible interpretation of the Buddha's teaching. However, in English the word 'desire' has great scope. A common sense of 'having a desire' is to be disposed to bring something about if one can. For instance, if I have desire to see a movie, then I have disposition to see it if I am able. In Buddhist texts, enlightened persons are commonly depicted as having dispositions to bring various things about. The Buddha himself is portrayed as being compassionate and hence as being disposed to bring it about that people gain enlightenment. So perhaps not every kind of desire produces suffering (however, we will see in later chapters that portrayals of the highest state of enlightenment are often not easily understood in terms of ordinary human psychology). In any case, there is no question that the Buddha thought that the primary sources of suffering are powerful and troublesome desires—cravings—both to gain what looks to be pleasing and to avoid what looks to be displeasing. A life consumed by craving, he thought, is a life of dissatisfaction, a life of suffering.

Craving itself is also said to have an origin, a form of delusion, specifically the mistaken belief that we are selves. If I am in pain and crave that it end, the suffering that comes with this has its source in thoughts such as "this pain is mine." It is the perspective of "I," "me" and "mine" that generates craving. By contrast, the discovery that we are not selves, the key discovery that constitutes enlightenment, eliminates this thought. If there is no "me" that possesses this pain, then the craving that this pain must end dissolves. An enlightened person (in this life) continues to have pain, but does not suffer because he or she no longer has the dissatisfaction connected with the insistent desire that his or her pain must end. Since the Buddha was compassionate, it would seem that there is a sense in which he desired that the pain of all living things end. However, he did not regard these pains as belonging to him—he did not think "these pains are mine"— and hence he did not crave their cessation. Realizing that we are not selves is critical to overcoming suffering.

The Third Noble Truth says that the cessation of suffering is the cessation of craving. Elsewhere this combination of cessations is called nirvana. This is the enlightened state of a person. Though attaining this state is clearly the focal point of the Buddha's teaching, little is said about nirvana, and what is said is often perplexing. Sometimes the term 'nirvana' refers to the enlightened state of a person after death: almost nothing is said concerning this except that the person will no longer be reborn. More is said about an enlightened person who is still alive. In the *Itivuttaka* we are told that, though this person "still experiences what is agreeable and disagreeable and feels pleasure and pain," he or she has destroyed the three roots of unwholesome *(akusala)* actions, namely attachment, hatred and delusion (Ireland 1997: 181). As we have seen, such a person is called an *Arahant*. Though the *Arahant* is often portrayed in the language of absence, especially as no longer craving and suffering, he or she is also portrayed in more positive terms. In particular, the *Arahant* is regularly depicted as being in a state of great peace or tranquility. This is said to be a blissful state and is clearly thought to be the highest form of happiness, certainly a higher form than is available to the unenlightened. In addition, though the *Arahant* is no longer participating in the karma system (generating degrees of happiness and unhappiness by performing morally good and bad actions), it seems clear that there is a sense in which he or she has the highest level of virtue (though, as we will see in Chapter 4, there is some difficulty in understanding what this means).

This is evident in accounts of the four "divine abodes" or "immeasurable deliverances of the mind": loving-kindness, compassion, appreciative joy and equanimity. These are presented both as forms of moral development (often involving meditation) and as the goals of this development—goals perfected in the *Arahant*. Buddhaghosa said that the divine abodes "bring to perfection all the good states" (*Vism.* IX 124). He also said that they "are the best in being the right attitude towards beings" (*Vism.* IX 106). The first two complement one another: loving-kindness *(mettā/maitrī)* is desiring the happiness of all creatures, and compassion *(karuṇā)* is seeking to abolish the suffering of these creatures. The third, appreciative joy *(muditā)*, means finding pleasure in the happiness of other creatures. Finally, equanimity *(upekkhā/upekṣā)* is a peaceful and neutral state, neither glad nor sad, that implies impartiality to all persons, whether dear, neutral or hostile (there is more discussion of the divine abodes in Chapter 9).

The Fourth Noble Truth describes the Eightfold Path, the way leading to enlightenment. As we have seen, this is depicted as a "middle way" between a life pursuing sensual happiness (the life of most people) and a life pursuing self-mortification (the life of the *samaṇas*). Each of the eight steps of the path is said to be a right or correct *(sammā)* way of proceeding. Sometimes the eight steps are grouped into three sections—wisdom *(paññā/prajñā),* morality *(sīla/śīla)* and concentration *(samādhi)*—but all of these have moral aspects. Moreover, the three sections are thought to support one another. For instance, we are told that "wisdom is purified by morality, and morality is purified by wisdom" (*DN* I 124). It appears that the eight steps are to be followed, not one after the other, but more or less simultaneously, even though at a given time some steps may need to be given more emphasis than others.

The section on wisdom contains right view and right intention. Right view *(sammā diṭṭhi)* basically means knowledge of the Buddha's teaching—especially the Four Noble Truths, the doctrines of karma and rebirth and Buddhist metaphysics (there is more about the last later). Suffering, craving and unwholesome actions are all associated with ignorance or delusion. Hence, it is to be expected that overcoming these requires knowledge. Right intention *(sammā sankappa)* is portrayed as "intention of renunciation, intention of non-ill will, and intention of non-cruelty" (*MN* III 251). In more positive Buddhists terms, these could be regarded as vows to live free of sensuality and in accordance with the virtues of loving-kindness and compassion.

The morality section includes right speech, right action and right livelihood. Right speech *(sammā vācā)* means avoiding speech that is false, malicious or harsh as well as not engaging in idle chatter. Right action *(sammā kammanta)* means not killing living beings, not taking what belongs to others and not taking part in "misconduct in sensual pleasures" (*MN* III 251). The last of these refers mainly to sexual misconduct (for monastics, this would be a violation of celibacy, and for laypersons, this would be activities such as adultery). Rather little is said about right livelihood *(sammā ājīva),* but it is clear that this means not earning a living in ways that are inconsistent with the Buddha's moral teaching such as by trading in weapons or intoxicants (see *AN* III 208).

The abstentions in right speech and right action bear some similarity in content to some of the prohibitions of the Ten Commandments. The Buddha also expected abstention from the consumption of alcohol and other intoxicants (though this is not an explicit part of the Eightfold Path). Taken together, these abstentions give us the five moral precepts that are often said to be the basic standards of morality for all followers of the Buddha: abstentions on speaking improperly, killing, stealing, engaging in sexual misconduct and consuming alcohol (see *AN* III 211–12). It is evident that the Buddha believed that following moral rules is quite important. In addition to the five precepts, which apply to all Buddhists, monastics were expected to follow more than 200 rules. However, as we have seen, the Buddha also endorsed moral values such as loving-kindness, compassion and generosity. These look to be moral virtues—morally admirable character traits—that are not simply abstentions and that cannot be usefully formulated in simple rules. Of course, there are connections between the five precepts and various Buddhist virtues. For example, abstaining from killing may be seen as an expression of compassion. Nonetheless, the Buddha's moral teaching was expressed in two rather different vocabularies: a set of rules to be followed (typically abstentions) and a set of virtues to be developed.

The final section of the Eightfold Path, the concentration section, has three components: right effort, right mindfulness and right concentration. Right effort *(sammā vāyāma)* is essentially a form of moral training: we are to strive to abolish and ward off unwholesome states (rooted in greed, hatred and delusion) and to bring about and encourage wholesome states (rooted in non-greed, non-hatred and non-delusion). This is ethical preparation for the remaining two steps of the path. These constitute two of the fundamental meditative disciplines in the early Buddhist tradition. Right mindfulness *(sammā sati)* is a set of contemplations (of the body, feelings and mind and mind-objects) while right concentration *(sammā samādhi)* involves that attainment of four increasingly refined meditative states *(jhānas).* Right concentration is sometimes considered a form of serenity meditation *(samatha-bhāvanā),* a practice that aims to calm and purify the mind, while right mindfulness is thought to be a form of insight meditation *(vipassanā-bhāvanā),* a mental discipline that brings about direct knowledge. Both are thought to be important to achieving genuine wisdom, to understanding the way things really are. Since wisdom and morality go together, these meditative practices are themselves both essential for moral development. From the perspective of the Buddha, they are part of ethical training. In addition, there are other kinds of meditation that are intended to develop moral character more directly. This is especially true of the meditations on the divine abodes (loving-kindness, compassion, appreciative joy and equanimity). For example, a well-known meditative technique described by Buddhaghosa involves directing loving-kindness to oneself, to a friend, to someone who is neutral and finally to an enemy. This is intended to develop a disposition to promote the happiness of all beings impartially (meditation and morality will be discussed at greater length in Chapter 9).

## Metaphysics

As we have seen, the Buddha taught that the cessation of suffering depends on the cessation of craving, and that this in turn depends on replacing delusion with wisdom, specifically the understanding that we are not selves. Thus, overcoming suffering requires knowledge of the true nature of things: it requires having a sound metaphysics. This is part and parcel of Buddhist enlightenment. Moreover, since only those who are enlightened attain the highest form of moral virtue, living a fully virtuous life also requires a sound metaphysics. For these reasons, the Buddha's no-self teaching is thought to have the highest practical importance. It may not be obvious that morality and metaphysics have much to do with one another, but in the Buddha's mind they were closely connected. Hence, understanding his moral thought requires an excursion into metaphysics (for discussion of issues in this section, see Siderits 2007a: ch. 3).

The claim that we are not selves depends on two ideas that have already surfaced and are fundamental to the Buddha's understanding of the world. The first is that all things are impermanent, are constantly changing. The second is that all things are causally conditioned or dependently arisen. The classic formulation of this idea says: "When this exists, that comes to be; with the arising of this, that arises. When this does not exist, that does not come to be; with the cessation of this, that ceases" (*MN* II 32). In both cases, the exception to these two generalizations is nirvana, which is depicted as being beyond change and causal conditioning. Whatever may be said about that, as applied to human beings, these ideas mean that, in every respect, human beings are in a state of constant change and are causally conditioned.

The Buddha thought that the belief that a human being is (or has) a self has three basic and related components. To begin (putting it

*[handwritten annotations: self ← same/identical over time ← Distinction B/T me ∧ not me / I decide me / have self-control]*

first-personally), to say that I am a self is to say that, no matter in what **# 1** ways or to what extent I may change, I am numerically the same person, *the same me,* throughout my life. For example, I may go to college, get married, start a career, get divorced, retire, and so forth. But it is the exact same person, me, who does these different things. I have, as contemporary philosophers might put it, strict identity through time. This is the *identity criterion* of being a self. Second, to say that I am a self is to say that there **# 2** is a sharp distinction between me and things other than me. For instance, I am me and so I am not you, or the tree across the street, or the chair I am sitting in. I am distinct from each of these other things. This is the *distinctness criterion* of being a self. Finally, to say that I am a self is to say **# 3** that, in at least most respects, what I decide and do is up to me. Decisions and actions are, at least typically, mine. For example, if I decide to go to a movie and then go, then it is me, myself, that determines that I do this. Even if someone else tells me what to do, or tries to coerce me into doing something, it is still up to me whether to comply or resist. In this sense, I have the capacity to control what I decide and do. This is the *self-control criterion* of being a self.

The Buddha's no-self teaching is that human beings are not selves in these three respects. A human being is not (and does not have) a self that has identity through time, that is truly distinct from other things, and that is in control of what it decides and does. The Buddha believed that we are not selves in these respects because of the ideas of impermanence and causal conditioning. Since everything is in constant change, nothing ever remains exactly the same through these changes. There is no strict identity through time. Moreover, if everything is causally conditioned by other things, then nothing is truly distinct from other things and nothing is fully in control of what it decides and does.

The Buddha developed these arguments in connection with a psychology according to which human beings consist of five aggregates *(khandha/skandha).* The first is material form *(rūpa).* This refers to the physical dimensions of a person. The other four aggregates refer to mental dimensions. Feelings *(vedanā)* are sensations. They are classified as pleasant, painful (or unpleasant) or neither pleasant nor painful. These are not feelings in the sense of emotions such as anger. They are sensations that have an affective quality. Perceptions *(saññā/samjñā)* are apprehensions of the world that involve sense-experience. They involve cognitive judgments about what we are experiencing. The next aggregate is *saṅkhāra/saṃskāra.* This is commonly translated as 'formation' or 'construction.' It is closely related to intention *(cetanā)* and refers to the ways in which we form or construct our dispositions and experiences through action. Finally, consciousness *(viññāṇa/vijñāna)* indicates the awareness dimension that is present in the other three mental aggregates.

The Buddha's basic argument for the claim that there is no self appears to be that there is nothing more to a human being than the five aggregates and that there is nothing in each of the five aggregates that is a self (according to criteria such as identity, distinctness and self-control). Versions of this argument are suggested in what is traditionally said to be his second discourse (see *SN* III 66–8). For example, with respect to identity, it is claimed that, for any aggregate, that aggregate is impermanent and subject to change. Observation of such things as feelings and perceptions are thought to make this evident: they are constantly changing. Hence, the proper thing to say about the aggregates is, "this is not mine, this I am not, this is not my self" (*SN* III 68). Since each aggregate is impermanent and since impermanence precludes identity through time, there is no self in the sense of identity associated with the aggregates. And if there is nothing more to a human being than the aggregates, then a human being is not a self in this sense.

A second argument in this discourse pertains to self-control. This argument states that, with respect to each aggregate (here represented by $A$):

> Bhikkhus, $A$ is nonself. For if, bhikkhus, $A$ were self, this $A$ would not lead to affliction, and it would be possible to have it of $A$: "Let my $A$ be thus; let my $A$ not be thus." But because $A$ is nonself, $A$ leads to affliction, and it is not possible to have it of $A$: "Let my $A$ be thus; let my $A$ not be thus."
>
> (*SN* III 66–7)

The suggestion seems to be that, if an aggregate $A$ were the self, then it could bring it about that it is or is not in a particular condition. Since it cannot do this, it is claimed, it is not a self. For example, we may suppose, the aggregate feeling cannot bring about what is and is not sensed (and because this sometimes is painful, this leads to affliction). It might be assumed that this is on account of dependent origination. So this aggregate is not a self, and likewise for the others.

It is obvious that there are possible responses to these arguments. For instance, it may be said that though there is much about a person that changes, there are some respects in which a person does not change (at least as long as the person exists). Again, it may be supposed that, though we do not control our condition in some respects, we do in others, such as in making decisions and acting. The Buddha's epistemological orientation was, broadly speaking, empiricist: the basic test of whether there is a self is whether we can observe it. However, Buddhist observation includes what can be observed through the meditative disciplines. Common sense appeals to what can be observed are not definitive. At the same time, as we will see in the next chapter, it was recognized early on that there is a role for philosophical reflection on these metaphysical and epistemological issues.

CHAPTER **2**

# The Development of Buddhism

After the death of the Buddha, his followers developed his thought and practice in India for well over one thousand years until Buddhism entered a period of decline in India, even as it took root elsewhere in Asia. The aim of this chapter is to provide a brief overview of this development with an emphasis on those aspects that are especially important for understanding Buddhist ethics. After a preliminary look at Abhidharma Buddhism, there will be a longer discussion of the emergence and growth of Mahāyāna Buddhism, primarily in India, but with a brief reference to Tibet and East Asia. In conjunction with Chapter 1, this will provide a basis for a more thorough consideration of Buddhist ethics and Buddhist moral philosophy in the remainder of the book.

## Abhidharma Buddhism

As we have seen, for several centuries after the Buddha's death his teaching was preserved in an oral tradition. It was probably around the first century BCE that this oral tradition was first put into written form. This is the historical basis of texts we have today such as the *Vinaya* and *Sutta* parts of the Pali Canon (respectively recording the rules of the monastic order and the conversations of the Buddha and his first disciples). But something else was going on during this time in addition to the preservation of the Buddha's teaching. His followers began to develop interpretations of it.

To some extent, it appears that the Buddha himself had encouraged this. In a text from the *Aṅguttara Nikāya* that is widely cited in contemporary discussions of Buddhism, the Buddha seemed to promote what might be considered a kind of autonomy of thought in response to a group of people, called the Kālāmas, who had expressed doubts about whether to accept the teaching of the Buddha because they had heard so many different views from different people. In response, the Buddha granted that they had reason to doubt and then added:

> Come, Kālāmas, do not go by oral tradition, by lineage of teaching, by hearsay, by a collection of scriptures, by logical reasoning, by inferential reasoning, by reasoned cogitation, by the acceptance of a view after pondering it, by the seeming competence [of a speaker], or because you think: "The ascetic is our guru." But when you know for yourselves: "These things are wholesome; these things are blameless; these things are praised by the wise; these things, if accepted and undertaken, lead to welfare and happiness," then you should live in accordance with them.
>
> (*AN* I 190)

It is probably best to interpret the first part of this statement as meaning that we should not *merely* follow oral tradition, lineage of teaching, and so forth because the Buddha's thought as a whole suggests that he did not reject the value of every item on the list in every context. At any rate, what is important here is the emphasis on knowing for oneself, at least in part through one's own experience. Unsurprisingly, when his followers took this advice in interpreting the Buddha's teaching, they differed in their interpretations in some respects and different doctrinal schools emerged over time. Though there are probably many reasons for the development of these schools, the encouragement of independent thought would seem to be one of them. In some cases, these differences were associated with different monastic communities with their own monastic codes. For example, the Theravāda school was connected with the Theravāda monastic community (the ancestor of contemporary Theravāda Buddhism). But there were many other schools (probably more than the traditional 18 referred to in some texts), and they were not all associated with particular monastic communities.

During this time a method of understanding and interpreting the Buddha's teaching developed that is called Abhidharma (the Pali term is 'Abhidhamma'). The word means higher, further or supplementary teaching. This method generated a more analytical and systematic expression of the Buddha's thought than is found in the *Sutta Piṭaka*. However, the method is rooted in the texts purporting to represent the Buddha's actual discourses. For example, as noted earlier, there are many lists in these texts. An indication of this is the fact that the *Aṅguttara Nikāya* is organized by how many items are on the lists it records—1, 2, 3 . . . all the way up to 11. These lists are the basis for the more extensive lists that emerge in the Abhidharma discussions (for an account of the Abhidharma approach, see P. Williams *et al.* 2012: 63–9).

The term 'abhidharma' also refers to sets of texts, especially two extant sets from the early monastic communities. The first set, referred to at the beginning of the last chapter, is the third basket of the Theravāda tradition's Pali Canon, the *Abhidhamma Piṭaka*. The second set is the third part of the canonical texts of the Sarvāstivāda community. The canons of texts of the Theravāda and Sarvāstivāda communities are similar in that they each have a Vinaya, Sutta and an Abhidharma part. However, whereas the first two parts of the two traditions are rather similar, the third—the Abhidharma parts—are completely different (even though each contains seven books). This is an indication of the fact that different interpretations had emerged. The Theravāda *Abhidhamma* has been the most widely discussed, at least in recent scholarship, because most of it has been translated into English. The Sarvāstivāda *Abhidharma* survives primarily in Chinese and has not been translated into English or other modern languages. Both collections were regarded by their respective traditions as in some sense representing the teaching of the Buddha, even though contemporary scholars believe that they were composed after his lifetime. There are also commentaries on these texts as well as manuals summarizing these. The best-known traditional manual in the Theravāda tradition is Buddhaghosa's "The Path of Purification" *(Visuddhimagga)* referred to in the last chapter. The most influential manual outlining the Sarvāstivāda Abhidharma is Vasubandhu's "Commentary on the Treasury of Abhidharma" (*Abhidharmakośabhāṣyam*; see Pruden 1988–90). Both of these manuals date from the fifth century CE and so summarize several centuries of Buddhist thought after the time of his death.

As a method, the Abhidharma approach aspired to provide a systematic, unified and technical account of all the types of factors, mental and physical, that are part of our experience of the world. Each event in our experience was understood to be an instantiation of one or more of these types. These instantiations were called dharmas, and they were taken to be the ultimate constituents of reality. The term 'dharma' could mean teaching, especially the teaching of the Buddha (as in the last chapter), but it could also mean what is ultimately real in our experience of the world. The

Abhidharma accounts had both an analytical dimension, precise descriptions of each type of dharma, and a synthetic dimension, accounts of how instances of different dharma types arise and cease in causal dependence on one another. In the Theravāda version of this dharma theory, there are 81 types of conditioned dharmas: consciousness *(citta),* 52 types of mental phenomena *(cetasikas),* and 28 types of physical phenomena *(rūpa).* The mental phenomena include such things as feeling, perception, intention, joy, mindfulness, wisdom, greed, delusion, shame, calmness, compassion, appreciative joy and so forth. The physical phenomena encompass such elements as earth, water, fire, wind, color, sound, odor, the life faculty, nutrition, space and so forth. In addition to the conditioned dharmas, there is a single unconditioned dharma, the very special case of nirvana, for a total of 82 types. The Sarvāstivāda version is somewhat different, containing 75 types of dharma.

In time, a philosophical doctrine called momentariness emerged in conjunction with this analysis of the basic types of dharma. According to this doctrine, each dharma is actual for only for a brief moment that has virtually no temporal duration: it ceases as soon as it arises. Hence, everything that happens in our experience of the world is nothing more than atomistic sequences of causally related moments, each of which is actual only for an instant. Momentariness is basically a philosophical attempt to make sense of the ideas of impermanence and dependent arising. In contemporary terminology, it is a kind of process philosophy. On this view, the world as we experience it consists, not of enduring substances, as we commonly suppose, but of sequences of evanescent events that are actual only momentarily, and are conditioned by and condition other such events.

This brings to the fore another feature of the Abhidharma approach. In part, it is basically intended to be a description of our conscious experience of the world, at least as revealed in meditation (it could also be seen as a guide to meditation, as the theoretical representation of the meditative disciplines). However, in part, it is also a philosophical theory, in fact several philosophical theories, that were intended to make sense of basic Buddhist ideas such as impermanence and dependent arising. In the Buddha's original teaching, for example in the texts of the *Sutta Piṭaka,* there are the rudiments of philosophical ideas and arguments, as was seen in the no-self arguments discussed in the last chapter. But in those texts these ideas and arguments are not developed philosophically. In the period of Abhidharma thought after the death of the Buddha, and beyond, Buddhist ideas and supporting arguments were put forward with increasing sophistication and complexity (for brief overviews of Abhidharma philosophy, see Westerhoff 2011 and P. Williams *et al.* 2012: ch. 4). There are three features of this progression that are worth noting here.

First, the Abhidharma analyses of our experience of the world required a distinction between what is ultimately true, according to a particular analysis, and what is conventionally regarded as true in everyday discourse (but is not ultimately true). This came to be called the distinction between ultimate truth *(paramattha sacca/paramārtha satya)* and conventional truth *(sammuti sacca/saṃvṛti satya)*. To some extent, this distinction was implicit in the Buddha's original teaching and is anticipated in some passages in the *Sutta Piṭaka* (for example, see *DN* I 202 and *SN* I 297). But in the Abhidharma period the distinction became explicit, and disagreements arose over its proper interpretation. But the basic idea is clear enough. For example, the theory of momentariness tells us that what is really going on in our experience of the world is a succession of ever-changing momentary dharmas that are causally conditioned by other dharmas. This is what is ultimately true. But this is not the way we ordinarily speak about the world. Rather, we say such things as 'the apple is on the table,' where we assume that the apple and the table are rather stable enduring entities in the world. Strictly speaking, from the perspective of momentariness, such occurrences in ordinary speech are assertions of statements that are never, ultimately, true. For these statements make no reference to the ultimate realities, the momentary dharmas, and they refer to entities such as enduring apples and tables that, from the standpoint of ultimate truth, do not actually exist. But of course we find it useful to talk about apples and tables. Moreover, from the standpoint of this useful speech, there is clearly a difference between the statement 'the apple is on the table' being true and being false, between the apple being on the table and not being on the table. This is the realm of conventional truth, the realm of ordinary, pragmatically useful discourse. Hence, we can say, and Abhidharma Buddhists did say, such things as that, though it is ultimately not true—in fact, not even meaningful—to say that the apple is on the table, it may be conventionally true.

The distinction between ultimate and conventional truth became a staple of Buddhist thought, and it was understood and applied in a variety of ways. One important way it was employed was to interpret the words of the Buddha. For example, sometimes in the discourses in the *Sutta Piṭaka* the Buddha appears to speak as if there is a self. This was interpreted as an instance of saying something that is conventionally true. In ordinary speech, it can be appropriate to speak of selves because this is a pragmatically useful way of speaking, just as it can be useful to speak of apples and tables. The enlightened as well as the unenlightened may talk about what is conventionally true; the difference is that the enlightened, but not the unenlightened, understand that it is merely conventionally true, a pragmatically useful way of speaking, and that it is not ultimately true. Of course, on other occasions the Buddha denied that there are selves. This was interpreted as saying something that is ultimately true because, in fact, there are no selves: there are only momentary dharmas. In this way, the distinction made it possible to resolve what appeared to be inconsistencies in what the Buddha said. More broadly, it was sometimes claimed that texts such as the *Sutta Piṭaka* often employed the language of conventional truth and so required interpretation, whereas the Abhidharma texts employed the language of ultimate truth and so did not require interpretation.

A second prominent feature of Abhidharma thought is the emergence of disagreements about doctrines that were put forward as the correct interpretation of the Buddha's teaching. Debates about these disagreements were often conducted in quite polemical terms. Here are two prominent examples of doctrines accepted by some Buddhists and rejected by others.

There were many issues about the ontological status of the dharmas that are central to Abhidharma reflections. In this connection, the Sarvāstivāda school was well known for claiming that the nature of a dharma always exists even though the dharma is actual only in the present moment, what was called the "all exists" doctrine (this is the meaning of the name 'Sarvāstivāda') The doctrine arose in connection with the attempt to makes sense of Buddhist impermanence and the notion of momentariness. But its basic rationale can be seen independent of this. Sometimes we make what we take to be true statements about what no longer exists or about what does not yet exist. It seems that these statements must be referring to something, but since there is a clear sense in which what they refer to no longer exists, or does not yet exist, it is puzzling what this might be. It is easy to see why proponents of momentariness would feel especially pressed by this concern. The Sarvāstivāda "all exists" doctrine is that there is something, the "own-existence" *(sabhāva/svabhāva)* or intrinsic nature of each dharma, that, in a sense, always exists—past, present and future. However, this intrinsic nature exists in another sense only in the present moment when, as they put it, it has activity *(sakāritra)* or is actual. The only things that are actual are things in the present moment. Everything else that was actual in the past or will be actual in the future exists as an intrinsic nature all the time. And this is what we refer to in statements about the past and the future, existing but non-actual dharmas (this is similar to a doctrine called eternalism in contemporary metaphysics). Nonetheless, many Buddhists objected to the Sarvāstivāda "all exists" doctrine. For them, the contention that the intrinsic natures of dharmas always exist did not sit well with the basic Buddhist commitment to the impermanence of all things.

A second example of a controversial philosophical view that was accepted by some Buddhists is the Pudgalavāda, or the person doctrine, the position that there is a real, enduring person *(pudgala)* who is neither identical to the five aggregates nor distinct from them. Other Buddhists rejected this. For example, from the Theravāda perspective, what we call a person is nothing more than the dharmas associated with the five aggregates. The proponents of the Pudgalavāda thought this was insufficient. Since everything associated with the aggregates is constantly changing, they thought that this reductionist view could not make sense of doctrines such as karma and rebirth, and the idea that a person attains nirvana. So the person cannot be nothing but the aggregates. However, if the person were distinct from the aggregates, it would appear to be indistinguishable from the self that Buddhists rejected. So adherents of the Pudgalavāda said the person was neither the same as the aggregates nor different from them. Similarly they said that the person was neither conditioned nor unconditioned. The person, they thought, was a unique kind of entity. But for others, such as the Theravāda Buddhists, this doctrine of the person was unacceptable. The person of the Pudgalavāda looked too much like a self to be allowed.

All of these doctrines—momentariness, the "all exists" doctrine, the person doctrine—and many others make it clear that some Buddhists in the Abhidharma period were engaged in serious philosophical reflection about the Buddha's teaching. Though they took themselves to be committed to basic features of this teaching, as they understood them, they recognized that the ensemble of these features presented some philosophical challenges, and they set out to resolve them through a more analytical, systematic and unified account of the Buddha's teaching than he himself apparently presented. The rudimentary ideas and arguments that he put forward were turned into something much more sophisticated.

However, and this is the third feature of Abhidharma thought worth noting, the philosophical reflection that developed was basically about metaphysics and epistemology. Some aspects of Abhidharma discussions did have a bearing on ethics. For example, as we have seen, the lists of dharma types include many categories relevant to ethics such as intention, greed, compassion, appreciative joy and the like. Moreover, one of the most important classifications of these categories is the distinction between wholesome and unwholesome types. The articulation of such categories and classifications might be seen as a kind of moral psychology (for more about this, see Chapter 9). Again, there was considerable concern about how to make metaphysical sense of the doctrines of karma and rebirth that were central to Buddhist ethics. Nonetheless, for the most part, there was little development of what might be called moral philosophy as a distinct discipline—for example, one concerned with the construction of a moral theory about the nature of the good, the criterion of moral rightness, the justification of morality, the nature of moral responsibility and other topics that have been central in the Western philosophical tradition. To a large extent, Buddhist philosophy in the Abhidharma discussions was centered on metaphysics and epistemology, but not on moral philosophy.

As will be seen, in all three respects Abhidharma Buddhism established a pattern that was to be followed throughout Indian Buddhism, including Mahāyāna Buddhism, to which we will turn next. In all of Indian Buddhism there was significant philosophical discussion of metaphysical and epistemological themes (and related issues in what are now called the philosophy of mind, philosophy of language and logic). In these discussions, the distinction between conventional and ultimate truth was of paramount importance (though it was understood in different and often incompatible ways), and there were significant doctrinal disagreements among Buddhists (as well as between Buddhists and non-Buddhists). All of this has significance for the Buddhist understanding of morality. But moral philosophy as a distinct enterprise—the explicit development of a moral theory such as we find in such canonical Western philosophers as Aristotle, Aquinas, Kant and Sidgwick—was largely absent.

## Mahāyāna Buddhism

There are two main branches of Buddhism in the world today: Theravāda Buddhism, which is practiced mainly in Sri Lanka and parts of Southeast Asia, and Mahāyāna Buddhism, which has followers throughout much of the rest of Asia. Theravāda Buddhism is the less innovative and more homogeneous of the two. Mahāyāna Buddhism has many forms and has the largest number of adherents. Both branches originated in India. Theravāda Buddhism is the sole surviving tradition of the kinds of Buddhism we have discussed so far. Other early forms such as the Sarvāstivāda tradition have all disappeared. Though Mahāyāna Buddhism began in India and has become the most common form of Buddhism in the world today, it may have remained a minority tradition throughout its history in India (for an overview of Mahāyāna Buddhism, see P. Williams 2009a).

The origins of Mahāyāna Buddhism are rather obscure, and there have been different views about them. There was no distinct Mahāyāna monastic order, and it was not itself a doctrinal school (though, as we will see, in time philosophical schools developed in connection with it). In any case, it is widely supposed that around the period from the first century BCE to the first century CE a new vision of Buddhism began to be expressed in texts written in Sanskrit. The best known of these is a collection of texts called the *Perfection of Wisdom Sutras (Prajñā-pāramitā Sūtras)* such as *The Perfection of Wisdom in Eight Thousand Lines* (Conze 2006) and *The Large Sutra on Perfect Wisdom* (Conze 1975). Though these books were evidently produced well after the life of the Buddha, they claimed at once to express "the word of the Buddha" and yet to espouse a kind of Buddhism that is superior to previous kinds. Proponents of this new teaching called it the Mahāyāna, meaning the Great Vehicle, and they contrasted it with the earlier forms of Buddhism, which they pejoratively called the Hīnayāna, or Lesser Vehicle. In this way, advocates of Mahāyāna Buddhism proclaimed a new hierarchy among followers of the Buddha. First, there are those merely seeking a better rebirth by living a morally decent life. Second, there are those seeking enlightenment for themselves by following the original teaching of the Buddha. Finally, there are those seeking enlightenment for the benefit of all sentient beings, the commitment that to a large extent is the defining aspiration of Mahāyāna Buddhism.

The importance of this aspiration is conveyed by the central role played by the figure of the Bodhisattva, in contrast to the *Arahant,* in Mahāyāna thought and practice. In the teaching of the Buddha presented in the Pali Canon, everyone is encouraged to become an *Arahant,* an enlightened being, in this or some future life. The Buddha was thought to have been a Bodhisattva (in Pali *Bodhisatta*) in past lives. That is, he was portrayed as having sought enlightenment over many lifetimes, in order to help all sentient beings overcome suffering, until he finally attained enlightenment in the life described in the last chapter. But this Bodhisattva commitment— to seek enlightenment for the sake of others—was not put forward as a model for everyone to follow. In Mahāyāna Buddhism, by contrast, this commitment was regarded as an ideal for all beings. Each one of us was encouraged to seek enlightenment, not just for oneself, but for the benefit of everyone. Each one of us was urged to strive for perfect Buddhahood so that all sentient beings may become enlightened themselves. In Mahāyāna texts, this point was made by way of a critique, often expressed in rather polemical terms, of the ideal of the *Arahant* in earlier forms of Buddhism. A person striving to become an *Arahant* was depicted as being less worthy because he or she is seeking enlightenment only for him or herself. The higher ideal was that of the Bodhisattva who strives for enlightenment for the sake of everyone.

From one perspective, this critique is perplexing since in the Pali Canon the *Arahant* is depicted as having compassion and loving-kindness for all beings. It may be hard to see how striving to become such a being could be regarded as a kind of selfishness. One explanation of the critique centers on the initial motivation for seeking enlightenment. In the Pali Canon it can sometimes appear as if, at least at the outset, I should seek enlightenment because it is in my self-interest, because it will enable *me* to overcome *my* own suffering. In Mahāyāna Buddhism it is not denied that there is a sense in which it is good for each person to be enlightened. What is emphasized, however, is that self-interest should be removed from the entire motivational structure of seeking enlightenment. It should not have a role even in our initial motivation for seeking it. A related explanation of the critique concerns the destiny of the *Arahant* after death. In the Pali Canon we are told that, when an *Arahant* dies, he or she will not be reborn and will instead attain final nirvana. Whatever this might mean exactly, it could appear as if the *Arahant,* though compassionate while alive, departs from the scene at death, enjoying the bliss of nirvana while the rest of us struggle with the suffering of the ongoing cycle of rebirth. By contrast, the Bodhisattva is committed to remaining in the cycle of rebirth indefinitely so as to help everyone else attain enlightenment and overcome suffering. It is easy to see how this could be thought of as a higher aspiration.

The basic impetus of the Buddha's teaching is that the concept of self-interest is rooted in a misunderstanding, namely, that there is a distinct self with its own interest. Once this lesson is fully absorbed—that there is no such self and so no distinct interest of the self—it would seem that the concern to overcome suffering could only mean overcoming suffering as such, wherever it may occur, not merely one's own suffering. Universal compassion would be seen as the heart of the Buddhist message (the connection between the realization of selflessness and the attainment of universal compassion is discussed in Chapter 8). Proponents of Mahāyāna Buddhism may be interpreted as supposing that they had grasped the full significance of this implication (more clearly than earlier forms of Buddhism had), and as a result had made universal compassion the core of Buddhist teaching. Hence, each of us is enjoined to become a Bodhisattva, to make our basic aspiration, from start to finish, to achieve enlightenment for the sake of all beings so that all suffering may be overcome. However, it was recognized that forming such an aspiration, what is called "the thought of awakening" *(bodhicitta),* was itself a considerable achievement that would require a regime of moral development over a series of lives.

In Mahāyāna literature, Bodhisattvas are sometimes portrayed as specific godlike beings, each quite distinctive, but always with enormous powers and extraordinary skills that are exercised in the service of universal compassion. In popular forms of Mahāyāna Buddhism, such cosmic Bodhisattvas as Kuan-yin *(Avalokiteśvara)* and Tārā have been regarded as sources of inspiration and addressees of prayer. Nonetheless, since each human being, in fact each sentient being, possesses what came to be called Buddha-nature *(Buddha-dhātu),* the capacity for enlightenment, becoming such an extraordinary being is considered a real possibility for each of us, at least in the very long run. We are encouraged to suppose that over countless lives of practice we could achieve this advanced Bodhisattva state. This is the ultimate vocation that summons us all. We are constantly called upon to begin, and to persist in, the lengthy and difficult path of a Bodhisattva. The delineation of this path is the main context in which the moral values of Mahāyāna Buddhism are expressed. The most fundamental moral value, the one that unifies all others, is compassion, the commitment to enable all beings to overcome suffering. However, as in earlier forms of Buddhism, there are numerous associated values, sometimes in the form of moral precepts and sometimes in the shape of virtuous character traits. These diverse values are classified in a number of different ways, but the most prominent classification is the Six Perfections *(pāramī/pāramitā)*: generosity, morality, patience, vigor, meditation and wisdom (for a discussion of these, see Wright 2009). There are accounts of these perfections in many different Mahāyāna texts (for example, see Conze 1975: 128–36 and 415–21, Conze 2006: 61–71 and Meadows 1986). Several of them are also featured in the great Mahāyāna ethical work, *The Bodhicaryāvatāra,* by Śāntideva (see Crosby and Skilton 1995).

In fact, the completion of the *full* Bodhisattva path is sometimes said to involve 10 perfections, the Six Perfections plus four additional perfections that concern cosmic stages of development. The Six Perfections themselves pertain to more recognizably human forms of moral development, albeit taken in a direction that, from many perspectives, might seem extraordinary. The Six Perfections bear considerable resemblance to the Eightfold Path discussed in the last chapter. It is a reasonable conjecture that proponents of the Mahāyāna approach developed the Six Perfections by refashioning the Eightfold Path in some respects. The content of the two is in many ways the same. One interesting difference is that right livelihood, a step on the Eightfold Path, is not featured in the Six Perfections. But there is probably no reason to think that right livelihood is any less important (except perhaps insofar as it might be taken as an implicit acknowledgement that the category of right livelihood is a bit out of place in a teaching directed primarily to monastics). Generosity and patience are central aspects of the Six Perfections. Though they are certainly considered moral virtues in the earlier tradition, they are not directly featured in the Eightfold Path. It is plausible to suppose that they are given more emphasis in Mahāyāna Buddhism. Wisdom has crucial importance on both lists, but Mahāyāna wisdom is rather different insofar as it centers on grasping the emptiness of all things (there is more about this later). Though the Six Perfections are commonly presented in a standard order (the order in the paragraphs that follow), we should not put too much weight on this. Sometimes they are presented as a progression. This might imply that we should follow them in order, starting from generosity and concluding with wisdom, but this order could also be more of an expository device than a recommended sequence of practices. Often it seems that the Six Perfections should be developed more or less simultaneously, with each reinforcing the other. From this perspective, none of the perfections is truly attained until wisdom is fully attained.

Since the basic Bodhisattva commitment is to compassion, it is natural that generosity *(dāna)* should be featured as the first perfection. Generosity is a familiar moral virtue, and in some respects this perfection is quite recognizable. For example, providing material goods to those in need can certainly be an expression of Mahāyāna generosity. More important, of course, is providing what might be thought of as "spiritual goods." The gift of the Buddha's teaching so as to promote progress to enlightenment is thought to be of greater value than merely providing material goods (though material goods may be needed to pursue enlightenment). A special aspect of Mahāyāna generosity, in contrast to earlier forms of Buddhism, is the concept of transferring karmic merit: it was thought that an advanced Bodhisattva with a great accumulation of benefits from a multitude of virtuous lives could transfer those benefits to other sentient beings. This was not the way the doctrine of karma was understood in the earlier tradition, and in fact it appears inconsistent with the earlier understanding since it violates the principle that the moral quality of each person's actions generate karmic results for that person and that person alone. But transferring karmic merit clearly expands the possibilities for generosity, at least among those with a great storehouse of merit. There was broad agreement with earlier forms of Buddhism that the mental state of the giver has great significance for its moral value. The highest forms of generosity are entirely selfless: they are based on an impartial concern for all sentient beings and involve no expectation of reciprocity.

Mahāyāna discourses on generosity (as well as other moral virtues) sometimes contain features that, from many standpoints, would be regarded as wrongheaded or preposterous. For example, a Bodhisattva might be portrayed as expressing generosity by benefitting foes before friends (see Goodman 2009: 74). Extreme acts of generosity have an ancient Buddhist lineage: in a story about one of the Buddha's previous lives, he is represented as giving away his wife and children (see Wright 2009: 37–8). Another way in which Mahāyāna discussions of generosity may seem surprising is rooted in the concept of emptiness. The highest form of the perfection of generosity involves the recognition that all things are empty of intrinsic natures, the key insight of the perfection of wisdom. This was taken to mean that distinctions that might be thought fundamental to generosity—such as the distinctions between the giver, the recipient and the gift—are recognized as illusory. It might be objected that without these distinctions we can no longer make sense of the virtue of generosity. In one respect, Mahāyāna Buddhists would agree: what we ordinarily mean by generosity is flawed by the failure to see the selflessness and emptiness of all things, and once we see correctly we really have something rather different from the commonsense notion of generosity. Many Mahāyāna Buddhist discussions of morality appear deeply paradoxical to outsiders because they reflect the implications of emptiness.

The second perfection is morality *(śīla),* a set of rules or percepts, commonly in the form of abstentions or prohibitions. The third section of the Eightfold Path (the section that includes right speech, right action and right livelihood) was referred to by the Pali version of this term *(sīla),* and the content is rather similar. Thus there are precepts proscribing such things as lying, using harsh speech, stealing, killing sentient beings and improper sexual acts. There are, in fact, numerous moral rules in Mahāyāna texts depicting the Bodhisattva path (for example, see Keown 1992: 142–5). This can create the impression that Mahāyāna Buddhist morality is basically a matter of following moral rules. However, though rules are very important, this impression is misleading in several respects. First, developing moral character, becoming morally virtuous, is clearly as important, and arguably more important, than simply following a set of rules. In fact, adhering to the rules may be seen as valuable, at least in large part, because this contributes to the development of moral virtues. Moreover, moral virtues involve much more than outer actions: they also involve such things as intention and motive (at least in stages of enlightenment that are still recognizably human). In addition, moral virtues also involve more than the abstentions depicted in many Buddhist moral precepts: for example, generosity cannot be fully understood as, say, abstaining from stingy actions. Finally, as will be seen later, some Mahāyāna texts suggest that sometimes a Bodhisattva might violate some moral rules as an expression of compassion.

The next perfection is *kṣānti,* which is often translated as patience, though it may also be rendered as forbearance or tolerance. Its primary concerns are various forms of adversity. These include all kinds of suffering, but the most important category is actions by other persons we regard as harming or abusing us, as being insulting, unjust, unfair and so forth. The most common responses to such actions involve emotions such as indignation, anger and even hatred. The perfection of patience means, at a minimum, overcoming all such emotions. Indignation is to be replaced by understanding, anger is to be exchanged for equanimity, hatred is to be converted into compassion and so forth. Patience may be seen as a Mahāyāna analogue to an aspect of courage: it means responding properly to what is challenging, difficult or threatening. In Mahāyāna discussions of this perfection, the difficulty of attaining it was fully acknowledged, and various exercises were offered for its development.

In contrast to the perfection of generosity, which has at least some continuity with what is usually regarded as a virtue, the perfection of patience may seem contrary to what is ordinarily considered virtuous. Are not such things as indignation and anger (and perhaps even hatred) something morally appropriate and even morally necessary? Various defenses of patience as morally proper and admirable were offered. Some of these, such as the claim that anger often has bad consequences, are familiar and have no distinctive Buddhist premises. But many of the reasons given for patience depend on key features of Buddhist teaching. For example, it was said that when a person acts unjustly toward us, the person's action is always conditioned by various factors external to the person, or that, on account of karma, the harms we suffer depend on our own past actions. Nonetheless, it may be objected that patience is basically a kind of passivity that often is not justified. The Buddhist response is that patience is activity, not passivity, but it is not the activity of retribution, retaliation or revenge. Rather, it is activity rooted in compassion, the commitment to overcome all suffering, including that of the wrongdoer. Once again, from a Mahāyāna perspective, fully grasping the rationale for this perspective requires an understanding of the selflessness and emptiness of all things (there is more discussion of patience in Chapter 9).

The perfections we have considered so far—generosity, morality and patience—are obviously ethical in nature, even if the ethics they embody is sometimes contrary to the moral outlook of many people. The remaining three perfections—vigor, concentration and wisdom—appear to be rather different. They do not depict in an obvious way what might ordinarily be thought to be moral virtues or moral rules. However, from a Mahāyāna standpoint, these last three perfections are crucial to the full moral development of a Bodhisattva. They each draw attention to states of mind that are involved in possessing the moral virtues. In addition, each corresponds to a step on the Eightfold Path.

The fourth perfection is *vīrya*. This is often translated as vigor, but its full connotations require many other terms such as energy, effort, persistence and strength. This perfection involves a variety of motivational aspects of moral virtue. Though the term is different, the perfection of vigor covers much of the same territory as right effort *(vāyāma)* in the Eightfold Path. In both cases, overcoming unwholesome states and fostering wholesome states are central. In addition to greed, hatred and delusion, unwholesome states include such things as envy, laziness, discouragement and attachment to what is vile. Wholesome states are such things as generosity, patience and ultimately compassion. The Bodhisattva path is depicted as long and full of hardship. In the face of this, positive sources of energy are needed—determination, persistence, enthusiasm for virtue and the like. These are the different dimensions of the perfection of vigor. Writing about this perfection, Śāntideva says that the "desire for what is good must be created" (*BCA* 7.46).

Meditation is as important in Mahāyāna Buddhism as in earlier forms of Buddhism, and so it is not surprising that the next perfection is meditation—here translating *jhāna/dhyāna* (one of several Buddhist terms for meditation). Many of the meditative disciplines from the older tradition are adapted to the Mahāyāna context, understood as crucial elements of the Bodhisattva path rather than the path to *Arahantship*. In both cases, the disciplines often focus on the attainment of concentration and tranquility as well as the development of wisdom. In addition, also as in the earlier tradition, some forms of meditation directly pertain to morality. In this connection, two meditation techniques depicted by Śāntideva are especially well known (see *BCA* 8.89 ff.). The first focuses on the fact that all persons are equal in trying to avoid suffering and striving to attain happiness. This is supposed to enable to meditator to see that he or she should be equally concerned with the suffering and happiness of all beings. The second meditation technique pursues a similar theme: one should aim to exchange oneself and the other so as to overcome attachment to oneself and to become equally concerned for the suffering of all.

The last of the Six Perfections is wisdom *(paññā/prajñā)*. For Mahāyāna Buddhists, the central feature of wisdom is the recognition that all things are empty of—lacking in—what is called "own-being" *(svabhāva)*. This means that nothing has an essential nature or inherent existence that belongs to itself. The concept of emptiness *(suññatā/śūnyatā)* is an interpretation, or development, of ideas associated with the Buddha's no-self teaching, in particular dependent arising, the contention all things are dependent on other things. Since everything is dependent, nothing has a nature or existence that can be said to be its own. Mahāyāna Buddhists thought that they were the first to understand the meaning and radical implications of emptiness (there is more about this later). We have already glimpsed some of these implications in the discussions of generosity and patience. More broadly, it is usually supposed that the other five perfections are brought to completion only when the perfection of wisdom is fully attained. In addition, a central theme in Mahāyāna Buddhism is that wisdom and compassion imply one another: the person who fully grasps emptiness and the person who is wholly compassionate are one and the same person. One is not possible without the other. Since universal compassion, the commitment to enable all beings to overcome suffering, is the heart of the Bodhisattva path, there is a sense in which nothing is more important to the fulfillment of this path than wisdom.

Two additional themes beyond the Six Perfections are important in Mahāyāna Buddhist ethics. The first is an ethical application of the concept of skillful means *(upāya-kauśalya)*. One way in which this concept is important in the Mahāyāna tradition is the claim that the teaching of Buddhas and Bodhisattvas varies in accordance with the needs and context of their audience. Hence, they are said to use different skillful means to convey the Buddhist message. In fact, on account of this, it is sometimes said that Buddhist teaching overall is provisional and should be justified, not as direct statements of doctrine, but in terms of its success moving people along the Bodhisattva path (see Schroeder 2001). The ethical application of the concept goes beyond this. It is sometimes suggested that a Bodhisattva, possessing wisdom and compassion, may on occasion be justified in violating basic moral precepts that are ordinarily expected to be followed strictly. For example, the Mahāyāna philosopher Asaṅga argued that a Bodhisattva may do things that are "reprehensible by nature" as long as the Bodhisattva has good intentions and the actions have good results. The reprehensible actions include lying, killing and stealing—in each case, a violation of a standard Buddhist moral precept (see Tatz 1986: 70–2). In such cases, he said, there is "no fault," but "much merit." Earlier Buddhist traditions did not suppose that there could be justified violations of these common moral precepts.

A second Mahāyāna theme introduces a different form of complexity. On the one hand, since the ultimate goal of the Six Perfections is to become a perfectly enlightened being, a Buddha, such a being would seem to be a morally ideal agent that we should aspire to imitate. On the other hand, Buddhas are sometimes depicted more as natural founts of goodness in the world, benefitting others, than as agents having characteristics such as perceiving a situation, making judgments about what to do, forming intentions and acting on them. Though a great deal of Mahāyāna moral thought and practice concerns what would ordinarily be thought to be the development of moral character, the ultimate goal of this development is a state of being that does not appear to be a state of character at all. Though this is also true of earlier forms of Buddhism, Mahāyāna moral discourse is often exceptionally paradoxical in its mode of expression. In many respects, these paradoxes are rooted in the philosophies of emptiness and non-dualism that flourished in the Mahāyāna tradition (there is more about these later). What is striking about the traditional texts of Mahāyāna Buddhism is that these paradoxes are often expressed enthusiastically with considerable flourish. In fact, at times, they seem intended to shock. Taken literally these statements might seem to undermine the entire enterprise. But taken as manifestations of Mahāyāna philosophies they are intelligible, even if surprising, expressions of its distinctive outlook.

## Some Mahāyāna Perspectives

Two schools of philosophy developed in Indian Mahāyāna Buddhism: the Madhyamaka school and the Yogācāra school (for an overview, see P. Williams 2009a: chs. 3 and 4). These schools grew out of the Abhidharma philosophies summarized earlier, developing many of their concerns, but also reacting against many of their characteristic positions in light of the *Perfection of Wisdom Sutras*. Though these schools were primarily concerned with metaphysical and epistemological issues, their outlooks have some relevance for the development of moral philosophy, and several authors in these schools wrote works specifically on ethical topics.

The Madhyamaka ("Middle Way") school is thought to have begun with the work of the philosopher Nāgārjuna (for a brief account of Nāgārjuna's philosophy, see Westerhoff 2010). Very little is known about Nāgārjuna, but he is often believed to have flourished in southern India in the second century CE. His most important work, and the central work of the Madhyamaka school, is *The Fundamental Wisdom of the Middle Way* (Garfield 1995). Several other works have been attributed to Nāgārjuna as well, though there are controversies about the accuracy of these attributions. One of these works, the *Precious Garland* (Hopkins 1998), explores ethical themes. There were several later proponents of the Madhyamaka perspective in the Indian Buddhist tradition, and some of these philosophers wrote works pertaining to ethics. The ethical texts of these authors include Āryadeva's *Four Hundred Verses* (Lang 1986), Candrakīrti's *Advice for Travelers on the Bodhisattva Path* (Lang 2003), and Śāntideva's *The Bodhicaryāvatāra* (Crosby and Skilton 1995) and *A Compendium of Buddhist Doctrine* (Bendall and Rouse 1971).

The primary concern of Nāgārjuna and the Mādhyamikas (the proponents of the Madhyamaka school) is the interpretation of emptiness *(śūnyatā),* the contention that all things are empty of *svabhāva,* what is variously translated as "own-being," "inherent existence," "intrinsic nature" and the like. The school is called the "Middle Way" because this position is said to be in between saying that things exist with *svabhāva* and saying that they do not exist at all. In saying that everything is empty of *svabhāva,* Nāgārjuna meant several different things. The most central is the contention that everything lacks independent (inherent, intrinsic) nature. That is, nothing has its nature "on its own," unconditioned by nothing else. This was thought to be an implication of the concept of dependent arising in the teaching of the Buddha. According to Nāgārjuna, "whatever is dependently co-arisen, that is explained to be emptiness" (Garfield 1995: 24: 18).

Nāgārjuna did not have a single argument for the emptiness of all things. Instead he repeatedly employed a familiar argument form, the *reductio ad absurdum,* to show that in whatever context we consider, if it is assumed that something has an independent nature, then absurd consequences follow. One of the best known and perhaps most central of examples concerns causality. It is common experience, and a key feature of the Buddhist outlook, that there are causal regularities in the world in which we suppose that something C is the cause of some effect E. For instance, striking a match causes fire. To simplify considerably, on the non-emptiness, independent nature view, either C and E are the same or they are not. If C and E are the same, then the effect is already in the cause. But this is absurd: fire is not already in the match (nor in the collection of conditions that make up the full cause). However, if C and E are distinct, then each of them has its own independent nature. But this means that neither depends on the other, and this too is absurd: if the effect does not depend on the cause, then there is no causal relationship. Since absurdity follows either way, the assumption that cause and effect have an independent nature should be given up (two other possibilities are also said to result in absurdities: C and E are both the same and not the same, and they are neither the same nor not the same). Hence, we can only make sense of causality on the assumption of emptiness.

Though emptiness as the absence of independent nature was rooted in an understanding of dependent origination, Nāgārjuna and the Madhyamaka tradition took this understanding in new directions. Beyond the claim that everything is dependent on causes or conditions (causal dependence), emptiness sometimes meant that parts and wholes depend on one another (mereological dependence) and, most importantly, that what something is depends upon the conceptual scheme we use to identify it (conceptual dependence). On this last view, everything that exists is a conceptual construct *(prajñaptimātra),* and so there is nothing that exists on its own, independent of any conceptual scheme.

One way to understand emptiness and the radical nature of the Madhyamaka stance is by comparing it to the Abhidharma doctrine of momentary dharmas discussed earlier. On the Abhidharma view, what we call the self (and other objects such as apples and tables) is a whole that consists entirely of—is nothing more than—the momentary events called dharmas. The self is thus a fictional or conventional entity that is useful for pragmatic purposes, but is not ultimately real. The only thing that is ultimately real is the ensemble of dharmas from which the self is constructed. Hence, on this Abhidharma view, there is a basic distinction between what is ultimately true, the dharmas that have primary existence *(dravysat/paramārthasat),* and what is merely conventionally true, those entities such as selves that have secondary existence *(prajñaptisat/saṃvṛtisat).*

Emptiness, as understood in Madhyamaka Buddhism, is the position that nothing is ultimately real, that everything that exists, exists only conventionally. There is thus no basic ontological divide between selves and dharmas as there is in the Abhidharma view. Selves and dharmas are both secondary existents because there are no primary existents. Everything is constructed all the way down: there is no bedrock of "unconstructed reality" from which secondary existents such as selves are constructed. Rationales for this position can be seen in the mereological and conceptual senses of emptiness noted earlier. Since parts depend on wholes as much as wholes depend on parts, parts and wholes are equally conventional. And since what something is depends on our conceptual scheme, that something is a dharma is as conventional as that something is a self. The only way anything can exist is conventionally.

This implies a different understanding of conventional and ultimate truth than in the Abhidharma tradition. In the Madhyamaka tradition, though the distinction between conventional and ultimate truth is of the utmost importance, the ultimate truth is, paradoxically, that nothing is ultimately true. Hence, there is a sense in which conventional truth is the only truth there is. This means that emptiness is not some kind of ultimate or noumenal reality beneath the appearances captured by conventional truth. This is one implication of what has been said to be Nāgārjuna's most significant claim: that emptiness is itself empty, that emptiness lacks *svabhāva*—independent nature—as much as anything else, and so emptiness also has only secondary existence (see Garfield 2002a: 39). The assertion of the universality of emptiness is only conventionally true, and arguments in favor of this assertion are sound only by reference to what is conventionally true. However, it was supposed, this is not a disadvantage: since the only truth there can be is conventional truth, the only way Madhyamaka philosophy could be true is by being conventionally true. Since it is conventionally true, it is as true as any philosophy could be (and likewise since philosophies denying emptiness are conventionally false, they are as false as any philosophy could be).

That Madhyamaka philosophy is only conventionally true is one of several statements in the tradition that appear quite paradoxical. Another such statement, perhaps the most striking, is Nāgārjuna's claim that "there is not the slightest difference between cyclic existence and nirvana" (Garfield 1995: 25:19). Since neither cyclic existence nor nirvana has an independent nature, there is no fundamental distinction between them. From the standpoint of the early Buddhist tradition, this would seem to be the most fundamental of distinctions. But from the standpoint of the Madhyamaka school, emptiness undermines all distinctions, including those employed in the Buddha's teaching. Another paradoxical statement is Nāgārjuna's claim that he has no view: "Emptiness is the relinquishing of all views. For whomever emptiness is a view, that one will accomplish nothing" (Garfield 1995: 13:8). As understood here, a view is a statement about the independent nature of things and so, if emptiness were a view, it would be an assertion that emptiness is a feature of the independent nature of things. But the whole point is precisely that there is no independent nature of things.

Nāgārjuna's philosophy is notoriously difficult to understand and has been diversely interpreted by contemporary scholars (the account just given does not square with all interpretations). Some have argued that it cannot escape being a form of nihilism (despite Nāgārjuna's claims to the contrary) and others have maintained that it is a kind of skepticism akin to Pyrrhonian skepticism. Another interpretation is that Nāgārjuna's dialectic gives rise to a kind of mysticism in which any discursive understanding of reality is inadequate, perhaps pointing to the need for a different form of understanding. In this respect, it is sometimes seen as a precursor of Chinese Ch'an and Japanese Zen Buddhism (there is a brief discussion of these later). Another interpretation, more in line with the aforementioned presentation, is that Nāgārajuna reaffirms conventional truth, but with the crucial realization that it is merely conventional and not an understanding of the independent nature of things (there being no such nature). On any reading, the realization of emptiness was regarded by Nāgārjuna as the one and only way to truly overcome suffering and gain universal compassion—the hallmarks of enlightenment for Mahāyāna Buddhism.

The Yogācāra school began a bit later than the Madhyamaka school. The term 'Yogācāra' means the practice of yoga (meaning the practice of the spiritual discipline of the Bodhisattva). However, the school is also known as the Cittamātra, or consciousness only, school, and this is an indication of the fact that it has often (though not always) been interpreted as endorsing a form of idealism. The Yogācāra school is traditionally said to have begun with two half-brothers, Asaṅga and Vasubandhu, who probably lived around the fourth and fifth centuries CE (though doctrines associated with Yogācāra appeared somewhat before this in works such as the *Saṁdhinirmocana Sutra*). Both figures were originally proponents of Abhidharma forms of Buddhism who then converted to the Yogācāra standpoint. In fact, Vasubandhu was probably the person of the same name who wrote the Sarvāstivāda "Commentary on the Treasury of Abhidharma" (referred to earlier in the discussion of Abhidharma Buddhism). In any case, the Yogācāra school is concerned with many of the central themes of the Abhidharma philosophers, though it is also in part a reaction to the Madhyamaka school. Asaṅga and Vasubandhu each wrote many works. One of these, Asaṅga's "Bodhisattva Stages" *(Bodhisattva-bhūmi),* contains an important ethical text, the "Chapter on Ethics" (see Tatz 1986). However, in accord with the Indian Buddhist philosophical tradition as a whole, most of these founding texts pertain to epistemological and metaphysical themes. With respect to these themes, Vasubandhu's work has received the greatest attention (for an overview, see Gold 2012).

The roots of the Yogācāra school in the Abhidharma philosophies are evident in its distinctive theory of consciousness. The Abhidharma tradition had distinguished six modes of consciousness: sight, hearing, smell, taste, touch and thought (or mind). To these familiar modes, the Yogācāra philosophers added two more, what they called storehouse or foundational consciousness *(ālaya-vijñāna)* and afflicted mind *(kliṣṭa-manas).* In postulating these additional modes of consciousness, their aim was to make sense of several basic Buddhist commitments: that our ordinary experience of the world is mistaken, that we nonetheless have a capacity for enlightenment, that the moral quality of actions conditions our future well-being (karma), and more broadly that there is some continuity within a life, across rebirths, and in the transition from the cycle of rebirth to nirvana (in all cases without supposing that there is a self).

The storehouse consciousness is the condition of all other modes of consciousness (even, they said, as the ocean is the condition of waves). Since it is present even when other modes of consciousness are not (for example, in sleep) it bears some similarity to what is called the unconscious or subconscious in contemporary thought. In itself the storehouse consciousness is neither subjective nor objective, but it is the ultimate source of the subject-object distinction that structures the other modes of consciousness (for example, in sight we suppose that a subject sees an object). Of course, the storehouse consciousness is not a self in the sense of being a substance that has identity through time and distinctness from other things. Rather, it is a stream of ever-changing processes, understood in terms of the doctrine of momentariness, that give rise to the false appearance of a self. These processes include the karmic seeds *(bījā)* that have been planted by previous actions and that will eventually mature and bear fruit in future experiences. The storehouse consciousness may be thought of as a repository of these seeds. The afflicted mind provides a kind of mediation between the store-house consciousness and the other six modes of consciousness. It actualizes the negative potential of the unwholesome karmic seeds by mistakenly interpreting the content of the other modes of consciousness in terms of the categories of subject-object dualism. Insofar as previous actions are based on ignorance, and so are expressions of attachment and grasping, they perpetuate the cycle of rebirth. But the storehouse consciousness also contains wholesome seeds that make enlightenment possible. Through purification processes such as the practice of the Six Perfections the unwholesome seeds are gradually eliminated and the wholesome seeds are cultivated. In the culmination of this process, enlightenment, the storehouse consciousness becomes "the great mirror cognition" that accurately reflects reality such as it actually is (without imposition of our misleading concepts based on subject-object dualism and the attachments to which it gives rise).

A second, related idea for which the Yogācāra school is well known is the doctrine of the three natures *(trisvabhāva)*. Mahāyāna philosophers were agreed in supposing that all things are empty of own-being, of inherent nature *(svabhāva)*, but they disagreed about how to understand and elaborate this fundamental notion. The Yogācāra contention that everything has three inter-related natures is an interpretation of emptiness that differs from the Madhyamaka approach. The first of the three natures is the imagined or constructed nature *(parikalpita-svabhāva)* according to which each thing is distinct. This is the way in which we ordinarily experience the world: we take it to consist of distinct, independently existing objects (distinct both from one another and from the perceiving subject). The second is the dependent nature *(paratantra-svabhāva)* according to which what we imagine to be distinct is in fact dependent on other things, in particular on the constructive activities of consciousness. This is the Buddhist doctrine of dependent origination as understood in the Mahāyāna tradition. Finally, the third is the consummate or perfected nature *(pariniṣpanna-svabhāva)* according to which the imagined nature is an illusion: though we experience things as distinct, they are not in fact distinct. The subject-object distinction, along with all other distinctions, has no reality. That is, every "thing" is empty of any inherent nature. Of course, it may seem odd to explain the absence of any inherent nature in terms of three natures. But, as we have seen, paradoxical modes of expression are common currency in Mahāyāna discourse, and the point was sometimes acknowledged by saying that what we really have here are three non-natures *(tri-niḥsvabhāva)*.

One final development in Mahāyāna Buddhism is worth noting here. During the third and fourth centuries CE a group of texts was produced in India that featured what was called Tathāgata-garbha (for discussion of these, see P. Williams 2009a: ch. 5). The term means the embryo or womb of the Buddha, and the basic contention of the Tathāgata-garbha perspective was that all sentient beings have the capacity for enlightenment. A similar point was made by saying that all sentient beings possess Buddha-nature *(buddha-dhātu),* meaning that they all have the potential to become a Buddha. The Tathāgata-garbha texts were primarily oriented toward spiritual practice. Central to their aim was to encourage practitioners to recognize that, despite obstacles, enlightenment was possible. They were not philosophical texts that defended a metaphysical theory. Hence, Tathāgata-garbha thought was not a philosophical school in the way that Madhyamaka and Yogācāra traditions were. But it was an important Mahāyāna orientation, and it was especially influential in the development of East Asian forms of Buddhism. Moreover, it was a key Buddhist perspective on our capacity for moral development insofar as this is an aspect of attaining enlightenment.

A central theme in all forms of Indian Buddhism is that greed, hatred and delusion are the three roots of unwholesome actions that must be destroyed in order to achieve enlightenment. However, these roots might seem so pervasive and intractable as to be unsurpassable obstacles to enlightenment. In Tathāgata-garbha thought, these roots and related phenomena were represented as insubstantial defilements that conceal our true nature, the embryo of the Buddha, which is always there ready to be uncovered by Buddhist practice. Enlightenment from this perspective is, in a sense, the realization of what already exists. We are always already Buddhas, but we fail to recognize this on account of the defilements. Since the defilements are not an essential part of our nature, but Tathāgata-garbha (or Buddha-nature) is, the process of enlightenment is the discovery of what we truly are. Though this claim is a Mahāyāna development, it may have been anticipated in the Pali Canon, where we are told that we have a "luminous" mind *(citta)* that is "defiled by adventitious defilements" until, through spiritual practice, it is freed of these defilements *(AN* I 10).

Tathāgata-garbha was characterized in a variety of ways. Sometimes it was associated with emptiness or nirvana, but other characterizations were more controversial. For example, in the *Śrīmālā-devi-siṃhanāda Sūtra* we are told that it possessed four "perfections," namely "permanence, bliss, self, and purity" (see S. B. King 1991: 12). Permanence? Self? It is easy to see why there has been opposition to Tathāgata-garbha thought by other Buddhists (for critical discussion, see Hubbard and Swanson 1997). It seemed to attribute an inherent nature to us, but of course any such attribution is contrary to the most fundamental of Buddhist teachings. The main response to this critique is that the central purpose of the Tathāgata-garbha tradition was practical, to promote enlightenment, not theoretical, to develop a metaphysics. Hence, though statements in Tathāgata-garbha texts might look like ascriptions of human nature that Buddhists could not accept, they should be understood pragmatically, as skillful means of encouraging the pursuit of enlightenment, or perhaps merely as expressions of conventional truth that are not intended as accounts of what is ultimately true (which in Mahāyāna Buddhism cannot be described in statements in any case).

In this respect, there is a connection between Tathāgata-garbha thought and the Yogācāra school. It is sometimes said that, from a Yogācāra perspective, the Madhyamaka school was inadequate because a more positive characterization of the Buddhist outlook is needed than simply maintaining the emptiness of all things. For this reason, the Yogācāra philosophers developed doctrines such as the eight modes of consciousness and the three natures. Something similar might be said about the Tathāgata-garbha thinkers. And in fact there were some historical connections between the two (see S. B. King 1991: 17–21). For example, in the *Laṅkāvatāra Sūtra* the Tathāgata-garbha is explicitly linked to the storehouse consciousness (see Suzuki 1999). Both notions convey something about our fundamental capacity for enlightenment.

## Buddhism Beyond India

For a variety of reasons, around the 12th century Buddhism largely disappeared from India, though in some limited respects it was revived in the 20th century. However, long before this, Buddhism started to spread beyond India to such places as Sri Lanka, Southeast Asia, Tibet, China, Japan and other parts of East Asia (for a brief account of these developments, see Harvey 1990: ch. 7). These are the main places in the world in which Buddhism has developed, and often flourished, throughout most of its history. Though to a large extent contemporary work in Buddhist moral philosophy tends to be oriented toward the Indian traditions described in this and the previous chapter, some of this work focuses on other Buddhist traditions, especially Tibetan Buddhism and some East Asian schools. Hence, it will be helpful to briefly introduce these other traditions here.

Buddhism entered Tibet in two waves, first in the seventh century CE and again, with more lasting results, in the 11th century CE. The form of Buddhism that took root in Tibet was grounded in Mahāyāna Buddhism, and the dominant philosophical outlook was that of the Indian Madhyamaka school. Four indigenous Tibetan Buddhist schools were established. The most influential of these, the Geluk ("system of virtue") school, was founded in the 15th century by Tsongkhapa, the most prominent Tibetan Buddhist philosopher. His work, *The Great Treatise on the Stages of the Path to Enlightenment (Lam Rim Chen Mo),* is an important source of Buddhist moral thought: the second volume contains an extensive discussion of the Six Perfections (see Tsongkhapa 2004: 85–224). The person entitled His Holiness the Dalai Lama is a significant figure in the Geluk school and monastic order. Since the 17th century, this figure has been the political as well as spiritual leader of Tibet. The person the world knows today as the Dalai Lama is the 14th such figure in Tibetan history (for more on the current Dalai Lama, see Chapter 11). In his numerous works, the 14th Dalai Lama presents and defends a version of Madhyamaka philosophy rooted in the Geluk tradition, with special emphasis on the Madhyamaka philosopher Śāntideva (for example, see Dalai Lama 1995). The prominence of Madhyamaka Buddhism in recent discussions of Buddhist moral philosophy is in some measure due to the influence of the Dalai Lama and Tibetan Buddhism in the Western world in the past half century.

An important characteristic of Tibetan Buddhism is that it is a tantric form of Buddhism (or what is sometimes called Vajrayāna Buddhism). Tantric Buddhism began in India and became an influential form of Indian Buddhism beginning around the eighth century CE (for an account of this, see P. Williams *et al.* 2012: ch. 7). Roughly speaking, it is a synthesis of Mahāyāna Buddhism and an ancient, independent Indian tantric tradition. Tantric Buddhism has a number of distinctive features. The most important of these with respect to ethical thought and practice is the suggestion that desires and emotions otherwise viewed quite negatively in Buddhist discourse (such as sexual desire and anger) may in special circumstances be used to attain enlightenment. Hence, actions ordinarily regarded as violations of basic moral precepts might sometimes be justified. One rationale for this is the belief that, on account of non-dualism, one should not be attached to the dual categories of the forbidden and permitted. This may also be related to the ethical employment of skillful means discussed earlier in this chapter according to which Bodhisattvas are sometimes permitted to violate the moral precepts in the name of compassion. In both cases, a form of moral complexity—justified violation of standard moral precepts—is introduced that was not envisioned in earlier Buddhist traditions.

Buddhism reached China around the first century CE. In time, numerous schools of Chinese Buddhism developed, often reflecting the interaction of Mahāyāna approaches with the indigenous Daoist tradition. One of these schools, Hua-yen Buddhism, has been influential in recent work in socially engaged Buddhism on account of its understanding of the interdependence of all things (a Mahāyāna interpretation of dependent arising)—especially as depicted in the metaphor of "Indra's net," an infinite net in which a jewel at each node reflects all the other jewels in the net (for a discussion of Hua-yen Buddhism, see Cook 1977). Another influential East Asian school is Chinese Ch'an Buddhism, along with its manifestation in Japan, Zen Buddhism. The Ch'an and Zen traditions are well known for their skepticism about the value of studying traditional texts and rationally reflecting on Buddhist ideas as well as for their emphasis on unique forms of meditation (the terms 'ch'an' and 'zen' are renditions of a Sanskrit term, 'dhyāna,' for meditation). These attitudes are expressed in a saying attributed to Bodhidharma, who is reputed to have brought this approach from India to China: "A special transmission outside the scriptures; without depending on words and letters; pointing directly to the human mind; seeing the innate nature, one becomes a Buddha" (Harvey 1990: 154).

Zen Buddhism was established in Japan in the 12th century (for an account of Zen, see Kasulis 1981). There are two main branches: the Sōtō school stresses purposeless "just sitting" meditation, not as a means to enlightenment, but as a way of, in some sense, already being enlightened, while the Rinzai school emphasizes the more familiar meditation on enigmatic statements and anecdotes called kōans. Despite its focus on meditation and its deep distrust of concepts and rational thought as inevitable distortions of reality, Zen developed a distinctive outlook that, at least in some presentations, has a philosophical dimension. The best-known figure in this regard is Dōgen, the 13th century founder of the Sōtō school and author of the *Shōbō-genzō,* a classic of Zen Buddhist philosophy. Since Zen largely inherits the ethical outlook of earlier forms of Mahāyāna Buddhism, one of Dōgen's concerns was how to understand this in light of the belief that concepts such as good and evil are as problematic as all other concepts. To some extent, this concern might naturally arise in any Mahāyāna outlook, given its emphasis on non-dualism and emptiness, but the worry is heightened in Zen in view of its strident suspicion of all forms of conceptual thought. On account of this suspicion and Zen's overall iconoclastic posture, questions have been raised about whether its perspective is basically antinomian or amoral (for discussion of this, see Brear 1974, Ives 1992, James 2004: ch. 2, Park 2008: ch. 9 and Whitehill 1987). Nonetheless, in recent years Zen has played a role in some discussions of socially engaged Buddhism, rather controversially in the case of war and violence (see Chapter 13) and more optimistically in the case of environmental ethics (see Chapter 14).

# CHAPTER 3

# What Is Buddhist Moral Philosophy?

The aim of this book is to provide an introduction to Buddhist moral philosophy. Hence, the book is about those features of Buddhism, especially Indian Buddhism, that pertain to morality, and the approach to these features is that of philosophy rather than, say, religion, history, sociology, anthropology and the like (though aspects of these other approaches may have some relevance to philosophical understanding). However, the phrase *Buddhist moral philosophy* immediately raises a problem or at least an initial concern. As has been seen, in the traditional forms of Buddhism in India, though morality was quite central and there was considerable philosophical work in areas such as metaphysics and epistemology, there was very little that could be considered explicit expressions of moral philosophy. Certainly, if by moral philosophy we mean the traditions of philosophical reflection about ethics that developed in the Western world from the time of the ancient Greek philosophers, and have endured in various forms more or less continuously until the present day, then as far as we know there is little in Indian Buddhism, or other traditional forms of Buddhism, that could be considered straightforward, systematic works of moral philosophy. This point is widely acknowledged (for example, see Clayton 2006: 21–2, Dreyfus 1995: 29, Goodman 2009: 89 and Kapstein 2001: 157, n. 4). This does not mean that there is nothing that counts as a philosophical discussion of a moral issue in Buddhist thought. Plainly there are such discussions. Nonetheless, there is a striking difference between Western philosophy and

Buddhist philosophy in this regard: virtually from the beginning, moral philosophy has been regarded as a distinct and important branch of philosophy in the Western tradition (see J. M. Cooper 2012: 2–5), but this cannot be said of Buddhist traditions.

Various reasons may be given to explain this difference. In a recent account focusing on the early Indian tradition, Damien Keown considers, but finds mostly inadequate, five possible explanations (see Keown 2006). First, perhaps there were traditional works in Buddhist moral philosophy, but they have been lost and not yet rediscovered. Keown thinks that this is unlikely since we have found so many other kinds of works in the Buddhist tradition. Second, there might be discussions of Buddhist moral philosophy, not as a distinct discipline, but distributed across different categories of knowledge. Keown says that, though in the Pali Canon there are some discussions of hard moral cases in the *Vinaya Piṭaka* and psychological classifications of states of consciousness in terms of their moral valence in the *Abhidhamma Piṭaka,* none of these texts resembles the ethical works of philosophers such as Plato and Aristotle. Third, it might have been supposed that, since the Buddha revealed the basic moral truths, there was no need for philosophical reflection about them. However, Keown observes that this rationale has not been accepted in every religious tradition. For example, the followers of Christ might also have supposed this, but there has been philosophical reflection about morality in the Christian tradition. Fourth, since Buddhism was originally a movement of renouncers, it was not especially concerned with the moral rules necessary for social life. Keown believes that this is somewhat persuasive, but not fully so because there was extensive interaction between the monastic and lay Buddhist communities. Fifth, moral philosophy was not recognized as a distinct discipline that was a part of a standard curriculum of learning: perhaps this is why no texts in moral philosophy were produced. Keown thinks that this explanation is more plausible than the others even though Buddhism clearly valued learning and embraced a curriculum that included such things as grammar, logic, medicine and theoretical forms of philosophy. Of course, it may be noted, this may explain the absence of texts in Buddhist moral philosophy, but the prior question why there was no such discipline in the curriculum would remain.

Keown also makes an interesting additional point. Perhaps what should surprise us is not the absence of moral philosophy in traditional Buddhism but the emergence of moral philosophy in the ancient Greek world. From the perspective of at least many intellectual quarters in the contemporary Western world, moral philosophy may seem to be an obvious and perhaps even inevitable form of human reflection. But when it emerged in the inquiries of Socrates in the fifth century BCE in Athens it was something altogether innovative and unique. Keown suggests that this was related to the development of democracy in Athens, something that has no parallel in the Indian world in which Buddhism was born and flourished. However, Athenian democracy was a brief moment in the history of Western political institutions, and moral philosophy endured as a central feature of the landscape of Western thought for centuries before anything resembling democracy returned to the scene. What is striking about Indian Buddhism is that, though ethics is pervasive and philosophy in the form of metaphysics and epistemology is common, no explicit tradition of moral philosophy developed. As far as we know, systematic works in Buddhist moral philosophy are not found in any ancient Buddhist tradition. There is some ground for perplexity in this, and we will have occasion to return to the issue (see especially the end of Chapter 7).

Nonetheless, something that is plausibly considered Buddhist moral philosophy is very much a part of contemporary Buddhist intellectual discourse. As a first approximation, Buddhist moral philosophy is a reflective endeavor that brings the concerns, perspectives and habits of thought of moral philosophy, as these have been developed in some tradition of the Western world, to bear on the understanding of ethics in Indian Buddhism or later Buddhist traditions that grow out of this. Buddhist moral philosophy in this sense takes diverse forms. At this juncture, it is important to distinguish two of these (noted earlier in the Introduction). First, Buddhist moral philosophy may be an *interpretation* of the commitments of Buddhist ethics, in some school or another, in terms of concerns, problems, concepts, principles or theories that are familiar in some tradition of Western moral philosophy. Second, Buddhist moral philosophy may be a *construction* of what purports to be a defensible Buddhist ethical outlook in terms of some concerns, problems and the like associated with a tradition of Western moral philosophy. Interpretation and construction are distinct enterprises. But they are often related to one another, in part because construction typically presupposes interpretation and interpretation often involves some measure of construction (or what is sometimes called reconstruction), and in part because it is common for both enterprises to be undertaken in the very same places (for example, by the same authors, in the same works). Nonetheless, it is helpful to keep the distinction in mind: it is one thing to claim that an Indian Buddhist text is best interpreted as being committed to a particular philosophical theory, and it is another thing to claim that a Buddhist philosophical theory is rationally defensible.

Buddhist moral philosophy, so understood, is in many respects a product of the modern world. In both its interpretive and constructive forms, there are important ways in which it may be seen as an instance of what is sometimes called Buddhist modernism. Hence, in order to better understand Buddhist moral philosophy, its aspirations as well as its potential limitations, it will be instructive to relate it to this broader cultural phenomenon.

## Buddhist Modernism

Buddhist modernism, as a category for understanding fairly recent Buddhist thought and practice in, or associated with, the Western world, has been featured in the work of a number of scholars such as Heinz Bechert (1984 and 1994), Jay L. Garfield (Forthcoming), Donald S. Lopez, Jr. (2002) and David L. McMahan (2008 and 2012). The term 'Buddhist modernism' (or sometimes 'modern Buddhism') is best seen as referring to a family of interpretations and developments of traditional forms of Buddhism that tend to emphasize ideas and values that are thought to be compatible with certain features of modernity and to de-emphasize, or even reject as "inessential," ideas and values that are thought to be incompatible with those features of modernity.

In this context, modernity is usually defined primarily in terms of the outlook connected with or inspired by the European Enlightenment of the 18th century. But the understanding of modernity is complicated in that it is sometimes taken to include earlier developments, such as the Protestant reformation and the scientific revolution, as well as subsequent developments, some of which were reactions against the Enlightenment—for example, Romanticism. Proponents of Buddhist modernism usually regard ideas and values drawn from this ensemble of viewpoints as important characteristics of the modern Western world.

Reacting in part to earlier 19th century pejorative European portrayals of Buddhism as nihilistic and pessimistic, advocates of Buddhist modernism often claim that in reality Buddhism is an ancient tradition that is especially well suited to the modern world. Sometimes they maintain that the Buddhism of Buddhist modernism is a recovery of the original teaching of Buddhism (or even of the Buddha himself) that existed prior to the later accumulation of alien or corrupt elements. However, to a large extent it would be more accurate to say that the Buddhism of Buddhist modernism is itself a hybrid form of Buddhism that has come into being only recently (roughly speaking, in the last century and a quarter) and that draws nearly as much on the outlooks of modernity as it does on the ancient traditions of Buddhism. At the same time, though, proponents of Buddhist Modernism are sometimes critical of certain aspects of the modern world (for example, with respect to issues concerning material consumption, technology and the environment), and they may present Buddhism as an important source of critique of modern values in these respects.

Buddhist modernism is by no means a homogeneous phenomenon. Its interpretations can take different forms, have different purposes and come from different sources. In many cases, these interpretations are not fully compatible with one another. Often they have been put forward by scholars of Buddhism or persons sympathetic to Buddhism in the West. However, this has not always been the case. Sometimes they have been developed by Asian Buddhist intellectuals (such as Walpola Rahula and K. N. Jayatilleke) or Asian Buddhist leaders (such as Thich Nhat Hanh and the Dalai Lama) who have been influenced by Western ideas. In any event, Buddhist modernism is very much an understanding of Buddhism of, and typically for, a modern world in which Western values and perspectives have tremendous currency.

A central theme of Buddhist modernism is that Buddhism is primarily a philosophy, or a psychology, that is based on experience and reason. Moreover, it is often claimed that Buddhism so understood is compatible with the methods, and sometimes even the doctrines, of modern science. It is sometimes said that the Buddha was a kind of empiricist and that Buddhist meditation is a form of empirical observation. On this view, Buddhism (or at least what is put forward as a defensible form of Buddhism) is fully in line with scientific naturalism, the contention that we should accept only what is supported by, or at least consistent with, the scientific understanding of the world (there is more discussion of Buddhism and naturalism in Chapter 4).

Another prominent theme of Buddhist modernism is that Buddhism is in harmony with many modern, Western political and moral values. In politics, it is often said that Buddhism is congruent with ideas such as democracy, equality, liberty and human rights (and also, in some anti-colonial contexts, nationalism). In morality, the Buddhist values of compassion, loving-kindness, generosity and patience are commonly put forward as well suited to a liberal moral outlook that many in the modern world embrace. Moreover, advocates of Buddhist modernism sometimes suggest that Buddhism is compatible with a form of individualism in which the experience, reason or intuition of each individual person may be regarded as a source of insight, understanding or wisdom.

Other aspects of Buddhist modernism stress the importance of lay persons and ordinary life (in contrast to monasticism), the value of meditation as a practice that can benefit virtually anyone, the significance of ancient texts (as opposed to practices of ordinary Buddhists), and sometimes—especially in connection with Zen Buddhism—the key role of Romantic themes such as creativity, spontaneity, simplicity and the identification with nature.

The claims of Buddhist modernists typically have some basis in Buddhist traditions: they are not fabrications. However, a misleading impression of these traditions may be created by the way the modernist themes are highlighted and, equally important, the way other aspects of these traditions thought to be out of sync with modernity—often much of what makes them look to be "religions"—are downplayed, ignored, reinterpreted or criticized. These latter aspects include rebirth and the cosmologies associated with rebirth (complete with realms of heaven and hell), prayers to cosmic Buddhas and Bodhisattvas, veneration of relics and images and a host of practices that may appear to involve magical, miraculous or supernatural features. These aspects of Buddhism are pervasive in many Buddhist traditions, and in the lives of many Buddhists today, but from the standpoint of Buddhist modernism they are usually on the margin of Buddhism (if they are not rejected entirely).

For this reason among others, the various expressions of Buddhist modernism are controversial and have been the subject of criticism by Buddhists and non-Buddhists alike. In this connection, it is important to draw a distinction that is similar to the distinction made earlier between Buddhist moral philosophy as interpretation and as construction. On the one hand, insofar as Buddhist modernists are making claims about the proper interpretation of some traditional Buddhist texts, teachings and practices, these claims might properly be criticized if they are inaccurate on account of distortion by modern ideas and perspectives. On the other hand, insofar as Buddhist modernists are making proposals about what Buddhism in the modern world ought to be like, they would not necessarily be subject to the criticism of inaccurate interpretation. For they may well grant that what they are proposing is at odds with certain features of the tradition and involves a synthesis of some aspects of traditional Buddhism and some ideas and values of the modern world. There might be objections to this as well, but the nature of these objections would be different. For example, it might be said that some Buddhist tradition is an integrated whole and so we should not pick and choose which features of the tradition to accept and which to reject. Or it might be argued that, since the modern outlook is problematic in many respects, there should be no attempt to synthesize Buddhism with it. In any case, Buddhist modernism has taken both of these forms: it has been put forward as an interpretation of what Buddhism has been or once was, and it has been presented as a proposal for what Buddhism ought to be (and, of course, it has sometimes been both).

It is helpful to situate Buddhist moral philosophy in the context of Buddhism modernism: in both its interpretive and constructive forms, Buddhist moral philosophy can often be understood as expressing one or more themes in the Buddhist modernist outlook. This is not to say that all Buddhist moral philosophers embrace all of these themes. There is too much diversity in the viewpoints of these philosophers to make any such generalization. Moreover, the themes themselves are not an integrated system, but a loose collection of sometimes overlapping features that are usually endorsed by people in various combinations and to differing extents. Nonetheless, a good deal of work in Buddhist moral philosophy exhibits one or more of the themes of Buddhist modernism. Here are three brief examples (each of which will be given substantial attention in later chapters).

The first is a recent debate about the doctrines of karma and rebirth. As we have seen, these doctrines are at the heart of Indian Buddhist ethical thought. They declare that morally good actions tend to increase the well-being of the person who performs them in this life or a future life, while morally bad actions tend to have the opposite effect. In the recent debate, some persons have maintained that these doctrines are untenable, at least in their traditional form, primarily because it is believed that they are incompatible with or at least not supported by the contemporary scientific view of the world or else because it is judged that they have problematic moral implications. Hence, much attention has been given to the question of whether these doctrines are really essential to Buddhism. A number of Western Buddhist philosophers and other followers of Buddhism have argued for a contemporary form of Buddhism that would reject, or at least not accept, or perhaps substantially reinterpret, karma and rebirth. These arguments are obvious manifestations of Buddhist modernism: commitment to modern science or a contemporary moral sensibility has led to a re-evaluation of ancient Buddhist doctrines that were virtually unquestioned in traditional Indian Buddhism and remain unquestioned by many Buddhists in the world today (for more discussion of this topic, see Chapter 4).

A second example of recent discussions of Buddhist moral philosophy that may be seen as an expression of Buddhist modernism is the literature on Buddhism and human rights. The belief that there are human rights and that they are an important part of moral and political life originates in Europe in the 17th and 18th centuries. This belief is quintessentially modern, and it is evident that ethical texts in classical Indian Buddhism, or any other traditional form of Buddhism, do not explicitly endorse or advocate human rights as such. Nonetheless, many contemporary scholars of Buddhism have argued that the values and principles in these texts either implicitly imply that there are human rights or are at least consistent with human rights. Moreover, many intellectual advocates of socially engaged Buddhism are deeply committed to human rights and maintain that a defense of human rights should be at the heart of a Buddhist moral and political outlook in the world today. Both of these contentions are clear expressions of Buddhist modernism (this issue is considered in Chapter 12).

A final example concerns normative moral theory. Though there is very little in classical Indian Buddhism that could be considered explicit articulations or defenses of normative moral theories as they have been understood in Western philosophy, some scholars of Buddhism have interpreted some of the texts of Indian Buddhism in terms of these theories. For instance, some scholars have argued that Indian Buddhist ethical thought is committed to a form of consequentialism, a normative moral theory that was expressly stated and developed only in the modern era. As an initial rough approximation, consequentialism is the position that what makes an action morally right is that it has appropriately valuable consequences. Insofar as scholars have claimed that Indian Buddhists were committed to consequentialism, their claim may be seen as an instance of Buddhist modernism: they are emphasizing the compatibility of Buddhism with a common feature of modern thought. Moreover, insofar as they have argued that contemporary Buddhist moral philosophy should be developed along consequentialist lines (irrespective of the commitments of the ancient Indian figures), their argument may also plausibly be regarded as a form of Buddhist modernism.

However, there is a complication in this picture. In recent debates, one of the main alternatives to the consequentialist understanding of Buddhism is a virtue ethics understanding (in terms of either interpretation or construction). In this context, virtue ethics is usually taken to be a normative moral outlook that originates in the ancient Greek world, especially in the thought of Aristotle. Hence, it is not a modern theory. In fact, the revival of virtue ethics in moral philosophy during the last several decades is often presented as a critique of modern moral theories such as consequentialism. From this perspective, it would seem to be a mistake to consider the virtue ethics understanding of Buddhist moral thought as an expression of Buddhist modernism (these different interpretations are discussed in Chapters 6 and 7).

This does show that understanding Buddhist moral philosophy as an expression of Buddhist modernism has limitations. It would be a mistake to think of it simply and exclusively in those terms. However, as we will see in the next section, contemporary normative ethics is commonly presented as centering on a debate about which theory of morally right actions is correct. The competing theories include both consequentialism and virtue ethics along with several others. Though these different approaches have various historical origins in the Western world, the supposition that an important task of moral philosophy is to determine which of these approaches is the correct moral theory is widely accepted in contemporary Western moral philosophy. Hence, to engage in a discussion about whether Buddhist ethical thought should be understood or developed in terms of one of these alternatives might be seen as another form of Buddhist modernism: it is an attempt to understand Buddhism in terms of what is currently thought to be important in Western moral philosophy.

It must be further acknowledged, however, that many contemporary proponents of virtue ethics would argue that virtue ethics is not a moral theory in competition with other moral theories such as consequentialism, but an alternative to such theories (for example, see Pincoffs 1986). In this view, the expectation that it is important to have a certain kind of moral theory—in particular, one that is centered on a basic principle that explains what makes actions morally right—is a feature of modernity that should be resisted. Virtue ethics, rooted in ancient figures such as Aristotle, represents a different way of conceiving of moral philosophy that emphasizes the importance of living a good life and having a good moral character. Understanding Buddhist ethics in terms of virtue ethics on this conception should not be seen as an expression of Buddhist modernism. It would be better to think of it as drawing on one current of anti-modernism that is part of the contemporary scene in moral philosophy.

To sum up, though much contemporary reflection on Buddhist morality, and especially Buddhist moral philosophy, participates in many of the tendencies of Buddhist modernism, there are complications in the nature and degree of this participation. As just noted, obvious modernist approaches such as the consequentialist understanding may exist alongside other approaches such as the virtue ethics understanding that resist assimilation to modernism. Moreover, some figures may be modernist in some respects but not in others. For example, the Dalai Lama defends human rights as compatible with a Buddhist moral outlook, but he also defends karma and rebirth. Nonetheless, if handled carefully, the framework of Buddhist modernism can provide one illuminating context for understanding much recent thought about Buddhist morality.

## Western Moral Philosophy

Since Buddhist moral philosophy in both its interpretive and constructive modes typically involves the employment of the concerns, perspectives, concepts, theories and the like of Western moral philosophy in understanding or developing Buddhist ethical thought, it will be helpful at this juncture to say something briefly about the nature of Western moral philosophy. Of course, there is not complete agreement about the characterization of the subject both in contemporary work and in discussions throughout its history. In fact, one way of portraying Western moral philosophy would be in terms of its development and transformations since the period of Socrates, Plato and Aristotle. However, a good deal of (though by no means all) work in Buddhist moral philosophy that is done today presupposes a conception of moral philosophy that is widely accepted in the English-speaking world in what is usually called the analytic tradition. In this conception, *philosophy* is a form of reflection and discourse on certain topics in which there is an emphasis on formulating arguments where premises and inferences are clearly and explicitly stated and defended. In supporting these arguments, philosophers stress the importance of maintaining consistency, carefully articulating distinctions, and responding to objections. The topics in philosophy are usually, though not always, rather abstract. In *moral philosophy* (sometimes called philosophical ethics or simply ethics) we can identify four main areas of concern. Though these areas are related in a variety of ways and many moral theories defended by philosophers involve more than one of them, it will nonetheless be helpful to delineate the main topics of each.

First, there are discussions about the meaning and possible truth-value of moral statements employing concepts such as good, right, ought and so forth (and sometimes more specific concepts such as justice or courage). These semantic discussions are usually closely connected to epistemological issues such as whether moral statements may be justified or known. And these epistemological issues are often related in turn to what may be considered metaphysical topics such as whether there are moral facts that are the truth-makers of moral statements. This ensemble of semantic, epistemological and metaphysical concerns is usually called *meta-ethics*. Debates about meta-ethics have been at the heart of much work in moral philosophy in the analytic tradition for over a century. There are many different meta-ethical theories, but it is customary to distinguish two broad outlooks. According to cognitivists, moral statements express beliefs that may be true or false (they are said to be "truth-apt"). Some cognitivists think that there are moral facts in the world in virtue of which moral beliefs are sometimes true and sometimes false (they are often called moral realists), while other cognitivists think that whether moral beliefs are true or false depends upon whether they would be generated by a suitably described rational procedure (they are usually called moral constructivists). According to non-cognitivists, moral statements are not expressions of belief, but of non-cognitive mental states such as attitudes, feelings, desires and the like. As such, they cannot be said to be true or false, at least not in the way in which ordinary cognitive statements are thought to be true or false. It is often supposed that a strength of cognitivism is that it can account for intuitions many people have to the effect that morality is in some way objective, while it is a weakness of non-cognitivism that it has difficulty doing this. By contrast, it is commonly thought that a strength of non-cognitivism is that it can make sense of commonly held intuitions that expressions of moral statements are motivating or action-guiding, while it is a weakness of cognitivism that it has trouble doing this. A meta-ethical position that in some ways straddles the distinction between cognitive and non-cognitive theories is moral relativism, the view that moral statements are true or false, not in an absolute sense, but relative to the perspective some group of people.

A second subject of central concern in moral philosophy is the nature of morally right and wrong actions and, more broadly, of morally good and bad persons. Related to this, especially in the case of actions, is a concern to specify a procedure or way of determining these things. This is the domain of what is usually called *normative ethics*. In contemporary discussions, the "textbook" short list of normative theories of the nature of right action often contains three entries. These may be stated briefly and rather simply as follows. Consequentialism is the view that an action is morally right if and only if, and because, it has appropriately valuable consequences. Deontology is the position that an action is morally right if and only if, and because, it is done out of respect for or at least in accord with our moral duties. Virtue ethics is the claim that an action is morally right if and only if, and because, it is what a virtuous agent would characteristically do. More would have to be said to relate these theories to accounts of how we should determine which actions are right.

It is important to recognize, however, that this common threefold division disguises several kinds of complexity in normative ethics. One of these complexities is that a more complete list of normative theories that are sometimes defended in contemporary discussions would include several other theories such as, for example, natural law theory, divine command theory and contract theory. Another complication is that there is considerable resistance within the field of normative ethics to the idea that it should feature a moral theory centered on a single fundamental principle as in the aforementioned three formulations. There are several sources of this resistance. One of these is skepticism about the role of general principles in moral life (what is often called particularism), and another is the belief that there is a plurality of basic moral values that cannot be reduced to a single moral principle (what is usually called pluralism). Virtue ethics itself, in Aristotelian and other forms, is sometimes presented as an alternative to the conception of moral theory usually presupposed in consequentialist and deontological theories. As observed in the last section, on this understanding, its proponents would not welcome the aforementioned formulation that represents it simply as another theory of what makes an action morally right. This is because the attraction of virtue ethics is often thought to be its broader emphasis on moral character and a morally good life, where these are not centered on following a fundamental moral principle. Another source of resistance is feminist ethics. In some of its expressions, such as the ethics of care, the center of ethical attention is our relationships with particular persons rather than adherence to a basic moral principle. In sum, contemporary work in normative ethics encompasses a wide variety of approaches.

There is another aspect of normative ethics that should be noted. Most normative outlooks presuppose some understanding of value, of what makes something such as a state of affairs, an experience, or a life as a whole, good or bad. Especially important in this regard are theories of what makes life go well or badly for a person (what are sometimes called theories of well-being or happiness). In contemporary discussions, four basic theories of well-being are commonly distinguished. Mental state theories depict well-being in terms of the positive or negative quality of a person's mental states (hedonism is the best-known version of this). Desire-satisfaction theories portray well-being as a matter of the satisfaction of a person's desires. For objective list theories, well-being concerns our participation in some set of objective goods such as knowledge, friendship, achievement and the like. Finally, according to nature-fulfillment theories, well-being has to do with the fulfillment of our human nature.

Normative ethics is sometimes understood as a rather abstract enterprise that typically operates at a fairly high level of generality. However, normative ethical theories as well as non-theoretical approaches to normative ethics often have practical implications for specific moral issues. Discussion of these implications is the province of a third area of moral philosophy, what is usually called *applied ethics* (or sometimes practical ethics). Moral philosophers in the Western tradition have long been concerned with the practical implications of general normative outlooks. For example, Aristotle wrote about the courage of soldiers, Aquinas discussed capital punishment, Locke examined tolerance, Hume considered suicide, Kant spoke about lying and Mill treated the subjection of women. But applied ethics, conceived as a distinctive branch of moral philosophy, is a rather recent development that came into prominence in the 1960s and 1970s (after a period in which such practical issues were mostly neglected by philosophers). Discussions in applied ethics tend to focus on rather specific moral topics about which there is some controversy in the sense that there are *prima facie* compelling arguments whose conclusions conflict with one another. Some of these issues pertain primarily to personal life, but they often have a public dimension that involves social, political, legal and economic considerations. Prominent areas of concern in applied ethics include, among many others, topics in environmental ethics, medical ethics (or bioethics) and the ethics of war and terrorism.

The distinction between normative and applied ethics might be thought of as a distinction between theoretical and practical forms of moral philosophy. However, though there is some truth to this, it is best not to put much weight on a sharp theory-practice distinction in this context. One reason, as already noted, is that the role of theory is a disputed topic within normative ethics. Another reason is that there is no distinctive method of applied ethics, in the sense of there being an approach that is ordinarily followed according to which the practical implications of a theory are determined. Rather applied ethics is an arena in which assumptions about method are often contested. For those who think there is a basic moral principle, a natural approach might be to establish the implications of the principle for particular cases. This top-down procedure is sometimes contrasted with a bottom-up procedure in which the principle is inferred from our judgments about particular cases. However, in recent years an approach more influential than either of these has been a variation of what John Rawls (1971: 48–51) called the method of reflective equilibrium. According to this approach, we begin with some convictions about a general moral principle (or principles) and some convictions about the proper understanding of some particular moral cases. We then look to see if the principle implies what we think is the correct understanding of the particular cases. When it does not, we make revisions either at the level of principle or at the level of particular (or both) until the principle does imply the proper results for particular cases. The thought is that when we have reached this state of reflective equilibrium we have done what we can to justify both the general principle and the particular result. On this approach, theory and practice go hand in hand. For those who embrace a non-theoretical approach to normative ethics, such as particularism or pluralism, there is even less room for a theory-practice distinction. From these perspectives, applied ethics focuses on the features of particular situations or persons, and theories and principles have little or no role to play.

The threefold division of meta-ethics, normative ethics and applied ethics is widely recognized in contemporary moral philosophy. There is also a fourth area of moral philosophy that is sometimes, but not always, distinguished from these that investigates different ways in which our moral judgments and practices assume, or have some relationship to, the psychology of human beings. This is commonly called *moral psychology*. Though topics in moral psychology have concerned Western moral philosophers since the time of Plato and Aristotle, the contemporary emphasis on these topics owes a good deal to the call by G.E.M. Anscombe (1958: 1) for "an adequate philosophy of psychology" more than a half century ago. More recently, it has been argued by some philosophers that moral psychology should pay more attention to the work of experimental psychology (this is a form of what is usually called experimental philosophy). However, work in moral psychology need not, and often does not, have this specific commitment. It often relies on other sources of understanding the psychology of human beings.

Several aspects of moral psychology may be distinguished. One of these is what is commonly called the problem of free will and determinism (though this is sometimes considered a topic in metaphysics). It is often thought that our moral practices, including especially our moral judgments about what to do and our ascriptions of moral praise and blame, presuppose that we have a free will and so are responsible for our actions. But free will and responsibility may appear to be threatened by determinism, the claim that all human actions are causally determined, and determinism may seem to be presupposed in a scientific understanding of human nature. The problem is how to adjudicate this apparent conflict. Another topic in moral psychology is related, but narrower in scope. As often understood, morality sometimes requires us to act contrary to our self-interest and in some cases it may require us to make extraordinary sacrifices. This would seem to assume that we are psychologically capable of doing these things, that we are able to be altruistic to a greater or lesser extent. But if, as is sometimes supposed, human beings always act so as to promote their own perceived self-interest, or a rather narrow extension of self-interest that encompasses only the interests of close friends and family members, then the requirements of morality might seem to be undermined. Hence, there is a question of whether the demands of morality can be reconciled with psychological facts about our capacity for altruism. This issue is connected to another topic: how to make sense of the fact that we sometimes know what we ought to do, but fail to do it (what is sometimes called *akrasia* or weakness of will). Yet another issue, or set of issues, in moral psychology concerns the nature, role, and importance of—as well as the relationships among—various kinds of mental states that appear significant in our moral life, such mental phenomena as perceptions, reasons, desires, emotions, intentions, motivations and the like. Proponents of virtue ethics have been especially concerned with these mental states, which they see as aspects of moral character, but most moral philosophers today would agree that all or most of these states have some significant role to play in morality. Finally, in connection with this, moral psychology sometimes develops an analysis of the nature and moral significance of specific emotions such as anger, resentment, guilt, remorse, gratitude, compassion, sympathy, generosity and the like.

As will be seen in the chapters ahead, there are forms of Buddhist moral philosophy that involve all four of these areas. There are meta-ethical considerations of the ways in which a Buddhist ethical outlook may be said to be true or justified. In addition, there are discussions of whether Buddhist ethics is or should be committed to a normative ethical theory (and about which theory this might be) as well as examinations of the nature of well-being from a Buddhist standpoint. There are also numerous debates about topics in applied ethics such as human rights, the ethics of war and environmental ethics, among many others (often, though not always, in connection with socially engaged Buddhism). Finally, there are analyses in Buddhist moral philosophy of topics in moral psychology such as the problem of freedom and determinism, our capacity for altruism, mental states associated with moral virtue such as intention, and emotions such as anger and hatred.

## Guidelines for Developing a Buddhist Moral Philosophy

Buddhist moral philosophy, in both its interpretive and constructive aspects, is a relatively recent enterprise that employs the perspectives of Western moral philosophy to understand or develop ethical thought in the Buddhist traditions. Though it has origins in the 19th and first half of the 20th centuries, Buddhist moral philosophy so understood has been pursued in earnest only in the past several decades. It is now beyond the stage of infancy, but is still in a rather early phase of development and is very much a work in progress. As such it will be helpful to consider some guidelines for thinking about what Buddhist moral philosophy has been and might be. This will give us some indication of its aspirations and promises as well as its potential obstacles and limitations (for discussion of the development of Buddhist moral philosophy, see Barnhart 2012, Ives 2008 and S. B. King 2005: ch. 3).

The identification of Buddhist moral philosophy as a distinctive form of inquiry presupposes that we have some confidence that there is something in Buddhist thought and practice that pertains to what we, in the modern world, would describe as *moral* or *ethical* concerns. In ordinary speech as well as in philosophical discourse these two terms, originating from Latin (*mōrālis*) and Greek (*ēthikos*) respectively, are commonly used more or less interchangeably as at least approximate synonyms. However, philosophers sometimes distinguish morality and ethics from one another, usually construing the former as narrower in scope than the latter. An example is Bernard Williams (1985: ch. 1) who considers ethics to be a response to what he takes to be Socrates's rather broad question "How should one live?" and morality to be an answer to a narrower question "What are our obligations (in a special sense of obligation most fully articulated by Kant)?" For the purpose of charting the terrain of Buddhist moral philosophy, it is better to think more in terms of the broad question rather than the narrower one, though there is no point abandoning the common expression 'moral philosophy' in light of Williams's terminological stipulation. Hence, the terms 'morality' and 'ethics' (and their grammatical variations) will be used largely interchangeably, as is common, but they will be understood to refer to the concerns of Williams's broad Socratic question about how one should live. Of course, the question may seem a bit too broad, but Buddhism certainly has a good deal to say about how one should live, while it is at least more debatable whether it supposes that we have obligations in the sense understood by Williams (and, he thinks, much modern thought). Likewise, the full range of topics delineated in the last section fit rather more comfortably within the wider rubric.

The classical Buddhist term most commonly translated as 'morality' or 'ethics' is *sīla/śīla*. This occurs in a variety of contexts, most prominently (as has been seen) in the part of the Eightfold Path that includes right speech, action and livelihood, and the second of the Six Perfections that contains a similar set of rules. These rules might be compared to what we would call moral obligations (or better, prohibitions, since they ordinarily refer to what we are *not* to do). However, since they are aspects of the path to enlightenment, they are sometimes considered commitments of someone who has undertaken the path rather than obligations we are all expected to follow. At the same time, however, pursuing the path is something everyone is ordinarily encouraged to do, at least eventually, and these rules correspond to how an enlightened person would behave, for the most part at any rate. In any case, Buddhism has much more to say about how one should live than is conveyed by following these rules.

As was seen in the first chapter, there are two pairs of evaluative terms in Buddhism that appear to have implications for how one should live, though their connotations are not precisely the same as those of our terms 'ethical' and especially 'moral.' First, actions that are *puñña/puṇya* are regarded as purifying or meritorious actions that benefit the person performing them (and those that are *apuñña/apuṇya* are the opposite). Second, actions that are *kusala/kuśala* are considered to be wholesome, healthy and skillful actions (while those that are *akusala/akuśala* are the contrary). Some scholars think that the first pair of terms is mainly connected with karma and the cycle of rebirth, while the second pair is usually associated with the pursuit of enlightenment. In addition, there are states such as the four divine abodes—loving-kindness, compassion, appreciative joy and equanimity—that are surely relevant to how one should live, along with character traits such as generosity and patience. Finally, from a Buddhist standpoint, aspects of the Eightfold Path and the Six Perfections such as wisdom and concentration are clearly regarded as centrally relevant to how one should live, even though they are distinguished from other aspects that might appear more obviously connected to morality or ethics as we understand them. At any rate, a Buddhist moral philosophy needs to be attentive to the ways in which Buddhist conceptions of how to live may, or may not, be similar to those assumed in Western moral philosophy.

Earlier in this chapter a distinction was drawn between two forms of Buddhist moral philosophy: it might be an interpretation of some Buddhist tradition, figure, text and the like, or it might be a construction of what purports to be a viable Buddhist ethical outlook. Both of these draw on the resources of what is sometimes called comparative philosophy (see Wong 2011) and, in some respects, what is often called comparative religious ethics (see Stalnaker 2013). Insofar as comparative philosophy (or religious ethics) is restricted to detailing the similarities and differences between two traditions such as Western moral philosophy and Buddhist ethical thought, it performs a valuable, albeit limited, service. Such comparisons may be interesting in their own right, and this is one form Buddhist moral philosophy might take. However, many who work in Buddhist moral philosophy have aspirations that go beyond comparison (and what is called comparative philosophy often include these aspirations). In its interpretive mode, the aim is to employ the resources of Western moral philosophy to interpret and thereby better understand Buddhist ethical thought (or, in the less common reverse approach, to use Buddhist perspectives to interpret moral philosophy in the Western traditions). This involves more than comparison. The same is true of the constructive mode of Buddhist moral philosophy. Here the aim is to create something that is in some respects new, a viable Buddhist ethical outlook that makes use of the resources provided by Western moral philosophy (or, with a somewhat different emphasis, to create a viable ethical outlook that employs the resources of both traditions). This constructive activity is related to what has been called fusion philosophy (see Siderits 2003: xi). Here problem-solving is conceived as fundamental to philosophy, and the aim is to use features of one tradition to solve problems in another tradition. This is a constructive activity, though not every constructive mode of Buddhist moral philosophy would put such an emphasis on problem-solving.

There are, in short, several intellectual enterprises that might be meant by the expression Buddhist moral philosophy, and other forms may well emerge in the future. Each of these different enterprises may have value and they need not exclude one another. Nonetheless, it is important to keep in mind that they are governed by rather different criteria of success. Comparison aims at accuracy in the depiction of similarities and differences. Interpretation seeks to go beyond this and increase our understanding. Construction goes beyond comparison in a different way and strives to create a defensible position. And fusion endeavors to solve specific problems.

All these activities are intellectual in that they focus on ideas and their articulation, development, explanation and defense—typically as expressed in texts. There is nothing surprising in this: both Buddhist traditions and Western philosophical traditions have rich textual histories. However, there is an objection to the emphasis on texts, namely, that Buddhism as represented in such texts is very far from Buddhism as experienced in the lives of ordinary persons (in the present or in the past). This is true enough: the rather abstract nature of most any philosophical thought relates to everyday life in at best rather indirect ways. However, this need not undermine the value of the undertaking. The various modes of Buddhist moral philosophy are ways of encountering the ethical dimensions of Buddhism that may be valuable for any number of reasons. But they are not the only ways of encountering these aspects of Buddhism and, for some purposes, they may not be the best ways. This objection should nonetheless remind us of an important point in developing a Buddhist moral philosophy: Buddhism in virtually any tradition is centered on practice, specifically on overcoming suffering, ultimately by attaining enlightenment, and it is important in studying texts to keep this practical context in mind.

Another objection to Buddhist moral philosophy is that there are dangers in employing the concepts, principles and perspectives of one tradition, Western moral philosophy, in order to understand or develop the outlook of another culturally distinct tradition such as Buddhism. One danger is that the Buddhism that emerges from the various forms of Buddhist moral philosophy will, because of the imposition of an alien framework, involve a misunderstanding of Buddhism by way of distorting some aspects of it, giving an improper emphasis to others and perhaps simply ignoring still others altogether. A second somewhat different danger, stressed in postcolonial studies, is that such enterprises may be exercises of power in which those in the Western world continue to dominate people in former colonies through "knowing" their culture in conceptual terms that primarily serve the interests of persons in the West.

These are important concerns that should not be ignored. However, taking them seriously need not mean abandoning Buddhist moral philosophy altogether. Rather, it should be pursued in ways that are alert to these dangers. This is one reason that it was situated in the context of Buddhist modernism earlier in this chapter. In its various modes, proponents of Buddhist moral philosophy aspire to increase our understanding and to develop better ways of thinking about the world. These goods are worth pursuing even in the face of the attendant dangers. Moreover, there are different dangers that would come with forgoing this pursuit entirely or with declaring the culture of "the other" to be so strange and incommensurable that it is simply beyond our comprehension. To a large extent, we can understand the viewpoint of others only through our own perspective. It is now widely recognized that there is no neutral "objective" standpoint available from which such cross-cultural understanding may be obtained. We cannot avoid the hermeneutical insight that, to a considerable extent, we can comprehend the outlooks of others only in terms of our own outlook and that, though our own perspectives may conceal those of others, they may also illuminate them. As Hans-Georg Gadamer (2000: 388) said, understanding involves a "fusion of horizons" based on conversation. On the second danger, it is true that Buddhist moral philosophy could be an expression of domination, but it might also be an opportunity for cooperation. This is an area in which there has been increasing collaboration between Western academics and scholars in Asian countries in which Buddhism has flourished. The participants in these discussions have a variety of backgrounds and standpoints. Some are committed Buddhists, some are not Buddhists but are sympathetic to some of its values, others are more critical in their approach and still others aspire to a more impartial stance. These voices, Western and Asian both, cannot be reduced to a single mold.

A characteristic feature of many voices of modernity is that they bring a high degree of critical reflection, often embracing or at least approaching forms of skepticism, to many characteristic features of human life, especially those concerned with religion and morality. This point is easily exaggerated: critical reflection was hardly absent from pre-modern traditions in ancient and medieval philosophy, and a critical stance is arguably insufficiently present in many expressions of modernity (where, it is sometimes claimed, it is rather selectively applied). Nonetheless, philosophy in the modern Western world rather commonly presents itself as taking a critical or skeptical perspective, and insofar as Buddhist moral philosophy is associated with modernity, it may share in this perspective. An example, already noted, is the concern expressed about the plausibility of karma and rebirth by many persons in the West who are often otherwise sympathetic to Buddhism. It may be objected that this rather skeptical perspective risks distortion in the understanding of Buddhism. For example, the Buddha said that the first of the "five factors of striving" is having "faith in the Tathāgata's [that is, the Buddha's] enlightenment" (*MN* II 95) and that the last of the "five hindrances" to proper concentration is doubt (see *MN* I 274–6). However, such passages need to be placed alongside others in which, for instance, the Buddha says that, subsequent to faith in the Buddha, a follower should examine the meaning of his teachings, gain "reflective acceptance" of them, and then scrutinize them further (see *MN* II 173). Hence, at least up to a point, the Buddha did encourage a critical stance. However, this stance probably did not encompass the skeptical pitch of many of the philosophical voices of modernity, and one of the challenges of Buddhist moral philosophy is to come to terms with this tension.

Another concern is rooted in the variety of forms of Buddhist thought and practice throughout its history and in the world today. As was seen in the first two chapters, there was considerable diversity in the Indian schools of Buddhism, both before and after the development of Mahāyāna Buddhism. As Buddhism spread elsewhere—to Sri Lanka, Southeast Asia, Tibet, China and Japan, among other places—this diversity only increased. Moreover, there are other kinds of variation than those tracked by historical and geographical measures. In view of this, there is reason to be cautious about generalizations concerning "the Buddhist view" of some subject. Buddhism is and has been many different things to many different people (for an overview of some differences, see Faure 2009). It is important to recognize different historical periods, traditions, schools, figures, texts and so forth as well as differences between the perspectives and aspirations of monastics and lay persons, and the differences in the manner in which Buddhism has related to various indigenous and originally non-Buddhist customs and practices in the places it has flourished. In connection with the last point, there are prominent examples of ways in which some forms of Buddhism have been profoundly transformed by their interaction with independent traditions such as tantric practices in India and Daoist perspectives in China.

In light of these concerns, it might seem that it would be unreasonable to make any generalizations about Buddhist ethics. However, this conclusion would be taking the concerns about diversity too far. There is no prospect of discovering an original or pure form of Buddhism, or of establishing a set of necessary and sufficient conditions for the essence of what Buddhism really is, independent of all traditions and cultures. There are, however, many common themes that are frequently, even if not always, found in various manifestations of Buddhism, though the importance, centrality, interpretation and connotations of these themes may differ. To employ the expression made popular by Ludwig Wittgenstein, the diverse forms of Buddhism often share family resemblances with one other. These resemblances sometimes make it possible to make meaningful generalizations qualified by expressions such as "for the most part" or "to a large extent." Though the focus in this book is primarily on the traditions of Indian Buddhism, and though it will often be appropriate to speak about specific schools, figures, texts and so forth, it is nonetheless true that qualified generalizations about Buddhism as a whole can sometimes have meaning and value. In view of this, it will be helpful to conclude this chapter by briefly stating the most common family traits relevant to Buddhist ethics:

- Human beings are caught in a cycle of rebirth driven by karma, a natural tendency in the world according to which the moral quality of our lives affects our future well-being.
- Lives in the cycle of rebirth may be better or worse, but all are characterized by suffering.
- However, it is possible to escape the suffering inherent in the cycle of rebirth propelled by karma by attaining enlightenment or nirvana (the state of the *Arahant* in Theravāda Buddhism and the Bodhisattva in Mahāyāna Buddhism).
- The primary obstacles to enlightenment are the three unwholesome roots: (1) greed or attachment, (2) hatred or aversion and (3) delusion or ignorance.
- A central way to overcome these obstacles is to follow the Eightfold Path (in Theravāda Buddhism) or the Six Perfections (in Mahāyāna Buddhism).
- These programs of development imply a distinction between a person pursuing enlightenment and person who has attained enlightenment, and both programs of development consist of three inter-related aspects involving morality, meditation and wisdom.
- The moral aspects include both moral precepts (such as not killing, stealing, lying or engaging in sexual misconduct) and moral virtues (such as compassion, loving-kindness, generosity and patience).
- The meditative aspects include various mental disciplines intended to develop high levels of tranquility, concentration, awareness, insight and virtue.
- The aspect pertaining to wisdom centrally involves the ideas of impermanence, dependent arising, no-self and (in Mahāyāna Buddhism) the emptiness and non-duality of all things.
- There is a distinction between conventional truth, which concerns the commonsense way of viewing the world, and ultimate truth, which pertains to the way the world is from the standpoint of (some understanding of) Buddhist wisdom.

- From the standpoint of Mahāyāna Buddhism, enlightenment is to be sought for the sake of all sentient beings (the Bodhisattva ideal), and all, or at least almost all, sentient beings have the capacity to attain enlightenment (sometimes referred to as Tathāgata-garbha or Buddha-nature).
- The sum of these teachings, called the Dharma, first began to be taught in human history by the Buddha (Śākyamuni), and they have been preserved and promoted ever since by the Buddhist monastic community called the Sangha.

It is certainly not the case that persons everywhere and always who might plausibly be considered to be Buddhists have accepted each and every one of these statements. Nonetheless, most traditions of Buddhism have implicitly or explicitly embraced these features in some form, so long as we take note of the basic differences between Theravāda Buddhism and the Mahāyāna Buddhist traditions (and recognize that there are many variations and dissimilarities as well). The ensemble of these ideas and practices provide the overall framework for the development of Buddhist moral philosophies in the world today.

# CHAPTER 4

# Karma, Rebirth, Nirvana and Other Topics
## Some Skeptical Concerns

In the chapters that follow, we will consider various ways in which a Buddhist moral philosophy might be developed, in an interpretative and/or constructive mode, largely from the standpoint of some of the standard perspectives of moral philosophy in the Western tradition. From the traditional standpoints of Buddhist thought and practice, however, ethical issues are often framed in a way that is quite foreign to the Western philosophical tradition and to most contemporary Western philosophers, including most scholars of Buddhist philosophy, within that tradition. The basic framework of Buddhist thought and practice is that human and other sentient beings are caught in a cycle of rebirth, *saṃsāra,* imbued by suffering and governed by karma, but it is possible to attain liberation from this cycle through a variety of practices that enable us to attain enlightenment, nirvana, and thereby overcome suffering. The Buddha's doctrine of liberation is at the heart of his teaching: it is said to be the core of what he discovered on the night of his enlightenment, and it was central to all Indian Buddhist traditions and has been fundamental to most other Buddhist traditions ever since. However, for many (though not all) persons in the West who are interested in and/or attracted to Buddhism, including scholars of Buddhist philosophy, as much as some features of Buddhism may seem valuable, various aspects of the doctrine of liberation are often regarded as problematic. As a result, a variety of strands of skeptical concern about this doctrine are an implicit, and sometimes explicit, dimension of a good deal of contemporary work in Buddhist moral philosophy by persons with Western philosophical training. This is one important way in which Buddhist modernism shapes scholarship in Buddhist moral philosophy. The doctrine of liberation—karma, rebirth and nirvana—is a source of unease in Western philosophical discussions of Buddhism in a way in which it has not typically been in earlier Asian Buddhist traditions. Before turning to the main topics of Buddhist moral philosophy, from a Western standpoint, it is important to examine the concerns about the liberation doctrine.

Many of these concerns pertain to karma and rebirth, and in this chapter we will consider some of the main grounds of skepticism about these doctrines. The hesitations about nirvana, and some related topics in Mahāyāna Buddhism, are somewhat different, and perhaps less pressing, but they are nonetheless worth examining as well insofar as nirvana would seem to be as crucial to the doctrine of liberation as anything could be. We will then explore some proposals to develop forms of Buddhist thought and practice that eliminate or significantly modify these doctrines. There is a danger that these discussions will degenerate into an unproductive debate about what is and is not essential to Buddhism or about what was or was not original to the teaching of the Buddha. Mindful of this concern, it is nonetheless important to recognize that, in putting forward the doctrine of liberation, the Buddha evidently believed that there is a certain kind of moral order in the universe. It is philosophically important to consider what Buddhist thought and practice might look like when informed by a modified understanding of this order.

## Concerns about Karma and Rebirth

In the Buddha's teaching, karma is the view that the moral quality of a person's actions, measured primarily by the person's intentions, causally determines the future well-being (or happiness) of the person: a person's morally good actions increase that person's future well-being, and a person's morally bad actions decrease that person's future well-being. Rebirth is the view that each of us has lived previous lives and will continue to live subsequent lives in a cycle of rebirth that will go on forever unless we escape it by attaining nirvana. Karma and rebirth are logically independent doctrines—one could be true without the other—but in the Buddha's teaching they are intimately linked: our well-being in this life causally depends on the moral quality of our past lives, and the moral quality of our current life causally determines our well-being in future lives. As we saw in Chapter 1, in the Pali Canon this causal correlation is situated within an elaborate, hierarchically ordered cosmology of 31 planes of existence.

Perhaps more importantly, the two doctrines are linked in another way. By all appearances, when we look at people in terms of a person's *single lifetime* we do not find the correlation between morality and well-being that the doctrine of karma, applied only to that lifetime, would have led us to expect: those who suffer greatly have not always led morally bad lives, and those who prosper have not always led morally good lives. Insofar as this is true, it would seem that the doctrine of karma could only be plausible on the assumption that karma operates across the series of lifetimes that rebirth makes possible. In short, without rebirth, it would seem much more difficult to accept karma as traditionally understood—at least this is the perspective of many Western observers.

Several years ago a prominent Western Buddhist intellectual, Stephen Batchelor, declared that he was an agnostic about rebirth: he neither affirmed nor denied this doctrine, he said, because he simply did not know if it was true (see Batchelor 1997). Though Batchelor was not raised a Buddhist, he had been a Buddhist monk for 10 years and had written persuasively, for many persons in the West, about the value of Buddhism. In light of this, his declaration was a source of controversy. In a debate with him in the pages of the Buddhist magazine *Tricycle,* Robert Thurman, a prominent scholar and proponent of Buddhism, challenged Batchelor and defended the importance of rebirth and karma for Buddhist practice (see Batchelor and Thurman 1997). From one perspective, it is easy to see the basis for Thurman's challenge. According to Richard Gombrich, another prominent Buddhist scholar, karma is "fundamental to the Buddha's whole view of life" (Gombrich 2009: 11). Moreover, it is often observed that for most "ordinary Buddhists," today as well as in the past, their basic moral orientation is governed by belief in karma and rebirth: they are mainly trying to live morally decent lives in the hope that this will increase their well-being in this or a future lifetime, with the project of directly pursuing enlightenment being reserved for some distant future lifetime (for example, see Faure 2009: 36–8). From this standpoint, the moral orientation of most Buddhists would seem to be undermined without karma and rebirth.

It is fair to say, however, that Batchelor stated a position shared by many (though certainly not all) Western followers of Buddhism: it is difficult to accept karma and rebirth as traditionally understood in Buddhist teaching, not simply because it is culturally foreign, but for significant philosophical, scientific and moral reasons (for an early Western critique, though not by a follower of Buddhism, see Griffiths 1982). Though a number of issues have been raised, there are three primary grounds of skepticism about karma and rebirth (it is best to consider the two doctrines together even though they are distinct ideas): these doctrines conflict with the Buddhist no-self teaching (consistency objection), they are contradicted or at least unsupported by the methods and doctrines of modern science (naturalism objection), and in various ways they are morally unacceptable (morality objection).

## Consistency Objection

The force of the first objection is obvious: If there is no self, then what is reborn and what bears the future karmic consequences of a person's actions? Unlike the other two objections, this objection was discussed early in the development of Buddhist thought. For example, as we saw in Chapter 2, it was a concern of Abhidharma philosophers such as the proponents of the Pudgalavāda (person doctrine) doctrine as well as Yogācāra philosophers who defended the foundational consciousness *(ālaya-vijñāna)* and afflicted mind *(kliṣṭa-manas)* doctrines (the Pudgalavāda doctrine was considered "heretical" by the Theravāda tradition, but its presence is a sign of a more general concern with the issue). These were efforts to develop a concept of the person that explains karma and rebirth without a self.

The issue arises because two features of persons that seem to be necessary for the doctrines of karma and rebirth are denied in the Buddhist no-self teaching: identity and distinctness. First, karma and rebirth appear to assume that a person has identity through time. Identity allows us to say that person (or being) Y is the rebirth of person X in the past, and that person Z in the future is the rebirth of Y: since X, Y and Z are all the same person, it makes sense to say that one member of the series is the rebirth of the previous member. Likewise, identity through time allows us to say that the moral quality of my actions in the past causally determined my well-being now, and similarly that the moral quality of my actions now will causally determine my well-being in the future. Without identity, it would seem, these claims lose their meaning. Second, karma and rebirth as traditionally understood seem to require that persons are distinct from one another. It is the moral quality of *my* actions, not the moral quality of *your* actions, that causally affects *my* future well-being. If I were not distinct from you, then it would appear that this claim does not make sense. (Even the Mahāyāna doctrine of merit transfer, in which a Bodhisattva can transfer some of his or her karmic benefit to another person, would seem to require a way of speaking of distinct persons, though this doctrine could be interpreted as pursuing the implications of the no-self teaching for the karma system.)

Different kinds of response to this objection can be made. Oftentimes similes were employed to explain karma and rebirth without a self. For instance, a temporal sequence of burning lamps, one lighting another, was said to be like the sequence of rebirths. In both cases, there is not strict identity across the members of the sequence, but they are causally related to one another. Hence, there is a kind of unity other than identity, and this is sufficient for karma and rebirth. According to a well-known Buddhist slogan, we can say of one member of the series in relationship to an earlier member that it is "neither the same nor another" (Mendis 1993: 39). A central project of the Abhidharma and Yogācāra philosophers was to develop (in contemporary terminology) a process philosophy of the person that would make sense of karma and rebirth without recourse to a substance metaphysics. For example, it may be said that what we call the person is nothing but a collection of ever-changing momentary events (such as the *dharmas* in the Abhidharma tradition) that are causally related to one another in such a way as to supply sufficient unification to provide substitutes for identity and distinctness. This was a central topic in the development of Buddhist metaphysics. But many philosophers are not convinced that karma and rebirth make sense without the self that Buddhists deny (for example, see Flanagan 2011: 132–3 and 222–5, n. 24, and Reichenbach 1990: 130–2). A particularly pressing worry is how to make sense of the continuity from one life to the next, such that there is a meaningful sense in which Z really is the rebirth of Y, without postulating an immaterial self to explain this.

A different kind of response to the consistency objection appeals to Buddhist ideas of conventional truth or skillful means. For example, it might be claimed that the doctrines of karma and rebirth are conventionally but not ultimately true. If in ultimate truth there is no self, but no karma and rebirth either, and in conventional truth there is karma and rebirth, but also a self, then the consistency problem may be solved. There is consistency at each level, and no issue of consistency arises between the levels since ultimate truth pertains to what is actually the case while conventional truth only concerns the world as represented in the categories of common sense. It might also be maintained that the teaching of karma and rebirth was an exercise in skillful means based on the assumption that acceptance of this teaching would motivate people to live morally good lives (and to move closer to enlightenment). This assumption is a common theme in Buddhist texts, and it might be supposed that this pragmatic consideration is the real basis of the teaching.

A rejoinder to both these responses, conventional truth and skillful means, is that they reveal the doctrines of karma and rebirth to be something other than what people thought they were and that understanding this analysis would undermine the belief in—and efficacy of belief in—these doctrines: once people realize that karma and rebirth are not ultimately true, or are justified only by their motivational value, they will stop believing them and they will no longer be motivated by them. Against this, it may be said, realizing that something is not what we thought it was need not undermine belief: for example, quantum physics tells me that the chair I am sitting on is not the solid object I take it to be, but I continue sitting on it because assuming it is solid is still a useful way of getting around in the world. With respect to the interpretation of the tradition, it may be more plausible to attribute pragmatic approaches to Mahāyāna rather than pre-Mahāyāna forms of Buddhism. In the Pali Canon, karma and rebirth are depicted as instances of right view in contrast to wrong view (see *MN* III 71–2), but in the influential Mahāyāna *Vimalakīrti Sūtra* these doctrines are represented as discourses by the Buddha designed to tame "wild and uncivilized" beings (see Thurman 1976: 82).

A related objection to the doctrines of karma and rebirth is that the no-self teaching denies that there is a self who is in control of what he or she decides and does. If everything is causally determined by past events, it may be wondered, then how can a person be held responsible for the goodness or badness of his or her actions, and be rewarded or punished accordingly in line with the doctrine of karma? There are two issues broached by this objection. The first is whether the doctrine of karma, and more generally the concept of dependent arising, involves a form of causal determinism, which conflicts with the freedom and responsibility that might be thought to be needed for reward and punishment to be appropriate. There are different interpretations of this issue, and we will discuss them in Chapter 10. The second issue is whether the doctrine of karma involves the concepts of moral responsibility and moral reward and punishment. These retributive concepts are sometimes invoked in discussions of karma, in a variety of contexts, but most interpreters think that this is based on a misunderstanding of the traditional view. As we saw in Chapter 1, the more common reading is that karma is not a form of desert, but is simply a natural process: morally good actions bring about greater well-being for the person who performs them, not because the person deserves this and should be rewarded accordingly, but simply because the universe operates according to this causal principle. On any interpretation, the doctrine of karma is not the view that there is some being in the universe administering cosmic justice.

## Naturalism Objection

The second line of objection to karma and rebirth is distinctively modern and is rooted in naturalism, which we may understand as the position that we should hold beliefs only if they are supported by, or at least consistent with, the methods and doctrines of the sciences (the term 'naturalism' is used in a variety of ways, in and out of philosophy, but this definition captures a common understanding). The basic objection is that the doctrines of karma and rebirth fail the scientific test of naturalism and so should not be accepted. But this objection can take different forms. One form is that we lack evidence for these doctrines, at least by the empirical standard of evidence assumed in the sciences (roughly speaking, we have good evidence only for what we can directly observe with the five senses or what is part of the best explanation of what we can directly observe). Another form is that these doctrines are not supported by, and perhaps conflict with, what we know about the world from pertinent sciences such as evolutionary biology and neuroscience.

It is interesting to note that the Dalai Lama himself has endorsed something close to naturalism. He writes:

> As in science so in Buddhism, understanding the nature of reality is pursued by means of critical investigation: if scientific analysis were conclusively to demonstrate certain claims in Buddhism to be false, then we must accept the findings of science and abandon those claims.
>
> (Dalai Lama 2005: 2–3)

However, in a comment on the Dalai Lama's position, his close associate Thupten Jinpa has stressed the importance of distinguishing between what has been *negated* by scientific method and what has *not been observed* by this method. According to Jinpa, rebirth has not been observed by science, but it has not been negated either (see Jinpa 2003: 77–8). Therefore, it passes the Dalai Lama's naturalist test. It is sometimes said that it is not possible to prove a negative, but by ordinary epistemic standards this overstates the case: surely, by these standards, endorsing a negative is sometimes the most reasonable stance to take (for example, that there is no elephant in my office at the moment). Hence, it is conceivable that scientific method could make it unreasonable to believe something, and one question raised by this claim is whether this method has made belief in rebirth unreasonable.

In fact, some have argued that there is a scientific basis for accepting rebirth. In particular, it has been maintained that there are children who report remembering details of the lives of persons from the past, and that the best explanation of these reports is that these children previously existed as those persons (see Stevenson 1987). Some Buddhists have endorsed arguments of this kind (for example, see Gunaratna 1980 and Thurman in Batchelor and Thurman 1997: 26). However, a variety of objections have been raised against such arguments: for example, the purported memories of the children might be explained by some alternative source of information about the deceased persons, or they might have been prompted by questioning in a cultural milieu in which belief in rebirth is common (for such objections, see Edwards 1996). In any case, it is not widely supposed among Buddhists that ordinary people can remember their previous lives or that this is the basis for accepting the doctrine of rebirth. The authority of the Buddha, who is said to have discovered karma and rebirth in his enlightenment experience (in which *he* remembered his past lives), is the primary reason followers of the Buddha have accepted these doctrines. As we saw in Chapter 1, though the Buddha responded to objections to karma and rebirth, he did not offer empirical evidence in support of these doctrines. They have not traditionally been put forward as a scientific theory that explains our experience (in the tradition, there were some philosophical arguments for rebirth, though not of a kind that would satisfy naturalists; see Arnold 2008).

Is there empirical evidence in support of the doctrine of karma? Part of the difficulty in answering this question is that the specific ways in which the morality of a person's actions are supposed to causally affect the person's future well-being are thought to be rather complex. In fact, the Buddha said "the result of karma is an inconceivable matter" (*AN* II 80). Different kinds of effects were envisioned. But one standard theme is that morally good actions result in such familiar goods as long life, health, wealth, beauty, influence and so forth, and morally bad actions result in the opposite (for example, see *MN* III 202–6 and *AN* II 202–5). This is what gives rise to the objection noted earlier: if we focus on a single lifetime, there is little reason to think that these causal relationships obtain. For example, there are people who live morally decent lives, but have very poor health, and there are other people who live morally very bad lives, but live a long time in good health and overall prosperity. As we saw in Chapter 1, the Buddha responded to this objection by appealing to future lives: the karmic consequences of our actions may unfold in this or some future life (see *MN* III 214). From a naturalist standpoint, there are two difficulties with this response. First, since it depends on the doctrine of rebirth, it inherits whatever doubts there might be about rebirth. Second, it renders the doctrine of karma virtually unverifiable (or unfalsifiable) by ordinary empirical standards. Choose your favorite incredibly evil person from the distant past: has this person since suffered the appropriate karmic consequences? There is no way to know because there is no way to know which beings this person was reborn as.

One form of the naturalist objection to karma and rebirth, then, is that there is no good evidence to support these doctrines. Could there be a stronger objection? Does contemporary science disprove or negate karma and rebirth? There is no simple way to answer this question. These doctrines certainly play no role in any of the sciences. For example, if we ask why a particular individual was born with some specific disadvantageous trait, the answer of biology might well be that the person has certain genes, and that these genes resulted from the parents' genes and so forth. It would not be that the person is the rebirth of such and such a person who lived his or her life, morally speaking, in such and such a way. The two kinds of explanation, heredity versus karma and rebirth, are entirely different (for discussion of this issue, see Reichenbach 1990: 35–8). From the standpoint of genetics, heredity has considerable empirical support and may provide sufficient explanation of the fact that a person was born with a specific trait. It would probably be too strong to say that genetics and related sciences negate karma and rebirth (where *negate* means something such as decisively refute), but it would also be too weak to say merely that they fail to observe them. These are not the only two options. There may be circumstances in which failure to observe permits some belief (presumably on other grounds), and there may be other circumstances in which failure to observe requires suspension of belief. But there could be circumstances in which failure to observe renders belief unreasonable (as in the aforementioned elephant example). From at least some naturalist standpoints, the difficulty with karma and rebirth is that, if they were true, there ought to be some observational evidence for them, but—it is claimed—there is no such evidence (or at least whatever evidence there might be is quite insufficient). In this circumstance, it might be argued, belief in these doctrines is unreasonable. If, as some naturalists suppose, we should accept only what is supported by the best empirical evidence, then it would seem that we should not accept karma and rebirth based upon what we know about the world through the sciences or other empirical means.

There are Buddhist responses to this naturalist critique. First, it was sometimes acknowledged that karma is not the only cause of well-being (see Ghose 2007 and Harvey 2007b: 50–3). Others causes include such things as bile and phlegm disorders, changes of climate, careless behavior and assault (see *SN* IV 229–31). In the Theravāda commentarial tradition, it was said that there are four kinds of causes *(niyāmas)* in addition to the causality of karma: seasons, seeds, mental processes and dharma. It has been suggested that this shows that Buddhist teaching is compatible with modern scientific explanations of why things happen (for discussion of this claim, see Crosby 2008, Jayatilleke 1974: ch. 11 and D. T. Jones 2012). The suggestion that there are, say, some "physical causes" (as understood in the sciences) in addition to karmic causes might allow us to say that the karma explanation and the heredity explanation are not in competition with one another, but in some way complement one another.

However, this proposal is not likely to alleviate naturalist concerns. First, the supposition that there are other kinds of causes does not address the worry that we do not have sufficient evidence for karmic causes. Second, this supposition raises an additional set of questions about how the different kinds of causality relate to one another. Do physical causes explain some events and karmic causes explain others? Are both kinds of causes necessary to explain any event pertaining to well-being? Are the different kinds of causes different orders of causality such that each may be the correct explanation of someone's well-being from a particular perspective (moral and physical respectively)?

A second Buddhist response to the naturalist critique comes from the Dalai Lama. Though he accepts a weak form of naturalism (we should give up what science disproves), he rejects a stronger form of naturalism, what he calls "scientific materialism," according to which "the scientific view of the world should be the basis for all knowledge." He says that scientific materialism cannot accommodate issues about "the meaning of life, or good and evil" (Dalai Lama 2005: 12–13). On this view, there are sources of knowledge besides science, and our knowledge of karma and rebirth is based on these other sources. In many ways, this view goes to the heart of the issue. Since traditionally karma and rebirth were not put forward as scientific explanations, the question is whether there is some other basis for accepting them. Naturalists who insist only that our beliefs be compatible with science, not necessarily that they be supported by science, might allow for this. But concerns would remain. Are karma and rebirth really compatible with the world as understood by science? For example, is the genetic explanation of my innate personality tendencies compatible with the karma and rebirth explanation? Can karma and rebirth be squared with what we know about the emergence of human life from evolutionary biology? And what is the alternative source of knowledge? Is it anything more than the authority of the Buddha? Could this authority be a source of knowledge? (In connection with the last three questions, see Arnold 2008.)

*Morality Objection*

The final objection to karma and rebirth is distinct from the naturalism objection, though it is often associated with it, and it is in any case rooted in modern moral sensibilities. The objection is really a group of closely related objections to the effect that the doctrines of karma and rebirth are in some way morally objectionable. Consider first an infant born with an incurable illness that is extremely painful and ultimately will be fatal. The Buddhist explanation of this in terms of karma and rebirth is that this child is suffering from this illness because he or she lived morally badly in a previous lifetime. It is clear that this explanation is implied by the Buddha's teaching on a literal reading. For example, he said that if someone "is given to injuring beings," then "wherever he is reborn he is sickly," and conversely if he is "not given to injuring beings," then "wherever he is reborn he is healthy" (*MN* III 204). It follows from the second of these that someone who is sick, and so not healthy, had been given to injuring beings. The point may be generalized to all sorts of misfortunes that young children suffer from—poverty, abuse, oppression and so forth. In all these cases, the karmic explanation is the moral quality of people's past lives.

Is this a morally objectionable claim? It is sometimes said that karma and rebirth mean that the child deserves his illness because of how he or she lived in a previous lifetime, that it is an instance of cosmic justice. However, as we have seen, this is not a standard reading the traditional doctrine: the contention is simply that a person's morally wrong actions will cause the person to suffer in the future, not that the person deserves to suffer. It is a doctrine of causal not moral responsibility. Suppose that within a single lifetime a person suffers on account of behavior known to cause such suffering: for example, the person is injured because he or she was intoxicated. In this case, it would not seem to be morally objectionable to think that the person suffered the injury because of what he or she did. This suggests that the fact that some people find it morally objectionable to say that the child is ill because of what he or she did in a past life is rooted in doubts about the doctrines of karma and rebirth. If we think the doctrines are false, then of course it will be objectionable to say something that presupposes that they are true—and it may be morally objectionable to think or say, for example, that the child could have prevented it or should have known better. But if this is the difficulty, then the objection begs the question: there is a problem with the implications of the doctrine only on the assumption that the doctrine is not true.

There is, however, another form of the objection that does not beg the question though it is related to doubts about karma and rebirth. It may be said that, since we do not—and perhaps cannot—know that karma and rebirth are true, it would be cruel to think or say that the child's illness was caused by what he or she did in the past. To treat the child as if he or she were even causally responsible for the illness—and so conceivably could have prevented it—when we cannot know that this is the case would be morally objectionable (this is one point where the morality objection may be allied with the naturalism objection, though there could be grounds for doubting karma and rebirth that do not depend on naturalism).

Another form of the morality objection, often expressed in the context of socially engaged Buddhism, is that belief in the doctrines of karma and rebirth, or the way in which they are interpreted, justifies or promotes attitudes of acceptance and passivity in the face of unjust institutions (see K. Jones 2003: ch. 3, Watts 2009b and Wright 2005 and 2009: ch. 2). Suppose that some people live in conditions of unjust poverty and oppression, as indeed many people do in Asian countries where followers of Buddhism are common. The doctrines of karma and rebirth mean that these persons live in these conditions because they lived morally badly in past lives, and the realization of this may lead them to believe that the unjust institutions cannot or should not be changed: these institutions are merely the instruments though which the law of karma is working. Since this law cannot be changed, it is pointless to try to improve these institutions (the law of karma would just find another way for these people to suffer on account of their past actions). Hence, it is concluded, unjust institutions must be endured with the Buddhist virtues of patience and equanimity in hopes of assuring a better rebirth in the future.

There is a response to the philosophical claim that the doctrines of karma and rebirth justify morally problematic attitudes. It would seem that the ideas of karma and rebirth *as such* do not imply that we should hold any moral attitudes: these ideas merely state that there is a certain kind of causal relationship in the world. However, Buddhist teaching as a whole clearly implies that we should live our lives in full cognizance of karma and rebirth. This is usually understood to have a twofold meaning: we should recognize that our present level of well-being is the result of the moral quality of our past actions (in this or previous lives), *and* we should realize that the moral quality of our present actions will causally determine our well-being in the future (in this or subsequent lives). On account of the first part, we cannot change the karmic results of what we have already done, but on account of the second part, we can affect future karmic consequences of what we do now and in the future. The first part by itself might provide the basis for an argument that we should simply accept our circumstances in life. But such an argument would be undermined by the second part. In Buddhist teaching, our ability to affect future karmic consequences is ordinarily presented as being very much under our control and is often used to motivate people to live morally good lives (there will be more discussion of this in Chapter 10). Hence, karma and rebirth in themselves do not imply that we should not try to change unjust institutions. It is true that patience and equanimity are standard Buddhist virtues, but so are compassion, loving-kindness and generosity. The extent to which Buddhist virtues taken as a whole provide a basis for reforming unjust institutions is a question for socially engaged

Buddhism (see Chapter 11). It is not an immediate consequence of the doctrines of karma and rebirth.

It has been argued, however, that in some Buddhist countries many people have attitudes of acceptance and passivity in the face of unjust institutions because they believe the doctrines of karma and rebirth support these attitudes. And it has been claimed that these attitudes are significant obstacles to social reform (for example, see Watts 2009b). These sociological claims about the effects of peoples' beliefs on their attitudes might well be true even if the philosophical claim that the attitudes are justified by the doctrines of karma and rebirth is not.

## Concerns about Nirvana and Bodhisattvas

What happened to the Buddha when he died? For pre-Mahāyāna forms of Buddhism, since the Buddha was enlightened, it is clear what did not happen to him: he was not reborn into another round of the cycle of rebirth with its attendant suffering. But what *did* happen to him? And what, according to the early tradition, happens to any enlightened person (an *Arahant*) who dies? It seems evident that, in some sense, *something* other than complete and utter nonbeing or nonexistence happens, but it is very difficult to say what (for discussion of this, see Collins 1998: 147–90). In the Pali Canon, a distinction was drawn between two nirvana elements, one with and one without a remainder of aggregates and grasping. What they have in common is the destruction of greed, hatred and delusion—and hence the elimination of suffering—a standard depiction of nirvana. The first element refers to an enlightened person who is still alive and still experiences pleasure and pain. The second element refers to an enlightened person who has died and has no such experiences. About this person, we are told only that at the point of death "all that is experienced, not being delighted in, will be extinguished" (Ireland 1997: 181). But what does this mean (assuming it is not simply nonbeing)?

Before he died, the Buddha was directly asked about his postmortem existence. However, this was one of the questions he would not answer (recall the discussion of the poison arrow story in Chapter 1). Specifically, he was asked whether after death the Tathāgata exists, does not exist, both exists and does not exist, or neither exists nor does not exist. The term 'Tathāgata' refers to the Buddha, but in this context it could be taken to refer to the existence of any enlightened person after death. When Vacchagotta asked the Buddha for his position on these propositions, the Buddha would not take a stand and described all these "speculative views" as a "fetter of views" each of which is "beset by suffering" and does not lead "to enlightenment, to nirvana." Vacchagotta then asked the Buddha where after death an enlightened person reappears, does not reappear, both reappears and does not reappear, and neither reappears nor does not reappear. Once again the Buddha would not take a position. He said that his teaching is "profound, hard to see and hard to understand, peaceful and sublime, unattainable by mere reasoning, subtle, to be experienced by the wise." By way of further explanation, the Buddha offered a simile: just as it does not make sense to ask in which direction a fire that has just been extinguished went, so it does not make sense to ask about the existence or reappearance of an enlightened person after death (*MN* I 483–9). Fire and the extinction of fire are prominent metaphors in the Pali Canon for suffering in the cycle of rebirth and overcoming suffering in enlightenment (see Gombrich 2009: ch. 8). The message of this text is evidently that we unenlightened persons cannot understand what happens to an enlightened person after death and should not concern ourselves with speculations about this.

There are, however, some texts that depict nirvana, albeit mostly in rather elusive ways. For example, about nirvana it is said, "this is the peaceful, this is the sublime, that is, the stilling of all formations, the relinquishing of all attachments, the destruction of craving, dispassion, cessation" (*MN* I 436). In another passage, nirvana is described as the unborn, unageing, unailing, deathless, sorrowless and undefiled "supreme security from bondage" (*MN* I 167). We are also told that nirvana "is the greatest bliss" (*MN* I 508). Some texts suggest that an enlightened person is beyond the moral categories that govern karma. For example, in the *Dhammapada,* a Pali Canon text, this person is said to be beyond "both the meritorious and the detrimental" (Carter and Palihawadana 2000: 412). Partly for this reason, it has been suggested that nirvana is a state beyond morality (what is sometimes called "the transcendency thesis"), but most commentators reject this interpretation (for instance, see Cooper and James 2005: 74–9 and Keown 1992: ch. 4). Overall, if we take the Buddha himself as our model, it seems clear that nirvana is, *in some sense*, the highest state of well-being and virtue, and yet it is quite perplexing what it means to be in this state once a person has died (for more discussion of this, see Chapters 5 and 6).

In Mahāyāna Buddhism, the source of perplexity is somewhat different. As we saw in Chapter 2, the Bodhisattva vows to seek enlightenment for the sake of all beings and to remain in the cycle of rebirth until everyone has attained enlightenment (the *Arahant* is criticized for selfishness in departing from the scene at death). Hence, the aforementioned issues with regard to nirvana are not at the forefront of concern. There are, however, two central features of Mahāyāna Buddhism that raise similar issues. The first is the prominence of cosmic Bodhisattvas such as Kuan-yin and Tārā, godlike beings of enormous compassion, knowledge and skill who populate and in various ways intervene in the world (for an account of these, see P. Williams 2009a: ch. 10). The second is the proliferation of paradoxical language, rooted in the philosophies of emptiness and non-dualism, in a variety of contexts. In particular, there is said to be no difference between the cycle of rebirth and nirvana, and perfectly enlightened beings—Buddhas—are portrayed as being in some sense ideal moral agents, and yet they can hardly be said to be either *moral* or *agents* in any ordinary sense of these terms.

In recent scholarship concerning Buddhist ethics, fewer concerns have been expressed about nirvana and related Mahāyāna issues than about karma and rebirth. In one way this is surprising since liberation from the suffering of the cycle of rebirth would seem to be of the highest importance in the Buddhist scheme of values. But in another way perhaps it is not surprising since nirvana, as an essentially unknowable state beyond death (at least for those of us in this life), cannot be judged in terms of our ordinary experience in the way that, in some respects, karma and rebirth can. Something similar may be said about cosmic Bodhisattvas (though their purported interventions in the world might be subjected to empirical scrutiny). Nonetheless, there are concerns about nirvana after death, and about Bodhisattvas, that parallel the concerns about karma and rebirth that we just considered. First, there are consistency questions: if there is no self, then what would it mean to say that a person attains nirvana after death, and in what sense can we speak of the Bodhisattva Kuan-yin reappearing in different phases of the cycle of rebirth? Second, there are naturalist concerns: if we are guided by the methods and doctrines of the sciences, what sense can be made of nirvana as a state in which we escape the cycle of rebirth and of the cosmic Bodhisattvas? Finally, from the standpoint of morality, how could a person who has attained nirvana after death be conceived in moral terms at all, and what are we to make of the paradoxical language of Mahāyāna Buddhism?

For the most part these questions have not been at the forefront of work on Buddhist ethics, and we will not pursue them further here. The first two issues, concerning consistency with the no-self teaching and naturalism, are quite similar to the discussion of these topics in connection with karma and rebirth. The issue concerning morality is somewhat different and deserves brief comment. As we will see in more detail in later chapters, a great deal of Buddhist teaching and practice concerns moral development. Though the ultimate goal of this development is not quite the same in Theravāda and Mahāyāna Buddhism, in both cases there is a conception of an ideal figure that is the fulfillment of such things as the Eightfold Path and the Six Perfections. It seems clear that there is some sense in which this ideal figure, however understood, exemplifies the highest forms of well-being and virtue. And yet it might be said that this figure is not really a human being at all, apparently lacking traits as such as agency, intention, perception, thought, consciousness and so forth that are ordinarily attributed to human beings. These attributes are thought to be lacking because of basic themes in Buddhist metaphysics, epistemology and philosophy of mind as well as portrayals of what it is like to be fully enlightened. It is easy to see how there could be skepticism about such a moral ideal (for discussion of how to make sense of it, see Finnigan 2011a and 2011b, Garfield 2006 and 2011b, and Hansen 2011). One response to this worry is to note that this ideal is on a distant horizon, very far from the immediate concerns of those on the paths of moral development. As will be suggested in the next chapter, much of the discourse in Buddhist ethics is directed to persons who have a more proximate, and more humanly recognizable, goal.

## Buddhism Naturalized

On account of some or all of the reservations about karma and rebirth, and about nirvana and related topics, discussed in the last two sections, some Western followers or interpreters of Buddhist thought and practice have proposed a qualified form of Buddhism that eliminates or substantially modifies these doctrines. This revised conception is sometimes called Buddhism naturalized. This is usually taken to mean at a minimum the rejection, or at least non-acceptance, of rebirth, and the acceptance of only a limited or revised understanding of karma. It may also extend to skepticism about such things as nirvana after death and Bodhisattvas. Here is the proposal of Owen Flanagan, a well-known proponent of the advantages of Buddhism naturalized:

> Imagine Buddhism without rebirth and without a karmic system that guarantees justice ultimately will be served, without nirvana, without bodhisattvas flying on lotus leaves, without Buddha worlds, without nonphysical states of mind, without any deities, without heaven and hell realms, without oracles, and without lamas who are reincarnations of lamas. What would be left? My answer is that what would remain would be an interesting and defensible philosophical theory with a metaphysics, a theory about what there is and how it is, an epistemology, a theory about how we come to know and what we can know, and an ethics, a theory about virtue and vice and how best to live.
>
> (Flanagan 2011: 3)

Flanagan calls this a "deflated secular Buddhism" (xi). What he finds attractive in Buddhism is basically an empiricist epistemology, a process metaphysics featuring impermanence, causality and selfless persons, and a eudaimonistic understanding of both well-being, emphasizing tranquility, and moral virtue, stressing compassion. In this view, there is no human life beyond what is immediately evident to us in our ordinary life from birth to death conventionally understood. Hence, there is no rebirth, no postmortem nirvanic form of existence for those who attain enlightenment and no cosmic Bodhisattvas (cf. Siderits 2001). All that remains of karma is a very "tame" concept according to which the intentional and unintentional actions of sentient beings have many effects (see Flanagan 2011: 77). There is a moral order in the universe only to the extent that certain ways of living featured in Buddhist teaching are likely to promote the well-being of oneself and others. This is a bold proposal for a mitigated form of Buddhism that naturalists could live with and perhaps even embrace (though Flanagan does not profess to be a Buddhist, he recommends Buddhism naturalized to contemporary Western philosophers as a position worthy of consideration).

Another somewhat less ambitious form of Buddhism naturalized has been suggested by Dale S. Wright (Wright 2005 and 2009: ch. 2). According to Wright (2005), "among Buddhists today, educated in a world of science and favorably disposed to contemporary standards for the articulation of truth, a naturalized concept of karma without supernatural preconditions will more likely be both persuasive and motivationally functional" (89). His naturalized concept of karma excludes rebirth as something we cannot know and includes features of the Buddha's teaching that he thinks can be defended. In the absence of rebirth, the most problematic feature of this teaching is that a person's morally good actions result in such things as health and wealth for that individual (for example, see *MN* III 170–8). Wright says that the most we could say here is that morally good actions make these benefits more likely. The most valuable part of the Buddha's karma teaching, Wright thinks, is that it is a doctrine of character-building: performing morally good actions are ways of becoming a morally good person (similar to Aristotle's doctrine of habituation). For example,

> Acts of kindness may or may not give rise to external goods such as rewards of money or prestige, but they do give rise to a transformation in character that makes us kind and concerned about the well-being of others.
>
> (Wright 2009: 69; cf. MacKenzie 2013)

Insofar as moral virtue is part of well-being on a Buddhist view (there is more about this in Chapter 5), morally good actions could be said to promote a person's well-being. Wright also proposes thinking about karma in collective or social rather than individual terms (cf. Hershock 2005). Although he grants that the dominant tradition in Buddhism has focused on individual karma (my good actions increase my well-being), he thinks that there is some basis in the tradition for the idea of collective karma (our good actions increase our well-being). Collective karma, he argues, has two advantages over individual karma: it is not in tension with the no-self teaching, and it is more likely to be true. The first point alludes to the consistency objection discussed earlier. The second point is that a society of virtuous persons is likely to have greater well-being than a society of vicious persons. Both themes—karma as character-building and collective karma—are *prima facie* plausible and are theories that in principle could be empirically tested and shown to be true. Though these are forms of moral order in the universe, they are forms that a naturalist might easily accept (a similar understanding of karma is developed in K. Jones 2003: ch. 3; cf. W. L. King 2001).

Buddhism naturalized is not an interpretation of traditional Buddhist ethics. It is a quintessentially modernist construction of what purports to be a plausible Buddhist outlook. The heart of Buddhism naturalized is Buddhism without rebirth and with forms of karma only when they have or might well have empirical support. It may also include rejection of other "supernatural" features of Buddhism such as nirvana as a state beyond death and cosmic Bodhisattvas. Such a position could respond to the skeptical concerns raised in the last two sections, and it could preserve a conception of a moral order in the universe that is limited to what each of us can achieve in this lifetime to enable ourselves and others to overcome suffering and otherwise attain well-being. But Buddhism naturalized is, by virtually any measure, a radical revision of traditional Buddhist thought and practice. As we have seen, many ordinary Buddhists past and present have lived their lives on the basis of a framework of karma and rebirth traditionally conceived. Moreover, though they may not be directly seeking enlightenment in this lifetime, it is important for these persons that liberation from the cycle of rebirth is possible (and for Mahāyāna Buddhists that there are cosmic Bodhisattvas who can assist us in our endeavors). For these persons, Buddhism naturalized may seem a pale imitation of what Buddhism means in their lives. On the traditional view, the doctrines of karma, rebirth and nirvana respond to significant human needs for an explanation of the distribution of good and bad fortune in human life and for hope that by living morally in this life one may bring about a better future life and eventually attain ultimate liberation (for classic Pali Canon presentations of these ideas, see the *Cūḷakammavibhanga Sutta* in *MN* III 202–6 and *Saccasaṃyutta* in *SN* V 420–31). These doctrines provide a framework of moral intelligibility that for many persons is deeply satisfying in responding to these needs. Buddhism naturalized does not do this. Perhaps for this reason, though it appeals to some modern Western Buddhist intellectuals, other such persons have resisted it (for example, Thurman).

PART **2**
# Theoretical Topics in
# Buddhist Moral Philosophy

# CHAPTER 5

# Well-Being

As we saw in Chapter 3, the nature of human well-being is an important topic in contemporary moral philosophy. Well-being also plays a role, arguably the central role, in the main traditions of Buddhist thought and practice. There are three primary ways in which Buddhism is committed to an understanding of well-being. First, according to the doctrines of karma and rebirth, there is a sense of well-being in which, over time, a person's well-being is causally determined by person's moral virtue. Second, there is a higher form of well-being that is unavailable to persons in the cycle of rebirth, but is gained when persons attain enlightenment and thereby escape the cycle of rebirth. Finally, central Buddhist moral virtues such as compassion and loving-kindness involve the promotion of the well-being of all persons, presumably in both of the aforementioned senses of well-being. However, despite the importance of well-being in contemporary philosophy and in Buddhism, the proper understanding of Buddhist well-being has received less direct attention from Buddhist moral philosophers than other topics, at least in terms of the standard categories of the Western well-being debate.

In this chapter, we will briefly summarize the contemporary philosophical debate about well-being, examine at greater length the Buddhist understanding of well-being for both unenlightened and enlightened persons, and then analyze the extent to which the contemporary debate might be employed to interpret the Buddhist understanding and construct a viable Buddhist position on well-being.

## The Contemporary Philosophical Debate about Well-Being

Contemporary philosophies of well-being analyze what we mean when we say that a person's life is going well or badly for the person whose life it is. In this sense, well-being pertains to what is good for a person or what has intrinsic value for a person. We presuppose the concept of well-being when we say that an action or event benefits or harms a person. Sometimes philosophers employ other terms as synonyms or near-synonyms for well-being, terms such as welfare, utility, prudential value, self-interest, quality of life, happiness and flourishing. Well-being is one kind of value that may be attributed to a person, and it is distinguished conceptually from other kinds of value that a person may possess such as moral or aesthetic value. Though some philosophies maintain that some of these other kinds of value are related to well-being, such claims are best seen as theories about what constitutes well-being and not as analyses of the meaning of the concept.

The widespread philosophical use of the term 'well-being' is relatively recent, but the Western philosophical discussion of well-being is very old. It is plausible to suppose that 'well-being' is an apt translation of the ancient Greek term *'eudaimonia,'* or at least that the ancient Greek and Roman philosophical debate about *eudaimonia* was centrally about the nature of well-being. In any case, it is widely (though not universally) thought that the concept of well-being is important because it plays a fundamental role in everyday prudential and moral reflection (concerning evaluation, deliberation, prediction, explanation and so forth).

Four basic types of theory of well-being are usually distinguished in contemporary discussions. First, *mental-state theories* declare that well-being is a matter of the positive or negative quality of a person's mental states. For example, hedonism, the best-known mental-state theory, says that well-being should be understood in terms of the balance of a person's pleasures and pains. Other relevant mental states might be enjoyment or contentment (and their contraries). Second, *desire-satisfaction theories* state that well-being is a matter of the satisfaction of an individual's desires (where these include both what is sought and what is avoided). The most common desire-satisfaction theories depict the desires relevant to well-being as those that a person would have insofar as he or she was rational and/or well-informed. Third, *objective-list theories* declare that well-being consists of participation in a set of purportedly objective goods such as friendship, knowledge and achievement (there is disagreement about which goods belong on the list, but these three are common). Finally, *nature-fulfillment theories* maintain that well-being consists of the fulfillment of the most important or distinctive features of human nature such as our capacities for rationality or social relations (for overviews of the debate about these philosophies, see Crisp 2013 and Haybron 2008: ch. 2).

Though this four-fold classification is useful, it is important to recognize that each of these four types of theory has many variations, and these variations often involve complications that mitigate the differences among the four types. For example, pleasure might be considered one of the objective goods in an objective-list theory, and knowledge might be regarded as the fulfillment of an important feature of human nature in a nature-fulfillment theory. There is also what are presented as hybrid (or mixed) theories that combine two or more of the basic four types. For instance, it might be claimed that well-being consists of participation in some list of objective goods, but only if the participation involves mental states that are largely positive (for example, participation in a good such as knowledge would contribute to well-being only if it were enjoyed).

Philosophical debates about these theories of well-being are sometimes informed by the defense of normative ethical theories. For example, consequentialism needs an account of well-being in terms of which we could judge which kinds of consequences make an action morally right. But these debates also answer to a variety of intuitions about well-being, some rather philosophical and some more commonsensical. From this perspective, a criterion of adequacy of a theory of well-being is thought to be its capacity to explain our intuitions. The disagreements about the four types of theory are partly based on a conflict of philosophical intuitions about the source of value, a conflict that informs many meta-ethical debates. In particular, does value depend on something in the mind of each subject, such as what a person desires or finds pleasurable, or does it depend on something independent of the mind of particular subjects, such as objective facts about things in the world or human nature? However, important as different intuitions about the correct answer to this question are, we should not lose sight of the fact that there is a good deal of common ground in contemporary debates about theories of well-being. In particular, it is widely assumed, as common sense assumes, that there is a set of what may be called *ordinary goods* that are central to at least most people's well-being. These goods include life, health, fulfillment of basic physical needs (such as food, clothing and shelter), pleasure and the absence of pain (physical and psychological), autonomy, friendship, marriage, children, various forms of status (such as honor, respect and esteem), knowledge and achievement.

These are the sorts of goods that typically appear on objective-list theories of well-being. But all the theories explicitly or implicitly acknowledge the importance of (at least most of) these goods for most people's well-being. They differ in that, while objective-list theories are usually content to assert this importance as a matter of manifest fact that is evident to any reflective person, the other theories offer further analysis of this importance: for hedonism these are considered ordinary goods because people typically find pleasure in them; for desire-satisfaction theories, it is because people usually desire them; and for nature-fulfillment theories, it is on account of our nature as human beings. The qualifications that are sometimes made in mental-state theories (for example, that pleasures with worthy objects contribute more to well-being than other pleasures) or in desire-satisfaction theories (for instance, that it is rational and informed desires that are the desires relevant to well-being) are designed in part to assure that the theory can accommodate the commonsense intuition about the value of ordinary goods.

Of course, there are other important differences among the four types of theory: mental-state and desire-satisfaction theories usually insist on, and objective-list and nature-fulfillment theories typically resist, the possibility that the well-being of *some* persons may diverge in significant ways from participation in the ordinary goods. For example, a hedonist might contend that an ordinary good does not contribute to the well-being of a person who finds no pleasure in it, and that something other than (or contrary to) an ordinary good does contribute to the well-being of a person if the person finds pleasure in it. In general, mental-state and desire-satisfaction theories allow for more variation across individuals in what contributes to well-being than do objective-list and nature-fulfillment theories. But these differences should not prevent us from recognizing the fact that virtually all the parties in contemporary philosophical debates about well-being grant the important role that ordinary goods play in most people's lives.

## Frameworks for Discussing Well-Being in Buddhism

In traditional forms of Buddhist thought there is no explicit philosophical theory of well-being either as part of an overall moral philosophy or as an attempt to explain everyday intuitions about well-being. There are Buddhist understandings of well-being implied by the practical concern to diagnose and cure the problematic nature of human life as summarized, for example, in the Four Noble Truths. However, these understandings are not expressed in a form that makes it easy to categorize them in terms of the contemporary theories.

An initial obstacle is presented by the Buddhist no-self teaching that what we ordinarily call a self or person is not a distinct substance with identity through time, but (as it is put in the Pali Canon) is nothing more than a causally related series of impermanent mental and physical elements or aggregates (the *khandhas/skandhas*). The difficulty is that most contemporary discussions of well-being assume that we are selves in the sense that Buddhism denies. In fact, the definition of the concept of well-being stated earlier—how well or badly a person's life is going for the person whose life it is—would ordinarily be understood to presuppose such a conception of the self.

There are different ways in which this obstacle might be overcome. The Buddhist understanding of well-being might be presented solely at the level of the aggregates, by referring only to momentary instances of feelings, perceptions, formations and the like, with no reference to a substantial self that possesses these things. This approach would follow the lead of the Abhidharma schools and would craft an account of well-being solely in terms of the dharmas, the ultimate realities, that make up the world. We would then have a Buddhist theory of well-being in an alternative framework that corresponds to the framework of the contemporary theories. Another approach would be to draw on the distinction between ultimate and conventional truth, and present an account of well-being at the level of conventional truth. Whereas the first approach would explain well-being at the level of ultimate truth (as understood in the Abhidharma schools), the second approach would explain well-being in terms of the commonsense categories of conventional truth, in which it is permissible to speak of a self that is distinct and has identity through time (as conventionally, but not ultimately, true). In Mahāyāna Buddhism, it is sometimes supposed, on account of emptiness, that nothing can be said about the ultimate truth or that the ultimate truth is that nothing is ultimately true (in the Madhyamaka school). On this approach, the only level on which we could speak of well-being would be that of conventional truth. In any case, in the Pali Canon, and in many texts in subsequent traditions, both Mahāyāna and non-Mahāyāna, well-being was often discussed in the commonsense language of conventional truth. By following suit, it may be possible to bring Buddhist views about well-being into somewhat greater proximity to contemporary concerns.

A great deal of Buddhist teaching presupposes a distinction between being unenlightened and being enlightened. Even when dualism as such is problematized in Mahāyāna contexts this distinction usually remains important, although it is qualified in some way such as being described as merely conventional or employed as skillful means. Moreover, it is often (though not always) supposed that the path from being unenlightened to being enlightened is a gradual one which encompasses several stages. For example, the Buddha said that "penetration to final knowledge occurs by graduate training, gradual activity, and gradual practice, not abruptly" (*AN* IV 201), and he distinguished the stages of the stream-enterer, the once-returner and the non-returner as leading up to the enlightenment of the *Arahant* (see *MN* I 141–2). In Mahāyāna Buddhism, we are sometimes told that there are 10 stages leading to the perfect Buddhahood to which the Bodhisattva aspires (however, in Zen there is resistance to this approach). Though we need not follow the specifics of these different models of the stages to enlightenment, it will be helpful in thinking about Buddhist understandings of well-being (and other topics in later chapters) to draw some distinctions regarding the path leading to enlightenment. In particular, it will be useful to think in terms of five basic categories (within which further distinctions might well be drawn; for a somewhat different classification, see Adam 2005).

First, there are unenlightened persons who have no knowledge of or interest in Buddhist teaching. These persons are not in any explicit or conscious sense on the Buddhist path at all. They may be called the *non-initiates*. Second, there are persons who have a basic commitment to some Buddhist ideas and values, but they are not at all close to being enlightened. In some of these cases, these persons may be committed to following the path to enlightenment in this lifetime, perhaps because they have taken a vow to do so, but in other cases they may simply be trying to live a decent life according to Buddhist standards, perhaps in the hope that this will lead to a better rebirth in which it will then be possible to seek enlightenment directly. In any case, these persons, though committed, have not gone far on the path to enlightenment. Let us call them *initiates*. Even those initiates who are committed in this lifetime to seeking full enlightenment are typically guided in more direct and concrete ways by a more proximate goal. This goal is, roughly speaking, to make significant progress along the path, a goal that is grounded in the recognition that such progress is necessary to attain full enlightenment even though it falls well short of it. Let us call persons who have attained this proximate goal *progressers*. Admittedly this is a vague category that encompasses a wide range of possibilities. Nonetheless, it is a useful category because a good deal of Buddhist literature may be interpreted as addressing initiates whose most immediate concern is to become a progresser of some kind. Such persons are in the cycle of rebirth and are not yet enlightened. But they are committed to the path, and their proximate though not final aspiration is to make some significant progress on the path.

In many respects, these three categories—non-initiates, initiates and progressers—fit fairly comfortably within both the Theravāda and Mahāyāna traditions (though they would not be understood in precisely the same way). However, as we go further to consider the movement from the stage of progresser to the final goal of full enlightenment, there are important differences between these two traditions. As we have seen, in the Pali Canon that is the root of Theravāda Buddhism, a distinction is drawn between enlightened persons who are still alive and enlightened persons who have died and escaped the cycle of rebirth (that is, *Arahants* before and after death). Both figures are fully enlightened, but there is a sense in which the former is still in the cycle of rebirth. Hence, in Theravāda Buddhism, the fourth category would be enlightened persons who are still alive, and the fifth category would be enlightened persons who have died and attained final nirvana (as it is sometimes called). In Mahāyāna Buddhism, the picture is somewhat different. In the 10-stage model of the Bodhisattva path, the completion of the sixth stage (corresponding to the Six Perfections) is similar in some ways to the *Arahant* at the point of death, except that there remain four additional stages of progress in cosmic realms before complete Buddhahood is reached (See Harvey 1990: 122–4). Hence, in Mahāyāna Buddhism, the fourth category would be an "advanced Bodhisattva" who is still alive, but the fifth category would encompass the remaining cosmic stages culminating in full Buddhahood (there are complications in that Bodhisattvas in the cosmic stages can reappear in some form in the cycle of rebirth).

Hence, we have the following five categories regarding the path to enlightenment:

1. Non-initiates who are not on the path,
2. Initiates who have some commitment to Buddhist values,
3. Progressers who have made significant progress on the path,
4. Living persons who either have attained enlightenment by Theravāda standards *(Arahants)* or have attained the sixth stage of the Mahāyāna Bodhisattva path, and
5. *Arahants* who have attained final nirvana from the Theravāda perspective or Bodhisattvas who in the Mahāyāna framework are in the final four stages culminating in Buddhahood.

Buddhism has something to say about the well-being of persons at each of these stages, though, as we shall see, at the final stage we cannot really speak of persons at all. Most Buddhist discussions of well-being pertain either to unenlightened persons in the cycle of rebirth (the first three categories) or to enlightened persons who are escaping or have escaped this cycle (the fourth and fifth categories). However, the two kinds of discussions are not entirely unrelated, and on this model there is a process of development from the unenlightened to the enlightened stages. This suggests the need for a unified framework. But the place to begin is with accounts of unenlightened well-being in the cycle of rebirth.

## Unenlightened Well-Being: The Role of Suffering

In the Pali Canon, the well-being of persons insofar as they are unenlightened is often understood in terms of participation in at least many of the ordinary goods such as long life, health, beauty, fulfillment of basic physical needs, pleasure and the absence of pain, marriage, children and influence or respect (for example, see *MN* III 202–6 and *AN* II 69–70 and 202–5). Sometimes these goods are portrayed as having instrumental value: for example, they may facilitate a life of virtue or the process of enlightenment (though they may do opposite when they are sources of craving or attachment). However, it seems clear that these goods are also presented as having intrinsic value, at least for unenlightened persons. At any rate, the idea that belief in the karma doctrine can motivate people to be virtuous seems to presuppose that people desire these goods for their own sake. On the karmic scale, greater well-being typically means greater participation in these ordinary goods, at least for human beings.

For unenlightened persons, both moral virtue and well-being are at best imperfect. Their virtue is limited insofar as, even if they have virtues such as love or compassion, these are deficient by being restricted to friends and relations. Their well-being is limited because every unenlightened creature, no matter how high up on the karmic scale, has some form of suffering, the standard translation of *dukkha/duḥkha*. Other translations include unsatisfactoriness, frustration, unease and "dis-ease." This array of terms suggests that for Buddhism there is ordinarily something deeply problematic in human life. The pervasiveness of suffering, to stay with the standard term, is a distinctive feature of the Buddhist account of well-being for unenlightened persons. According to the First Noble Truth:

> Birth is suffering, aging is suffering, illness is suffering, death is suffering; union with what is displeasing is suffering; not to get what one wants is suffering; in brief, the five aggregates subject to clinging are suffering.
>
> (*SN* V 421)

In elaborations, suffering often appears to be understood by reference to ordinary goods: it is said to involve their absence, or loss or the threat of their loss. For example, the loss or danger of the loss of property needed for fulfillment of basic physical needs is a commonly cited instance of suffering (see *MN* I 85–7). But this is not the whole nor even the main part of the story: even those who fare well with respect to ordinary goods, those at the top of the karmic scale, are to some extent plagued by suffering. By contrast, those who are enlightened have overcome suffering. This is the most important difference between unenlightened and enlightened well-being.

This analysis points to a disparity between the Buddhist perspective on well-being and a common assumption in the contemporary philosophical debate about well-being. For Buddhism, unenlightened persons may have more or less well-being in terms of participation in ordinary goods, but their lives are always fundamentally problematic until enlightenment is attained, at which point a form of well-being is achieved that is superior to any level of well-being that is available to the unenlightened. In the contemporary debate about well-being, there is no such contention and usually it is tacitly denied. Hence, Buddhism may be seen as implying a critique of contemporary discussions: they fail to recognize, or at least to be concerned with, both the flawed nature of most people's well-being and the possibility of something better. In order to comprehend the well-being of both unenlightened and enlightened persons from a Buddhist perspective, we need to say more about what Buddhism says about suffering.

The Buddhist understanding of the nature of suffering and what it would mean to overcome it requires some interpretation. In addition to depictions of suffering in terms of the absence or loss of ordinary goods, we are given some general characterizations. As was seen in Chapter 1, suffering is often associated with impermanence. A basic teaching of Buddhism is that all things are impermanent, and it is not difficult to see the connection with suffering. On account of impermanence, we may be anxious about losing the good things we possess and about encountering the bad things we have so far managed to avoid. Analyses of this kind are common in Buddhism. If we think that genuine well-being would be permanently possessing the good things and permanently avoiding the bad things, then in a world in which all things are impermanent such well-being would be impossible. This might be thought to imply that a form of suffering is inevitable.

However, it is not clear that impermanence as such is the main problem. People are not always anxious about the impermanence of things, and some enjoyments presuppose impermanence (for example, people often enjoy athletic events, the change of seasons and the growth of their children). Moreover, enlightened persons in the fourth category are still living in a world of impermanence. In addition, if some things that are bad were permanently endured, that might well be a source of suffering. Hence, it is not obvious that impermanence as such is necessary or sufficient for suffering. Impermanence is clearly an important occasion for suffering in Buddhist teaching, and is an important part of the arguments for no-self. But it may be less central to the analysis of suffering as such than it sometimes appears to be.

What is more central is our mental response to what happens to us. In Buddhist texts such as the aforementioned First Noble Truth, suffering is often depicted in terms of the frustration of desires and what we find displeasing. These depictions are parts of enumerations of factors associated with suffering. They are not themselves analyses of the nature of suffering. But they suggest that a key part of suffering is our mental state: it involves some form of dissatisfaction or discontentment. By implication, insofar as well-being is associated with overcoming suffering, well-being would imply freedom form such mental turbulence.

In order to see this, consider the suffering involved in sickness. We usually regard sickness as a form of suffering because it often involves physical pain, and it prevents us from doing things we would like to do. But it seems that for the Buddha these things by themselves are not suffering since we are told that an *Arahant* who is alive (the fourth category above) nonetheless "still experiences what is agreeable and disagreeable and feels pleasure and pain" (Ireland 1997: 181). Moreover, the Buddha himself is said to have experienced "sharp pains" during an illness just prior to his death (see *DN* II 99 and Collins 1998: 156). Hence, it would seem that the suffering of sickness must be something more than, or other than, pain and disability. This might seem problematic since pain is sometimes listed as an instance of suffering. However, the Buddha addressed this problem by referring to an "uninstructed worldling" and an "instructed noble disciple" who both have painful feelings. About the first person, he said:

> When the uninstructed worldling is being contacted by a painful feeling, he sorrows, grieves, and laments; he weeps beating his breast and becomes distraught. He feels two feelings—a bodily one and a mental one . . . . Being contacted by that same painful feeling, he harbours aversion towards it.
>
> (*SN* IV 208)

By contrast, the instructed noble disciple who experiences a painful feeling does not sorrow, grieve and the like. "He feels one feeling—a bodily one, not a mental one." And "he harbours no aversion towards" the painful feeling (*SN* IV 209). In this text, at least, there is a distinction between pain and our mental response to it. The unenlightened and enlightened persons both feel bodily pain, but they have different attitudes toward it: the unenlightened persons feel distress and aversion, but the enlightened persons do not.

In the case of sickness, then, the suffering that the Buddha purports to alleviate is not the physical pain or disability of sickness itself. His teaching is analogous to medical treatment; it is not a substitute for it (in fact, the Buddha had a physician and monastics were allowed a form of medicine). Medical treatment might relieve us of the physical pain and disability of sickness. Buddhist teaching promises relief, not from this, but from troublesome reactive attitudes such as being distraught when we are sick and feeling aversion to possible future sickness (see Gowans 2010).

This is evident in the Second Noble Truth and related texts where we are told that the proximate cause of suffering is charged forms of desire such as craving, clinging, attachment, greed, lust, hatred and so forth. Some texts give the impression that desire as such is the source of suffering. For example, the Buddha says, "desire is the root of suffering" (*SN* IV 329). This would seem to imply that overcoming suffering means eliminating desire altogether. With respect to the final stage of enlightenment, the aforementioned fifth category, this may well be true (there is more about this later). However, as we saw in Chapter 1, for those who are enlightened while still alive, the fourth category, this is more problematic. At any rate, in one familiar sense of the term 'desire,' to desire that something happen is to have a disposition to bring it about. Enlightened persons such as *Arahants* and advanced Bodhisattvas have the virtues of compassion and loving-kindness, and these would seem to involve having dispositions to bring about certain things. The Buddha himself is represented as having desires in this sense during the 45 years he taught the Dharma. This suggests that, at least for the most part, the source of suffering is forms of desire that are especially urgent or powerful such as craving (for an account of desire in the Pali Canon, see Webster 2005).

Suffering, then, is the dissatisfaction that accompanies pressing and often unfulfilled desires that particular states of affairs that are regarded negatively disappear or not arise, and that states of affairs that are regarded positively continue or arise. The Buddhist teaching is that, as long as we are in the cycle of rebirth, we are prone to such dissatisfaction. At times it may overwhelm and dominate our consciousness, but even when it does not, this prospect is always on the horizon. This does not mean that the degree of suffering is the same for all persons at all times. In particular, on a gradualist model of attaining enlightenment, suffering will generally decline as an unenlightened person travels the path toward enlightenment.

The deeper source of craving and suffering is the delusion that we are selves. For example, the craving that the pain must end, and the suffering that accompanies this craving, originates in the connection of the pain with the perspective of "I," "me," and "mine"—as in the thought "this pain is mine." Likewise, the realization that we are not selves, the key to enlightenment, undermines this thought—there is no "me" to whom this pain belongs—and hence eliminates the craving that this pain must end. We might wonder, of course, why the presence or absence of the belief that we are selves should have such a powerful effect. Would not the pain be just as annoying with or without this belief? The Buddhist view appears to be that this belief significantly affects our aversion to the pain (as well as our craving for pleasure). But why should this be?

One answer is that suffering needs to be understood at a more holistic level. Mark Siderits has proposed that suffering in Buddhism refers not merely to pain but to "existential suffering," the alienation and despair that come from thinking one's life lacks meaning, value or purpose (see Siderits 2007a: 19–21; cf. 2003: 29–31 and 99–101). In this analysis, this thought may be occasioned by the realization of one's own mortality or, on the assumption of karma and rebirth, the sense of pointlessness that comes from the belief that one will live an endless series of lives. Either way, the realization that one is not a self (that could be mortal or have endless lives) undermines the thought that one's life is meaningless and hence eliminates existential suffering. This interpretation lends a rather contemporary flavor to Buddhist suffering, describing it in a vocabulary that is associated with the distinctive concerns of some 20th century Western intellectuals. But it may nonetheless capture part of what Buddhists have had in mind.

Another view is that thoughts such as "this pleasure *is mine*" or "this pain *is mine*" are sufficient to generate craving and suffering, not because of concerns about meaning and purpose, but because the delusion of self-hood propels us into feverish attractions (to unite myself with what seems good) and aversions (to separate myself from what seems bad). In a famous text often called the "Fire Sermon," the Buddha says, "all is burning." Each of the senses, he says, is "burning with the fire of lust, with the fire of hatred, with the fire of delusion; burning with birth, aging, and death; with sorrow, lamentation, pain, displeasure, and despair" (*SN* IV 19). On this interpretation, what is problematic about the cycle of rebirth is not that it goes on and on without purpose, but that throughout it is a driven and hence inherently unsatisfactory state of being. This interpretation may closer to the traditional Indian Buddhist sources, though we might wonder again whether the sense of "mine-ness" could have this kind of effect.

In any case, in Buddhist thought, though the well-being of unenlightened persons is typically portrayed in terms of participation in at least many of the ordinary goods, that participation is always marred by suffering to some extent. For unenlightened persons, dissatisfaction is always on the scene no matter what happens. Hence, they have a defective form of well-being.

Since a crucial feature of suffering is a mental state such as dissatisfaction or discontentment, the Buddhist understanding of the well-being of unenlightened persons implies that it is defective at least in part because of this mental state.

## Enlightened Well-Being

The well-being of enlightened persons is thought to be superior to the well-being of unenlightened persons at least in large part because enlightened persons have overcome suffering. But how are we to understand enlightened persons? Let us begin with persons who are enlightened and still alive (our fourth category). In the Pali Canon, this person is characterized as follows:

> His five sense faculties remain unimpaired, by which he still experiences what is agreeable and disagreeable and feels pleasure and pain. It is the extinction of attachment, hate and delusion in him that is called the nirvana-element with residue left.
>
> (Ireland 1997: 181)

This is the depiction we would expect given the aforementioned analysis of suffering. The enlightened person is not without feelings of pain and experiences of what is disagreeable. But this person does not suffer because he or she is without craving and related forms of troublesome desires (attachment and hate). The enlightened person is also characterized as being dispassionate, mentally unperturbed and free of many emotions such as anger and fear. Just as suffering is a second-order dissatisfaction that accompanies craving, so overcoming suffering would seem to be the absence of this dissatisfaction no matter what happens, even if what happens is painful or disagreeable. In this respect, suffering and overcoming suffering are both depicted in terms of mental states that persons may or may not have regarding their experiences.

In view of this, it seems clear that the well-being of an enlightened person involves a mental state. Let us call this state *contentment*. There are at least two ways in which this might be understood. It might be argued that there is nothing more to contentment than the absence of suffering. In this view, the relevant mental state of enlightened persons is simply a state of *non-dissatisfaction*. However, enlightened persons are often portrayed in more positive terms than merely living without suffering. In fact, one of the most common portrayals of enlightened persons is that they are in a state of profound peace, calm, tranquility, equanimity and the like (for example, see *MN* I 431). They are also said to be in states of extraordinary bliss and delight (for example, see *MN* I 504 ff.). These depictions suggest that contentment includes, but is more than, the mere absence of dissatisfaction: it has a positive dimension that is at once tranquil and joyful. Putting these together, we might say that contentment is a state of *joyful tranquility*. This is a state that is the opposite of—and not merely the absence of—the dissatisfaction that characterizes suffering (similar to the way in which it might be said that pleasure is the opposite of pain, not simply the absence of pain). In any case, it is evident that, just as the well-being of unenlightened persons is always defective on account of suffering, a crucial feature of which is a mental state such as dissatisfaction, so the well-being of enlightened persons is always superior on account of contentment, where this may be understood either as mere non-dissatisfaction or as joyful tranquility.

Contentment is not the only feature attributed to enlightened persons. Such persons are also standardly said to possess two other characteristics: wisdom and virtue. In brief, wisdom is the correlate of the delusion or ignorance that is said to be the source of craving and hence suffering. It refers primarily to the realization that we are not selves or, in Mahāyāna Buddhism, to the realization of the emptiness of all things. Virtue in this context would seem to be some state near ethical perfection. Sometimes this is depicted in negative terms as the absence of such things as greed and hatred. But often it is portrayed in positive terms as the presence of specific virtues such as compassion (striving to eliminate the suffering of all beings) and loving-kindness (striving to promote their well-being). Are wisdom and virtue part of well-being or something in addition to well-being? There may not be an explicit and unambiguous answer to this question in the tradition. If they are something in addition to well-being, then the well-being of enlightened persons would simply be a state of contentment (either the absence of dissatisfaction or the presence of joyful tranquility). However, these three states—contentment, wisdom and virtue—are often portrayed as implying one another and as being the three constitutive features of the state of enlightenment. This might be thought to support the view that the well-being of enlightened persons who are still alive (our fourth category) consists of all three of these states together—what might be called a tripartite interpretation of enlightenment well-being.

But what about the well-being of enlightened persons beyond this life (our fifth category)? What about the well-being of "the nirvana-element without residue" or of the Buddha himself after he died, as understood in Theravāda Buddhism? Or about the well-being of one who attains full Buddhahood by fulfilling all of the 10 levels of perfection in Mahāyāna

Buddhism? To some extent we are encouraged to suppose that the well-being of the enlightened beyond death is similar to the well-being of the enlightened during this life except that it is in some sense more purified, elevated or perfect. However, very little is said about these ultimate states of enlightenment and what is said is quite elusive. Moreover, what is said is paradoxical in that, on the one hand, it seems clear that these are descriptions of the highest form of well-being from a Buddhist perspective and yet, on the other hand, they can hardly be said to be descriptions of a form of *human* well-being at all (or even a form of well-being that the rest of us can hope to understand). The question "What is it like to be in a fully enlightened state?" is not easy to answer.

Depictions of this state are deeply perplexing. In the Pali Canon it is said that the "happiness" of nirvana is a state in which "nothing is felt here" (*AN* IV 415). The Theravāda commentator Buddhaghosa says: "Let us dwell in bliss by being without consciousness here and now and reaching the cessation that is nirvana" (*Vism.* 705). And the Mahāyāna philosopher Śāntideva says in what is traditionally taken to be a reference to the state of nirvana: "when neither entity nor non-entity remains before the mind, since there is no other mode of operation, grasping no objects, it becomes tranquil" (*BCA* 9.34). Such passages make it clear that the ultimate state of enlightenment, and hence the ultimate form of well-being, is utterly different from any form of human consciousness that is ordinarily known to us. On the one hand, this is a state of happiness, bliss and tranquility—which is recognizable as an account of well-being. On the other hand, this is a state in which nothing is felt, there is no consciousness, and there is no object before the mind—which is not easily recognizable as a theory of well-being. From a philosophical standpoint, these passages may strike us as puzzling.

Of course, efforts may be made to clarify these passages philosophically. No doubt some light could be shed upon them by exploring the ideas of no-self and emptiness. But there is a significant strain of Buddhist thought, beginning in the Pali Canon and continuing in many traditions, that discourages us from pursuing this endeavor. As we saw in Chapter 4, the Buddha refused to answer questions about his postmortem existence (specifically, the existence of the Tathāgata after death) on the ground that speculations about this topic are "beset by suffering" and do not lead to enlightenment. In this regard, he declared that his teaching is "profound, hard to see and hard to understand, peaceful and sublime, unattainable by mere reasoning, subtle, to be experienced by the wise" (*MN* I 485–7). This may be why so little is said about the ultimate state of enlightenment. Though this state is always on the horizon of Buddhist practice, it is ordinarily on a very distant horizon, and much more attention is given to what it would mean for living human beings to attain enlightenment and how those on the path might move toward this.

## Is There a Unified Account of Buddhist Well-Being?

If we set aside the ultimate form of Buddhist well-being (our fifth category), we could summarize the last two sections as follows. The well-being of persons insofar as they are unenlightened consists of some measure of ordinary goods, the more the better, but this is always imperfect because suffering is always present. By contrast, the well-being of persons insofar as they are enlightened precludes suffering and consists of contentment—and perhaps wisdom and virtue as well. There is a common denominator here pertaining to our mental state: suffering as dissatisfaction and contentment as either mere non-dissatisfaction or joyful tranquility are crucial determinants of the extent to which a person does or does not possess well-being. But in other respects this account might suggest a dualistic conception of well-being: for unenlightened persons, ordinary goods are central, while for enlightened persons, at least on the tripartite interpretation, wisdom and virtue are crucial. These appear to be quite different (even though in karma theory more virtue is said to result in more ordinary goods and on occasion these goods are said to include some form of wisdom). In one way this is not surprising. The dichotomy of unenlightened and enlightened persons is often fundamental in Buddhist thought. But a dualist account of well-being may appear perplexing. We may well wonder: Do wisdom and virtue play any role in the degree of well-being of unenlightened persons or, more significantly, in the well-being of persons who are in transition from being unenlightened to being enlightened? And do ordinary goods play any role in the well-being of enlightened persons?

The answer to the first question is surely that, if the tripartite interpretation is correct for enlightened persons, then wisdom and virtue make a difference to the well-being of unenlightened persons as well. That is, if wisdom and virtue contribute to the well-being of the enlightened, then presumably the lack of wisdom and virtue contributes to the lack of well-being of the unenlightened. Moreover, in the transition from an unenlightened to enlightened life, in the movement from the first to fourth categories, there is presumably a gradual increase of wisdom and virtue—and so of well-being as well. Hence, for those not yet enlightened, well-being would depend on the level of participation in ordinary goods, the proportion of dissatisfaction and contentment and the measure of wisdom and virtue.

The answer to the second question, whether ordinary goods play any role in the well-being of enlightened persons, is less obvious. It would seem that, if we are speaking of enlightened persons in our fourth category, one enlightened person might participate in more ordinary goods than another enlightened person. Would the first person have greater well-being on account of this? There are several possible answers to this question.

In its more ascetic manifestations, Buddhist texts often seem to be committed to a negative answer, that participation in ordinary goods makes no real difference to the well-being of enlightened persons. Various reasons might be given for this. One would be that the value of enlightened life in terms of wisdom, virtue and contentment is so extraordinarily high that participation in ordinary goods is not significant enough to make any real difference to it (just as a drop of water in a lake would not make a real difference to its water level). Another rather different reason would be that (at least many of) the so-called ordinary goods are not really goods at all for anyone: they merely appear to be goods to the unenlightened, and their invocation in standard accounts of the karma doctrine is a form of skillful means designed to motivate people to live morally better lives. In pre-Mahāyāna Buddhism this would probably appear to be a rather unorthodox suggestion, but it is easier to see how it could find purchase from a Mahāyāna perspective.

A possible difficulty for the view that ordinary goods make no real difference to the well-being of enlightened persons is that these persons would be indifferent to these goods (at least with respect to one another), and it might be hard to understand what a life of such indifference would be like and why it would be the highest form of well-being. Though the value of wisdom, virtue and contentment might well be recognized by many people (at least in some forms), a life of indifference to the ordinary goods surely would not be regarded as a fully good life by most people. However, it might be said in response that this is simply another respect in which the lives of enlightened persons cannot be understood from the unenlightened perspective of most of us.

There are other strands within Buddhist thought—for example, the middle way motif—that might be taken to suggest that participation in at least some ordinary goods does affect the level of well-being of enlightened persons (recall that the Buddha said that the Eightfold Path was a middle way between the sensuous lives of most people and the ascetic lives of the samaṇas). In this view, participation in more rather than fewer ordinary goods of some kinds increases the level of well-being of enlightened persons. One form this view could take would be to say that every enlightened person participates in these ordinary goods to the greatest extent possible (so that the aforementioned suggestion that they might differ in ordinary goods would be incorrect). This might be thought of as a natural extension of the karma doctrine: since greater virtue results in greater ordinary goods, the highest level of virtue would result in the highest level of ordinary goods. However, traditional Buddhist texts do not typically portray enlightened persons in this way. They are more likely to be depicted as being indifferent to ordinary goods than as enjoying maximal participation in them.

Another form this view could take would be to say that participation in ordinary goods increases the well-being of enlightened persons, but some enlightened persons participate in more ordinary goods—and so have greater well-being—than other enlightened persons. It could still be maintained, as often seems to be implied, that the well-being that consists in wisdom, virtue and contentment is fundamentally—and perhaps incommensurably—higher than the well-being that consists in participation in ordinary goods. Nonetheless, in this position, some enlightened lives are better than others on account of greater participation in ordinary goods. This might be regarded as the most realistic of the alternatives on this issue. However, in allowing for gradations of well-being among the enlightened, it might not sit well with the superlative rhetoric that seems to imply that enlightenment is something such as "the best state" or "the highest perfection."

In any case, there is little reason to think that much consideration was given to this question in Indian forms of Buddhism or subsequent traditions. It was probably thought that what really mattered—either altogether or else most—was the state of enlightenment that consists in contentment, and perhaps wisdom and virtue as well. And it may have been thought that pursuing concerns about the status of ordinary goods would only encourage the craving that is the root of suffering.

## Buddhist Well-Being and the Contemporary Philosophies

Let us now consider the question how the Buddhist understanding of well-being might relate to the contemporary philosophical theories of well-being, focusing first on those elements that might be thought to be central to the well-being of enlightened persons: contentment, wisdom and virtue. Though traditional Buddhists were not directly concerned with developing a philosophical theory of well-being, we might wonder whether the Buddhist position can be interpreted as committed to, or at least can be illuminated by, one of the contemporary theories.

The least plausible possibility is the category of desire-satisfaction theories according to which a person's well-being is simply a matter of the satisfaction of the person's desires (or at least the desires the person would have insofar as he or she were rational and/or fully informed). Of course, a central theme in Buddhism is that frustration of desires, as an occasion for suffering, detracts from well-being. But this does not mean that well-being consists in the satisfaction of desires. It is clearly not the case that for Buddhism the highest form of well-being consists in the fulfillment of desires, even those of a rational and fully informed person. The enlightened person has contentment, wisdom and virtue irrespective of the satisfaction of desires. As seen earlier, some Buddhist texts seem to imply that an enlightened person would have no desires at all. This may well be the case for fully enlightened persons in the fifth category. For them, well-being can hardly consist of the satisfaction of desires. However, even if enlightened persons in the fourth category have some desires (for example, that others overcome suffering), as was suggested earlier, this does not imply that the well-being of these enlightened persons consists in the satisfaction of those desires. There is no indication that contentment, wisdom or virtue contribute to well-being simply because we desire them.

There is more plausibility in the idea that the Buddhist understanding of well-being has some similarity to mental-state theories according to which well-being is a matter of the negative or positive quality of our mental states. The suffering that detracts from the well-being of unenlightened persons involves mental states such as dissatisfaction, and contentment is a mental state that is a crucial part of the well-being of enlightened persons. Hence, negative and positive mental states are surely relevant to well-being from a Buddhist perspective. In fact, it might be argued that Buddhist well-being is nothing more than contentment, either non-dissatisfaction or joyful tranquility (for suggestion of a position close to the former, see Siderits 2007b: 292). However, whether contentment is all or part of Buddhist well-being, there is an important difference from what is usually intended in contemporary mental-state theories such as hedonism. The assumption of these theories is often that different people find pleasure and pain in rather different things. Hence, what would bring me pleasure and hence well-being (listening to the Grateful Dead) may be very different from what would bring you the same (say, listening to Johann Sebastian Bach). Proponents of these theories commonly suppose that it is an advantage of their positions that they allow for this kind of diversity. The Buddhist understanding of well-being does not have this implication. Suffering and contentment are ultimately a function, not of the diverse ways in which different persons happen to respond to various states of affairs, but of whether a person is enlightened. Hence, whatever music they hear, unenlightened persons as a class are dissatisfied to some extent and enlightened persons as a class are content. Moreover, if wisdom and virtue are also features of the well-being of enlightened persons, it would not seem that they contribute to well-being simply insofar as they are positive mental states. These considerations might be thought to suggest that Buddhist well-being is better understood by one of the other two contemporary theories of well-being.

It has been argued that Buddhism is committed to an objective-list theory in which well-being consists of participation in a set of objective goods, that is, goods that are good for everyone. There are disagreements among contemporary objective-list theorists about what belongs on the list of objective goods, and there are also disagreements among interpreters of Buddhist well-being about what goes on the list. For example, according to Keown, life, knowledge and friendship are basic goods in Buddhism (see Keown 2001: 42 ff.), while for Goodman virtue and worldly happiness are the main Buddhist goods (see Goodman 2009: 61–2 and 80–1). Moreover, in light of the tripartite interpretation someone might suggest that the three basic goods are contentment, wisdom and virtue. These theories are obviously not the same, though they may be somewhat less different from what these lists suggest. For example, Keown (2001) associates friendship with virtues (51–2). Hence, all three lists make some reference to virtue.

In any case, there is an objection to an objective list interpretation. Proponents of contemporary objective-list theories typically assume that the goods on the list are to a large extent distinct and independent of one another. This is why the word 'list' is an apt term for the theory. Moreover, they commonly think that a person may have one of the goods, but not another. It might be argued, however, that at least many aspects of well-being associated with Buddhist enlightenment are not best interpreted as distinct goods. For example, the holism that inspires the tripartite interpretation suggests that wisdom, virtue and contentment are best thought of as three aspects of a single, unified state of being. They can be distinguished conceptually, but the existence of each implies the existence of the other two. Hence, a person could not be truly wise, but lack the virtue of compassion. On a gradual model of enlightenment the three features may be gradually acquired, but ordinarily it is not supposed that they are acquired in sequence (though sometimes presentations of the Eightfold Path or the Six Perfections might give this appearance). Insofar as this is true, there is a difference between the Buddhist understanding of the well-being of enlightened persons and the usual understanding of objective-list theorists. In response, it might be countered that this is not a serious difference since objective-list theorists are not opposed to the idea that there may be relationships among the various goods. Moreover, it might be said that the goods on the lists proposed by Keown and Goodman are somewhat independent of one another.

A final possibility is that the Buddhist understanding of well-being might be interpreted as some kind of nature-fulfillment theory. According to this theory, well-being consists of the fulfillment of the most significant or characteristic features of human nature. A proponent of a nature-fulfillment theory might agree with a proponent of an objective-list theory about which specific goods constitute well-being. But they would differ in that the nature-fulfillment theorist thinks these goods constitute well-being because they fulfill our nature whereas the objective-list theorist offers no such explanation (he or she might think that all that can be said is that, in light of our experience, it is self-evident that these goods are forms of well-being). Nature-fulfillment theories are often thought to have some kinship with Aristotle. As will be seen in the next chapter, one prominent interpretation of Buddhist normative ethical thought is that it is similar to Aristotle's virtue theory. An understanding of the Buddhist account of well-being as a nature-fulfillment theory might go hand in hand with this approach. Several commentators have suggested that it is fruitful to interpret Buddhist viewpoints on well-being in terms of an Aristotelian eudaimonistic framework, though they all emphasize various ways in which Buddhist thought differs from Aristotle (for example, see Cooper and James 2005: ch. 4, Flanagan 2011 and Keown 1992: ch. 8).

There is, however, an objection to this approach. It has been claimed that the no-self teaching precludes understanding the Buddhist account of well-being or ethics as rooted in human nature in a way that is similar to Aristotle (see Goodman 2009: 70–1 and Siderits 2007b: 292). The objection in terms of well-being is that, if there is no self, then there is no entity that has a human nature, and if there is no human nature, well-being cannot be understood as the fulfillment of it. There is no question that Buddhism in virtually every tradition supposes that in ultimate truth there is no self. At this level, this might seem to be a compelling objection. However, as was suggested earlier, in Buddhist texts well-being is often discussed in the commonsense language of conventional truth. In fact, discussions of wisdom, virtue and contentment themselves appear to presuppose the language of conventional truth. At this level, it is permitted to speak of the self as something that is conventionally (but not ultimately) real. Hence, at this level, perhaps we may be permitted to speak of well-being as the fulfillment of human nature.

At the level of conventional truth, the Buddhist understanding of well-being may be thought to conform to a nature-fulfillment theory in the following way: the apparent de facto condition of human beings makes us prone to suffering, but we have the capacity to attain enlightenment and thereby overcome suffering. The highest form of well-being is thus the fulfillment of a central human capacity. In this respect, the understanding of Buddhist well-being is based on an analysis of human nature and the human condition. This analysis grounds the dominant narrative of much Buddhist teaching, and such an analysis is a distinguishing feature of a nature-fulfillment theory in contrast to an objective-list theory.

Moreover, as was seen at the end of Chapter 2, in Mahāyāna Buddhism, our capacity for enlightenment is sometimes depicted in terms of our Buddha-nature or Tathāgata-garbha (embryo or womb of the Buddha). A central theme in this tradition is that such things as the three unwholesome roots (greed, hatred and delusion) are insubstantial defilements that conceal our true nature—our Buddha-nature—according to which we are already Buddhas and have only to realize this. On this view, the process of attaining enlightenment is the process of realizing what we truly are. However the well-being of enlightenment is construed, it might be thought of as the fulfillment of our nature. Of course, the traditions of Buddha-nature and Tathāgata-garbha have been controversial within Buddhism itself precisely because they appear to attribute an inherent nature or self to us. One response to this critique is that statements in the texts of these traditions attributing this nature to us are expressions of conventional truth or are simply practical ways (skillful means) of encouraging enlightenment. So understood, a Buddhist nature-fulfillment theory of well-being would clearly have a different metaphysical status than is ordinarily associated with contemporary nature-fulfillment theories, especially those closely associated with Aristotle (there is more about this in the next chapter). This is an important difference, but this interpretation might nonetheless show that there is a way in which the nature-fulfillment theory has some affinity with Buddhist thought.

As we have seen, in addition to the features of enlightenment that might be associated with well-being such as contentment, wisdom and virtue, Buddhist texts often suggest that there is a lower form of well-being that consists of participation in ordinary goods (though it is not clear how these figure in the well-being of enlightened persons). We might also wonder whether the Buddhist understanding of these goods could be interpreted vis-à-vis the contemporary theories. If it can, it might be supposed that this interpretation would align with the understanding of the goods associated with enlightenment. Once again, a desire-satisfaction theory is not a likely candidate for a Buddhist understanding of the value of ordinary goods. There is nothing in Buddhist thought that suggests that the fact that a person desires something makes it good. However, a Buddhist mental-state theory might be more plausible. It would maintain that ordinary goods contribute to well-being insofar as they promote positive mental states. This would be similar to the claim of contemporary mental-state theories such as hedonism. If the well-being of enlightened persons consists of contentment, but not wisdom and virtue, then this might provide a unified Buddhist understanding of well-being. Moreover, it might be a natural ally of consequentialist interpretations of Buddhism since in consequentialist theories the value of consequences is often understood in terms of a mental-state theory—for example, in Bentham and Mill (see Chapter 6). An objective-list theory would claim that ordinary goods belong on the list of objective goods. In this case, there would not seem to be an objection to supposing that the goods are independent of one another. Finally, a nature-fulfillment theory would state that these goods contribute to the fulfillment of our nature in some way. This would face the same objection as before, that it conflicts with the no-self teaching, and it might seem less plausible in this case to appeal to something such as Buddha-nature since it is not obvious that participation in ordinary goods fulfills this nature (this relates to the question how these goods might relate to the well-being of an enlightened person).

CHAPTER **6**

# Normative Ethics
## Buddhist Ethics as a Theory of Right Action

One of the central topics in Western moral philosophy is the nature of morally right and wrong actions as well as the procedure for determining which actions are right and wrong. This topic has received considerable attention in contemporary discussions of normative ethics. Moreover, several recent interpreters have argued that at least some expressions of Buddhist ethical thought may be understood in terms of one of the standard Western theories of right and wrong action. The main candidates have been deontological theories, consequentialist theories and virtue ethics theories, especially the last two. These interpretations are the topic of this chapter. However, as we will see in the next chapter, some interpreters have argued, in opposition to all of these approaches, that Buddhist ethics is not committed to any such theory and has more kinship with pluralist, particularist or other non-theoretical approaches to normative ethics. In many ways, these debates about Buddhism and normative ethics have been at the heart of work in Buddhist moral philosophy. For this reason, we will discuss them at some length.

As an initial statement, the three aforementioned theories might be distinguished as follows: deontological theories emphasize duties, consequentialist theories stress consequences and virtue ethics theories focus on virtues. By itself this is not a very helpful characterization. It is widely supposed that Kant, Sidgwick and Aristotle are paradigmatic exponents of these three respective theories. But each of these philosophers thinks that duties, consequences and virtues all have moral importance in some contexts. In order to see the three theories as *alternatives,* they need to be characterized as different views about what has primary importance in relationship to other considerations. This might take the form of a strict foundationalist theory according to which the featured concept (or principle) is basic in that it is not derived from any other ethical concept and all other ethical concepts are derived from it. Or this might be expressed with less precision and strength by saying simply that the featured concept is what has the most explanatory significance vis-à-vis other ethical concepts.

With these considerations in mind, it is more helpful to begin with the following brief characterizations of these three theories:

- *Deontology.* An action is morally right if and only if, and because, it is done out of respect for or at least in accord with our moral duties.
- *Consequentialism.* An action is morally right if and only if, and because, it has appropriately valuable consequences.
- *Virtue Ethics.* An action is morally right if and only if, and because, it is what a virtuous agent would characteristically do.

These formulations are still quite simple and more elaboration would be needed to make clear all the differences among these theories. However, understanding the theories in these ways allows us to see that they are alternatives. Moreover, it enables us to see how a proponent of deontology could hold that consequences and virtues have some importance, but only insofar as they are based on or construed in relationship to our moral duties. For example, it might be said that fulfilling some duties requires us to take consequences into account or that virtue is a disposition to act out of respect for our moral duties, and similarly for proponents of consequentialism and virtue ethics. More broadly, as we will see, advocates of these three theories have much richer positions than these simple formulations indicate. Hence, we need to keep in mind both the basic differences among the theories and the complex ways in which each of them have been developed.

As we have seen, writers in Buddhist ethical traditions cannot plausibly be said to have explicitly articulated or defended one of these three theories (or any alternative theory of morally right actions). However, it has been argued that some of these writers were implicitly committed to one of these theories or at least that it is illuminating to interpret them in terms of one of the theories. Let us now consider the deontological, consequentialist and virtue ethics interpretations in turn, keeping in mind both the main distinctions between them and the complexity of the issues raised by each. We can then discuss, in the next chapter, some contrasting interpretive approaches that propose that Buddhist ethical thought is best seen as having some non-theoretical stance that rejects the idea that we need a theory of morally right actions that features a foundational or primary concept.

## The Deontological Interpretation

Interpretations of Buddhist ethics as a form of deontological ethics have sometimes been discussed, but have rarely been defended (however, see Davis 2013a and Olson 1993). Since deontology emphasizes the importance of moral duties, and the many rules in Buddhist ethics might be thought of as statements of moral duties, the lack of support for this interpretation may seem surprising. But a deontological interpretation has difficulty giving a Buddhist account of the kind of importance usually assigned to moral duties, in relationship to other moral considerations, in standard deontological theories. Moreover, much of Buddhist ethics does not appear to correspond to other features often associated with deontological approaches. Before considering what may be said for and against a deontological interpretation, it will be helpful to characterize more fully the deontological approach—or approaches—to morality (for an overview, see McNaughton and Rawling 2006).

As defined in the aforementioned brief statement, deontology is the view that an action is morally right if and only if, and because, it is done out of respect for or at least in accord with our moral duties. However, there are different ways of elaborating the emphasis on moral duties. The term 'deontology' comes from the Greek term *deon* meaning what one ought or must do—that is, a duty. Deontological accounts typically feature a threefold deontic vocabulary that distinguishes what is morally forbidden (a duty not to do something), morally obligated (a duty to do something), and morally permitted (neither forbidden nor obligated). An action that is in accord with our moral duties, on this view, is one that is obligatory or permissible and so is not forbidden. The category of the morally forbidden (or prohibited) is often thought to be especially important. A common characterization of deontological ethics states that there are kinds of actions that are always (or nearly always) wrong to perform. These usually involve ways of intentionally harming people. Hence, it is said to be wrong to kill, torture, betray or lie to a person. In order to distinguish the deontological account from other theories, it is said that the wrongness of these kinds of action does not depend on their consequences and or on the fact that virtuous agents would not perform them. Sometimes the first of these points, about consequences, is expressed more broadly by saying that in a deontological theory "the right is prior to the good." That is, which actions are right (obligatory or at least permissible) and wrong (forbidden) is independent of the goodness and badness of their consequences. They are right and wrong in themselves. Of course, we might wonder how we are to determine which actions are right and wrong on a deontological theory. There are different views about this. For example, sometimes it is said that it is self-evident or a matter of common moral understanding which actions are right or wrong, but sometimes it is said that this is known on the basis of some general moral principle that does not involve any form of consequentialism or virtue ethics.

Deontological theories are commonly contrasted with consequentialist theories for the reasons just given. Sometimes they are also contrasted with at least simple forms of consequentialism because they maintain that we should not perform a wrong action even to bring about a very great good or to avoid a very great evil. In this view it would be wrong to kill one person in order to save the lives of five other persons (for example, by transplanting the organs of the first person to the other five persons who would otherwise die). This is an implication of saying that these actions are always wrong, and in this example most people are likely to agree. But other cases often elicit different reactions: suppose the only way we could discover the location of a nuclear bomb soon to explode in a very large city would be by torturing an innocent person, say the young daughter of the terrorist responsible for the bomb, who has knowledge of its whereabouts. Would torture be wrong in this case? Some (but not all) proponents of deontological theories have granted that there is a "catastrophe proviso" according to which actions that are wrong (or would otherwise be wrong) may or should be performed if that was the only way to avert something such as a nuclear disaster.

The emphasis on avoiding wrong actions is sometimes linked to an understanding of morality according to which we are morally permitted to do whatever we want as long as we perform no wrong actions such as intentionally harming others. In this view, morality may not be very demanding and may leave persons with a good deal of freedom to live their lives in the large space of the morally permissible. However, some deontological theories—including those of Kant and Ross about to be discussed—include positive obligations to promote the well-being of other people (ordinarily as long as we do nothing wrong as a means to this end). Depending on how extensive these obligations are, a deontological morality may turn out to be quite demanding.

There are many proponents of deontological theories. Kant's moral philosophy in the *Groundwork of the Metaphysics of Morals* is usually interpreted as one of the most prominent examples (for an overview of Kant's ethics, see Hill 2006). Kant believed that we have "perfect duties" not to perform certain kinds of actions such as committing suicide, making a false promise and telling a lie. He famously thought that these kinds of actions were always wrong. Hence, it would be wrong to lie to a would-be murderer to prevent him from killing someone. But Kant also thought that we have "imperfect duties" to promote ends such developing our talents and promoting the well-being of other persons. Hence, we ought to pursue these ends to some extent and in some way so long as we violate no perfect duties as means to doing so. Kant thought that all of these duties were justified by the Categorical Imperative. Though he presented this as a single foundational principle of morality, he formulated several rather different versions of it. Perhaps the best-known formulation says: "act only in accordance with that maxim through which you can at the same time will that it become a universal law" (Kant 1998: 4:421) Another well-known formulation states: "So act that you use humanity, whether in your own person or in the person of any other, always at the same time as an end, never merely as a means" (Kant 1998: 4:429). By 'humanity' Kant meant our capacity to act on the basis of reasons, and it is clear that for Kant the fact that we are rational beings is the foundation of the Categorical Imperative in all its formulations and the moral duties he thought it sanctioned.

A rather different theory that is deontological in that it makes moral duties central was defended more recently by W. D. Ross (1988) in *The Right and the Good*. Ross identified seven *prima facie* duties concerning fidelity, reparation, gratitude, justice, beneficence, self-improvement and non-maleficence. He thought that it is self-evident that we have these various duties. They are not justified by a more fundamental moral principle such as the Categorical Imperative. By a "*prima facie* duty" he meant a feature of an action that counts in favor of doing it and would render the action an actual duty if the action did not have any other feature that was a conflicting *prima facie* duty. Ross supposed that such conflicts of duty were rather common. For example, we may need to break a promise in order to help someone in distress (fidelity conflicts with beneficence). Though Ross believed that some kinds of *prima facie* duties were generally more stringent than others, in the end he thought that when *prima facie* duties conflict we need to decide which is more stringent or binding in that particular case—what our actual all-things-considered duty is then and there—not on the basis of a general rule, but on the basis of a "considered opinion" that is at best probable and is never certain.

Let us now consider the deontological interpretation of Buddhist ethics. The primary consideration in support of it is that Buddhist ethics includes many moral rules that might plausibly be thought to be statements of moral duties. The most prominent of these rules are the five precepts that enjoin us to abstain from lying and other improper forms of speech, killing human beings and other sentient creatures, taking what does not belong to us, engaging in sensual misconduct and consuming alcohol. In the tradition, all Buddhists were expected to follow these rules. In addition, Buddhist monastics were supposed to follow more than 200 rules. Hence, there is no question that moral rules play an important part in Buddhist ethics.

It is sometimes said that Buddhism lacks a concept of moral obligation and that Buddhists are required to follow these rules only insofar as they voluntarily promise to do so (see Goodman 2009: 52). This would mean that the rules are not statements of moral obligation or duty. Even if this were true, however, there would still seem to be one obligation that does not depend on this promise, namely the obligation to fulfill the promise. Moreover, though there clearly are rules in Buddhism that persons are to follow only because they have agreed to do so (most obviously the rules governing the monastic communities), there also appear to be rules that it is supposed everyone ought to follow whether they have agreed to or not. In discussions of karma and rebirth in the Pali Canon, actions that are "not in accordance with the Dharma" are said to result in unhappiness. These actions include such things as killing living beings, taking what does not belong to one and misconduct in sensual pleasure (see *MN* I 285–6). These are kinds of actions that all persons, not simply Buddhists, are expected to refrain from: it would be wrong to perform them in the sense that it would be contrary to the Dharma. It does not seem implausible to consider rules to this effect as statements of what we would call moral duties or obligations. These rules are not, of course, commands of a divine lawgiver. But this is not required for the common understanding of the concept of duty or obligation, and deontological theories do not necessarily presuppose this.

For this reason, it may seem plausible to suppose that moral duties are an important part of Buddhist ethics. In some contexts, it is evident that these duties are to be performed no matter what. For example, we are told that there are "five impossible things" for an *Arahant*. He

is incapable of (a) deliberately taking the life of a living being; (b) taking what is not given so as to constitute theft; (c) sexual intercourse; (d) telling a deliberate lie; (e) storing up goods for sensual indulgence as he did formerly in the household life.

(*DN* III 235)

Taken at face value, the first of these, concerning killing, would seem to imply a form of pacifism according to which it is always wrong to kill a human being (there is more about this in Chapter 13). The fourth, pertaining to lying, looks to be an absolute moral prohibition similar to those Kant accepted. Such absolute restrictions are characteristic of some deontological theories.

In other contexts in the Pali Canon, however, a less restrictive position seems to be taken. For example, when King Pasenadi said that he was "able to have executed those who should be executed" the Buddha said that his words were "monuments to the Dharma" (see *MN* II 121–4). This might be taken to imply that killing human beings is sometimes morally required, if not for *Arahants,* at least for kings. Moreover, as we have seen in Chapter 2, in Mahāyāna Buddhism there is an even greater willingness to allow that some moral rules may or should be broken. For instance, Asaṅga maintained that a Bodhisattva may do things that are reprehensible—including killing, stealing and lying—if he or she has good intentions and these actions have good results. But this more flexible understanding of moral rules could also be accommodated to a deontological theory such as that of Ross by interpreting them as statements of *prima facie* duties.

As noted earlier, some deontological theories are rather undemanding, leaving us morally free to live our lives as long as we do not intentionally harm anyone. It might be objected that this is not compatible with the demanding moral requirements associated with most conceptions of Buddhist morality. However, although these requirements are real enough in Buddhism, not all deontological theories are undemanding. In fact, both Kant and Ross thought that there were positive duties to promote the well-being of others. Ross even endorsed, as a broad *prima facie* duty, "the general principle that we should produce as much good as possible" (Ross 1988: 27). Hence, the demanding nature of many conceptions of Buddhist ethics is not inherently incompatible with a deontological approach.

These considerations may be taken to favor, or at least not rule out, a deontological interpretation of Buddhist ethics. But they are not sufficient to establish the primacy of moral duties in Buddhist ethics as a whole. Though these duties obviously have a place in the program of attaining enlightenment in most Buddhist traditions, there is much more to this program than acting in accord with or out of respect for these duties. The threefold deontic vocabulary of the morally forbidden, obligatory and permitted is not the dominant moral vocabulary of Buddhist ethical thought. There are at least two reasons for this. First, the liberation program as a whole is oriented toward the elimination of suffering and the achievement of enlightenment. This might be taken to support a consequentialist interpretation in which the duties are justified solely in terms of promoting these ends. Second, attaining enlightenment is centrally a matter of developing moral virtues such as compassion, loving-kindness, generosity, patience and the like. On the face of it, these virtues involve much more than adhering to moral duties in that they concern character traits having to do with dispositions, motivations, intentions, actions and so forth. This might be thought to lend credence to a virtue ethics interpretation in which virtues rather than duties are morally fundamental. Arguments in favor of either a consequentialist or a virtue ethics interpretation of Buddhist ethics are effectively objections against a deontological interpretation since they purport to show that something other than moral duties is fundamental. These two interpretations will be explored in the next two sections.

Other issues arise when we consider specific deontological theories such as those of Kant and Ross. There are some respects in which it may be argued that Buddhist ethics has some affinities with Kant's moral outlook. For example, Kant thought that what is most important—the only thing that is good without qualification—is having a good will, and this bears some resemblance to the idea expressed in the Buddhist doctrine of karma that the moral quality of our intention *(cetanā)* is primarily important (see Chapter 1). Moreover, Kant believed that the antithesis of a good will is a will motivated by self-love, and this contrast has a parallel in the Buddhist contention that an enlightened person would act on the basis of universal compassion and not at all on the basis of self-love. Finally, related to this, Kant often suggested that desires and inclinations were morally problematic, declaring in the *Groundwork* that we would rather not have them (see Kant 1998: 4:454–8), and this may have some similarity with the Buddhist critique of craving, attachment, greed, lust and so forth as well as the suggestion that a fully enlightened person would be free of all desire.

Nonetheless these similarities are in many ways overwhelmed by other differences. The most fundamental of these differences is the crucial role that reason plays in Kant's moral philosophy. Though Kant was concerned to articulate the limits of reason, he thought that the fact that human beings are rational beings is the source of both our moral worth and our moral understanding. The various formulations of the Categorical Imperative such as those stated earlier are diverse ways of expressing this fundamental conviction. The universal law formulation is derived from the idea that the practical principles of a rational being must have the form of universal law, and the humanity as an end formulation is based on the notion that human beings should be respected as ends in virtue of their capacity to act on the basis of reason. Moreover, additional formulations of the Categorical Imperative relate these ideas to the fact that human beings are autonomous and have a free will. This complex ensemble of ideas is the unifying foundation of our moral duties for Kant.

There is little, however, in any Buddhist tradition that looks much at all like this outlook. The Buddha did not deny that human beings are rational, and there are different interpretations about whether he presupposed that we have a free will in some sense (for debates about Buddhism and free will, see Chapter 10). But to whatever extent these attributes may be acknowledged, they are not featured as the source of our moral understanding, our moral worth or our moral duty in the way envisioned by Kant. It is difficult to see anything in Buddhist moral thought that resembles or plays the role of any of the formulations of the Categorical Imperative. The universal law formulation is sometimes compared with the Golden Rule (though Kant denied that they were the same), and at one point the Buddha seemed to endorse this Rule. He asked: "How can I inflict upon another what is displeasing and disagreeable to me?" (*SN* V 354; cf. *Vism.* 297). However, even if there is a thought here in the neighborhood of Kant's Categorical Imperative, this rhetorical question was offered as a bit of moral advice and not as a statement of the foundation of the Buddha's moral outlook. It has been suggested that the Bodhisattva vow to help others overcome suffering is a vow to enable others to become Bodhisattvas and that this implies a model of collective agency, with each Bodhisattva contributing equally to the liberation of all, that is similar to Kant's kingdom of ends formulation of the Categorical Imperative (see Davis 2013a: 287–93). In this kingdom, Kant says, each free and rational being is the source of universal moral laws (see Kant 1998: 4:433–4). It may be objected, however, that even if the Bodhisattva vow implied some concept of collective agency, the notion that morality has its source in the laws of free and rational beings is very different from the idea of Bodhisattvas working together to enable all to overcome suffering.

The problem here is not simply that Kant's understanding of human beings is very different from that suggested by the Buddhist no-self teaching. The main problem is that even when Buddhists speak of a self at the level of conventional truth, and of morality in connection with this self, they do not portray the morality of this self in ways that resemble Kant's understanding. The various accounts of the Buddhist path to enlightenment, which commonly employ the language of conventional truth, do not valorize the triumph of pure practical reason in ways that would be expected in any account with serious affinities with Kant (for sharply contrasting comparisons of Buddhist ethics and Kant, see Goodman 2009: ch. 11 and Olson 1993).

The situation is rather different with respect to Ross. Once again, there are some points of possible similarity. Ross thought that it was self-evident to a person with "sufficient mental maturity" who pays "sufficient attention" that we have the *prima facie* duties he identified. And he believed that these duties expressed a "moral order" that is a part of "the fundamental nature of the universe" (Ross 1988: 29). With regard to the first point, if we substitute the phrase "sufficient level of enlightenment" for "sufficient mental maturity," perhaps it could be said from some Buddhist perspectives that it is self-evident to such a person what his or her moral duties are. As for the second point, it might be thought to have affinity with the notion, referred to earlier, that the Buddhist moral precepts are rooted in Dharma, a term that may connote the nature of the universe (for more on this issue, see Chapter 8). Moreover, it might be claimed that at least some Buddhist perspectives would allow that there is no general rule for resolving conflicts of duties, as Ross supposed, and perhaps they might also allow that, at least to the extent that persons are not enlightened, they would need to make these determinations on the basis of Ross's probable opinion.

The main difference between Ross and Buddhist ethical thought is Ross's insistence on moral pluralism. He thought that there were seven irreducibly different kinds of *prima facie* moral duties (though he wavered about the number). It is difficult to reconcile this with a Buddhist moral outlook. First, if we were to think of such an outlook as a form of moral pluralism, with irreducibly different moral elements, then it would have to include more than moral duties. As noted earlier, moral virtues are just as important as duties in Buddhist ethics, and these virtues involve more than duties. Second, more importantly, Buddhist moral outlooks have more unity than Ross's moral pluralism allows. Once again, as noted earlier, the fundamental goal of eliminating suffering and attaining enlightenment suggests an integrated framework that is foreign to Ross's pluralism (there is more discussion of these issues in the next chapter).

## The Consequentialist Interpretation

There is a long tradition in modern scholarship of interpreting Buddhist ethics as implicitly committed to a form of, or at least something close to, consequentialism, usually more specifically utilitarianism (for recent examples, see Goodman 2008 and 2009 and Siderits 2003, 2007a and 2007b). This is not surprising insofar as the dominant motif in the Buddhist soteriological project is the elimination of suffering and the promotion of enlightenment. It is fundamentally oriented to bringing about these ends. However, there are objections to these interpretations in part because of the importance of duties and virtues in Buddhist thought and in part because of questions about whether Buddhism understandings of well-being are easily accommodated to standard consequentialist theories. Before discussing these issues, it will be helpful to explain more fully the nature of consequentialism. The term refers to a large family of theories with numerous variations and complications, but for our purpose it will be sufficient to indicate some elementary forms (for a discussion of consequentialism, see Brink 2006).

The term 'consequentialism' was first employed by Elizabeth Anscombe in the mid-20th century (see Anscombe 1958). It is now widely used to refer to a range of theories that have developed out of discussions of the classical utilitarian theories of the 19th century. According to the simple definition given at the beginning of the chapter, consequentialism is the view that an action is morally right if and only if, and because, it has appropriately valuable consequences. This captures a necessary feature of a consequentialist theory of right action, but there is ordinarily much more to consequentialist ethical theories than this (and in some cases they are theories of something other than right actions). For the purpose of our discussion, the best way to begin is with a brief statement of the classical utilitarian theories suggested by Jeremy Bentham, John Stuart Mill, and Henry Sidgwick.

Classical utilitarianism is a consequentialist theory with four additional specifications. First, the consequences relevant to evaluating the moral rightness of an action are the consequences that bear on the well-being of all human beings and perhaps all sentient beings (a *universality* doctrine). Second, the well-being of each human being counts equally (an *impartiality* doctrine). Third, what makes an action morally right is that, in comparison with available alternatives, it maximizes the well-being of all human beings counted equally (a *maximization* doctrine). Finally, well-being is happiness where this is understood solely in terms of the pleasure and pain of each human being (a *hedonism* doctrine, one of the mental-state theories considered in the last chapter). By putting these features together, we can define classical utilitarianism as the view that an action is morally right if and only if, and because, among available alternative actions it has the best overall consequences in terms happiness (the balance of pleasure and pain) for all human beings impartially considered. Mill tried to capture this idea when he said that the morally right action is the action that produces "the greatest amount of happiness altogether" (Mill 1957: 15–16).

The intuitive plausibility of utilitarianism is based on its claim that morality is simply a matter of making the world a better place. What could be more obvious and compelling than that? However, there are many objections to utilitarianism and the attempts to respond to these objections have resulted in the wide range of consequentialist theories on offer today. An initial objection is practical: a direct application of classical utilitarianism would require each person on each occasion of action to determine the value of the consequences of each available action for all human beings and to determine which alternative action has the best consequences overall. As a practical matter this would seem to be virtually impossible to do.

There are several responses to this objection. For our purpose, the most important response is to draw a distinction between utilitarianism as a theory of moral rightness (telling us what makes an action morally right) and utilitarianism as moral decision procedure (telling us how to decide which action is morally right). According to this response, classical utilitarianism as defined earlier is the correct theory of moral rightness. However, we should not suppose that directly applying this theory is the correct moral decision procedure. Rather, the proper way to decide which action is morally right is to follow the set of moral rules that are justified on utilitarian grounds, namely, those rules the adherence to which would produce the best consequences as understood by classical utilitarianism (there are somewhat different ways of specifying the utilitarian basis of the rules). It is often said that the rules are based on the accumulated wisdom of human beings throughout history in determining which kinds of actions have the best consequences, and that these are by and large the rules of common-sense morality. Since we need only to follow the rules in deciding what to do, the impracticality objection is answered.

This response employs a distinction between *act-utilitarianism* (classical utilitarianism as an account of what makes actions right) and *rule-utilitarianism* (utilitarian-justified-rules as an account of the correct decision procedure). Both Mill and Sidgwick defended a utilitarian position of this kind. Nowadays this is sometimes called a two-level theory, with one foundational level that establishes the criterion of right actions and another level based on this for deciding what to do (see Hare 1981). There are various ways in which this theory may be filled out. For instance, it is often said that when rules conflict people need to decide which rule to follow by determining as well as they can which course of action has the best consequences in that particular case. However, it is also sometimes said that utilitarianism so understood is self-effacing, meaning that overall the best consequences will come about if people do not generally understand that the rules are justified on a utilitarian basis (for example, if they think that actions prohibited by the rules are simply wrong in themselves).

A very different kind of objection is that classical utilitarianism conflicts with a variety of moral beliefs that many people find very compelling. As we will see, the distinction between act-utilitarianism and rule-utilitarianism may be employed to respond to this objection as well. Here, in brief, are three common forms this objection can take.

First, it seems that there are some occasions when violating standard deontological prohibitions on such things as lying or breaking promises would have the best consequences. However, it is supposed, at least for the most part we should not lie or break promises even if doing so would have the best consequences. These prohibitions are "deontological constraints" on the production of good consequences, and the objection is that classical utilitarianism cannot account for this *(deontological constraints objection)*. The two-level response is that *overall* the best consequences will come about if everyone just follows the rules. Hence, ordinarily this is what everyone should do, even when they can see in a particular case that breaking a rule would have better consequences. The fact that most people think it is always wrong to break the rule is a good sign on this view because overall better consequences will result from people thinking this than from people thinking that sometimes it is alright to break the rule for consequentialist reasons.

Second, the impartiality doctrine of classical utilitarianism says that the well-being of each human being counts equally. But in most contexts we think that it is morally much more important that we promote the well-being of friends and relations than that we do so for strangers. For example, most parents are much more concerned about the well-being of their own children than they are about the well-being of other people's children. According to this objection, this is as it should be, and the impartiality doctrine of classical utilitarianism conflicts with this *(partiality objection)*. Once again, the two-level response is that overall the best consequences for everyone, impartially considered, will come about if each parent is much more concerned with the well-being of his or her own children. This is because parents are in a much better position to take care of their own children and would do less good overall if they tried to be equally concerned with the well-being of all children. Hence a rule justifying partiality toward one's one children has an impartial utilitarian justification.

Finally, the maximization doctrine of classical utilitarianism implies that on each occasion we should try to do that which will have the best consequences for all human beings. But, it is claimed, this is far too demanding a conception of morality. If I am thinking about going to a movie, it seems that I could bring about better consequences if I gave the ticket money to charity instead. However, according to this objection, even if I should sometimes give to charity, surely it is not the case that I should never go to a movie or do anything similar because it would virtually always be the case that I could bring about better consequences by doing something else *(demandingness objection)*. There are different responses to this, but one two-level response is that the rules of morality need to take into account that fact that people are strongly disposed to favor their own interests. A rule demanding extraordinary efforts to promote well-being in the world is unlikely to be effective, and attaching internal sanctions to increase compliance (such as educating people to feel guilty otherwise) might well be counter-productive. Hence, the rule that is most likely to have the best consequences overall is a much less demanding rule such as one that says we are often permitted to pursue our own personal interests, but sometimes we ought to give to charity.

We now have a sense of how the two-level approach yields responses to a variety of objections and thereby brings utilitarianism closer to common-sense understandings of morality. However, some utilitarians and consequentialists resist this strategy and argue that we should accept a conception of morality that sometimes requires breaking deontological constraints, that expects us to promote well-being impartially, and that is often quite demanding (for an example, see Singer 2000). Hence, utilitarianism has been taken in two very different directions. Sometimes it is presented as mostly compatible with commonsense morality, as a theory that explains and on occasion reforms this morality, but largely leaves it in tact. But sometimes utilitarianism is presented as a theory that radically challenges commonsense moral beliefs.

As we will now see, these are important considerations in consequentialist interpretations of Buddhism. Another significant consideration is an objection that is often thought to be implicit in some of those already considered: as John Rawls said, since all that matters for utilitarianism is the impartial maximization of well-being, it "does not take seriously the distinction between persons" (Rawls 1971: 27). Rawls and many others have thought that this is a serious problem for utilitarianism. But it is easy to see how, from the standpoint of the Buddhist no-self teaching, this could be considered a positive feature and not a defect.

Let us now look at the reasons supporting a utilitarian or at least a consequentialist interpretation of Buddhist ethics. One reason that is sometimes suggested is based on the doctrine of karma. As we have seen, according to this doctrine, morally right (wrong) actions bring about happiness (unhappiness) for the person who performs them. It is sometimes implied that this shows that Buddhists, in accepting this doctrine, are committed to some form of consequentialism according to which actions are evaluated by their karmic consequences (for example, see Dreyfus 2001: 39 and Tillemans 2011: 363 and 366). On this view, actions are right (wrong) because they bring about happiness (unhappiness) for the person who performs them. However, this is not the most common interpretation of the doctrine of karma. The more common view is that actions that are right by whatever standard makes actions right—say because they are "in accordance with the Dharma" (*MN* I 285)—in fact bring about happiness for those who perform them (for example, see Harvey 2000: 17 and Keown 1992: 178). This does not imply consequentialism, but it does not rule it out as being the standard of rightness. On this interpretation, it might be said to someone that he or she should be moral because of karmic consequences. But this would be offering a self-interested reason for being moral, not a reason in terms of what makes the action right.

The main reasons supporting a utilitarian or consequentialist interpretation may be seen by considering Buddhist ethics in terms of the different features of classical utilitarianism. The first feature is that the moral rightness of actions depends on consequences and only on consequences. Certainly if we consider the exemplars of Buddhist moral virtue, the *Arahants* and especially the Bodhisattvas, there can be no question that their basic ethical aim is the elimination of suffering and the promotion of enlightenment. This is evident in the divine abodes of compassion, seeking to abolish suffering in all beings, and loving-kindness, trying to bring about the happiness of all beings. The entire moral framework of the fully virtuous is structured by a commitment to achieving these ends. Hence, consequences are surely crucially relevant to the moral rightness of actions. Whether they are the *only* relevant consideration will be discussed momentarily, but this orientation also makes clear that the relevant consequences have to do with well-being. As we have seen, the suffering that is to be eliminated detracts from well-being and the enlightenment that is to be attained is the highest form of well-being.

Moreover, it is evident that the well-being of all human beings, and often of all sentient beings, is the primary concern. Compassion and loving-kindness embody a universality doctrine. In addition, another of the divine abodes, equanimity, makes it clear that the fully virtuous person embraces an impartiality doctrine as well. According to Buddhaghosa, the function of equanimity is "to see equality in beings" so as to promote "neutrality" toward them (*Vism.* 318). Universality and impartiality are fundamental features of the Buddhist ethical outlook. This is especially apparent in the Bodhisattva, who seeks enlightenment for the sake of all beings, but it is equally present in non-Mahāyāna forms of Buddhism as well. Of course, the classical utilitarian claim that well-being is happiness understood in terms of pleasure and pain (hedonism) may seem less obvious as a feature of Buddhism. In the last chapter, however, it was suggested that Buddhist well-being might be understood in terms of a mental-state theory, and that on most any plausible interpretation Buddhist well-being includes a mental state since suffering is a form of dissatisfaction and enlightenment includes contentment. Hence, positive and negative mental states play a crucial role in the Buddhist account of well-being. Finally, since the ultimate aim, particularly for Bodhisattvas, is to eliminate *all* suffering and to bring about the enlightenment of *all* beings, there appears to be an implicit commitment to some maximization notion in this ethical orientation.

In short, there are considerable affinities between classical utilitarianism and Buddhist ethical thought. According to Goodman, one of the most prominent defenders of a consequentialist interpretation, all the features of classical utilitarianism may be found in this passage from the *Compendium* of the Mahāyāna writer Śāntideva:

> Through actions of body, speech, and mind, the Bodhisattva sincerely makes a continuous effort to stop all present and future suffering and depression, and to produce present and future happiness and gladness, for all beings. But if he does not seek the collection of the conditions for all this, and does not strive for what will prevent the obstacles to this, or he does not cause small suffering and depression to arise as a way of preventing great suffering and depression, or does not abandon a small benefit in order to achieve a greater benefit, if he neglects to do these things even for a moment, he is at fault.
>
> (as translated in Goodman 2009: 89–90)

On the basis of this and other passages, Goodman argues that Śāntideva is best interpreted as an act-consequentialist whose position is quite close to classical utilitarianism.

One consideration in favor of this interpretation is based on the Buddhist no-self teaching. If selves are not truly distinct from one another, then it might be argued that I have as much reason to end the suffering of all others as I do to end my own suffering. According to Śāntideva: "Without exception, no sufferings belong to anyone. They must be warded off simply because they are suffering" (*BCA* 8.102). From this standpoint, the absence of a distinction between persons is taken, not as an objection to utilitarianism, but as a reason in support of it (there is more on this in Chapter 8). Buddhist metaphysics, it has been maintained, naturally lends itself to a utilitarian outlook. Moreover, once we realize that we are not distinct selves, objections to utilitarianism that depend on this distinction (such as the deontological constraints and partiality objections) will no longer appear as raising fundamental problems. In addition, the objection that utilitarianism is too demanding because it requires us to maximize overall well-being will also be embraced as a positive feature of the position.

Considerations along this line can support an interpretation of at least some forms of Buddhism as a version of utilitarianism or consequentialism that radically challenges commonsense moral beliefs. One of the main challenges for this interpretation, however, is the importance in Buddhism of rules that appear to be statements of moral duties. As we have seen in the discussion of the deontological interpretation, at least sometimes violations of these duties are taken to be wrong irrespective of consequences. There is, however, a response to this objection: these duties are implicitly justified on a consequentialist basis. For example, Goodman thinks that the best interpretation of Theravāda ethics is that it is committed to a form of rule-consequentialism (see Goodman 2009: ch. 3). Though Buddhist ethics so understood can still be rather demanding, the importance of obeying strict rules is preserved on the ground that following these rules will have the best consequences overall.

In Mahāyāna Buddhism the view emerges that a Bodhisattva might violate the rules at least partly on consequentialist grounds. Recall that Asaṅga thought that sometimes Bodhisattvas could kill, steal or lie as long as they had good intentions and their actions had good results (see Chapter 2). A similar view can be found in Śāntideva. He said: "One should always be striving for others' well-being. Even what is proscribed is permitted for a compassionate person who sees it will be of benefit" (*BCA* 5.84). This Mahāyāna perspective might be interpreted as an indication that, over time, there was an increased awareness of the consequentialist basis of Buddhist ethics. It might also be suggested that as a person progresses along the path to enlightenment, from initiates to progressers to enlightened persons (in the terminology introduced earlier), there is increasing awareness of this consequentialist basis such that those who are less advanced follow the rules while those who are more advanced realize that sometimes the rules should be broken for consequentialist reasons. In any case, a rule consequentialist or utilitarian position can provide a *prima facie* plausible basis for explaining the importance of what appear to be deontological constraints in much of Buddhist ethics.

Another objection is that moral virtues are at the center of Buddhist ethical thought and the consequentialist or utilitarian interpretation cannot account for this. However, a similar response is available to this objection: virtues are indeed important, but they are justified on consequentialist grounds. In some cases, the consequentialist orientation of the virtues seems obvious: compassion is directed toward ending suffering and loving-kindness aims to promote happiness. Something similar might be said about other virtues such as generosity, the first of the Six Perfections. In other cases, though, it is less obvious that the sole justification is in consequentialist terms. A common theme in Buddhist thought is that an enlightened person would never be angry. For example, Buddhaghosa says that, "if you are angry now, you will be one who does not carry out the Blessed One's teaching" (*Vism.* 299). Moreover, the Mahāyāna perfection of patience is substantially about the elimination of anger. But from a consequentialist standpoint it would seem that a more moderate position on anger would be put forward: anger is unjustified when it has bad consequences and justified when it has good ones. What often appears to be a deep and fundamental opposition to anger would not make sense (there is more on this in Chapter 9).

Classical utilitarians accepted a hedonist theory of well-being according to which well-being is happiness understood solely in terms of pleasure and pain. As we have seen, there is an important aspect of Buddhist understandings of well-being that involves a mental state: the dissatisfaction of suffering and the contentment of enlightenment. To this extent, there may be an affinity with hedonism. However, as we have also seen, there may be more to Buddhist well-being than mental states. For example, it might be argued that it consists of contentment, wisdom and virtue—and possibly some ordinary goods as well. Goodman claimed that well-being consists of happiness and virtue (what he considers an objective-list theory). He called this position "character consequentialism" (see Goodman 2009: 70; cf. Clayton 2009). In this view, good character is one of the positive consequences to be promoted. Since a consequentialist theory could be formulated in terms of accounts of well-being that include a complex set of goods, a consequentialist interpretation of Buddhism might defended in these terms (though it would not be a classical utilitarian interpretation in this respect).

There is, however, a possible difficulty with such a consequentialist interpretation if it includes a maximization doctrine. Maximization requires that the value of the consequences of our actions can be added up and compared so that a meaningful overall judgment about which action has the best consequences can be made. One of the reasons the classical utilitarians were attracted to hedonism is that pleasure and pain seemed to lend themselves to such a utilitarian calculus (though Mill's doctrine of more and less valuable pleasures put some pressure on this). But if well-being consists of a complex set of goods, it may be more difficult to make sense of maximization. For example, Keown has argued that Buddhism is committed to three "basic goods"—what he calls life, knowledge and friendship—that are irreducible and incommensurable. Since the goods have these features and consequentialism requires commensurable goods, he claimed, consequentialism is an inadequate interpretation of Buddhist ethics (see Keown 2001: 55–6; for other expressions of this concern, see Cooper and James 2005: 86 and Vélez de Cea 2010: 232). Similar issues may arise for the aforementioned interpretations of Buddhist well-being: if well-being includes virtue, happiness and/or the ordinary goods, then these values would need to be commensurable if the rightness of moral actions ultimately depends on maximizing them. In response, it might be said that at least sometimes there are signs of a willingness to engage in the kind of calculations that maximizing requires, as in the passage from Śāntideva discussed earlier in which he speaks of foregoing a small benefit in order to gain a greater benefit (see Clayton 2009: 24–5).

## The Virtue Ethics Interpretation

In recent years, interpretations of Buddhist ethics as implicitly committed to some form of virtue ethics have received considerable support (for example, see Cooper and James 2005, Fink 2013, James 2004, Keown 1992, 1996 and 2007, Sahni 2008, Vélez de Cea 2013, Whitehill 1994 and Wright 2009). It is easy to see the reason for this. Moral virtues such as compassion, loving-kindness, generosity and the like appear to be at the heart of both the path to Buddhist enlightenment and, in perfected form, the state of enlightenment itself. Many of these interpretations stress affinities specifically with Aristotle's eudaimonistic conception of virtue ethics. Once again, it is easy to see the reason for this. For Aristotle, a good life is oriented to the attainment of *eudaimonia,* a life of well-being centrally constituted by a set of virtues. Likewise for Buddhism it is plausible to suppose that a good life is oriented to the attainment of enlightenment, arguably also a life of well-being centrally constituted by a set of virtues. Nonetheless, there are numerous objections to this line of interpretation. Aside from the importance assigned to duties and consequences in Buddhist ethics, as just seen, Aristotle's understanding of human nature, which is central to his eudaimonism, appears to be at odds with the Buddhist account of human beings. Moreover, the moral virtues featured by Aristotle are different and often contrary to the moral virtues featured in Buddhism. As a result, Aristotle's ideally virtuous person is quite different from any conception of an ideally virtuous person in Buddhist thought. Before examining the debate about this interpretation, it will be useful to describe more fully the virtue ethics approach (for an overview, see Annas 2006).

In the mid-20th century, it was generally supposed in Anglo-American moral philosophy that the main theories of normative ethics were forms of the deontological and consequentialist approaches we have just discussed. This began to change in the late 1950s when Anscombe, Philippa Foot and others argued for the importance of virtue ethics as an alternative (see Anscombe 1958 and Foot 1978: ch. 8). Their proposal received renewed attention with the publication of Alasdair MacIntyre's very influential *After Virtue: A Study in Moral Theory* in 1981 (see MacIntyre 1984) so that by the end of the 20th century it was widely agreed that virtue ethics is a viable alternative to deontological and consequentialist theories.

But an alternative in what sense? At the outset of this chapter, virtue ethics was defined as a theory of right action according to which an action is morally right if and only if, and because, it is what a virtuous agent would characteristically do. So defined virtue ethics is a theory of right action that directly contrasts with the theories of right action of deontology and consequentialism. Virtue ethics can certainly be understood in these terms, and its proponents sometimes represent it as implying a theory of right action (for example, see Hursthouse 1999: ch. 1; cf. Statman 1997). However, virtue ethics is often understood as an alternative in a rather different sense, not as another theory of right action, but as an approach to normative ethics in which the main concern is not to explain morally right actions but to explain more broadly what it means to be—and to become—a morally good or virtuous person (Hursthouse herself thinks that virtue ethics is primarily about moral character even though it provides a theory of right action). We will return to this latter understanding in the next chapter. For the time being, we will focus primarily on the narrower understanding in which virtue ethics is taken to be a theory of right action in direct contrast to deontological and consequentialist theories.

On any understanding, virtue ethics emphasizes the importance of moral virtue, where this is taken to be a rich, multifaceted concept encompassing attributes of human beings such as dispositions, thoughts, attitudes, motives, intentions, emotions, desires and actions. Advocates of virtue ethics often maintain that moral theory should consider a person as a whole, not simply what a person does. Moreover, they sometimes claim that moral theory should focus on the entire life of a person, on what it would mean for a person to live a morally good life as a whole. For these purposes, moral virtues—considered as enduring character traits involving all or most of the aforementioned attributes—need to be at the center of attention. Part of the argument in favor of the virtue ethics approach is the contention that an adequate moral theory should have this broad scope. From this perspective, morally right actions could only be explained in terms of what a morally virtuous person would do.

Proponents of virtue ethics usually suppose that there are several moral virtues such as courage, justice, charity, honesty and trustworthiness, to name only a few. They ordinarily contrast these with a set of moral vices, character traits that are in some way opposed to the virtues, such as states of being cowardly, unfair, stingy, dishonest and unfaithful. There is not, however, complete agreement about which character traits are the virtues and vices, about how to characterize each of them and about which are most important. This is partly because theories of virtue ethics draw on a variety of contemporary and historical perspectives. Though some of these theories are influenced by philosophers such as David Hume and Friedrich Nietzsche, among others, most of them are inspired primarily by Aristotle. Moreover, most of the scholars who advocate an interpretation of Buddhist

Ethics in terms of virtue ethics think mainly in terms of Aristotle's, or an Aristotelian, virtue ethics (and sometimes, relatedly, of the eudaimonistic virtue ethics of Hellenistic philosophers in the Stoic or Epicurean traditions). In order to evaluate this interpretation, we need to know something about Aristotle's specific form of virtue ethics.

A distinctive feature of Aristotle's approach in the *Nicomachean Ethics* is that it was framed in terms of a teleological conception according to which there is a highest or primary good of human life. Aristotle thought that all of us throughout our lives implicitly aim for this good, that which formally speaking is the final end of all our actions and which, when attained, would leave us in need of nothing else. He believed that everyone agrees that the good in this sense is *eudaimonia,* which may be translated as happiness, flourishing or—as will be done here—well-being. Aristotle thought that people disagreed about what is needed for well-being, and he argued that, contrary to what many people think, genuine well-being consists primarily of a life of virtue (along with some measure of "external goods" such as friends, wealth and power). In short, Aristotle's virtue ethics is eudaimonistic in that a virtuous life is presented as the best way to attain well-being.

Aristotle is well known for defining moral virtue or excellence of character *(ēthikē aretē)* as a disposition to decide and act with respect to affective states such as fear or pleasure, in an intermediate state or "mean" between excess and deficiency, as determined by the reason of a person possessing the intellectual virtue of practical wisdom (for this definition see Aristotle 2002: bk. II, ch. 6). An implication of this definition is that for each virtue there are two vices, one corresponding to the excess and one to the defect. Since the intermediate state involves many factors, Aristotle said that the virtuous person has affective states and acts at the proper time, in the proper way, to the proper extent, about the proper things, for the proper people, for the proper reason, toward the proper end and so forth. According to Aristotle, since human beings are distinctive in having a rational nature, our function as human beings is to reason well, and virtuous persons reason well precisely by correctly determining throughout their lives what is proper in these various respects. Practical wisdom *(phronēsis)* enables them to do this. Aristotle is also well known for claiming that human beings have a capacity for moral virtue, but this capacity must be developed by practice or what he called "habituation." For example, we become a just person by repeatedly doing just acts. In this and other ways, the *Nicomachean Ethics* implies a program for the cultivation of the virtues.

Aristotle emphasized the importance of three moral virtues in particular: bravery, moderation and justice. Bravery concerns the affective states of fear and boldness in the face of death, but only in the finest circumstance, namely war. The brave person is not fearless, but stands firm in battle without being rash. Moderation (or temperance) pertains to the bodily pleasures of touch and taste, namely those of food, drink and sex. As the term implies, Aristotle thought that the moderate person would neither abstain from nor indulge in these pleasures. Finally, though Aristotle's overall account of justice is rather complex, justice in one sense has to do with fairness in such activities as the distribution of goods and the rectification of injuries. In contexts involving these activities, the just person allocates what is appropriate, neither too much nor too little, to the relevant parties.

Though he gave them less attention, Aristotle also thought that there were several moral virtues besides these three. Some are unsurprising, at least up to a point. For example, generosity concerns giving (but also acquiring) wealth. The generous person is said to give the right amount, to the right people, at the right time and so forth, being neither avaricious nor wasteful. Even-temperedness (or mildness) has to do with anger. The even-tempered person is thought to be angry with the right people, on the right occasion, to the right extent and so forth, being neither irascible nor slavish (in the sense of overlooking insults). Other virtues may seem more surprising. Munificence is a virtue for the wealthy. According to Aristotle, the munificent person spends a great deal for important civic projects such as building a temple or giving a feast when it is appropriate to do so. Magnanimity is also a virtue for a special class of persons in a different sense, namely those who are worthy of receiving great things, especially honor for their virtue. The magnanimous (great-souled) person realizes that he is indeed worthy of this and expects it.

This is a sufficient account of Aristotle's ethics for our purpose. Let us now look at some reasons that have been offered for interpreting Buddhist ethics as a form of virtue ethics, in particular as an ethics with some kinship to Aristotle's virtue ethics. As noted earlier, one of the most obvious reasons is the centrality of moral virtues in Buddhist ethical thought. There is no denying the importance of character traits such as compassion, loving-kindness, equanimity, generosity, patience and the like in virtually all Buddhist traditions. And there is no denying that these are moral virtues in some sense: they are clearly portrayed in a morally positive way, as wholesome states that are crucial elements on the path to enlightenment and, in perfected form, of enlightenment itself (and they are contrasted with various corresponding vices or unwholesome states). Moreover, Buddhist ethical thought was very much concerned, as was Aristotle, with the development of moral character, with the cultivation of moral virtues in our lives (see Harvey 1995). In addition, and most importantly for proponents of this interpretation, Aristotle's eudaimonism has a structural similarity with Buddhist soteriology: in Buddhism we are encouraged to strive for a highest or primary good, namely enlightenment or nirvana, just as in Aristotle we are encouraged to strive for a highest or primary good, namely *eudaimonia*. According the Keown, one of the best-known proponents of the Aristotelian virtue ethics interpretation of Buddhism, "*eudaimonia* and nirvana are functionally and conceptually related in that both constitute that final goal, end and *summum bonum* of human endeavor" (Keown 1992: 195). In particular, as Keown noted, for both Buddhism and Aristotle the highest good—well-being—includes moral virtues as well as wisdom. For Keown (1992), Buddhist ethics is a theory of morally right actions in which "rightness is predicated of acts and intentions to the extent that they participate in nirvanic goodness" (177).

In addition, though it would be difficult to find a detailed definition of moral virtue in Buddhist texts that could be compared with Aristotle's definition, it does seem that the different attributes of human beings involved in moral virtues in Aristotle's and other accounts have a key place in Buddhist moral psychology. That is, there is a concern with a variety of mental states such as dispositions, attitudes, intentions, motives and emotions. For example, Śāntideva said about the perfection of generosity that "the perfection is the mental attitude itself." Similar things are said about the perfections of morality and patience (see *BCA* 5.10–12). Again, as we have seen, in the doctrine of karma, our mental state is crucial for the moral quality of our actions. The Buddha said: "It is volition *(cetanā)*, bhikkhus, that I call karma. For having willed, one acts by body, speech, or mind" (*AN* III 415). Keown, translating *cetanā* as choice, proposed that it plays a role very similar to the role of *prohairesis,* which is often translated as decision, in Aristotle's account of moral deliberation. In both cases, cognitive and affective states are involved in bringing a person to the threshold of action (see Keown 1992: 210–22). Whatever may be said about the details of this comparison (*cetanā* and *prohairesis* are each complex terms), it is clear that both Aristotle and Buddhist ethical thought regarded elements of our mental life involving such things as motive, choice and intention as morally significant for the determination of moral virtue.

Another similarity may be seen in the Buddha's contention that the Eightfold Path is a "middle way" between a life in pursuit of sensual happiness and a life devoted to self-mortification. This appears to bear considerable resemblance to Aristotle's virtue of moderation, which also charts a middle course between the extremes of hedonism and asceticism. Moreover, the notion of the Buddha's teaching as a middle way develops into something of a motif in Buddhist thought with numerous applications beyond this specific point. This orientation might be compared to Aristotle's proposal that the moral virtues all involve the notion of finding the proper intermediate state. In addition, the claim in some Mahāyāna texts that "skillful means" might on some occasions justify a compassionate person in violating one of the moral precepts could be seen as having an affinity with Aristotle's insistence that determining the intermediate state is a difficult intellectual process that requires focusing on the particulars of the situation and cannot be reduced to following a set of rules (see Aristotle 2002: 1109a20–1109b27).

There are, then, several reasons for supposing that Buddhist ethical thought is similar to virtue ethics and especially the virtue ethics of Aristotle. However, there are also a number of important objections to this interpretation. Some of these objections relate to the previous interpretations. Hence, it may be said that a virtue ethics interpretation cannot account for the fundamental importance of moral duties in Buddhism. In response, it might be said that Aristotle himself thought some kinds of actions such as theft or murder were wrong in themselves and would never be performed by a virtuous agent (see Aristotle 2002: 1107a8–13). According to the definitions given at the beginning of this chapter, the key question is whether such actions are wrong because a virtuous agent would not perform them (the virtue ethics explanation) *or* a virtuous agent would not perform them because they violate our moral duties, where these duties are established independently of virtue (the deontological explanation). Though it is not obvious that Buddhists texts would definitively support either of these options, it is clear that there is much more emphasis on following a set of moral precepts in Buddhism than there is in Aristotle. It might also be objected that a consequentialist justification can be given for the Buddhist moral virtues: they are virtues precisely because they produce good consequences. In response, as we saw earlier in this chapter, though this explanation is plausible for some Buddhist virtues, it is less evident that it can account for all the Buddhist virtues. Some virtues such as the Mahāyāna perfection of patience seem to require the elimination of anger, and it may be wondered whether this categorical stance could be justified on consequentialist grounds.

There are two more fundamental objections to an interpretation of Buddhist ethics as similar to Aristotle's ethics. We saw the basis of one of these objections at the end of the last chapter. According to Aristotle, human beings have a nature and the most important feature of our nature is rationality. Moreover, our well-being consists in fulfilling our nature. Hence, we fulfill our nature and attain well-being when we reason well, and for Aristotle reasoning well is the heart of moral virtue. The objection is that this eudaimonistic account is incompatible with the Buddhist no-self teaching: if there is no self, then there is nothing that has a nature. Hence, Aristotle's contention that a life of virtue fulfills our nature as rational beings is fundamentally at odds with the key feature of Buddhist metaphysics (see Goodman 2009: 70–1 and Siderits 2007b: 292).

As we saw in the last chapter, there are Buddhist responses to this objection. One response is that we are permitted to speak of selves at the level of conventional truth. Hence, at this level there is no obstacle to a Buddhist thinking of a virtuous life as fulfilling our nature in a way that parallels Aristotle. A second response is that this model of a virtuous life fulfilling our nature is already suggested in the Mahāyāna claim that we all possess Buddha-nature—or Tathāgata-garbha (embryo of the Buddha)—and that enlightenment is simply the process of revealing this nature, of revealing that by nature we really are Buddhas (despite the apparent unwholesome defilements that conceal this). Revealing that we are already Buddhas is not quite the same as Aristotle's actualizing our potential as rational beings, but there is some affinity in that the life of virtue is closely related to what we really are by nature. However, there is still a difference here. Though the attribution of Buddha-nature or Tathāgata-garbha was a prominent Mahāyāna tradition (sometimes connected with Yogācāra Buddhism and very popular in East Asian forms of Buddhism), it may seem to attribute an inherent nature to us that conflicts with the no-self and emptiness doctrines. Hence, it could not be presented as ultimately true, but only as conventionally true—or perhaps as one more pragmatic employment of skillful means for promoting enlightenment (see S.B. King 1997: 181). These qualifications are significant departures from Aristotle that an Aristotelian virtue ethics interpretation would need to acknowledge.

There is, however, another aspect to the human nature objection. For Aristotle, our function as human beings is to reason well. This is why practical wisdom is a crucial element in every moral virtue. Though Aristotle differs from Kant in a number of ways, he shares with Kant the conviction that reason is the most important feature of human nature and so is central to our moral lives. As we have seen, the Buddha did not deny that we are rational beings, but rationality does not have the central place in Buddhist ethical thought that it does in Aristotle. In Buddhism, enlightened persons have wisdom, a metaphysical understanding of the way things really are in terms of ideas such as no-self and emptiness, but they appear to have no analogue of Aristotle's specific virtue of practical wisdom, the intellectual virtue necessary for living well. Moreover, the meditative disciplines that are so important in Buddhist conceptions of living well (see Chapter 9) have no counterpart in Aristotle's ethical thought.

The second more fundamental objection is that Aristotle's eudaimonism is a kind of egoism that directly conflicts with the universal compassion that is at the heart of Buddhist ethics. The reason Aristotle is thought to be committed to some form of egoism, it is claimed, is that Aristotle's virtuous agent is virtuous only because this is the best way to attain his own well-being. Hence, at bottom, the Aristotelian virtuous agent is self-interested. And this, of course, is incompatible with Buddhist ethical teaching, which often requires great self-sacrifice of virtuous agents (see Goodman 2009: 54–5). The objection that Aristotle's eudaimonism is a form of egoism is a common one. However, there are responses to this objection. First, many of Aristotle's virtues such as bravery and generosity require that the virtuous agent be concerned about the well-being of others. In fact, bravery might require sacrifice of the agent's life and it is hard to see how this can be understood as a self-interested action in any normal sense of the term 'self-interested.' Second, more generally, though for Aristotle well-being is best attained by living a virtuous life, a virtuous life requires being directly concerned about the well-being of others. Hence, the motive of the virtuous agent is basically altruistic, and someone who was "virtuous" for self-interested reasons—only because he thought this would promote his own well-being—would not in fact be virtuous on this view. At any rate, Aristotle is often interpreted in this way.

There is, however, another difficulty in the neighborhood of the egoism objection that is more compelling: Aristotle's ideally virtuous person is very different from any ideally virtuous agent presented in Buddhist ethical thought (a point that is commonly acknowledged by proponents of Aristotelian interpretations; for example, see Cooper and James 2005: 83–4). There are many indications of this. For example, the ideal of overcoming attachment that is so important in Buddhist thought has no counterpart in Aristotle. But the difference is most evident in the respective virtues featured in each account. First, though Aristotle's moderation and generosity may seem similar to Buddhist virtues, they are in fact quite different. The Buddha taught a middle way, but the mode of life he prescribed for monks and nuns was far more ascetic than that of Aristotle's moderate person (even granting that, by many people's standards, moderation for Aristotle is rather austere). The Buddha's middle way was in the middle only because the extraordinary self-depravation of the Buddha's earlier life—and of the Jains—was at one of the extremes. Likewise, as we saw in Chapter 2, generosity was often portrayed in remarkable ways quite out of step with anything Aristotle envisioned. For example, we are presented with the model of the Buddha in an earlier life expressing generosity by giving away his wife and children. This story may not be intended for literal imitation, but the ideal of extraordinary self-sacrifice for the benefit of other beings is central to Buddhist ethical thought. The difference from Aristotle can be seen in a passage from Śāntideva. According to Śāntideva, "one should consume in moderation and share with those in need." Aristotle would no doubt have agreed with this. But Śāntideva concludes the passage by declaring that one should "give away everything" (*BCA* 5.85), and Aristotle clearly would not have agreed with this.

Second, many other Aristotelian virtues such as bravery (mainly a virtue of soldiers), justice (often a virtue of government officials), even-temperedness (a virtue prescribing anger when appropriate), munificence (a virtue of the very wealthy) and magnanimity (a virtue for those who expect to be honored) are clearly contrary to moral profile of the *Arahants* and Bodhisattvas usually featured in Buddhism. These figures are animated by compassion, loving-kindness, patience, equanimity and the like—virtues that are centered on a universal, impartial concern for the well-being of all sentient beings, and that have no correlates in Aristotle. To a very large extent, *Arahants* and advanced Bodhisattvas, and the monks and nuns who are committed to attaining their enlightened standing, are very different from the persons who are most suited to exemplify many of Aristotle's virtues—primarily upper-class men who are soldiers and political leaders. This contrast might be mitigated to some extent by consideration of Buddhist attitudes toward war and politics (see Chapter 13) or by attempts to broaden the scope of Aristotle's virtues (for example, see Nussbaum 1993). But the basic contrast in moral ideals is striking nonetheless. Buddhist ethical thought promotes as an ideal a radical transformation of our lives that is not envisioned in Aristotle's or most other forms of virtue ethics in Western philosophy.

There is one final objection to a virtue ethics interpretation, Aristotelian or otherwise, that deserves attention. As we saw in Chapter 5, portrayals of the highest stage of enlightenment (our fifth and final category), though infrequent, are quite elusive. For instance, we are told that in this enlightened state nothing is felt, there is an absence of consciousness and there are no objects before the mind. In that discussion, the question was posed whether this can be considered as a human form of well-being. Here a similar question may be raised, whether being in this state can be considered a form of moral agency and hence a kind of character. If it cannot, if the final goal of the Buddhist path cannot be understood as a state of moral virtue, then it might seem to be problematic to interpret Buddhist ethics in terms of virtue ethics (for discussion of these issues, see Finnigan 2010 and P. Williams 2009b). In response, it could be said that for most persons on the Buddhist path the most immediate goals are to make significant progress or to attain enlightenment in this life (our third and fourth categories), and these goals are represented in recognizable ways as states of moral virtue. Hence, if we prescind from the final state, a virtue ethics interpretation could be viable. However, though this may well be correct, the fact remains that the ultimate state of Buddhist enlightenment is something radically different from anything ordinarily envisioned in Western discussions of virtue ethics.

CHAPTER **7**

# Normative Ethics
## Anti-Theoretical and Other Interpretations

In the Chapter 6, we examined interpretations of Buddhist ethics in terms of three major normative theories of morally right actions that in contemporary philosophy are often thought to be major theoretical alternatives. In simple form, each of these theories explains morally right actions in different ways: as what is in accord with our moral duties (deontology), as what has appropriate consequences (consequentialism) and as what a virtuous agent would characteristically do (virtue ethics). We considered what may be said for and against interpreting Buddhist ethical thought on the basis of each of these theories, both in their simple forms and in the more complex positions defended by some of the primary proponents of these theories. There is little doubt that moral duties, consequences and virtues all have some role to play in Buddhist ethics. The central question in the last chapter was whether any one of these has a foundational status that gives it primacy over the other two and, more generally, whether the richer theories associated with these three approaches provide useful models for interpreting Buddhist ethics. From this discussion, a complicated situation emerged: though there are arguments in support of each interpretive approach, there are also significant objections.

An assumption shared by defenders of each of these three interpretations is that Buddhist ethical thought is implicitly committed to and exemplifies some unified and systematic normative structure. For example, Keown

147

emphasizes the importance of "elucidating the foundations and conceptual structure of Buddhist ethics" (Keown 1992: 196) and Goodman stresses the need to understand the "theoretical unity" of Buddhist ethics (Goodman 2009: 59). But perhaps these convictions represent a bias of Western philosophy, or maybe a prejudice of modernist currents within Western philosophy, that are foreign to anything that can be found, implicitly or explicitly, in traditional expressions of Buddhist thought. In any case, some scholars of Buddhist ethics have challenged the assumption generating the interpretations in the last chapter. On their view, none of these interpretations is correct because, in the various traditional discussions of Buddhist ethics, we find no evidence of acceptance of the idea that there is a unified and systematic normative structure of ethical thought, either because authors in these discussions simply lacked this commitment or, more strongly, because they were opposed to thinking about ethics in these terms.

In this chapter, we will examine this alternative approach to understanding Buddhist ethical thought. Of course, as we will see, this approach is sometimes influenced by some prominent "anti-theory" perspectives in contemporary Western moral philosophy. These perspectives are not opposed to anything that might be considered an ethical theory, but to certain conceptions of moral theory that have been dominant in modern philosophy such as the theories of moral rightness we discussed in the last chapter (for critical discussion, see Louden 1992). The main question is whether these anti-theoretical orientations shed more light on Buddhist ethics than the theoretical approaches we have just considered. There are in fact several variations of this alternative approach. We will focus on four of these. The first emphasizes the plurality of ethical considerations in Buddhist thought (pluralism). The second stresses the importance in Buddhism of looking at the particular features of each ethical situation (particularism). The third points to affinities between Buddhism and an understanding of virtue ethics, not as a theory of right action, but as an approach to normative ethics that emphasizes what it means to be and become a morally good or virtuous person (virtue ethics). And the fourth focuses on the practical dimension of Buddhism as oriented to solving the problem of suffering (Buddhist ethics from its own point of view). These four approaches are not necessarily mutually exclusive, but they draw attention to different features of Buddhist ethical thought.

## Pluralist Interpretations

It is widely (thought not universally) acknowledged that duties, consequences and virtues all play some role in Buddhist ethics. Each of the three interpretations in the last chapter claimed that one of these values was foundational or primary in relationship to the other two. If these interpretations each have difficulty sustaining this claim, perhaps this is because writers in the Buddhist traditions did not think that these values were unified in this way. Perhaps they thought that all these values were important and were related to one another in a variety of ways, but did not think that they were systematically ordered in terms of one foundational or primary value—or at least they did not think that it was important to determine whether there is such an order. This is one prominent way in which a pluralist interpretation of Buddhist ethics could be formulated. Peter Harvey exemplified this pluralist attitude by saying that "overall, the rich field of Buddhist ethics would be narrowed by wholly collapsing it into any single one of the Kantian, Aristotelian or Utilitarian models (Harvey 2000: 51; cf. Harvey 2010 and Vélez de Cea 2004 and 2010). In order to assess this and other pluralist interpretations, it will be helpful to begin with a brief account of how moral pluralism is understood in recent philosophy (for an overview, see Mason 2011).

Moral pluralism is now a standard category of contemporary normative ethics, but it is understood in different ways. Its basic definition is that there is a plurality of moral values that cannot be reduced to a single value (as the contrary position, moral monism, supposes). However, this insistence on plurality can be applied in a variety of contexts. In one prominent form, moral pluralism is a theory of the moral rightness of actions. Ross's claim that there is a plurality of *prima facie* duties is commonly taken to be the pre-eminent example of this. Though Ross's account can be understood as a form of moral monism in that it explains moral rightness solely in terms of moral duties (as was done in the last chapter), it includes a pluralist account of the *prima facie* moral duties (namely, fidelity, reparation, gratitude, justice, beneficence, self-improvement and non-maleficence). Ross did not think these duties could be justified on the basis of a single principle such as Kant's Categorical Imperative or classical utilitarianism with its hedonistic theory of value. However, moral pluralism (or what is sometimes called ethical or value pluralism) is often understood in broader ways than this. For example, Thomas Nagel proposed that there are five fundamentally different kinds or sources of ethical value: obligations to persons or institutions; rights possessed by everyone; ways in which actions may benefit or harm people; the value of scientific, artistic or other achievements; and commitments to our own personal projects. Nagel allowed that these five kinds of value might be reduced to two basic kinds—what he called personal or agent-centered values versus impersonal or outcome-centered values—but he did not think that any further reduction was possible because he thought that goodness is not unitary (see Nagel 1979).

Contemporary forms of moral pluralism are usually presented as reactions against the perceived moral monism of Kant, classical utilitarianism and other moral theories. They are critical responses to reductionism in ethics. For instance, Bernard Williams, referring to "the desire to reduce all *ethical* considerations to one pattern," argued "in ethics the reductive enterprise has no justification and should disappear" (B. Williams 1985: 16–17). However, as just noted, moral pluralism can take different forms, and the anti-reductionist impulse need not be expressed across the board. Ross thought that moral rightness was always a matter of following duties (monism), but he thought that there is a plurality of different kinds of duties. Likewise, a consequentialist could claim that moral rightness is always explained by the value of consequences (monism), but maintain a pluralist theory of this value (as in objective-list theories). And a proponent of virtue ethics could believe that moral rightness always depends on what a virtuous agent would do, but hold that there is a plurality of moral virtues (as in most virtue theories there are). In any case, at whatever level pluralism is applied, the main arguments in its favor typically appeal to our moral intuitions: if we reflect on what we find to be morally important in some context, we will realize that the various factors cannot be reduced to a single element.

Now, to return to the interpretation of Buddhism, it cannot plausibly be argued that the authors of classical texts pertaining to Buddhist ethics explicitly defended some form of moral pluralism any more than it can be argued that they explicitly defended one of the three theories of moral rightness discussed in the last chapter. Moral pluralism is a sophisticated philosophical position that is committed to a rejection of some form of moral monism: its defense would require arguments in favor of pluralism over monism in the relevant context. It is hard to see that the classical proponents of Buddhist ethics articulated such arguments. However, it might plausibly be maintained that some or all of these proponents were *implicitly* committed to some form of moral pluralism. The primary argument in favor of this interpretation is twofold: there are a variety of ways in which a plurality of moral values is affirmed in Buddhist texts, and there is little concern or effort to show that these values are unified in the way that moral monism would require. Hence, the most illuminating way to read these texts is to suppose that they implicitly presuppose some kind of moral pluralism.

We have already seen two ways in which Buddhist ethical texts appear to affirm a plurality of moral values. First, each of the three basic moral concepts featured in the last chapter is important: duties (as shown in the moral precepts), consequences (as shown in the commitment to eliminate suffering and promote enlightenment) and virtues (as shown in the various positive character traits). Hence, it could be maintained that insofar as Buddhist ethics is committed to an account of the moral rightness of actions, the account is that moral rightness may depend on whether the action is in accord with the precepts, the consequences of the action and/or the intention or other aspects of the moral character of the agent performing it. Second, within each of these three categories there is a plurality of moral values: it is obvious that there are several different precepts and virtues, and it might be argued that the elimination of suffering and the attainment of enlightenment includes several different elements such as wisdom, virtue and contentment (as was seen in Chapter 5). Hence, moral rightness further depends on whether an action is in accord with each moral precept, is an expression of a variety of virtues and/or contributes to different aspects of well-being.

A variety of pluralist interpretations are possible along these lines. In some cases, some values may be emphasized more than others: for example, it is common in recent discussions to stress that both virtues and consequences are important. Again, a pluralist interpretation could maintain that there are systematic ways in which the diverse values relate to one another. This might be called a "hybrid theory" that combines two or more values in some fashion (for both of these, see Clayton 2006: chs. 5 and 6, and 2009). But a pluralist interpretation might reject this and hold that, though in a particular context one or another of these different values may be identified as especially important for some reason, there is no overall theory about how in general these values contribute to moral rightness. This would be structurally similar to both Ross's and Nagel's pluralism and would conform to what is often meant by pluralism in contemporary philosophy. We will discuss this option more later.

Manifestations of moral pluralism in Buddhism may be seen in the tendency, especially prominent in the Pali Canon, to provide lists of factors pertaining to some ethical phenomenon supplemented by no further analysis. For example, as we saw at the beginning of Chapter 2, in his advice to the Kālāmas the Buddha said:

> But when you know for yourselves: "These things are wholesome; these things are blameless; these things are praised by the wise; these things, if accepted and undertaken, lead to welfare and happiness," then you should live in accordance with them.
>
> (*AN* I 190)

Here the Buddha says that there are four factors that we should take into account in deciding how to live. No subsequent analysis in this particular text points to a unifying feature of the factors, makes it clear whether they are intended to be necessary and sufficient conditions, or explains what we should do in cases where they appear to conflict (for instance, if a wholesome action leads to suffering). We are simply given a list of considerations to take into account, a frequent practice in the teaching of the Buddha.

Issues of pluralism and monism also arise in connection with the Buddhist understandings of well-being discussed in Chapter 5. As we saw, there are several candidates for being a feature relevant to well-being in Buddhist thought. These include the ordinary goods referred to in discussions of karma, characteristics of enlightened life such as wisdom and virtue and the dissatisfaction of unenlightened life along with the contentment of enlightened life. There are different analyses of the overall Buddhist position on well-being. Both desire-satisfaction theories and mental-state theories may be regarded as monist theories of well-being. Though it is not plausible to interpret Buddhism in terms of a desire-satisfaction theory, a case might be made for claiming that Buddhist well-being can be understood entirely by reference to mental states. The nature-fulfillment theory could also be considered a monist theory of well-being in that it maintains that fulfillment of our nature is the one factor relevant to well-being, and we saw that there are interpretations of Buddhist understandings of well-being as being committed to such a theory. By contrast, the objective-list theory might be regarded as a pluralist account of well-being, and an interpretation of Buddhist well-being along this line could be considered as a pluralist approach. An objection to this approach, however, is that there is often more unity to the Buddhist understanding of well-being than pluralism would allow: for example, it may be said, the main attributes of enlightened life (wisdom, virtue and contentment) are commonly presenting as states that imply one another.

There is a more general issue here: in Buddhist texts, we are sometimes presented with what appear to be mere lists of factors, as in the Kālāmas passage earlier, but sometimes we are given lists that clearly have a greater measure of unification. For instance, a dominant theme in Buddhist ethical writing is that there are three roots of unwholesome *(akusala)* actions: greed, hatred and delusion. These are sometimes said to be the primary obstacles to enlightenment, but they are unified in that greed and hatred correspond to the two basic forms desire can take (desire to attain something and desire to repel something) and delusion relates to the misunderstanding (the mistaken belief that there is a self) that underlies these two forms of desire. Hence, the three roots of unwholesome actions form a unified set. In general, as much as there is an emphasis on lists of values in Buddhism there are also a various ways in which these values are sometimes related to one another. Moreover, all these values are unified insofar as they are part of the overall soteriological project of overcoming suffering and attaining enlightenment (for example, in the Eightfold Path and the Six Perfections). This unification may not imply moral monism, but moral pluralism, as often understood in contemporary philosophy, assumes that the plurality of different values is not unified in this way.

One way in which a plurality of values might be unified is for them to be ordered in some fashion. Even if a set of values cannot be reduced to a single value, it might be maintained that some values in the set are higher than other values. According to Abraham Vélez de Cea, in the *Nikāyas* of the Pali Canon there is sometimes a "lexical order of values" such that some are higher than others. For example, "the value of spiritual pleasures is superior to the value of sensual pleasure" (Vélez de Cea 2010: 232). In line with this, it might be said that the well-being of enlightened persons is of a higher order than the well-being of unenlightened persons, where this is understood to mean that distinct kinds of goods are involved in the two forms of well-being, and one form is higher than the other. It is conceivable that similar things could be said about some moral values. For instance, it might be claimed that respecting the life of a person is of a higher order than respecting the property of a person. However, there does not seem to have been much concern in Buddhism to provide an overall ranking of the precepts, or other moral values, in this way (though in the monastic codes some violations of rules are clearly considered to be more serious than others).

In recent defenses of moral pluralism in Western philosophy, the tendency has been to resist such rankings and to argue, controversially, that different kinds of values are incommensurable with one another and, sometimes, that there are moral dilemmas on account of this (for instance, see Nagel 1979). However, the term 'incommensurable' can mean at least two different things, and this gives rise to two kinds of moral dilemmas. In one sense of 'incommensurable,' if two actions A and B are conflicting (meaning that it is not possible to do both, though it is possible to do each) and each action ought to be done for incommensurable reasons, then the moral value of A and B is *incomparable,* where this means that there is no basis for choosing one over the other. This is the sense of 'incommensurability' that directly conflicts with ranking. In another sense of the term, if two conflicting actions A and B each ought to be done for incommensurable reasons, then the moral value of each is *inconvertible,* where this means that doing one does not make up for the failure to do the other, and so the person will do something morally wrong no matter what (for example, if it turns out I cannot keep both of two promises, then it might be said that I will inevitably do wrong by breaking one of them). These two senses of incommensurability and moral dilemmas—irresolvable moral decisions and inescapable moral wrongdoing—raise distinct issues (for further explanation, see Gowans 1994: 147–8). Even if there were no basis for choosing A or B, it might be claimed that as long as a person does one or the other there is no moral wrongdoing (the only obligation is the disjunctive obligation to do A or B). Conversely, even if there were a basis for choosing one over the other, it might be argued that moral wrongdoing could still be inevitable (A might be morally the best thing to do, all things considered, but still be wrong because it involves a violation of an obligation).

Now, is there any reason to think that ethical texts in Buddhism addressed the issue of moral dilemmas in either of these two senses? It cannot be said that the Buddha was particularly concerned with moral conflicts (see Gombrich 2009: 170). However, it was acknowledged in the tradition that there are moral decisions in which it is difficult to determine which course of action is morally the best all things considered, though it is not clear that it was ever supposed that there are dilemmas in the sense of there being no basis for a decision (on account of incomparability or for some other reason). Although, as we have seen, a plurality of morally relevant values was often affirmed in various ways, the issue of irresolvability on account of this was never thematized as a philosophical problem. The situation is somewhat different, however, with respect to the second sense of moral dilemmas. There are some texts in Mahāyāna Buddhism pertaining to the violations of the precepts and the employment of skillful means in which the issue of inescapable moral wrongdoing appears to be at least implicitly broached.

As we saw in Chapter 2, in the *Chapter on Ethics* Asaṅga thought that there were cases in which a Bodhisattva might be justified in violating a precept in order to prevent great harm. For example, he might kill a robber in order to prevent the robber from killing many Bodhisattvas and "other magnificent beings" (and thereby also preventing the robber from suffering great negative karmic consequences). Is this a case in which wrongdoing is inescapable because either a precept is violated or great harm is not prevented? Asaṅga said that such killing by the Bodhisattva is "reprehensible by nature" and he represented him as thinking, "If I take the life of this sentient being [the robber], I myself may be reborn as one of the creatures of hell" (Tatz 1986: 70). This would seem to imply that it is wrong for the Bodhisattva to kill the robber and so this action could result in negative consequences for the Bodhisattva on account of the doctrine of karma. However, Asaṅga might be interpreted as denying this because he also said that in this case the bodhisattva "acts with such skill in means that no fault ensues." Perhaps the conjunction of "reprehensible by nature" and "no fault" could be interpreted as meaning morally wrong, but not blameworthy, in which case it might be thought that moral wrongdoing is inevitable (though it might be wondered whether there would be negative karmic consequences if the action is not blameworthy). But it is not obvious that there is an affirmation of inescapable wrongdoing here.

In a related scenario in the *Upāyakauśalya Sūtra* (see Tatz 1994: 73–7), the Buddha in a past life as a Bodhisattva in the role of a sea captain named Great Compassionate faced a similar though somewhat more complex situation in which he could kill a robber both in order to prevent him from killing many Bodhisattvas and to prevent the intended victims from killing the robber if they were told of his plan (in both cases also in order to prevent the would-be killers from going to hell on account of their actions). The Buddha then kills the robber even though he envisions that he, the Buddha, will be reborn in hell for a very long time as a consequence of this action. Once again, the willingness to undergo the negative karmic consequences of killing even to prevent killing might suggest that moral wrongdoing is inevitable here. However, we are also told that this action was done "with great compassion and skill in means" (Tatz 1994: 74). Moreover, the story says that the Buddha did not actually suffer the negative karmic consequences he was willing to undergo (for some different interpretations, see Gethin 2004: 188–9, Harvey 2000: 135–6, Jenkins 2011: 315–18 and Tatz 1994: 107, n. 148).

In any case, Mahāyāna texts such as these are primarily intended to show that the great compassion of a Bodhisattva could conceivably justify violating the precept forbidding killing in those cases in which this would prevent others from killing and other bad consequences (see Chapter 13). The reference to the Bodhisattva's willingness to suffer negative karmic consequences for this action may be intended to demonstrate the willingness of the Bodhisattva to make a great sacrifice in order to help others rather than to show that sometimes moral wrongdoing is inevitable.

## Particularist Approaches

Scholars of Buddhist ethics who have rejected theoretical interpretations such as those we considered in the last chapter have sometimes argued that Buddhism is implicitly committed to a form of moral or ethical particularism (for instance, see Barnhart 2012, Bartholomeusz 2002: 25–7 and Hallisey 1996). In contemporary philosophy, the central thought animating moral particularism is that there are no general principles explaining the moral rightness of actions or that we should not employ general principles in trying to determine which action is morally right in specific cases of deliberation (for a discussion of the contemporary debate about moral particularism, see Lance and Little 2006). Discussions of moral particularism raise a broad set of issues about the role that general principles should play in the explanation of the moral rightness of actions as well as in moral deliberation. Particularism as it is understood in these discussions is a sophisticated philosophical position that is contrasted with generalism, the view that there are general principles explaining the moral rightness of actions or that we should rely on such principles in moral deliberation. Once again, it is not plausible to suppose that traditional proponents of Buddhist ethics explicitly defended a moral particularist theory. However, perhaps it could be argued that they, or at least some of them, were implicitly committed to some particularist theory. An obvious objection to this interpretation is the importance of the moral precepts in Buddhist ethical thought. These look to be general moral principles, and a particularist interpretation would need to take these precepts into account (for critical discussions of particularist interpretations, see Keown 2013b, Schilbrack 1997 and Vélez de Cea 2005; Hallisey responds to Schilbrack in 1997).

Prior to the recent discussions of moral particularism, Roderick Chisholm employed the term 'particularism' to refer to a position in a debate in epistemology. Charles Hallisey, in the 1996 paper cited earlier that inaugurated the particularist interpretation of Buddhist ethics, began with a consideration of Chisholm's understanding of particularism. Chisholm was concerned with a fundamental epistemological issue he called the "the problem of the criterion" (see Chisholm 1982). The problem is based on a skeptical argument that we cannot have knowledge of the way things really are because in order to distinguish true appearances from false appearances we would need some procedure, and in order to know if our procedure is a good one we would need to know if it succeeds in correctly distinguishing true frxom false appearances, which would require that we already know which appearances are true and which are false. The problem is how to escape this circle and establish that we have knowledge. According to Chisholm, there are two contrasting non-skeptical responses to this problem. Particularists hold that we begin with particular cases of knowledge and then formulate general principles (criteria) that explain why those are cases of knowledge, while methodists maintain that we begin with general principles of knowledge and judge particular cases on the basis of these principles. Chisholm argued that both these approaches have limitations, but he defended a form of particularism.

Hallisey argued that some texts in Theravāda Buddhism affirmed particularism over methodism because they focused on instances, in the form of stories, of auspicious things such as the five precepts rather than offering a general criterion of auspiciousness. It is certainly true that there are many occasions in Buddhist texts in which particular instances of some moral phenomena are put forward without any explicit reference to an overall criterion. There is, however, a difficulty with this argument. Particularism as Chisholm understood it is not the view that general principles (criteria) are non-existent or unimportant. Rather, it is the view that general principles must be established on the basis of an assumed prior knowledge of particular instances. Hence, to show a Buddhist acceptance of Chisholm's particularism would require showing an attempt to establish a general principle on the basis of particular instances.

That Hallisey did not attempt to show this suggests that his real concern was not particularism in Chisholm's sense but particularism in the sense stated at the beginning of this section, the position that there are no general moral principles or that we should not employ them in deliberation. Hallisey's main interest was in showing that in at least some cases Buddhist texts were concerned with focusing on particular cases rather than employing or establishing criteria such as those provided by moral theories. The importance of a particularist interpretation of Buddhist ethics is the suggestion that some Buddhist authors may be similar to some recent proponents of moral particularism in downplaying the importance of general moral principles.

In recent discussions, moral particularism has been closely associated with the work of Jonathan Dancy and others (for example, see Dancy 2004). Moral particularism, as Dancy understands, is a strong and controversial thesis based on holism, the view that, for any property relevant to action, in one situation the property can be a reason for an action, but in another situation the same property may not be a reason for the action and may in fact be a reason against the action (for example, that something causes pleasure may count in favor of doing it in one case and count against doing it in another case). For this reason, there are no general moral principles. Hallisey suggested that there are cases in the Theravāda tradition that exhibit an adherence to holism. For example, the Buddha sometimes encouraged monks to support their parents and sometimes encouraged them to keep their distance (Hallisey 1996: 42; cf. Barnhart 2012: 32–3).

There are generalist responses to Dancy's holism that are relevant to this interpretation. First, it may be argued that we can account for the fact that pleasure can be a reason for an action in one case and against the action in another case by formulating more complex but still general principles (for example, that pleasure is a reason for action in circumstance C1 but is a reason against an action in circumstance C2). Second, it may be claimed that there are some properties that always count in favor of an action or always count against an action (contrary to Dancy), but also claimed that these reasons are sometimes overridden by other considerations. Hence, it may be said that the fact that an action causes pleasure always counts in favor of it, but that sometimes we should not do what causes pleasure because another consideration overrides this (thereby accounting for at least part of what made Dancy's particularism seem plausible). This second position is similar to that of Ross, discussed in the last chapter, who held that fulfilling a *prima facie* duty always counts in favor of an action even though in a particular circumstance this may be overridden by another *prima facie* duty favoring an incompatible action.

In this debate, as just summarized, there are (at least) three possible positions: Dancy's holism-based particularism, a generalist's defense of complex principles, and a generalist's defense of *prima facie* principles. Is there reason to think that traditional proponents of Buddhist ethics took a stand in this debate, even implicitly, by allying themselves with one of these positions in contrast to the others? The most plausible initial response to this question is that at some place or another support might be found for a Buddhist acceptance of each of the three positions. In addition to passages supporting a particularist reading such as those invoked by Hallisey, there are aspects of the Buddhist monastic codes that contain rather complex moral rules and there are many places in which adhering to the moral precepts appears to always counts in favor of an action even though (it is sometimes allowed) this may be overridden. From these considerations it might be concluded that different Buddhists took different positions in this debate (or perhaps that in different contexts different positions were taken). But it might also be concluded that, though there are various apparent manifestations of these different positions, there is insufficient evidence to suppose that any of these manifestations was even an implicit affirmation of one position in contrast to others.

Another aspect of Dancy's particularism is a model of moral deliberation in which, rather than subsuming particular cases under general principles, we carefully examine all the properties of each situation, discern what is morally salient in these properties in this situation, and determine what is the morally correct action based on the overall configuration of what is morally salient here and now. Since this model presupposes that there are no general principles, Buddhist ethics could be interpreted in terms of it only on the assumption that Buddhist ethics supposes there are no general principles. That is one possible interpretation of Buddhist moral deliberation, but as we have seen there are others. It is worth noting, however, that there are aspects of the particularist model of deliberation that could be employed by some generalists with the qualification that discerning what is morally salient is a matter of determining which general principles are morally relevant. An example of this would be the position of Ross: we determine which *prima facie* duties are relevant to a given situation and we then form a "considered opinion" about what our actual duty is all things considered. Often in Buddhist ethical teaching it is suggested that we simply follow the moral precepts, and the tacit assumption seems to be that this is a rather straightforward matter of subsuming particulars under a general principle. But sometimes, as in the cases of killing the robber at the end of the last section, we have a scenario that might be interpreted as similar to Ross's position in that there are something like conflicting *prima facie* duties (for example, not to kill and to save lives) and a judgment needs to be made about what all things considered ought to be done in this particular situation. Though, as we have seen, this scenario might be interpreted in terms of consequentialism or some other theory (see Keown 2013b), an alternative "non-theoretical" interpretation would be to regard it as exemplifying something in the neighborhood of Ross's pluralism of values and intuitive model of adjudicating conflicts. Though Buddhist ethics is more unified than Ross's outlook, it might be claimed that it is nonetheless similar in these respects.

## Virtue Ethics Approaches

In the last chapter, we saw that virtue ethics could be understood as a theory of moral rightness that directly contrasts with deontological and consequentialist theories of morally right actions. But we also saw that virtue ethics could be regarded in another way, not primarily—and perhaps not at all—as a theory of moral rightness, but as a very different approach to normative ethics in which the central emphasis is what it means to be and become a morally good person. From this perspective, the main focus is not on the rightness or wrongness of particular actions, but on the whole of what a person is throughout his or her lifetime. It is for this reason that the multifaceted concept of moral virtue is regarded as important: by including discussion of such things as dispositions, thoughts, intentions, motives and emotions, as well as actions, as situated within a person's entire life, accounts of moral virtue encompasses a much broader range of morally relevant considerations than many theories of right action typically do. Moreover, virtue ethics is sometimes understood as implying a critique of the preoccupation of some theories of right action with establishing a decision procedure for determining right action. Proponents of virtue ethics often deny that there is any such decision procedure and maintain that determining what to do is a matter of the good judgment or perception of the virtuous person with practical wisdom.

Virtue ethics understood in this way may be considered as yet another anti-theoretical voice in normative ethics (see Pincoffs 1986 and for critical discussion Louden 1992), and Buddhist ethics may be interpreted as a form of virtue ethics so understood. Of course, this interpretation will share some of the advantages and disadvantages, discussed in the last chapter, of interpreting Buddhist ethics in terms of a virtue theory of right action. The extent to which this is true will depend in part on the extent to which Aristotle is invoked as a central paradigm of virtue ethics (as was done in many of those interpretations). Though Aristotle may be interpreted as providing a theory of the moral rightness of actions, he is often considered a source of anti-theoretical conceptions of virtue ethics. However, virtue ethics as depicted in the last paragraph need not be closely associated with Aristotle. In particular, virtue ethics on this understanding, and an interpretation of Buddhist ethics in terms of it, need not accept Aristotle's eudaimonism or his specific conception of the ideally virtuous person. Moreover, an anti-theoretical understanding of virtue ethics might share some features of the positions discussed earlier in this chapter. For example, it might suppose that virtue involves a plurality of moral considerations and that in moral deliberation there needs to be a sensitivity to the relevant features of particular situations and an intuitive judgment about what is morally best all things considered.

Anti-theoretical virtue ethics interpretations of Buddhist ethical thought may thus be taken in a number of different directions. For example, they might be developed in a more Aristotelian fashion by following themes developed by MacIntyre such as the relationship between virtue and community (see MacMillan 2002 and Whitehill 1994). Or, by contrast, they might be pursued in a way that is not closely related to Aristotle, but still pursues issues central to any virtue ethics outlook such as the development of moral character. In view of the importance of the Eightfold Path and the Six Perfections in Buddhism, it is natural to stress character development. For instance, Buddhism could be seen as providing the basis for a "philosophy of spiritual self-cultivation," as Wright did in an analysis and contemporary articulation of the Six Perfections in Mahāyāna Buddhism (see Wright 2009: 16). Wright described the end of these Perfections as what the Greek philosophers called "the conception of the good life." But he did not draw on the specific theoretical commitments of Aristotle or others figures in that tradition in spelling out his position. According to Wright, the Six Perfections are not a set of principles or rules that state our moral duties or may be used to solve moral problems. Rather, the Perfections provide "an ethical training program" analogous to a physical fitness training program (see Wright 2009: 8–9). The goal of this program is to develop the qualities of an excellent or enlightened character, embodying practical wisdom, and based on the various concrete images of the Bodhisattvas in Buddhist stories and texts.

This approach certainly captures something central and important in Buddhist teaching: its practical orientation and its emphasis on moral development as part of a program of seeking enlightenment. It is a further question, however, to what extent this practical orientation may include or preclude consideration of, or commitment to, theoretical philosophical positions in ethics. Most of the Greek philosophers thought that philosophy had a practical aim. Aristotle said that he was examining moral virtue "for the sake of becoming good" (Aristotle 2002: 1103b28–9). And Epicurus famously wrote:

> Empty are the words of that philosopher who offers therapy for no human suffering *(pathos)*. For just as there is no use in medical expertise if it does not give therapy for bodily diseases, so too there is no use in philosophy if it does not expel the suffering of the soul.
>
> (Long and Sedley 1987: 155)

This might well be compared to the portrayals of the Buddha as a physician and depictions of the Four Noble Truths as offering a medical diagnosis (see Chapter 1). In both cases, it may be argued, Greek philosophy and Buddhist Dharma had as their practical aim the attainment of well-being—which for Epicurus and other Hellenistic philosophers, as well as for Buddhism, meant eliminating suffering (other similarities between Buddhist thought and the Hellenistic philosophers will be discussed at greater length in Chapter 9). However, most of the Greek philosophers clearly believed that a rather robust conception of philosophical theory, including ethical theory (though perhaps not a theory of moral rightness), was necessary to attain this practical end (see J. M. Cooper 2012). As we saw in Chapter 3, there is little reason to think that Buddhists writers shared this conviction. Our question, in this and the previous chapter, concerns the extent to which these writers had any implicit philosophical commitments pertaining to ethics and, if they did, the extent to which these commitments can be understood or illuminated by reference to normative ethical theories in Western philosophy. The fact that they had a practical orientation emphasizing the development of moral character does not necessarily preclude such commitment. As we will see, this issue also arises for the next and final interpretation we will consider in this chapter.

## Buddhist Ethics from Its Own Point of View

We have now considered three ways in which those who reject interpretations of Buddhist ethics as a theory of moral rightness could draw on some anti-theoretical currents in contemporary philosophy to develop an alternative reading emphasizing pluralism, particularism or a form of virtue ethics. There is another way in which an alternative to interpretations based on theories of moral rightness might be developed: it could be argued that we should interpret Buddhist ethics from the point of view of Buddhism itself. This is the interpretive proposal of Jay Garfield (Unpublished; cf. Edelglass 2013). For Garfield, there is something that may be called Buddhist moral theory, but it is not any form of Western moral theory. He rejects deontological, consequentialist and virtue ethics interpretations as failing to recognize that in Buddhist ethical thought there are many features of moral life and no overall interest in establishing a unified basis for moral evaluation. Hence, though aspects of the forms of evaluation emphasized in the three Western theories may be found in Buddhism, they are not unified in any foundational model such as we considered in the last chapter.

What is Buddhist ethics from the Buddhist standpoint? Garfield takes his cue from the Four Noble Truths: Buddhist teaching is concerned, first and foremost, with the problem of suffering identified in the First Noble Truth, and it offers a solution to this problem in the remaining three Noble Truths. Buddhist ethical thought must be understood within the framework of solving the problem of suffering. On Garfield's view, the metaphysics of interdependence is central to the Buddhist analysis of suffering. Specifically, suffering arises because our actions are conditioned by attachment and aversion, and these are conditioned by the "confusion" that we are distinct, substantial selves (that is, the three roots of unwholesome actions). The realization of interdependence, and hence of no-self, allows us to overcome suffering. However, since we have a deep instinctive tendency to believe that we are selves, the Eightfold Path identifies "areas of concern" (not prescriptions, duties, rights or virtues) that are needed to bring about the complex cognitive, affective and behavioral changes required for this realization. This is consequentialist only in the "thin sense" of aiming to make things better by overcoming suffering.

In this view, Buddhist ethical thought is centrally about the development or cultivation of moral character, as it is for Wright. However, in an interpretation of Śāntideva, Garfield (2010) argues that the heart of Mahāyāna ethics is compassion, rather than the Six Perfections, and in particular the Bodhisattva's commitment to promote the well-being of all sentient creatures (based on the realization, grounded in an understanding of interdependence, that suffering as such is bad no matter whose suffering it is). He calls Śāntideva's approach a "moral phenomenology" that depicts the experience of moral development from the "terror and unreason" of unenlightened persons to the "confidence and clarity" of awakened life (Garfield 2010: 349). This is not an attempt to interpret Śāntideva in terms of the philosophical tradition inaugurated by Edmund Husserl, but to draw attention to Śāntideva's emphasis on moral experience (in line with the use of the term 'moral phenomenology' in analytic philosophy to refer to an approach focusing on various moral experiences). Buddhist moral theory, in this view, is nothing more than this experiential account of the cultivation of moral sensibility on the path of the Bodhisattva. However, though Garfield rejects attempts to assimilate this to standard normative theories in Western moral philosophy, he allows that a contemporary Buddhist might employ, as a form of skillful means, theories of rights, virtues or utility to advance the aims of the Bodhisattva (an example of this is discussed in Chapter 12). Hence, he envisions the possibility of a constructive interaction between these two traditions form this perspective.

In one respect, Garfield is obviously correct: there is no doubt that Buddhism is centrally about solving the problem of suffering, and any understanding of Buddhist ethics needs to take this into account. In another respect, however, it may not be obvious that Garfield is correct: proponents of Buddhist ethics as a theory of moral rightness may agree that Buddhism is fundamentally about solving the problem of suffering, but argue that it is still illuminating to interpret Buddhist ethical thought, for example, as implicitly committed to a form of consequentialism or virtue ethics. The two are not necessarily incompatible. Moreover, though there is no denying that Buddhism is crucially concerned with moral development, and with the experiential aspects of moral development, it may be argued that this does not mean that it does not tacitly presuppose a moral theory similar to one of those featured in Western moral philosophy.

This response takes us back to the issues discussed in the last chapter. A possible rejoinder, beyond reconsideration of those issues, is that Buddhist writers implicitly supposed that a moral theory such as we find featured in Western philosophy is neither needed for, nor even helpful in, living morally and especially attaining enlightenment. In Garfield's terms, it may be said, a moral theory of this kind plays no important role in, and perhaps could distract us from, solving the problem of suffering. Recall the poison arrow example explained in Chapter 1. The Buddha was asked some philosophical questions (about the relationship of soul and body, and about the existence of the Tathāgata after death, among others), and he refused to answer these questions. Just as a doctor attending a man wounded by a poison arrow need not answer his patient's question "who shot me?" in order to heal him, the Buddha said, he need not answer these philosophical questions in order to teach the way to attaining enlightenment and overcoming suffering. Declaring an answer to these questions would not be beneficial to achieving enlightenment, and so he did not do so. What would be beneficial to achieving enlightenment, the Buddha said, is understanding the Four Noble Truths. And that is why he taught these truths: they are what we need to overcome suffering (see *MN* I 426–32). The poison arrow example does not include questions about moral theory. But it could be argued that the best interpretation of the Buddha's teaching, and of subsequent traditions of Buddhist ethical thought, is that it was implicitly supposed that having a philosophical theory of morality would not be beneficial to attaining enlightenment—and this is why there are no explicit attempts to develop such a theory in classical forms of Buddhism. This interpretation could apply to the theories of moral rightness discussed in the last chapter and perhaps also to some of the "anti-theoretical" but nonetheless very philosophical accounts of morality considered in this chapter (such as Dancy's particularism). In more radical form, this line of thought might lead to the deeply anti-theoretical stance of Zen as well as to post-modernist perspectives that see some kinship with Zen (for example, see Park 2008).

In this reading, what is required to attain enlightenment are the Eightfold Path, the Six Perfections or any number of other practices taught by Buddhist traditions. It is true that wisdom stands at the heart of all these practices, and wisdom means understanding dependent arising, impermanence, no-self and (in Mahāyāna Buddhism) emptiness. Moreover, in at least many traditions, a philosophical understanding of these ideas is regarded as important (Śāntideva evidently thought this). But this understanding, in conjunction with the various moral and meditative disciplines featured in Buddhist practices, is all that is needed. The tacit assumption was that issues such as resolving moral conflicts would be taken care of on a case-by-case basis by those progressing on the road to enlightenment, not by recourse to moral theory, but as a natural result of overcoming the unwholesome roots of attachment, aversion and delusion. This is not to say that there was a conviction that moral theory is not possible, only that it is not needed and that trying to develop it would get in the way of seeking enlightenment. In this interpretation, the Buddhist attitude toward moral theory sharply contrasts with that of the Greek philosophers.

Of course, this is yet another interpretation of Buddhist ethical thought, to be considered alongside those interpretations we have already examined. But it suggests a quite different orientation to reading the texts expressing this thought. Proponents of interpretations that regard Buddhist thought as tacitly committed to some moral theory often identify particular passages as, in effect, the tips of an iceberg of a presumed moral theory believed to be just beneath the surface of the text, informing its content without being directly and fully expressed. From this alternative perspective, however, such passages are more likely to be read as exercises of skillful means, as helpful things to say in some particular context to promote enlightenment. There is no temptation to see them as manifestations of a moral theory.

It is another question whether it would be worthwhile in the contemporary world to *construct* a Buddhist moral theory modeled on ideas in Western philosophy. Even if the tradition would have considered such an enterprise to be unhelpful or counter-productive, it might be that it would be valuable in the circumstances of the world today. In fact, construction of such a theory might be considered a form of skillful means in current conditions. One reason for this is that Buddhism, through its encounter with Western culture, is now confronting a world in which moral theory is often considered important. Hence, it might be advantageous to the communication of Buddhist perspectives to express its message in languages familiar to that world. Another reason, more limited in scope, is that some people in the modern, Western world are highly reflective and inclined to think in more theoretical ways (even though others are not). Hence, in order to communicate with these particular persons, it would be helpful to develop a Buddhist moral theory in terms of Western philosophical ideas.

CHAPTER **8**

# Moral Objectivity

In contemporary Western philosophy, meta-ethics refers to an ensemble of concerns about the meaning of moral statements, whether—and in virtue of what—these statements have truth-value, and the possibility of justifying or knowing these statements. As a starting point, it is common to distinguish two approaches: cognitivist positions hold that moral statements affirm beliefs that may be true or false in some robust sense, and non-cognitivist positions maintain that moral statements do not affirm such beliefs, but express some non-cognitive mental states such as attitudes, feelings or desires. Cognitivists often claim that their position shows that morality may be objective in some way (when combined with the thesis that some moral beliefs are true and justified, cognitivism can yield the view that there is objective moral knowledge), while non-cognitivists often assert that their position shows why moral statements may be motivating or action-guiding. It is sometimes supposed that a successful meta-ethical theory would establish, in some sense, both the objectivity of morality and its capacity to direct us to action. For more than a century, issues such as these have dominated Anglo-American moral philosophy (for an overview of meta-ethics, see Sayre-McCord 2012).

As we have seen, traditional Buddhist ethical texts are replete with a variety of moral statements. Moreover, sometimes these statements appear to have been put forward as truths and arguably as truths that we can know. For example, in early Buddhism the Four Noble Truths include moral precepts against killing, stealing, lying and the like (in the last Noble Truth, commonly called the Eightfold Path), and it is often suggested that we can know these Truths. Elsewhere, especially in Mahāyāna texts, there are some indications that moral statements may be understood rather differently, for example as exercises in "skillful means" rather than as assertions of truths, and this implies that there was an emphasis on the acting-guiding function of these statements. There was, in any case, considerable interest in a variety of traditions in motivating people to act on these moral statements. For instance, this was the concern of right effort *(vāyāma)* in the Eightfold Path and the perfection of vigor or energy *(vīrya)* in the Six Perfections. Hence, it might seem that the materials of meta-ethics were available in traditional Buddhist thought. Beyond this, as Buddhist philosophy developed, considerable work was done in metaphysics, epistemology and the philosophy of language, the disciplines of philosophy that are so central to meta-ethics. In particular, much attention was devoted to the distinction between ultimate and conventional truth (and the different ways in which this distinction could be understood). In spite of these factors, however, there is little in traditional Buddhist ethical thought that could be considered an explicit meta-ethical theory that looks much at all like meta-ethical theories in contemporary Western philosophy.

In recent years, philosophers interested in interpreting and reconstructing Buddhist ethics have begun addressing meta-ethical themes. In a fashion similar to debates pertaining to normative ethics, arguments have been made either about the implicit meta-ethical commitments of some Buddhist school or thinker, or about the way in which a Buddhist position could be developed into a meta-ethical theory. Sometimes these meta-ethical analyses have been connected with the debates regarding normative ethics (for example, see Finnigan 2010), but often they have been largely independent of these. In comparison with other work in Buddhist moral philosophy, however, these meta-ethical discussions are at a relatively early stage. Perhaps for this reason, there is little direct reference to developed meta-ethical theories in Western philosophy.

A natural entrée into these discussions is a claim, common to many Buddhist traditions, that there is an important connection between wisdom and morality. Though wisdom and morality are sometimes understood in different ways, it is often said that a full understanding of fundamental metaphysical ideas such as impermanence, dependent arising, no-self and (in Mahāyāna Buddhism) emptiness goes hand-in-hand with the attainment of the central values of compassion, loving-kindness and the like. Many traditional Buddhist texts assert or imply that in various ways Buddhist wisdom brings about Buddhist morality. For example, in *The Large Sutra on Perfect Wisdom,* a Mahāyāna text, we are told "in this deep perfection of wisdom all the perfections are contained." (Conze 1975: 456). The other perfections include, of course, generosity, morality and patience. However, saying that wisdom contributes to, brings about or perfects moral virtues may mean different things. By far the most common suggestion is that it refers to some kind of *psychological* connection: as a matter of psychological fact, those who attain wisdom become, on account of that attainment, morally virtuous. But sometimes it might be implied, though this is much less clear, that it refers to an *epistemological* connection: metaphysical knowledge provides a justification or reason for the ethical values. These two claims, affirming a psychological and an epistemological connection between metaphysical wisdom and morality, suggest one way in which Buddhist meta-ethics might be understood. In light of this, it has often been proposed that Buddhism has something to say about what, in Western philosophical terms, is sometimes called the relationship between *is* and *ought* (or between *facts* and *values*), usually that in Buddhism there is an aspiration to derive an *ought* from an *is,* or else that there is no need to do so because the distinction is not recognized (for example, see Burton 2004: ch. 4, Clayton 2001, Gombrich 2009: 161, Kalupahana 1995: ch. 3, S. B. King 2005: 43–51, P. Williams 1998 and P. Williams *et al.* 2012: 28–9 and 44).

Our main concern in this chapter will be the possibility of an epistemological connection because the justification of morality has been a central topic in Western meta-ethics and a primary concern in recent scholarship on Buddhist meta-ethics. Since the understanding of wisdom—and the corresponding understanding of the distinction between ultimate and conventional truth—are quite different in the early Abhidharma schools and in the later Mahāyāna schools (especially Madhyamaka), we will consider these separately. We will then address some issues pertaining to the purported psychological connection.

## Early Buddhism: Does Metaphysics Justify Morality?

In the Buddhism of the Pali Canon and the Abhidharma schools, a variety of ethical or moral statements are affirmed or clearly implied. Prominent among these statements are that suffering is bad and enlightenment good (views about well-being), that we ought not to kill, steal and lie (moral precepts) and that we ought to be compassionate, loving and patient (moral virtues). From a meta-ethical perspective, we might wonder whether these statements are put forward as objective moral truths. A good deal in early Buddhism suggests that the answer is yes. For example, we are told that there are 10 kinds of conduct that are "not in accordance with the Dharma, unrighteous conduct." These are killing, taking what is not given, misconduct in sensual pleasure, speaking falsehoods, speaking maliciously, speaking harshly, speaking uselessly, being covetous, being hateful and having wrong views. Likewise, abstaining from each of these (not killing, etc.) is said to be "conduct in accordance with the Dharma, righteous conduct" (*MN* I 285–8). The term 'Dharma' has different meanings in Buddhist thought. But one of them is "the law of the universe" (Gombrich 2009: xii). In the Pali Canon, we are told that in his enlightenment experience the Buddha discovered the Dharma (see *MN* I 167), and he urged his followers to take refuge in it (see *DN* II 100). All this might be taken to suggest that the moral precepts above are presented as objective moral truths in the sense of being laws of the universe. According to the Theravāda scholar Phra Prayudh Payutto, the moral precepts taught by the Buddha are "objective principles established in accordance with natural law" (Payutto 1995: 249; see also Keown 2001: 20).

If the moral precepts (and perhaps other Buddhist moral values) are objective moral truths, then we might wonder what makes statements affirming these true and how we can know that they are true. Very little is said in the traditional texts that directly responds to these concerns. Of course, it might be claimed that it is self-evident that these statements, or at least some of them, are objectively truth. This might suggest a form of what is usually called moral intuitionism, the position that moral knowledge rests on a foundation of self-evident moral truths (recall that Ross thought that it was self-evident that we have *prima facie* duties; for an account of intuitionism, see McNaughton 2000). In some cases, this might strike us as plausible. For example, it may seem self-evident that suffering is bad. But in other cases, this might appear rather less convincing. For instance, it may not seem self-evident that we ought to eliminate the suffering of all beings or that we should never be angry (as in the virtues of compassion and patience respectively). There is a good deal in Buddhist ethics that is counter-intuitive to many people, and this would make it difficult to defend the claim that all or most of Buddhism's central ethical claims are self-evident—at least to ordinary people. In any case, there is no defense of moral intuitionism as a meta-ethical theory in early Buddhism. The most that could be said is that some Buddhist thinkers were implicitly committed to intuitionism or perhaps that their thought is best explained on the assumption that they accepted it.

The claim that wisdom (meaning knowledge of Buddhist metaphysics) supports morality in some fashion might be taken to suggest that Buddhism has some kinship with natural law ethics, where this is understood as the view that moral truths are objective in that they are, in some sense, part of the natural world (the expression 'natural law ethics' has a variety of meanings, but this understanding captures a central theme in the tradition; for an overview of natural law ethics, see Buckle 1991). Sallie B. King has defended this position on the basis of an interpretation of Payutto and an earlier Thai thinker Buddhadāsa Bhikkhu (see S. B. King 2005: 43 ff.). According to Buddhadāsa, Dharma implies both the "laws of nature" and that it is "a person's duty to act in accordance with the laws of nature" (Buddhadāsa 1989: 128). The natural law tradition is commonly thought to assert that there is a sense in which an *is* may imply an *ought* (or a *fact* may imply a *value*). Whether this is true will depend on the sense of these terms at issue. In some cases, it is clearly not true. For example, that there is a glass of water in the kitchen (a statement of what is the case) does not *by itself* imply anything about what anyone ought to do. In order to reach some prescriptive conclusion—for example, that I ought go into the kitchen to get the glass—we need at least to add a premise such as that it would be good for me to drink some water. But then we would have derived an *ought* from a statement of fact conjoined with a statement of value. In the natural law tradition, it is often claimed that there are certain kinds of facts that do by themselves imply values. Thus it might be said (following Aristotle) that human beings have a function by nature and from this it might be inferred that human beings ought to fulfill this function. For example, just as a carpenter ought to saw and hammer well because his or her function is to build houses so human beings ought to think properly about living their lives because their function is to reason (see Aristotle 2002: 1097b22–1098a21).

When we turn to early Buddhist metaphysics the central "facts" concern impermanence, dependent arising and no-self. None of these are facts about functions and so it seems clear that nothing similar to the function argument just noted could be based upon them. Impermanence is the view that everything constantly changes. But neither a commonsense understanding of this nor the philosophical understanding in the momentariness doctrine of some Abhidharma schools entails, by itself, any kind of prescriptive or evaluative statement. A common claim in the Pali Canon is that "what is impermanent is suffering" (*SN* IV 1). Even if this were true, however, we would not have a value claim unless we also said that suffering is bad or ought to be eliminated, and the fact of impermanence alone would not establish this. It might be said that it is obvious that suffering is bad and ought to be eliminated. But simply asserting this would effectively be a form of intuitionism in which Buddhist metaphysics plays no role. It might also be said that impermanence shows why attachment is bad. Again, however, this only follows with additional premises such as that attachment in a world of impermanence will only lead to frustration, and frustration is bad. It is hard to see, then, how impermanence could provide a basis for a Buddhist ethical outlook without the assumption of some independent value claims.

Dependent arising is the position that everything depends on something else. In the classic formulation: "When this exists, that comes to be; with the arising of this, that arises. When this does not exist, that does not come to be; with the cessation of this, that ceases" (*MN* II 32). As with impermanence, it is not easy to see how values are implied by this claim alone, either commonsensically understood or as interpreted in the philosophical theory of momentariness. Nonetheless, an important instance of dependent arising is the doctrine of karma, and this doctrine might be considered a natural moral law. According to Payutto: "*Sīla*, or the Buddhist system of ethics, is a universal set of objective principles established in accordance with natural truths . . . which involves observing mental processes and contemplating the outcome of certain behaviors, habits, and personality traits" (Payutto 1995: 249). The reference here is to the doctrine of karma that morally right (wrong) actions bring about greater (lesser) well-being for the person who performs them. This might be considered a "natural moral law" insofar as it states that there is a causal connection between morally right actions and well-being. However, the doctrine of karma could not establish that the moral precepts (that we ought not to kill, etc.) are objective moral truths unless this doctrine was interpreted as a theory of moral rightness according to which an action is morally right for a person *because* the action brings about well-being for the person who performs it (and similarly for wrong actions). As we saw in Chapter 6, this is a possible interpretation of the doctrine of karma. In effect, it suggests that Buddhist morality (at least in this respect) is a form of ethical egoism: right actions are the actions that promote a person's long-term self-interest. On this reading, facts about what serves a person's self-interest are the objective basis of the moral precepts (of course, a question might still be raised about what constitutes our self-interest). This, however, is not the most common understanding of the doctrine of karma. The more usual understanding is simply that there is a causal relationship between morally right actions and well-being, and it is a further and independent question what makes something a morally right action. From this perspective, the karma doctrine does not by itself address issues about the truth and justification of the moral precepts (or other Buddhist moral values).

This is not to say that the principle of dependent arising is irrelevant to Buddhist ethical thought. The principle is at the heart of the Buddhist analysis of the human situation both in the doctrine of karma and in the Four Noble Truths. To simplify, these Truths establish suffering as the main problem, give a diagnosis of the cause of suffering as craving, identify a state free of suffering (nirvana) and present a set of practices (the Eightfold Path) that will bring a person from suffering to nirvana. This is a causal analysis (recall the medical analogy discussed in Chapter 1). Those who have emphasized this fact and the ways in which it resembles some forms of pragmatism in this respect have drawn attention to an important feature of Buddhism (for example, see Kalupahana 1995: ch. 3 and Neeman 2010). Early Buddhist thought constantly urges us to analyze the causes of suffering and to determine ways in which we might act to overcome them (see also the discussion of causes in the last section of this chapter). However, this does not mean that the principle of dependent arising by itself answers foundational meta-ethical questions such as why suffering is bad, why nirvana is good or why we should be concerned to alleviate the suffering of all other beings.

It might seem that the no-self teaching would have some relevance to the last issue. Selfishness often stands in the way of concern for others and the realization that we are not selves would seem to undermine selfishness (see Perrett 1987). In the absence of this obstacle, it might be supposed, we would have a basis for concern for others. But why exactly would this be? Siderits has argued that a passage in Śāntideva (*BCA* 8.97–103) shows how the no-self doctrine can provide a rational basis for universal compassion (see Siderits 2003: 102–3 and 2007a: 80–3; cf. Clayton 2001). Here is a key part of the passage:

> The continuum of consciousness, like a queue, and the combination of constituents, like an army, are not real. The person who experiences suffering does not exist. To whom will that suffering belong? Without exception, no sufferings belong to anyone. They must be warded off simply because they are suffering. Why is any limitation put on this? If one asks why suffering should be prevented, no one disputes that! If it must be prevented, then all of it must be. If not, then this goes for oneself as for everyone.
>
> (*BCA* 8.101–3)

Though Śāntideva is a later Mahāyāna writer in the Madhyamaka tradition, this argument appears to be defended from the perspective of Abhidharma thought, and so it is appropriate to consider it here. To simplify a bit, on Siderits's (2007a: 82) reconstruction of Śāntideva's argument, we begin with the assumption "that we are each obligated to prevent only our own suffering." But the no-self doctrine shows that "it cannot be ultimately true that some suffering is one's own and some suffering is that of others." Hence, the belief we began with is ungrounded insofar as it refers only to one's own suffering. In view of this, either we have an obligation to stop all suffering or we have no obligation to stop any suffering. But since "every-one agrees that at least some suffering should be prevented (namely one's own)," we should agree that there is an obligation to stop all suffering. This conclusion may be understood as an endorsement of universal compassion.

This argument has the advantage of providing an explanation of the intuitive thought that the realization of selflessness provides a basis for compassion for others. Still, it does not claim that the no-self doctrine by itself entails an ethical conclusion. What it claims is that the conjunction of this doctrine and an ethical premise with which "everyone agrees" entails an ethical conclusion. The role of the no-self doctrine is not to generate a concern for suffering, but to shift us from a partial to an impartial perspec-tive. The argument assumes that we all agree that at least some suffering is to be prevented. If everyone does agree with this, then it might be supposed that this is a significant result. But does everyone agree that "at least some suffering should be prevented (namely one's own)"? That everyone agrees is asserted at a stage in the argument when it has already been shown that in ultimate truth there is no self. But at this stage the phrase "one's own" has no grounding. Perhaps it is to be understood in terms of conventional truth. From that standpoint, there are distinct persons: the belief that one's own suffering is to be prevented presupposes this. Hence, the belief that some suffering should be prevented would seem to be a consequence of the belief, from the perspective of conventional truth, that the suffering in question is one's own. It might be objected that, once it is realized that, in ultimate truth, it does not make sense to suppose it is one's own, it is not obvious what belief about preventing suffering a person might have.

Of course, it might be said that it is self-evident that suffering as such is to be prevented (even if it exists impersonally without selves). To this it may be replied that we think that suffering is to be prevented only because it is the suffering of someone: if there is no one to whom the suffering belongs, then there is no reason to prevent it—or at least it is not clear that there is a reason (in this connection, see S. Harris 2011: 109–13). But a Buddhist might respond to this objection by claiming that it is a prejudice rooted in conventional truth. From the perspective of conventional truth, this may be the only way we can understand the need to prevent suffering. But once we realize that in ultimate truth there are no selves it will be self-evident to us that suffering as such is to be prevented wherever it is found (see Barnhart 2013). This would still be a form of intuitionism, but the claim would be that it is self-evident to those who are enlightened that suffering as such is to be prevented, not that it is self-evident to those who are unenlightened. It might also be said that suffering is a concept that allows us to bridge the divide between *is* and *ought*. On this interpretation, though it is not a functional concept (in Aristotle's sense), suffering does have as an inherent feature that it is to be prevented wherever it is found (of course, some forms of suffering may be said to have a biological function of alerting us to harm, but this is not relevant to an argument for preventing suffering as such). Hence, that there is suffering somewhere implies that we ought to prevent it (at least if we can and there is no overriding reason not to). Perhaps this is why it is evident to the enlightened that suffering is to be prevented. Though the rest of us may not see this clearly, given the distortions of thinking in terms of what is mine and is not mine, the enlightened do see it.

In a critique of the Śāntideva passage quoted earlier (from *BCA* 101–3), Paul Williams argued that Śāntideva effectively "destroyed the bodhisattva path" (P. Williams 1998: 104). He gave several reasons for this. One is that the argument requires the denial of the existence of the self at both the ultimate and conventional levels of truth. This is because, if there were still selves at the conventional level, then it would still be possible to favor preventing one's own pain over preventing the pain of others (P. Williams 1998: 111). In response to this, it might be said that the point of Śāntideva's argument is not to establish that, with the realization of selflessness (in ultimate truth), it is not possible to show preference for one's own pain because there is no basis for distinguishing it (in the framework of conventional truth), but that it is not rationally justified to show this preference. Hence, the argument need not deny acknowledgment of a self at the level of conventional truth (for related responses, see Clayton 2001: 91–2 and Siderits 2000a: 416–17). It is certainly common in Buddhist thought to allow for the existence of selves at the level of conventional truth, however this might be understood (as Williams granted).

A second reason why Śāntideva's position is incoherent, Williams thought, is because it requires that there can be pains without subjects and "pain has a *necessary* connection with a subject who is in pain" (P. Williams 1998: 140). That is, there cannot be "free-floating" pains without a subject who is in pain. This criticism brings to light a deep and important question about the overall plausibility of the Buddhist no-self teaching. The issues it raises go well beyond what is immediately relevant to Buddhist ethics and what can be considered here. A natural response to this claim, from a Buddhist standpoint, is related to the first criticism in that it involves the distinction between conventional and ultimate truth: it may be said that at the level of conventional truth pains require subjects, but at the level of ultimate truth they do not (see Siderits 2000a: 418–19). There are several other aspects of Williams's critique of Śāntideva, and the different dimensions of this critique have been widely discussed (for other responses, see

S. Harris 2011, Pettit 1999 and Wetlesen 2002; in addition, see the response to Siderits 2000a in P. Williams 2000 and the reply to it in Siderits 2000b). It is worth noting that the passage from Śāntideva occurs in a chapter on meditation. It has been suggested that Śāntideva was not trying to provide an argument for universal compassion in this passage, but was instead putting forward a meditational technique that is intended to help bring about universal compassion (see Clayton 2001 and S. Harris 2011).

If the well-being of persons consists simply of the absence of suffering (non-dissatisfaction), then there might be no reason to justify anything more than the need to prevent suffering (or pain). But Buddhist depictions of enlightenment often suggest that there is more to well-being than this. For example, as we saw in Chapter 5, the well-being of enlightened persons might be thought to include wisdom, virtue and the positive state of joyful tranquility. Moreover, it is commonly said in Buddhism that both compassion (which concerns preventing suffering) and loving-kindness (which concerns promoting happiness) are important. This might also be taken to suggest that there is more to well-being than the absence of suffering. However, if the well-being of enlightened persons has a positive dimension, then we might wonder if there is a rational basis for saying that it is a good state that is to be promoted (even as suffering is a bad state that is to be prevented). In this case, it might seem that the intuitions of the unenlightened are not likely to be helpful. They have no experience with this state, and it is often suggested that they cannot expect to understand it. It would seem that the most that could be said is that it is self-evident to the enlightened that this is a good state to be in.

## Mahāyāna Buddhism: Does Metaphysics Justify Morality?

In Mahāyāna Buddhism, moral statements are expressed as often as they are in earlier Buddhist traditions, though typically with the characteristic Mahāyāna emphasis on the centrality of compassion within the context of the Bodhisattva path. It might seem natural to understand these statements as assertions of moral truths, but this interpretation needs to take into account the fact that in Mahāyāna Buddhism the notion of truth is problematized in fundamental ways and, relatedly, the employment of skillful means is sometimes understood to encompass virtually all Buddhist teaching. In any case, several new themes are introduced in Mahāyāna Buddhism that have sometimes been thought to have some relevance to issues concerning the truth and justification of moral statements. These themes include Buddha-nature, interdependence and—most importantly—emptiness.

As we saw in Chapter 2, Buddha-nature *(Buddha-dhātu)*—and the closely related "embryo of the Buddha" *(Tathāgata-garbha)*—refers to the capacity of sentient beings for enlightenment or Buddhahood. These ideas were introduced, at least in part, in order to emphasize the fact that, despite the defilements of the unwholesome roots greed, hatred and delusion, human beings really could hope to achieve enlightenment. The purpose of these notions was primarily practical rather than theoretical. Nonetheless, as we will see later, in recent years the capacity for enlightenment has been appealed to as a ground for assigning dignity and basic rights to human beings (see Chapter 12) and also as a basis for valuing sentient beings—and sometimes all beings—in the natural world (see Chapter 14). These arguments might be understood as proposing a metaphysical basis for evaluative and prescriptive moral judgments. For example, it might be said that since human and other sentient beings have Buddha-nature they have special value and for this reason we ought to be concerned to prevent their suffering.

There is, however, a difficulty with this suggestion. In Mahāyāna Buddhism, in ultimate truth everything is empty of inherent natures. Hence, it cannot be the case in ultimate truth that sentient beings have Buddha-nature as their inherent nature. Understood as a metaphysical theory, Buddha-nature would seem to conflict with the most basic philosophical commitment of Mahāyāna Buddhism. However, according to Sallie B. King, "Buddha-nature is a soteriological device and is ontologically neutral" (S. B. King 1997: 190). On this understanding, it is not in conflict with the notion of emptiness. But if it is merely a soteriological device, a form of skillful means to encourage the pursuit of enlightenment, then it cannot provide a metaphysical basis for value judgments. Either way, Buddha-nature would not seem to offer an avenue for justifying Buddhist values: as a metaphysical theory it conflicts with emptiness and so cannot be accepted (in Mahāyāna Buddhism), and as a soteriological device it makes no metaphysical assertions that could support an argument for values.

It might be argued that the doctrine of conventional truth offers a way out of this dilemma. At the level of ultimate truth, emptiness prevails and so it cannot be asserted that Buddha-nature is our inherent nature. But at the level of conventional truth, it might be maintained, this could be asserted. Some texts about Buddha-nature suggest that it has metaphysical properties. For example, as we saw in Chapter 2, it was said to have the perfections of permanence and self (see S. B. King 1991: 12). In this interpretation, these statements should be understood as conventional truths. Hence, discourse about Buddha-nature can be seen as a metaphysical theory that can have a legitimate place in conventional truth and can then be employed in an argument for Buddhist values within this context (we should relieve the suffering of beings with Buddha-nature since they are inherently valuable).

It might be objected that, since this argument is within the realm of conventional truth, it does not really establish anything: the conclusion is not, after all, ultimately true. In response, it might be said that nothing is ultimately true and thus the only way for something to be true is conventionally true (as is sometimes said from the perspective of Madhyamaka Buddhism). Hence, the conclusion that we ought to relieve the suffering of all beings is true in the only way that anything can be true. Though the argument may be an employment of skillful means, there is a sense in which this is true of all Buddhist arguments and so is not a disadvantage in this case (there is more about this later). Of course, the question can still be raised why we should suppose that all sentient beings have Buddha-nature at the level of conventional truth. This would not seem to be self-evident. Is it simply a matter of faith, accepted on the authority of certain texts, or is there some rational basis for believing this?

A second theme in Mahāyāna Buddhism that has been supposed to have some bearing on the truth and justification of moral statements is a development of dependent arising according to which all things are interdependent. As we will see in Chapter 14, in discussions of Buddhist environmental ethics this idea has often been appealed to in support of the claim that we should value all things in the natural world. Interdependence is a stronger notion than dependent arising: that each thing depends on every other thing says much more than that each thing depends on something else (see I. Harris 2000: 124–5 and Schmithausen 1997: 13–14). However, interdependence was widely accepted in East Asian Buddhist schools (especially Hua-yen) and represents an important strand of Mahāyāna thought. But why should we think that interdependence gives us reason to value other things? After all, someone might well respond to the recognition of interdependence with annoyance rather then compassion, for example by wishing for independence and regretting that he depends on other people and that they depend on him. This might lead to frustration, insofar as we actually are interdependent in this way, but the most this would provide would be an argument that we have self-interested reasons to accept (or not resist) the fact that we are interdependent. At most this might provide a preliminary argument for following some Buddhist values. But it is hard to see that it would be a sufficient basis for the universal compassion of a Bodhisattva. It might be suggested that the fact of interdependence implies that we should live in harmony with other things (see S. B. King 2005: 46–7). However, if harmony is a normative concept such that some ways of living are harmonious and so better, and some are not (as it needs to be in order to be relevant to morality), then it is not evident why interdependence implies that we should live harmoniously. It might be said that this would be in the interest of all sentient beings. Though this might well be true, the question would still remain why the interest of all sentient beings should matter to us, and interdependence as such would not seem to establish that they should matter. Hence, it is not obvious that interdependence as such has any direct normative implications, though as was noted earlier with respect to dependent arising it may play an important role in Buddhist ethical thought in connection with other values (for example, if we already have the Bodhisattva commitment, then recognition of interdependence would suggest a variety of ways in which we could help others overcome suffering).

The signature theme of Mahāyāna metaphysics is emptiness, the contention that all things lack an essential nature or inherent existence. This was thought to be an implication of dependent arising: since everything depends on something else, nothing has a nature or existence that could be said to be its own. In Mahāyāna texts, it is frequently said that the full realization of emptiness and the attainment of universal compassion go together. Why should this be? Could understanding emptiness give us a reason for having compassion for all beings? Or might it undermine the possibility of any such reason?

In recent discussions pertaining to Buddhist meta-ethics, the interpretation of emptiness that has received the most attention is that of Nāgārjuna and the Madhyamaka school. As we saw in Chapter 2, an important respect in which the Madhyamaka school differed from the pre-Mahāyāna Abhidharma schools was the understanding of the distinction between conventional and ultimate truth. According to the Abhidharma momentariness doctrine, everyday objects of experience such as persons and chairs are partite wholes that in fact consist of nothing more than momentary events called dharmas. On this view, in ultimate truth, these dharmas have inherent existence. However, objects such as persons and chairs do not have inherent existence: these objects exist at the level of conventional truth as useful fictions. By contrast, in the Madhyamaka view, nothing has inherent existence. What, then, are we to say about the distinction between ultimate and conventional truth? For Mādhyamikas, at least on one interpretation, nothing is ultimately true (since nothing has inherent existence) and so the only way anything can be true is conventionally. This means that the basic stance of Madhyamaka philosophy, that everything is empty of inherent existence, is itself only conventionally true. Since conventional truth is the only truth there is, this is not a defect. Moreover, philosophies that assert the ultimate truth of inherent existence contradict themselves (as shown by Nāgārjuna's *reductio* arguments) and so they are conventionally false. Or so at least some Mādhyamikas claim (for discussion of conventional truth in Madhyamaka thought see Cowherds 2011).

There is no doubt that Nāgārjuna and other Madhyamaka philosophers affirmed the basic values of the Mahāyāna ethical orientation (for example, see Hopkins 1998). Two central questions have been raised about the epistemic status of these values. First, does the Madhyamaka understanding of the two truths undermine the possibility of a philosophical justification of these values? Second, if it does not, is there any sense in which the Madhyamaka understanding of emptiness could provide a philosophical basis for these values? The Indian Madhyamaka school did not thematize these questions, but they have been addressed in recent philosophical interpretations of the school.

Some interpreters have argued that Madhyamaka philosophers cannot provide a fundamental justification for their ethical claims. For Davis (2013b), Mādhyamikas are committed to thinking that virtues such as compassion are valuable in themselves, and this commitment requires a robust conception of moral truth, specifically moral realism (a form of moral cognitivism according to which moral statements have truth-value in virtue of some kind of objective facts). The value of compassion, or at least of some Buddhist virtues, cannot be defended merely as an exercise in skillful means if this is understood as a non-epistemic form of persuasion. Rather, there must be a justification by reference to ultimate—and not merely conventional—truth. This is what moral realism requires, but this is precisely what a Mādhyamika cannot provide. As we will see shortly, however, many proponents of the Madhyamaka approach do not accept the contention that its ethical commitments require moral realism as Davis understands it.

According to Bronwyn Finnigan and Koji Tanaka (2011), the Mādhyamikas did not thematize questions about justification because they were primarily concerned with practice and believed that they could not justify their basic moral commitments in a manner that is consistent with their understanding of emptiness and the two truths. However, while Davis sees this as a fundamental problem, they do not. Hence, in line with the emphasis on practice, they explore how the commitment to compassion could be fulfilled in a framework of conventional truth. It is, in any case, widely acknowledged that, from a Madhyamaka perspective, it is not possible to rationally justify the ethical orientation of Mahāyāna Buddhism by reference to ultimate truth. It is hard to see how there could be a justification, as it were, simply on a foundation of the *absence* of entities with inherent existence or intrinsic nature. But could there be justification of this orientation in terms of conventional truth? For Davis this would be insufficient since he thinks that Mahāyāna ethics requires a more robust conception of moral truth than conventional truth could provide, while Finnigan and Tanaka are skeptical about the prospects of justifying this orientation even within conventional truth. But other philosophers have been more optimistic about the value and prospects of this enterprise.

It might seem that justification in terms of conventional truth would not really be *justification* since conventional truth as a whole is a kind of delusion. But for the Madhyamaka school conventional truth is only a delusion insofar as it is supposed that it accurately represents the intrinsic nature of things—as ordinary people commonly do. As long as we realize that, on account of emptiness, the realm of conventional truth does not represent the intrinsic nature of things and is warranted only insofar as it is useful to us, we may properly operate within this realm—as the enlightened do. Bodhisattvas recognize that what is considered "real" within the conventional realm has no intrinsic nature and depends on our constructive conceptual activities guided by pragmatic purposes. Yet they continue to guide their lives—and their efforts to help all sentient beings overcome suffering—on the basis of these "realities." Moreover, Garfield has argued from a Madhyamaka viewpoint that within the conventional framework there is a distinction between truth and falsehood, between what is conventionally true and conventionally false, and there are epistemic standards for determining which is which (see Garfield 2011a). In particular, by means of "epistemic instruments" such as perception and inference, claims may be justified as conventionally true or shown to be conventionally false. The overall mode of justification is coherence: the epistemic instruments are themselves justified by reference to "epistemic objects."

This approach suggests that, from the perspective of Madhyamaka, there might epistemic resources for justifying Buddhist moral claims as conventionally true (again, from this perspective, the only way that they could be true). One possibility is that there are different ethical conceptual frameworks employed by different people, and we can speak of what is conventionally true and false, and may be justified as such, only relative to some particular framework. Hence, an ethical statement might be true and justified in one framework, but not in another. If there were no framework-independent way to rationally justify one framework as superior to others, we would have a familiar form of moral relativism. One way in which this might be understood is by supposing that some Buddhist ethical claims could be true and justified within a Buddhist framework, but not (necessarily) within a non-Buddhist framework. It might objected that this approach is inconsistent with the fact that Buddhists have often attempted to show that their ethical views are superior to the ethical views of non-Buddhists (see Tillemans 2011). A response to this is that relativism need not rule out the possibility of rationally convincing persons in non-Buddhist frameworks of the value of the Buddhist perspective, but this would have to be done by making arguments rooted in the non-Buddhist frameworks. That is, non-Buddhists might be convinced to change to a Buddhist perspective on the basis of premises they already accept in their non-Buddhist framework. This might require a conversion or gestalt shift at some point, but it need not be rationally unmotivated. Of course, it might be wondered whether this would be possible with respect to all non-Buddhist frameworks. At any rate, it may be contended that the more basic objection to a relativist interpretation of Buddhist ethics is that Buddhists have commonly supposed that Buddhist Dharma is universally valid and not simply true and justified relative to one framework but not others (for discussions of moral relativism and Buddhism, see Burton 2004: ch. 4, Davis 2013b, Dreyfus 2011, Finnigan Forthcoming and Finnigan and Tanaka 2011).

It has been argued that our ability to understand one another ensures that there is sufficient agreement about basic moral values to preclude moral relativism (see Cooper 1978 and, in reference to Buddhism, Siderits 2003: 205–6). Whether for this reason or on the basis of observation, it might be supposed that there is a broad framework of beliefs and standards that is accepted by more or less everyone in the world—what might be called the framework of "common sense" or what philosophers sometimes call "folk" beliefs and practices—and basic Buddhist moral commitments could be justified on the basis of this shared framework (interpreted as the realm of conventional truth). For example, it has been argued that these commitments might be established on the grounds of "what the world acknowledges" *(lokaprasiddha)* understood as conventionally true (see Tillemans 2011).

However, there are objections to this approach (see Finnigan Forthcoming). For example, what people ordinarily acknowledge might be understood as commonly accepted moral views of everyone, but it is not clear that there is enough stability in these views, or that they are the right kind of views, to support a Buddhist moral outlook. There might be an appeal simply to the widespread moral view that suffering is bad (recall the earlier argument from Śāntideva). But then there would be a question why this one—and only one—view was featured in this way (different and sometimes conflicting moral intuitions might be as widespread and deeply felt, such as the belief that serious wrongdoing should be punished). If the belief that suffering is bad were simply posited as the epistemic starting point, this would seem ad hoc (and it would not fit well with a coherentist epistemology). Another approach might be to take what people ordinarily acknowledge to refer, not to moral views, but to beliefs people have about the world such as that sentient beings are aversive to pain. But this would then require an inference from the fact that they are pain-aversive to an evaluative claim that pain is bad and so should be prevented—and this might seem to be an illicit inference from fact to value.

Even if there were some framework within which it was intelligible to suppose that a Mādhyamika could offer a justification of Mahāyāna ethical values, it would be a further question whether the realization of emptiness could play a crucial role in this justification. It might be supposed that this realization justifies Buddhist compassion in that it removes any obstacles to compassion (see Gómez 1973: 372–3). It is a common Mahāyāna theme that this realization destroys afflictions *(kleśas)*, such as greed and hatred, which prevent compassion. Though this is usually understood as a claim about psychology, it might be put in epistemic terms: if realizing emptiness undercuts all reasons against compassion, then perhaps we have as much justification as we need. However, it might be objected that the absence of reasons against compassion is logically compatible with other attitudes such as indifference. A valid argument would seem to require a "burden of proof" premise to the effect that we should be compassionate unless we have reasons to the contrary. It is not clear what the basis for this premise would be. In general, it is hard to see how the realization of emptiness by itself could provide a direct justification of compassion.

There have been suggestions, however, that this realization may contribute to justification in some fashion. For example, Siderits has proposed that there are ways in which the Madhyamaka understanding of emptiness could support the Bodhisattva path (see Siderits 2003: ch. 9). The argument he defended based on the Śāntideva passage (in the last section) can no longer be accepted insofar as it presupposed the Abhidharma view that dharmas have inherent natures. But the argument could be accepted insofar as, conventionally, the no-self view is regarded an improvement over the view of most people that there is a self. Though there is no ultimate truth about what persons are, some views are conventionally better than others. Beyond this, Siderits argues, the realization of emptiness can help us overcome the attachment that might stand in the way of pursuing the Bodhisattva path. Since both persons and the objects of attachment (of desire and aversion) are conceptual fictions with no inherent nature, attachment makes no sense. Moreover, the Abhidharma view that the dharmas have an inherent nature could foster an attachment to the ultimate nature of things whereas the Madhyamaka view that there is no ultimate nature of things would undermine this attachment. In addition, the recognition that persons are empty makes it possible to practice properly Śāntideva's "exchange of self and other" meditation (see *BCA* 8.120 ff.) that is intended to bring about universal compassion (the exchange involves imaginatively occupying the position of other persons).

Of course, it might be objected that the Madhyamaka view is a kind of nihilism that would inspire fear rather than compassion. The claim of Madhyamaka, however, is that it is a middle position between the view that that are inherent natures (realism) and the view that nothing exists (nihilism): it affirms the existence of the objects of common sense understanding as being real in the only way anything could be real, as conceptually constructed objects that play a role in human practices. According to Siderits, there is no ground for fear here, but there is a basis for an "ironic engagement" in which we continue our personal interactions with one another, though with the realization that these are meaningful only in terms of ordinary "lifeworld activities" and not because of some ultimate reality about the meaning of our lives. The overall theme of Siderits's argument is that understanding emptiness provides a stronger ground for universal compassion than understanding the no-self teaching in the Abhidharma schools.

## The Psychological Connection

Buddhist texts regularly refer to connections between wisdom and morality. So far in this chapter, we have been concerned with the question of whether wisdom, meaning an understanding of fundamental Buddhist metaphysical ideas, provides some kind of reason or justification for morality, meaning central Buddhist ethical values. This question is important insofar as in Western meta-ethics the epistemological issue of whether there is an objective basis for morality has been a paramount concern. However, it cannot be said that this issue was a primary concern in Indian and other Buddhist traditions. The exploration of whether there might be an epistemological connection between Buddhist wisdom and morality has mainly been an interest of recent scholars with Western philosophical training who have offered interpretations or reconstructions of traditions of Buddhist thought. In the traditions themselves, there was much more interest in a rather different question, the ways in which attaining wisdom *brings about* moral virtues such as compassion. Traditional Buddhist discussions of connections between wisdom and morality center on psychological issues about how one causes the other more than epistemological concerns about how one justifies the other. This is a reflection of a more general phenomenon: in discussions of the mind and mental states as they bear on ethical concerns, there is much more interest in causes than reasons (for example, see Heim 2014: 129–30). There is a great deal more emphasis on moral psychology, as we will see in the next chapter, than there is on moral epistemology.

The assertion that wisdom brings about virtues such as universal compassion raises both philosophical and psychological issues. We will discuss some of these in the section on meditation in the next chapter. One issue that pertains to the concerns of this chapter as well as the next, and so may serve as a natural point of transition, is the suggestion that knowledge of a certain kind is sufficient for action. Knowledge of the way things really are, according to Buddhist metaphysics, is presented as bringing about, not simply understanding how to live, but actually living that way. This may be seen as a very strong form of the view that acceptance of moral statements is motivating. For example, we are often told that attaining Buddhist wisdom is sufficient for becoming a compassionate person. In this respect, the Buddhist position might seem to be similar to the view attributed to Socrates, and discussed by Aristotle, that no one who knows what is good would act contrary to the good. As Aristotle pointed out, it would seem to be common experience that some people—*akratic* persons who lack mastery over themselves—know the good and yet sometimes fail to act well because they are overcome by some desire or emotion (Aristotle 2002: 1145b21 ff.). It might seem that Buddhists are susceptible to a similar criticism (for discussion of one form of this critique of Buddhism, see Burton 2004: 63 ff.).

As Aristotle recognized, one response to this criticism is that different senses of knowledge may be involved in the Socratic claim that knowing the good is sufficient for being good and the counter-claim of ordinary experience that people often know what is good but fail to do what is good. The sense of knowledge assumed in the counter-claim is some state such as "solid conviction" or "belief without doubt," a state that many people have concerning what is good and bad or right and wrong (as when we say something such as "I certainly knew it was wrong"). It seems evident that in this sense of knowledge people often know what they ought to do but fail to do it: we do not doubt that lying is wrong, but lie nonetheless on account of embarrassment, shame, fear, greed and the like. By contrast, those who put forward the Socratic claim usually have in mind a sense of knowledge that is not ordinarily possessed and represents a high level of intellectual achievement. It is only knowledge in this sense, whatever this may be, that is said to be sufficient for action. Aristotle himself thought that a practically wise person acts on his or her knowledge (see Aristotle 2002: 1152a6–9). From this perspective, the dispute may be resolved, though whether it is possible to attain a form of knowledge with such power, as it were, that it is immune to the ordinary temptations of desire and passion is a large question. In any case, Buddhist responses to the objection of everyday experience would be, at least in part, to assert that it is only knowledge of a rather extraordinary kind, namely Buddhist wisdom, that results in actually being compassionate.

However, from Buddhist standpoints, in an important respect the way in which this issue is often conceived in Western philosophical discussions is misplaced. In particular, in these discussions, it is commonly assumed that we can usefully distinguish reason, emotion and desire, and an ideal is put forward according to which reason ought to rule over emotion and desire (an example of this view is Plato's threefold division of the soul in the *Republic*). There is a sense in which Buddhist thought may be said to be concerned with issues similar to *akrasia* that interested Socrates, Plato and Aristotle. In fact, in Buddhist texts there is acute awareness of, even preoccupation with, the ways in which such states as anger or lust can lead us to perform actions that we, in some sense, recognize to be wrong. Nonetheless, Buddhist thought does not conceptualize these issues in the same fashion as is common in much of Western philosophy. Examples of this can be seen in the elaborate typologies of mental states in Abhidharma works such as the *Dhammasaṅgaṇī,* the first text in the *Abhidhamma Piṭaka* in the Pali Canon (see Rhys Davids 1900). The 52 kinds of mental dharmas classified there are not categorized in terms of the threefold scheme of reason, emotion and desire—or anything similar to this (for a chart displaying these dharmas, see Heim 2013: 380–1). Moreover, enlightenment is not portrayed as a state in which reason rules over desires and emotions. Beyond this general point about ways of conceptualizing the issues, it is important to consider the multifaceted understanding of moral development in Buddhist teaching.

The typical Buddhist claim is not simply that wisdom results in morality, but that wisdom and morality promote one another and, in their highest forms, are always found together. This is evident in this passage from the Pali Canon:

> For wisdom is purified by morality, and morality is purified by wisdom: where one is, the other is, the moral man has wisdom and the wise man has morality, and the combination of morality and wisdom is called the highest thing in the world.

> *(DN* I 124)

The thought expressed in this text reverberates throughout many Buddhist traditions. It is not simply that understanding brings about goodness: goodness also brings about understanding. More broadly, it is often supposed that a variety of kinds of factors work together to promote enlightenment and the virtuous life an enlightened person lives. This can be seen in common training programs suggested by the Eightfold Path and the Six Perfections. These programs include following basic moral precepts, working to destroy the roots of unwholesome actions, generating enthusiasm for and commitment to virtue, cultivating diverse meditative disciplines and developing an intellectual understanding of such ideas as no-self and emptiness. From the perspective of these programs, moral development is seen as proceeding on numerous interacting fronts involving a variety of mental (and even physical) states. A person on the path to enlightenment, but far short of enlightenment, may well succumb to something akin to *akrasia:* recognizing that something is wrong, but still doing it on account of lust, anger or other hindrances. Moreover, on common Buddhist models of the path to enlightenment, there is no suggestion that philosophical understanding of a sound argument for no-self or emptiness, or for universal compassion, would by itself make a person compassionate. The intellectualism sometimes associated with the Socratic claim, that a purely rational understanding of what is good would be sufficient for actually being good, has no counterpart in these Buddhist perspectives. The enlightened person may be said to have an integrated set of mental states that are not torn by internal conflict (at least this is true of enlightened persons at the fourth level of development distinguished in Chapter 5). To this extent there is some similarity with the ideal of harmony presented in Plato's *Republic* and advocated by other Greek philosophers. But the instrument of integration is not reason as such, but a form of wisdom conceived in very different terms (for example, meditative states are a central part of it).

CHAPTER **9**

# Moral Psychology

In contemporary Western philosophy, moral psychology refers to a rather diverse range of topics in which moral philosophy is thought to relate in some way to the psychology of human beings. We will discuss one of the most prominent of these topics, the relationship between freedom, responsibility and determinism, in the next chapter. Here we will consider several other themes in moral psychology that bear on Buddhist ethical thought and practice. Though there are many aspects of work in moral psychology in Western philosophy that might illuminate Buddhist ethical concerns, we will do better in this arena to take as our guidelines, not the common frames of reference of Western philosophers, but some standard topics emphasized in Buddhist traditions. Since there are numerous issues that pertain to Buddhist moral psychology our approach will need to be selective. We will focus on three important and interrelated issues: first, the four "divine abodes" (loving-kindness, compassion, appreciative joy and equanimity), second, the unwholesome state anger and the corresponding perfection patience and finally, meditation practice.

Each of these three topics brings out a distinctive feature of ethical life from Buddhist perspectives. The first two topics concern what may be considered moral virtues that directly involve our relationships with other persons. The divine abodes pertain to ways in which we are to care about people, but they raise a question about how modes of concern that might commonly be thought to involve forms of passion (loving-kindness, compassion and appreciative joy) relate to a state that appears to connote dispassion (equanimity). For example, we might wonder how a person could be at once compassionate and equanimous. This has not been a central concern in recent discussions in Western philosophy, but an aspect of this issue—the relationship between partiality and impartiality—has been featured in these discussions. There is also a sense in which the second topic, the unwholesome state anger and the corresponding perfection patience, is relevant to recent Western philosophical work, primarily in connection with P. F. Strawson's reactive attitudes. The dominant Buddhist position, that we are to replace anger with patience, appears to challenge the importance assigned to the reactive attitudes by Strawson and his many followers. The last topic, meditation practice, pertains more to the development of virtue than to virtue itself. In many Buddhist traditions, it is supposed that meditation is a central aspect of moral development. This is partly because meditation is crucial to cultivating moral character traits directly and partly because it is essential to attaining wisdom (which is a central aspect of these traits). Though there is almost nothing in contemporary Western philosophy that pertains to such meditative disciplines, there are philosophical questions about the nature of meditation and the ways in which it can contribute to the development of moral character.

A striking feature of these three themes in Buddhist moral psychology is that, though they are often out of step with contemporary philosophical perspectives, they are much closer to the outlooks of the Hellenistic philosophies of the Stoics, Epicureans and Pyrrhonian Skeptics. In Chapter 7 it was observed that Buddhist thinkers and the Hellenistic philosophers both had a practical orientation. A number of commentators have noted several other similarities (in addition to references later in this chapter, see Cooper and James 2005: ch. 4, Gowans 2003: ch. 4, Kuzminski 2008 and McEvilley 2002). As we will see, for each of our three topics, some Hellenistic philosophers held positions similar to those proposed in some Buddhist texts.

## The Four Divine Abodes

One natural way to approach Buddhist moral psychology is to ask what it would be like to be an enlightened person. As we have seen, if we ask what the highest stage of enlightenment is like (the fifth of the five categories distinguished in Chapter 5), then it is very difficult to say anything meaningful in recognizable human terms. But if we set this aside and ask what it is like to be a person who has made significant progress on the path to enlightenment, or to be a living person who has either attained enlightenment by Theravāda standards or reached the sixth stage of the

Mahāyāna bodhisattva path (the third and fourth of these categories), then there is much more to say. One helpful way to think about what it is like to be these persons is to consider the four "divine abodes" (or "immeasurable deliverances of the mind"): loving-kindness, compassion, appreciative joy and equanimity (for a classic discussion of these in the Theravāda tradition, see Buddhaghosa's *Visuddhimagga*, Ch. IX; for a more recent account, see Aronson 1980). In the Buddha's teaching and in many later traditions, these are presented both as central kinds of moral development and, in more perfected forms, as goals of this development. In many respects, these abodes take us to the heart of the Buddhist understanding of the ideal moral and emotional life. They also raise an interesting question about this life. The last divine abode, equanimity, suggests a life of peace and tranquility, and the importance of this is a dominant theme in Buddhist teaching. But we might wonder how this comports with the other three abodes—loving-kindness, compassion and appreciative joy—which seem to connote a life with a rather different, and perhaps conflicting, emotional character. Several years ago, David Wong criticized Buddhism, or at least some manifestations of it, for its emphasis on emotional detachment and tranquility (Wong 2006). Is this a fair criticism, or do states such as compassion point to a more nuanced and plausible picture?

There is no question that tranquility and detachment—a less misleading word might be non-attachment—are important in Buddhism. As we have seen, in the Pali Canon, nirvana is regularly described with expressions such as peace, dispassion, the end of craving, and the relinquishment of all attachments (for example, see *MN* I 436). These themes reverberate throughout virtually all Buddhist traditions. This is another important respect in which there appears to be a striking similarity to the Hellenistic philosophical tradition. The main schools of this tradition each supposed that tranquility *(ataraxia)* was a key feature of well-being or happiness *(eudaimonia),* and they typically connected this with a life of virtue and wisdom (for the Skeptics the latter statement requires some qualifications). This was especially true of the followers of the Hellenistic schools in the Roman period. As diverse as Buddhist and Hellenistic philosophers were metaphysically and epistemologically (and the differences in these respects were quite significant), they were united in finding a life of mental peace and calm attractive.

Now, it might be supposed that such a life would be free of emotional turbulence (for discussion of this issue, see Griswold 1996). In fact, the Stoics are well known—indeed infamous—for their advocacy of a dispassionate life (though they did think there were some "good emotions"), and we will see shortly that Stoics and Buddhists both advocated a life free from anger. Nonetheless, in Buddhist ethical thought, as important as peace and calm were, it was not supposed that this precludes everything we might regard as emotion or passion. For example, the Buddha did not think that peace and tranquility were opposed to states such as compassion. To the contrary, he thought that we attain a peaceful condition precisely by developing all four of the divine abodes (see *MN* I 284).

As we saw in Chapter 1, loving-kindness means wishing for the well-being or happiness of all beings, compassion means striving to eliminate the suffering of these beings and appreciative joy means taking pleasure in or being glad about the happiness of other beings. Each of these three abodes involves caring about how other beings fare with regard to happiness or suffering, and for this reason it might be thought that each of them is, or at least implies, an emotion. George Dreyfus (Dreyfus 2001) has argued that, though there is no Buddhist term that is the equivalent of the English word or concept 'emotion,' there are many mental states in Buddhist teaching that are what we would ordinarily call emotions (his focus is Tibetan Buddhism, but the point has more general application; see also P. de Silva 1995 and Heim 2008). In many Buddhist traditions, a central interest in this connection is to distinguish mental states that are unwholesome, such as greed, hatred and ignorance (or delusion), from mental states that are wholesome such as non-attachment, loving-kindness, compassion and wisdom (there are also mental states that are considered neutral, meaning neither unwholesome nor wholesome). In the Abhidharma schools, much attention was devoted to classifying mental states according to these categories: unwholesome states are those that are detrimental to the person's future well-being (according to karma doctrine) and create obstacles to enlightenment, while wholesome states increase future well-being and are conducive to enlightenment. Moral psychology, understood as the elaboration of this and related classification systems, may be said to be at the heart of much Buddhist ethical thought (for example, see Rhys Davids 1900). Some of the mental states on these lists would probably not be regarded as emotions. For example, greed (and related states such as lust and craving) seems closer to desire, and wisdom is more cognitive than affective. However, other states are by and large what we would call emotions. Some of these emotions are unwholesome and hence to be eliminated (for instance, hatred or anger). But other emotions are wholesome and so are to be cultivated and perfected. These include the divine abodes loving-kindness, compassion and appreciative joy. This means that in whatever sense the pursuit of enlightenment, and the state of enlightenment itself (at least at the fourth stage), are thought to be states of peace and tranquility, those states were intended to be compatible with these emotions. In fact, it has been argued, in contrast to Wong, that Buddhist moral development is not "a Stoic eradication of the emotions" (Frakes 2007: 119) and can include the cultivation of "passionate emotions" such as compassion (see McRae 2012a: 119).

But how should we understand this? A common answer emphasizes the importance of the last divine abode equanimity (a theme emphasized in Dreyfus, Frakes and McRae). As we have seen, equanimity has a phenomenological aspect: it is a peaceful state that involves neither pleasant nor painful feelings. In addition, according to Buddhaghosa, equanimity promotes "the aspect of neutrality toward beings" and "its function is to see equality in beings" (*Vism.* IX 96). Hence, equanimity embodies an attitude of impartiality toward all beings (they are all equally important), and it is apparently on account of this impartial stance that it is a peaceful state. In effect, equanimity reinforces the fact that the other three divine abodes all involve an attitude of impartiality as well. Thus, loving-kindness means desiring the well-being of all beings equally, compassion means seeking to eliminate the suffering of all beings equally, and so forth. So the divine abodes are emotions in that they are ways of caring about other beings, but they embody a sense of peace insofar as they are impartial in their outlook. Equanimity is not indifference or passivity, but it is not emotional volatility either. The reason it is not volatile may be brought out by what Buddhaghosa calls its "far enemies" or completely opposite states: greed and resentment. These are forms of two of the three unwholesome roots involving attachment and aversion (the other root is ignorance or delusion). Each of these states involves a form of partiality: I am greedy for what this person has that I do not have, and I resent what that person has done to me. In Buddhist teaching, troublesome emotional states that result in suffering are closely related to viewing the world in terms of what is me and mine in contrast to what is you and yours. This provides a basis for partiality, for showing preference for myself or for a person I love, and likewise for showing aversion for other persons I dislike or hate. By contrast, the divine abodes, rooted in the realization of selflessness, are ways of caring about all beings impartially without any such preferences.

Of course, love and compassion are commonly experienced and expressed in partial ways: I love this specific person and feel compassion for that particular person, and I want my children to be happy and my best friends not to suffer. In each case, the love and compassion are directed to some particular persons I care about, not to all beings or even to all human beings. This is not necessarily to say that I do not care about others or want them to be unhappy. It is simply that love and compassion, on one common understanding, are focused on the limited number of people who

192 • Topics in Buddhist Moral Philosophy

are especially important to us. In the traditional Buddhist teaching on the divine abodes, these are not genuine—or at least the highest—forms of loving-kindness and compassion precisely because they are partial. And it is easy to see how these emotions in their partial forms can be sources of distress, for example, when my child is disappointed or my best friend remains ill. It might be objected that the shift to an impartial standpoint in which a person cares about the happiness and suffering of all beings equally would not eliminate this distress and in fact would only exacerbate it: if I am distressed because the few people I care about are not faring well, then I will be even more distressed when I care about everyone equally and realize how poorly they are faring. The primary Buddhist response to this objection is that the impartial perspective makes a crucial difference in this regard because the realization of selflessness liberates us from obsessive attachments (craving, greed, lust and so forth) and aversions (anger, hatred, cruelty and so forth) predicated on partialities and thereby enables us to care for all equally without emotional turbulence—that is, to be equanimous in the Buddhist sense.

A different objection emphasizes the importance of intimate, personal and inescapably partial relationships of love and friendship for human well-being. In recent moral philosophy, it has been argued that moral theories that make impartiality the heart of morality (as consequentialist and Kantian theories are usually understood to do) are inadequate because they cannot account for the importance of these partial relationships in our lives (see Stocker 1976 for a classic statement of this objection). For example, friendship means having special concern for a particular person for that person's own sake. But if morality requires us to justify our actions from an impartial standpoint in which all persons have equal moral standing, then the inherent partiality of friendship would seem conflict with morality. Even if there were an impartial basis for these partial relations (for example, if these relationships were often the best way to maximize good consequences impartially considered), that would still provide the wrong kind of reason: friendship means caring for my friend for his or her own sake, not because this turns out to be the best way to maximize goodness in the universe. A similar objection might be made against the Buddhist conception of impartiality embodied in the divine abodes.

Another source of this objection may be found in an influential outlook in psychology called attachment theory. Though this theory was originally formulated to explain the importance of children's relationships with parents in early stages of development, it has grown to emphasize the importance of attachment in healthy, mature adult relationships as well (for example, see Mikulincer and Shaver 2007). According to the theory, these relationships require attachment bonds that allow the parties in the relationships to turn to one another for support and protection in times of need and distress. As understood in the theory, these bonds would seem to be inherently partial: an attachment figure is a particular person one can turn to because there is a loving relationship that makes this possible. If human beings require these relationships for a decent life, then it might be supposed that the Buddhist emphasis on impartial love cannot allow for this (for a discussion of attachment theory in relationship to Buddhism, see Aronson 2004: ch. 11).

Emily McRae has argued that there is a "non-ideal" sense of equanimity rooted in the divine abodes that provides a response to objections such as these (see McRae 2013). Her focus is on the 19th century Tibetan Buddhist thinker Patrul Rinpoche, but her argument is rooted in Buddhaghosa's discussion of the divine abodes. For McRae, equanimity is centrally about eliminating craving and aversion so as to generate an even-minded attitude. She thinks that equanimity so understood does not undermine partial relationships of love and friendship and can in fact inform and enhance them. This is because craving and aversion are destructive of these relationships, and even-mindedness creates emotional space for loving and caring for intimates. McRae grants that equanimity is based on the recognition of the moral equality of all beings. But she understands this to require, not the elimination of partial relationships, but an expansion of our concerns beyond these relationships to encompass more and more people. However, this "does not demand that we must deny the needs of loved ones in order to meet the more pressing needs of strangers," though it may be compatible with this on some occasions (McRae 2013: 460).

There is, however, a significant aspect of Buddhist ethical thought that suggests a different response to objections that emphasize the importance of partiality and attachment. In his account of the divine abodes, Buddhaghosa's central theme is that one is to overcome distinctions between oneself, a dear person, a hostile person and a neutral person so as to realize the moral equality of all persons (see *Vism.* IX 307). This has been interpreted as supporting the impartiality of classical utilitarianism (see Goodman 2009: 50). Rather than seeking to make room for partial attachments within this framework, as contemporary consequentialists have often tried to do, one might see the framework as challenging the importance of personal relationships. It might be argued that this is basically what Buddhaghosa does. He says that each divine abode has a "near enemy" as well as a "far enemy." A near enemy is a state that is similar to the abode in some respect, but nonetheless opposed to it, and Buddhaghosa says that near enemies are often "based on the home life" (see *Vism.* IX 318–20).

This draws attention to the fact that the Buddha thought that the home life—essentially a life of marriage and child-raising—is not conducive to seeking and being enlightened. The Buddha left his wife and child in order to seek enlightenment and he did not return to them upon attaining enlightenment. Instead, he founded a monastic community that he thought was the ideal environment for pursuing enlightenment. Though this community was less austere in its lifestyle than that of other *samaṇas* he had known (and hence was a "middle way"), it was nonetheless intended to free its members from the partial attachments of the home life. Of course, there could still be friendships within a monastic community that might not be free of all partial concerns (see the account of the relationship between the Buddha and his attendant Ānanda in Heim 2008: 29–30). Nonetheless, this renunciation model has been very influential in Theravāda Buddhism and many Mahāyāna traditions ever since. From this perspective, the moral ideal expressed in the divine abodes requires strict impartiality, and an attempt to accommodate these abodes to the partial attachments of the home life would indeed be less than ideal. This is not to say that the home life has no value at all from a Buddhist standpoint. The Buddha clearly thought that it did have some value and he taught to laypersons as well as monastics (for example, see *DN* III 180–93). Moreover, the importance of laypersons is often stressed in later Mahāyāna traditions (for example, the central figure of the popular *Vimalakīrti Sutra* is a layperson). Nonetheless, throughout Buddhism monastic life has often been regarded as morally higher than lay life.

The divine abodes have had currency in many Buddhist traditions. There is a sense in which they do show that there is a place for positive emotions in Buddhism. However, at least in Buddhaghosa's classic presentation, they also exemplify a significant dimension of Buddhist thought that challenges the value of intimate, personal and partial relationships that most people take for granted. As we are about to see, Buddhist discussions of anger question another dimension of human relationships that many people value.

## Anger and Patience

Buddhism is well known for its opposition to anger. There are numerous statements of this outlook in the Pali Canon. For example:

> How can anger arise in one who is angerless, in the tamed one of righteous living, in one liberated by perfect knowledge, in the Stable One who abides in peace? One who repays an angry man with anger thereby makes things worse for himself. Not repaying an angry man

with anger, one wins a battle hard to win. He practices for the welfare of both—his own and the other's—when, knowing that his foe is angry, he mindfully maintains his peace.

(*SN* I 162)

In the Theravāda tradition, Buddhaghosa discusses anger at length because it has to be overcome in order to develop loving-kindness. He says that anger is contrary to the teaching of the Buddha and "is not the kind of deed to bring you to full enlightenment" (*Vism.* IX 301). In Mahāyāna Buddhism, as we have seen, the opposition to anger is even more pronounced. One of the six perfections, patience *(kṣānti),* centrally involves the elimination of anger. In a chapter devoted to this perfection, Śāntideva states, "there is no sense in which someone prone to anger is well off," and "on account of anger . . . I have benefited neither myself nor others" (*BCA* 6.5 and 6.74). In short, the dominant Buddhist position is that anger is unwholesome and we should strive to eliminate it. Of course, as we have seen, in Mahāyāna Buddhism it is sometimes suggested that we may be justified in violating moral precepts in special circumstances. This stance might allow that anger could be justified in some situations. But this would nonetheless be an exception to what is ordinarily the case. Moreover, in Tantric Buddhism it is thought that various mental states that are ordinarily regarded in a negative way in Buddhism, such as anger or sexual desire, may be employed by some persons as instruments of enlightenment. But such transgressive practices are for quite exceptional persons and circumstances, and they presuppose that these are ordinarily negative mental states (see Dalai Lama 1995: 101–2 and P. Williams *et al.* 2012: 150 and 178–80). These qualifications notwithstanding, Tsongkhapa, the great Tibetan philosopher, speaks for the mainstream Buddhist position when he says that perfecting patience means attaining "a state of mind wherein you have stopped your anger and the like" (Tsongkhapa 2004: 152; see McRae 2012b).

The Buddhist view that anger is to be eliminated is quite similar to the Stoic view of anger defended by philosophers such as Seneca and Marcus Aurelius (for this comparison, see Gowans 2010 and Vernezze 2008). For example, in "On Anger" Seneca says, "instead of moderating our anger, we should eliminate it altogether" (Seneca 1995: 114). These elimination views of anger contrast with the more widely accepted view that anger is not to be eliminated but regulated. According to this moderation view, though many instances of anger are problematic for various reasons (for example, they are irrational, self-destructive or morally wrong), many other instances of anger are not only good but also in some sense morally required (for instance, we should be angry in the face of significant injustice). An important defense of a moderation view in Western philosophy may be found in Aristotle's discussion of the virtue of mildness or even-temper *(praotēs)*. Aristotle says approvingly that "a person is praised if he gets angry in the circumstances one should and at the people one should, and again in the way one should, and when, and for the length of time one should." He also says that persons with the vice of deficiency in this virtue are "foolish" or "slavish" (Aristotle 2002: 1125b32–1226a9) Though there are aspects of Aristotle's view that are controversial (such as the importance he puts on responding to the slights of inferiors with anger), his overall moderation outlook has been very influential and arguably articulates a commonsense view. For example, a similar position was accepted by Aquinas in the medieval period and has been endorsed by Martha Nussbaum in recent years. In a criticism of the Stoics, Nussbaum says that anger "is an appropriate response to injustice and serious wrongdoing" (Nussbaum 2001: 394). Elsewhere she relates a story from Elie Wiesel about the anger of an Allied soldier upon first entering a Nazi death camp. She asks: Is not this soldier's anger "an assertion of concern for human well-being and human dignity?" Would not its absence be "at best 'slavish' . . . at worst collaboration with evil?" (Nussbaum 1994: 403).

The moderation view of anger is also a prominent feature of P. F. Strawson's "Freedom and Resentment," what is probably the most widely discussed essay in contemporary moral psychology. Strawson argues that it is a "commonplace" that in "ordinary inter-personal relationships" we typically regard one another as "morally responsible agent(s)" who are "member(s) of the moral community" and hence are appropriate objects of "participant reactive attitudes" such as resentment, anger, gratitude, love and forgiveness (P. F. Strawson 1974: 5–6, 10 and 17). Strawson claims that these attitudes are "natural human reactions." For example, resentment is the natural reaction to offense or injury by another person, and we withhold resentment only in special cases in which we do not regard the person as a fully responsible agent (for instance because he or she is a child or is schizophrenic). In these special cases, we adopt what Strawson called "the objective attitude" in which we regard the person as an appropriate object of treatment or social policy (rather than as an object of the participant reactive attitudes). However, Strawson thinks that the participant attitude is deeply ingrained in human nature and society. Within this framework there may be reasons to modify our attitudes in various ways. But the framework as a whole can neither be given up nor justified. It is simply an inevitable feature of human relationships.

These moderation views of anger pose two serious challenges to the Buddhist elimination view. Nussbaum and the Aristotelian tradition maintain that anger is sometimes morally required in response to serious moral wrongdoing, and Strawson holds that anger and other participant attitudes are a fundamental part of human relations and so cannot be eliminated. How might the Buddhist position be defended against these challenges? In order to answer this question, let us turn to Śāntideva's defense of patience in chapter 6 of *The Bodhicaryāvatāra*. This chapter endeavors to convince the reader of the importance of overcoming all anger, and to provide therapeutic techniques for doing so, in order to develop the perfection of patience. It is featured in many contemporary discussions of the Buddhist stance on anger (for example, see Bommarito 2011, Dalai Lama 1997 and Vernezze 2008).

Let us consider first what it would mean to eliminate anger. It is plausible to suppose that, in at least most cases, anger has three aspects: a belief that a person has wronged someone (the cognitive component), a painful and agitated mental state brought about by this belief (the affective component) and—at least often—the desire to harm, or that harm come to, the wrongdoer as proper desert for the wrongful action (the retributive component). There is a sense in which Śāntideva thinks that eliminating anger would mean eliminating all three of these components. Though he clearly believes that some actions are morally wrong, his appeals to dependent arising suggest that beliefs about one person wronging another need to be reinterpreted: since dependent arising undermines agency, strictly speaking there is no agent who can wrong another. Moreover, he seems to think that the elimination of the cognitive component brings about the elimination of the affective component. For example, he says, "even if one sees a friend or an enemy behaving badly, one can reflect that there are specific conditioning factors that determine this, and thereby remain happy" (*BCA* 6.33). As for the retributive component, Śāntideva appeals to the Bodhisattva's commitment to universal compassion to challenge this: "If I did retaliate [against those who injure me]," he says, "they would not be protected and I would fail in my practice, with the result that those in torment would be lost" (*BCA* 6.51).

Śāntideva offers numerous reasons for eliminating anger. Some of these draw attention to the respective effects on oneself of anger and overcoming anger through patience. For example, anger results in rebirth in hell (see *BCA* 6.74) while patience results in "serenity, freedom from disease, joy and long life, the happiness of an emperor, prosperity" (*BCA* 6.134). These arguments presuppose the doctrines of karma and rebirth. The same is true of an argument that anger is unjustified because we have brought on ourselves the harm inflicted on us by others because we have harmed people in the past. Our suffering at the hands of others now is a karmic result of our own wrongful actions in the past (see *BCA* 6.42, 6.45–6 and 6.68). A rather different argument, alluded to in the last paragraph, is based on the commitment of a Bodhisattva to help others (a commitment presumed to have been made by the reader): "After arousing the Awakening Mind out of the desire for the happiness of every being, why are you angry at them now that they have found happiness for themselves?" (*BCA* 6.80). Since anger involves the desire to harm the wrongdoer, and for Śāntideva often involves hatred, a person who is committed to eliminating the suffering and promoting the happiness of all sentient beings would not be angry. In fact, Śāntideva goes further and says that we are fortunate to have persons who harm us because they provide us with the opportunity to develop the perfection of patience. Hence, we should honor and worship these persons rather than be angry with them (see *BCA* 6.106–111; for discussion of this view, see Fitzgerald 1998).

Several other reasons for not being angry are invoked, but it is widely supposed that the most important of these philosophically is implied in the following passage: "As I do not become angry with great sources of suffering such as jaundice, then why be angry with animate creatures? They too are provoked by conditions" (*BCA* 6.22, here following the translation in Dalai Lama 1997: 40). This passage suggests the following argument: since we are not angry with inanimate sources of suffering (and presumably think we should not be), and both animate and inanimate sources of suffering are alike in being conditioned, we should not be angry with animate sources of suffering either (for discussion of this argument, see Bommarito 2011). The argument clearly appeals to the Buddhist doctrine of dependent arising. Someone might object that there is a difference between persons and other inanimate sources of suffering on the ground that only persons are autonomous sources of action and so appropriate objects of anger. But Śāntideva rejects this: in all cases, persons and otherwise, "all arise through the power of conditioning factors, while there is nothing that arises independently" (*BCA* 6.25). In short, we should not be angry on account of the doctrine of dependent arising and the purported fact that this undermines the idea of an autonomous self (see the critique of the self-control criterion of the self in Chapter 1).

This argument shows that Śāntideva has a response to Nussbaum and Strawson. Though their perspectives are not identical, they both think that anger is sometimes appropriate because anger and its expression are ways of holding people responsible for their actions. On this view, when someone intentionally wrongs me, I suppose that the action was up to the person and through anger I hold the person accountable: I expect that the wrongdoer should suffer on account of this action or at least should answer for it in some fashion. But if, as Śāntideva supposes, the action, even though intentional, was conditioned and so not really up to the person, then such anger no longer makes sense. Moreover, if we are committed to alleviating suffering, we should strive to help rather than harm the person. In short, Śāntideva is proposing a fundamental reorientation of our relationships with other human beings (from that assumed by Nussbaum and Strawson, and arguably by many common sense moral outlooks). Recall that Strawson thought that in special cases we withhold participant reactive attitudes and adopt an objective attitude in which we regard persons as objects of treatment or social policy. In effect, Śāntideva would seem to be suggesting that we—or at least we insofar as we are enlightened—should do this in virtually every case. Following a common Buddhist tradition, he employs a medical analogy: "I am medicine for the sick. May I be both the doctor and their nurse, until the sickness does not recur" (*BCA* 3.7). The sickness is the life of suffering in the cycle of rebirth, but this includes wrongdoing. Rather than expressing anger at those who are sick in this way, we should try to help them: "even if people are extremely malignant, all that is skillful should be done for them" (*BCA* 6.120).

In this respect, Śāntideva's critique of anger and defense of patience raise several fundamental philosophical issues. One of these is whether, as this discussion might seem to suggest, Buddhism is committed to determinism and the complete denial of freedom and responsibility (we will return to this question in the next chapter). Another issue is whether such a wholesale reorientation of human relationships is possible. As we have seen, Strawson thinks that it is not possible because the participant reactive attitudes are too deeply ingrained in our nature. Buddhists such as Śāntideva grant that this reorientation is extremely difficult, indeed they are acutely aware of this, but they think it is possible in the long run through practices promoting the development of the Six Perfections (there is more about this in the next section on meditation). In fact, Galen Strawson (the son of P. F. Strawson) pointed to Buddhism as a counter-example to his father's claim about impossibility (see G. Strawson 1993: 97–9). Another issue is whether we would lose something morally important by abandoning the reactive attitudes. Some philosophers such as Stephen Darwall think these attitudes are at the heart of morality insofar as they express second-person demands that members of the moral community rightly make on one another (see Darwall 2006: 15–17). In this connection, we might wonder whether there might be a Buddhist perspective in which these attitudes could play a role in some contexts. For example, perhaps they could have a place in conventional truth, wherein it may be said that our actions are up to us, on the ground that practices of holding one another accountable are ways of helping people overcome suffering. Darwall would probably resist this as being the wrong kind of reason, but Buddhists might resist it on other grounds. A pervasive theme in Buddhist discussions is that anger is extremely dangerous both in threatening our own moral development and in leading us to harm others (there is a similar outlook in Seneca). Remember Śāntideva's statement that through anger "I have benefitted neither myself nor others" (*BCA* 6.74). Perhaps an advanced Bodhisattva could employ anger (or some simulacrum of anger) wisely, but the dominant Buddhist teaching is that most persons on the Buddhist path should strive to be free of all such states. Buddhaghosa warns that "this anger that you entertain is gnawing at the very roots of all the virtues that you guard" (*Vism.* IX 300).

## Meditation and Morality

In the Western world, Buddhism is probably better known for its emphasis on meditation than for any other reason. Though the extent to which ordinary Buddhists throughout the world engage in meditative practices is often exaggerated, there is no question that in the textual traditions we have been considering meditation is presented as extremely important. In particular, meditation is often regarded as essential to attaining enlightenment. An indication of this importance is the fact that meditation is featured in both the Eightfold Path and the Six Perfections. Moreover, a pervasive theme in many Buddhist traditions is that the pursuit of enlightenment has three basic dimensions—morality, wisdom and meditation—sometimes called the "Three Forms of Training" (see *MN* I 301 for an early expression of this). It is a common understanding that these three aspects are mutually supporting, meaning that the successful pursuit of each aspect requires the successful pursuit of the others. This means that for Buddhism meditation is a crucial part of moral development (and conversely moral virtue enhances meditation). From this perspective, understanding meditation is an important part of Buddhist moral psychology.

As we have seen, there are many different kinds of Buddhist meditation. In the Pali Canon, two meditative practices are especially important: mindfulness *(sati)* and concentration *(samādhi)*. In the classic text on mindfulness meditation, the *Satipaṭṭhāna Sutta,* we are told that it has four foundations—contemplations of the body, feelings, mind and mind-objects—that are the "direct path" to attaining nirvana (see *MN* I 55–63; there is a longer version at *DN* II 290–315). Regarding the first foundation, we are instructed to abide "contemplating the body as a body, ardent, fully aware, and mindful, having put away covetousness and grief for the world" (*MN* I 56). Similar instructions are given for the other three foundations. It is worth noting that the first foundation, contemplations of the body, includes a meditation on one's breathing. We are to observe the in-breaths and the out-breaths, the long ones and the short ones and so on and so forth (the idea is to observe, not control, breathing). The Buddha practiced this meditation while seeking enlightenment and apparently continued throughout his life (see *SN* V 317 and 326). He strongly recommended it, and it is widely considered to be the most fundamental form of Buddhist meditation (for accounts of this, see *MN* III 78–88 and Goodman 2013: 556–8).

Concentration involves the attainment of four progressively higher meditative states *(jhānas/dhyānas)*. These begin with "applied and sustained thought," but then transcend this and eventually culminate (at least in some accounts) in "the cessation of perception and feeling" (see *MN* I 174–5). Mindfulness and concentration appear to be quite different forms of meditation. Mindfulness is sometimes regarded as achieving insight *(vipassanā/ vipaśyanā),* while concentration is believed to bring about serenity *(samatha/śamatha)*. These are related in different ways in the texts, but a common view is that concentration resulting in serenity is a preparation for what is most important—mindfulness that attains insight. However, the relationship between the two forms of meditation is by no means obvious, and there have been debates about whether they are fully compatible with one another since it seems that mindfulness involves conceptual cognition and concentration in its higher forms does not (for discussion of this, see Shulman 2010: 409–19).

Numerous other forms of meditation have been developed in various Buddhist traditions. In his discussion of the divine abodes, Buddhaghosa describes a meditation in which a person directs loving-kindness to himself or herself, a dear person, a hostile person and a neutral person. This is supposed to develop our capacity to promote the happiness of all beings impartially. A similar meditation involving compassion is meant to develop our capacity to eliminate the suffering of all beings impartially (see *Vism.* IX 297–8 and 314–15). In Mahāyāna Buddhism, Śāntideva explains two meditations, one focusing on the equality of all beings and the other involving an exchange of oneself and others, that are intended to have similar effects: to generate concern for the suffering and happiness of all beings equally (see *BCA* 8.89 ff.). In the Ch'an and Zen traditions still other meditative disciplines developed such as meditations on apparently enigmatic *kōans* (for example, "What is your original face before your mother and father were born?") and Dōgen's non-conceptual "without-thinking" meditation (see Kasulis 1981). There are many other kinds of Buddhist meditation, but these are central examples.

There is little in Western philosophy that correlates with Buddhist meditative practices and the important connections these are thought to have with developing morality and wisdom. However, once again a possible point of contact is the tradition of Hellenistic philosophy—in particular, the Stoics and Epicureans—especially as interpreted by Pierre Hadot. According to Hadot, for the Hellenistic philosophers, philosophy was a "way of life" devoted to the pursuit of a wisdom that promised "to cure mankind's anguish" by bringing about "peace of mind *(ataraxia)*, inner freedom *(autarkeia)*, and a cosmic consciousness" (Hadot 1995: 265–6). Moreover, this end was to be achieved by undertaking an ensemble of "spiritual exercises." Some of these exercises were intellectual, directed toward proper understanding (including the rational analysis of philosophical ideas). Others were ethical, aimed at the development of good moral habits, especially with regard to desires and passions. But others had a more overtly spiritual dimension. These included memorization of maxims, examination of conscience, training for death and above all, "attention to the present moment" *(prosoche)*—what Hadot calls "the key to spiritual exercises" (Hadot 1995: 84) According to Hadot:

> Philosophy in antiquity was an exercise practiced at each instant. It invites us to concentrate on each instant of life, to become aware of the infinite value of each present moment, once we have replaced it within the perspective of the cosmos. The exercise of wisdom entails a cosmic dimension. . . . the sage never ceases to have the whole constantly present to mind. He thinks and acts within a cosmic perspective. He has the feeling of belonging to a whole which goes beyond the limits of his individuality.
>
> (Hadot 1995: 273)

Hadot's interpretation of Hellenistic philosophy is controversial (for a critique, see J. M. Cooper 2012: ch. 1). Nonetheless, Matthew T. Kapstein has proposed that Buddhist philosophy bears some similarities to Hellenistic philosophy as understood by Hadot (see Kapstein 2001: 7ff.), and Hadot himself has acknowledged that there are some common features (see Hadot 2002: 232–3 and 278–9). Many of the Hellenistic spiritual exercises depicted by Hadot have counterparts in Buddhist thought and practice. Moreover, the "attention to the present moment" stressed by Hadot in the aforementioned passage appears to have some resemblance to Buddhist mindfulness meditation (though other aspects of the passage go beyond this). It is also worth noting that some of the therapeutic techniques attributed to the Hellenistic philosophers by Martha Nussbaum (1994) and Richard Sorabji (2000) have some relationship with Buddhist meditative practices. For example, the Stoic Hierocles, in an effort to promote universal altruism, put forward an image of concentric circles emanating from oneself, to other persons, and finally to "the whole human race," that bears some similarity to Buddhaghosa's loving-kindness and compassion meditations described above (see Long and Sedley 1987: 349).

Some of the forms of Buddhist meditation described earlier have an obvious connection with moral development. This is especially true of the techniques of Buddhaghosa and Śāntideva that strive to expand our capacity to promote happiness and eliminate suffering in all beings. But other forms of Buddhist meditation, including mindfulness meditation, are also thought to promote moral development, and it may not be initially evident why this is. Dreyfus has argued that once we recognize the affinities between Buddhist ethics and the virtue ethics approach of the Hellenistic philosophers, with their emphasis on moral character, emotions and internal attitudes (he also refers to Hadot), we can see how various forms of Buddhist meditation are morally significant (see Dreyfus 1995). Though Dreyfus focuses on the lam-rim (stages of the path) literature in Tibetan Buddhism, his central argument has broader applicability to other Buddhist traditions that stress a gradualist approach to enlightenment.

One central way in which meditation is thought to contribute to moral development is by enabling a person to attain the key Buddhist recognition of the selflessness of persons. According to Dreyfus:

> When the meditator realizes selflessness, she loses her self-centered attitude and attachment to herself. This in turn leads to the abandonment of negative emotions such as attachment, hatred and pride, which are all based on ignorance, that is, a self-grasping attitude.
>
> (Dreyfus 1995: 39)

As we have seen, there are philosophical arguments for the no-self teaching in Buddhism, but it is commonly supposed that genuine understanding of this teaching comes only with the successful practice of meditation: when we direct calm and focused attention to everything that we take to be a self, we realize experientially that there is no self to be found. This realization then brings about the decrease and eventual elimination of self-centered emotions such as greed and hatred and at the same time fosters impartial moral virtues such as loving-kindness and compassion (see also Goodman 2013: 562 and Repetti 2010a: 193). Hence, Buddhist wisdom, founded in meditation, brings about moral virtue. For many Buddhist traditions, there is no more important practical truth than that the meditative disciplines result in a morally transforming wisdom.

Another way in which meditation techniques such as mindfulness meditation are thought to contribute to moral development is that they enable us to become more attentive to morally relevant features of situations, such as that someone who is suffering is in need, features that we often overlook on account of various emotional obstacles such as fear, anger and indifference. Mindfulness, according the Dreyfus, enables us to recognize and overcome problematic emotions and attitudes, and it thereby allows us to understand what is morally appropriate in a given circumstance. That is, it provides us with a heightened form of attention that may be directed both inwardly and outwardly in morally valuable ways. Of course, it is not supposed that mindfulness does this on its own: it only works in conjunction with the full range of Buddhist practices such as the Eightfold Path or the Six Perfections.

In a more recent article, Garfield makes related points about the moral importance of mindfulness and tries to explain how mindfulness can unite what might seem to be two contradictory models of moral action (see Garfield 2012). According to the first model, moral action should be spontaneous, non-calculating and non-reflective action that (in its Aristotelian form) naturally emanates from one's moral character or (in its Ch'an form) issues from a non-dual and non-conceptual perception involving compassion. According to the second model, moral action requires paying deliberate and thoughtful attention to a situation and what one is doing in it. For Garfield, the way to bring these models together is to realize that for moral agents (though perhaps not for a Buddha) spontaneity involves forms of thought and attention that are analogous to what is sometimes exhibited by persons in athletic competitions and musical performances. Mindfulness training, the disciplined development of our capacity for attention, makes spontaneity in this sense possible. Though the training requires great effort, its goal is to become "mindful of ourselves, of others, of the moral landscape and of our actions so that we can act with the effortless virtuosity of a jazzman bodhisattva" (Garfield 2012: 22)

Buddhist accounts of the importance of meditation for morality involve two central claims: meditation is a source of knowledge, and it brings about a positive moral transformation (in both cases, in conjunction with other Buddhist practices). The most important knowledge that Buddhist meditation is supposed to secure is the knowledge that we are not selves (or in Mahāyāna traditions that all things are empty of inherent natures). How is it supposed to do this? A common narrative in many Buddhist traditions suggests a plausible answer: through concentration forms of meditation the mind is calmed and purified of distractions, and then through mindfulness forms of meditation the mind has insight into the way things really are (no-self, emptiness and so forth). Purged of mental turbulence, the mind apprehends the reality of selflessness. Of course, there may be skeptical challenges to this claim. It is widely supposed that objective knowledge requires intersubjective verification, and it might be thought that this is lacking here (the rest of us cannot see that the meditators have it right). A Buddhist response might be that there is intersubjective verification by those properly trained in meditation (in other cases, such as seeing the significance of an X-ray, training is also required). Nonetheless, there might still be the worry that what is experienced in Buddhist meditation is not simply what is always already there to be apprehended, but what one expects to see only on account of Buddhist training (for an interpretation of Buddhist meditation that might inspire this worry, see Shulman 2010). In response, it might be said that all experience is conditioned by training, expectations and the like, but it is not necessarily unreliable simply for this reason. These are but a few indications of the many questions that may be raised about the epistemic status of meditation (for discussion of some of these, see Goodman 2013: 566–71 and Tillemans 2013).

It is commonly claimed in many Buddhist traditions that various forms of Buddhist meditation promote the development of moral virtues such as loving-kindness and compassion. In recent years, some psychologists have begun to test these claims empirically, and there is some evidence that the claims are correct. In one study (Weng *et al.* 2013), subjects underwent a compassion meditation training similar to the meditations of Buddhaghosa described earlier (mentally extending compassion to a loved one, oneself, a stranger and a difficult person). The subjects were then presented with a "redistribution game" in which they were given the opportunity to spend some or all of their own $5 to induce a "dictator" to pay more to a penniless "victim" the dictator had just treated unfairly by giving only $1 out of the $10 he had available: whatever the subjects spent of their own $5 would compel the dictator to give twice that amount (for example, if a subject gave $2, then the dictator would give $4). Those undergoing compassion training were compared with a group of subjects who underwent reappraisal training instead (involving the reinterpretation of stressful events so as to decrease negative affect) and were then presented with the redistribution game. The result of the experiment was that those with compassion training spent significantly more money to help the victim than those with reappraisal training ($1.14 compared with $0.62). The experimenters concluded that the compassion training increased altruistic behavior.

Another recent study established a similar though somewhat more complex result, but in a different way (Condon *et al.* 2013). Here two groups of persons underwent a mindfulness meditation training that involved focusing and calming the mind, but only one of the two groups underwent a form of this that included compassion meditation training (similar to but more extensive than that in the previous experiment). A third group of persons did not undergo any meditation training. Each member of these three groups was then placed in a situation in which he or she sat in one of three occupied chairs in a waiting room (the other two were occupied by female confederates placed by the experimenter, and there were no other chairs). A fourth person then appeared who was visibly suffering and in need of a chair (she was on crutches, had a walking boot, winced and sighed in discomfort). The two confederates were instructed to do nothing and so the subject in the third chair was given the opportunity to offer his or her chair to the person on crutches. The result was that persons in the two meditation groups were more than five times more likely than persons with no meditation training to offer their seat to the person on crutches. However, those with meditation training that included compassion training were not more likely to offer their seat than those with meditation training without compassion training. The experimenters concluded that meditation does increase spontaneous compassionate behavior.

In both experiments there was an attempt to employ meditation techniques that are close to those found in Buddhist traditions (in the second, these were led by a Tibetan Buddhist lama). For this reason, these results provide some support for the claim that Buddhist meditation can increase compassion (though it is interesting that in the second experiment calming meditation alone was sufficient to achieve this result and the emphasis on compassion meditation made no difference). Nonetheless, there are several factors that suggest the need for caution in interpreting the significance of these results for Buddhist practice. First, the meditation practice did not last long (2 and 8 weeks respectively) and the test for compassion was a single event at the end. This contrasts with the common Buddhist understanding that both meditation practice and its results are expected to be long-lasting—ideally lifelong. Second, the meditation practice was not conjoined with any Buddhist teaching (or other Buddhist practices), and there is no indication that any of the participants came to accept any Buddhist ideas such as no-self, dependent arising, emptiness and so forth. For instance, though the compassion trainings could be said to directly counter selfishness, they were not directly promoting the realization of selflessness as this is understood in Buddhism (namely, the metaphysical view that there is no distinct and autonomous self with identity through time). It is common Buddhist teaching that it is this realization, or the realization of emptiness, that brings about universal compassion. The experiments did not test this claim. Finally, the number of participants in these experiments was rather small (41 and 39 people respectively) and the test of compassion was quite limited. The redistribution game was rather artificial, and it is hard to know what the results would imply for real-world situations calling for compassion. The seat scenario was more realistic, but also limited in that little sacrifice is ordinarily involved in giving up one's seat. Still, despite these qualifications, the link between meditation and compassion shown by these experiments is in line with what Buddhist traditions would lead us to expect. It is worth noting that there have also been numerous experiments that have shown that mindfulness and other forms of Buddhist meditation promote the well-being of subjects in a variety of ways (for information about this research, see Davis and Hayes 2011 and the Cognitively-Based Compassion Training program at http://tibet.emory.edu/cbct/index.html).

CHAPTER **10**

# Freedom, Responsibility and Determinism

In contemporary Western philosophy, what is often called the "problem of free will and determinism" is routinely presented as an obvious and pressing problem that requires a solution. Since the problem closely relates to concerns about moral responsibility, it is sometimes considered an issue in moral psychology (though it is also classified as a topic in metaphysics). In whatever category it is placed, philosophers in the West typically consider the problem of free will and determinism to be of tremendous importance. There is an enormous philosophical literature concerning it (for a sample, see Kane 2011). As usually conceived, the problem, in brief, is this: we ordinarily believe that we have free will and that on account of this we are morally responsible for our actions. But modern science suggests that everything in the world is causally determined. Yet if this were true, then it would seem that we do not have free will and so assigning moral responsibility makes no sense. Instructors of introductory philosophy courses in the Western world usually have little difficulty convincing their students that this is a problem worthy of their attention.

In traditional Buddhist philosophy in India and elsewhere, there is no direct discussion of this problem. This may seem unsurprising insofar as there was no explicit concept of free will in Buddhist thought and there was obviously no knowledge of modern science among Buddhists many centuries ago. For these reasons, it might be supposed that there is no basis for expecting that this problem would have been discussed by ancient Buddhist thinkers. For other reasons, however, it might be thought that it is perplexing that they did not consider this problem. It has been argued that assumptions pertaining to free will and moral responsibility may be discerned in some traditional Buddhist texts, and that Buddhist thought is committed to a form of determinism, especially on account of the doctrine of dependent arising. In view of this, we might expect that there would have been some awareness of the problem among traditional Buddhist writers. Yet it is generally agreed that there was little or no awareness of it.

Nonetheless, in the last few decades there have been a number of analyses of ways in which Buddhism might be interpreted or reconstructed in terms the Western debate about free will and determinism. In particular, it has been argued by various scholars that Buddhism rejects determinism and accepts some notion of free will and responsibility, that Buddhism endorses a form of determinism that is incompatible with free will and responsibility, and that Buddhism is committed to a kind of determinism that is compatible with free will and responsibility. In this chapter, we will first consider how the problem of free will and determinism is conceived in Western philosophy, and we will then review some considerations in Buddhist thought that have been believed to have some bearing on this problem. This will make it possible to discuss the main approaches to this issue in recent Buddhist scholarship. As will be seen, though Mahāyāna authors such as Śāntideva have played a role in these debates, much of the discussion has focused on early forms of Buddhism in the Pali Canon and the Abhidharma traditions that followed (perhaps because of the emphasis on psychology in these texts).

## The Problem of Free Will and Determinism in Western Philosophy

Let us begin by outlining the basic contours of the debate about the problem of freedom and determinism as it is usually understood in contemporary Western philosophy (for an overview, see the Introduction in Kane 2011). The problem is thought to arise because it is widely supposed that there are prima facie reasons to believe each of the following three statements:

- Human beings have free will,
- Everything that happens is causally determined, and
- Free will and determinism are incompatible with one another.

Since these three statements are inconsistent, a resolution of the problem requires abandoning or qualifying at least one of them. The difficulty is to determine which one since there seem to be good reasons for each.

In contemporary discussions, the second statement, affirming determinism, is usually thought to be an important feature of the scientific understanding of the world. For determinism so understood, everything that happens at a given time is a necessary causal consequence of prior states of the universe according to the laws of science (there are also theological forms of determinism that maintain that everything that happens is a necessary causal consequence of God's will). It is true that determinism seems to be denied by quantum physics, which is often interpreted as maintaining that the elementary particles of the universe cannot be explained by deterministic laws, but it is supposed that sciences concerned with human behavior at the macroscopic level (psychology, biology, neuroscience and so forth) presuppose a deterministic universe. An implication of this view is that all human choices and actions are causally determined by prior states of the universe according to the laws of these sciences.

That human beings have free will is usually thought to be the position that (to put it in the first person) my choices and actions are "up to me." As a matter of history, Augustine of Hippo defended the belief in free will in the fourth century CE. It is disputed whether any such notion was accepted by the Greek philosophers prior to Augustine, but it has been affirmed in some form by many (though by no means all) Western philosophers since his time. In contemporary discussions, two fundamental considerations are thought to give us reasons to believe in free will. First, it is claimed that, in a wide variety of circumstances, each of us has a strong feeling or sense that our choices and actions are typically up to us. Sometimes this point is made by saying that, when thinking about what to decide and do, I cannot help but believe that my choices and actions are up to me. This seems to be true in small matters, such as which flavor of yogurt to choose, as well as in major concerns, such as whether to pursue a career in law or medicine. Second, we regularly hold persons morally responsible for their choices and actions through practices such as praise and blame, reward and punishment and the like. However, it is supposed, it does not make sense to hold me morally responsible unless my choices and actions are up to me.

If this last point is correct, then the larger problem is that determinism appears to be incompatible with both free will and responsibility (for this reason, concerns about responsibility are often as important as concerns about free will in this debate). The incompatibility of free will and determinism is commonly thought to be shown by the following argument: if my choices and actions are causal consequences of prior states of the universe as determined by the laws of science, then my choices and actions are not up to me since these prior states and laws are obviously not up to me.

Hence, these choices and actions are not free and I am not responsible for them (on the assumption that responsibility requires freedom).

There are three basic positions that have been taken in the debate about free will and determinism (each of which has numerous variations). Two of these positions affirm incompatibility, but they draw different conclusions from this. *Hard determinists* accept determinism, but reject free will (and usually responsibility) as being incompatible with this. *Libertarians* take the opposite stance: they accept free will (and usually responsibility), but reject determinism as being incompatible with these. The third position, that of *compatibilists,* is that determinism is actually compatible with free will (and usually responsibility as well). Sometimes compatibilists are called "soft determinists" because they accept determinism, but do not see it as challenging free will and responsibility. Compatibilists often differ from incompatibilists (whether hard determinists or libertarians) in their understanding of free will. The classic compatibilist outlook is that we are free as long as we have the ability to do what we want (consistent with ordinary human capabilities). Adult human beings ordinarily have this ability unless they are constrained or impeded in some fashion by internal factors (such as paralysis) or external factors (such as physical restraint). These compatibilists argue that free will in this sense is fully compatible with determinism. For incompatibilists more is required for freedom: they think that a choice and action are free only if the person could have chosen or acted otherwise than he or she did. This is often taken to mean that, immediately prior to the choice and action, the person had alternative possibilities that could have been taken (though I chose the raspberry yogurt, it was possible for me to have chosen the peach yogurt instead). However, alternative possibilities appear to be precisely what determinism rules out: if whatever happens is causally necessitated by prior events according to scientific laws, then at each moment of decision there is only one possibility.

Each of the three standard positions faces a distinctive challenge. Since hard determinists deny free will as well as responsibility insofar as it is taken to presuppose free will, they need to explain both why we are mistaken in assuming these notions and what it would mean to live without them. Insofar as our belief in free will is based on an intuitive sense that we are free, it might be claimed that this is simply a delusion. The greater challenge is to explain what it would mean to live in a world in which it no longer makes sense to hold one another morally responsible because we freely choose what to do. Would this undermine praise and blame, reward and punishment, and the like? Or would there be an intelligible way to continue with these practices? The challenge for the libertarian is to make sense of free choice and action that is not determined. If something is not determined, then it might seem to be a chance event, but it is widely acknowledged that a chance event is not what is needed to make sense of our beliefs about freedom and responsibility: we do not suppose that a person acts freely insofar as the person's action is random (for this reason, it is usually granted that quantum physics does not help the cause of those who believe in freedom and responsibility). Libertarians sometimes appeal to a notion of agency to make sense of freedom: for example, an agent is the first cause of actions (this is usually called agent causation). But how can there be such first causes in a world in which everything else is causally determined by prior states of the universe? For compatibilists the question is whether freedom as the unimpaired exercise of our abilities gives us a sense of freedom that makes sense of our responsibility practices. If everything is causally determined, it may be argued, there is no genuine sense in which my actions, even if unimpeded, are up to me, no deep way in which I am ultimately responsible for them. There are now a variety of new compatibilist attempts to articulate a sense of freedom that captures what we mean consistent with determinism: for example, we are free and responsible insofar as we endorse our desires, can respond to reasons or are appropriate objects of reactive attitudes such as resentment or gratitude. But in each case we may ask: if determinism were really true, would this approach give us a bona fide sense of freedom and responsibility?

## Why Was the Problem of Free Will and Determinism Not Recognized in Buddhist Thought?

It is widely acknowledged that nothing resembling the problem of free will and determinism, as just described, was recognized in traditional Buddhist thought as a problem that needed to be solved. In view of the importance that is assigned to this problem in contemporary Western philosophy, we might wonder why there was no awareness of it among Buddhist thinkers. According to Garfield, the reason is that the concept of free will is a peculiar artifact that arose from the theological concerns of Augustine and has influenced Western thought ever since (see Garfield 2014). In *On Free Choice of the Will,* Augustine introduced the concept of free will as an undetermined first cause in order to explain evil in a way that preserves God's goodness (see Augustine 1993). The basic idea is that evil originates in our free choices, not in God. On Garfield's interpretation, though many persons in the contemporary debate about free will and determinism do not have Augustine's specific theological worries, they are nonetheless influenced by his concept of free will, and this animates concerns about determinism rooted in the scientific conception of the world. Since these issues did not arise in Buddhist traditions (because there is no God), there was no problem of freedom and determinism to address (Garfield's focus is on the Madhyamaka school, but the point may be generalized to other Buddhist traditions).

Nonetheless, several scholars of Buddhist thought have argued that at least some Buddhist outlooks are either implicitly committed to a position in the free will and determinism debate or have the resources for constructing such a position (for an overview of some of these discussions, see Meyers 2010: ch. 1 and Repetti 2010b, 2012a, 2012b and 2014). In some cases the motivation for these arguments is simply to determine what Buddhism could say about this Western philosophical problem. But in other cases the motivation is the belief that something akin to the problem of free will and determinism was tacitly implied by Buddhist thought even though it was not explicitly recognized. For this to be the case, there would have to be something in Buddhism that would give rise to the notion of free will and something that would give rise to the concept of determinism.

The second of these is the more obvious contention. Several features of Buddhist thought might be supposed to imply a commitment to some form of determinism. The first of these is the doctrine of karma. It might be believed that this doctrine concerns not only well-being, but also actions. This would mean that my actions at any given time are causally determined by previous actions. The second is a twelvefold series of conditions described in the Pali Canon that traces the origin of suffering back to ignorance. It might be thought that each element in this series causally determines the next element. The final and most important feature is the doctrine of dependent arising. This might be considered a general statement of causal determinism according to which each event that occurs is causally determined by some prior event. Though each of these interpretations has been disputed, these are the main reasons why some scholars think that the determinism side of the problem of free will and determinism was present in traditional Buddhist thought (these reasons will be discussed later).

The free will side of the problem is somewhat more difficult to discern. Since there is no self in Buddhist teaching, there is surely no place for what Augustine and many contemporary libertarians regard as a free will understood as an agent that is the first cause of choices and actions. Any doctrine of free will that presupposes a self in the sense that Buddhist teaching denies that there is a self is obviously incompatible with this teaching. However, it has been proposed that in a variety of ways Buddhist texts seem to imply ideas that have been the source of a free will doctrine. For example, there are many passages in which it is suggested that actions are up to or initiated by a person, and there are other texts in which persons are regarded as morally responsible for their actions. These might be taken to indicate a tacit commitment to a psychological phenomenon that is akin to what in Western thought is conceptualized as a free will. Though this interpretation has also been disputed, it is the main reason why it has been supposed that there is a commitment in Buddhism to some notion of free will and responsibility (this interpretation will also be discussed later). From this perspective, it might also be said that the "up to me" intuition is a common human experience that does not depend on anything resembling Augustine's theological concerns and creates a *prima facie* problem in any context in which determinism is assumed.

If Buddhists assumed some form of determinism, and if they also presupposed that our actions and choices are up to us and that we are morally responsible for them, then that would seem to be enough to establish that there was a *prima facie* problem of freedom and determinism implicit in Buddhist thought even though it was not acknowledged. In any event, in recent years there have been several interpretations or reconstructions of Buddhist positions that have addressed this issue. A striking feature of these works taken together is that something close to each of the three main positions in the contemporary Western debate has been put forward as a Buddhist response to the problem. That is, there have been libertarian, hard determinist and compatibilist approaches. In order to see this, let us look at those Buddhist texts that have been thought to indicate some notion of freedom and responsibility and then consider those texts that have been believed to suggest some form of determinism. These texts will provide a basis for examining the three aforementioned approaches to Buddhist thought on this issue.

## Considerations Thought to Suggest Freedom and Responsibility

Several reasons may be given for thinking that there is a commitment to some notion of free will in the Buddha's teaching. For example, actions are sometimes attributed to specific persons. In a discussion of karma, it is said (in a story told by the Buddha) "this evil action was done by you yourself, and you yourself will experience its result" (*MN* III 180). The assumption here seems to be that the action was up to the person in question. Again, the Buddha said that there is "self-initiative" and "initiative taken by others" on the ground that we come and go on our own (see *AN* III 337–8). Moreover, throughout Buddhist ethical discourse people are regularly urged to do or refrain from doing something so as to achieve enlightenment or at least a better rebirth. At the time of his death, the Buddha urged his followers to "live as islands unto yourselves" by engaging in contemplative practices so as the attain enlightenment (see *DN* II 100–1). In the *Dhammapada* we are told: "Oneself, indeed, is patron of oneself, oneself is one's own guide. Therefore, restrain yourself, as a merchant, a noble steed" (Carter and Pali-hawadana 2000: 380). All such admonitions might be taken to presuppose that, in some sense, it is *up to me* whether I live well or badly, whether I seek to attain enlightenment. If my choices and actions were not up to me, then there would seem to be no point in urging me to act one way rather than another.

Another consideration that might be thought to suggest a commitment to free will is that in Buddhist texts it is often assumed that people are morally responsible for their actions, and moral responsibility presupposes some concept of free will (see Jayatilleke 1974: 248). There are at least two ways in which Buddhist thought might be regarded as committed to a notion of moral responsibility. The first is that the doctrine of karma might be understood as meaning that we are morally responsible for our actions insofar are we experience the fruits of these actions. If this understanding were correct, then it might be argued that we could not be morally responsible for our actions unless they were freely chosen (see Nanayak-kara 1979: 280). However, against this, it may be objected this is not a plausible understanding of the doctrine of karma (see Garfield 2014: 176). As usually interpreted, this doctrine is not a retributive account according to which the good are rewarded and the bad are punished. Rather, it is an account of the natural causal relationships that obtain between the good and bad actions of a person and the future well-being of that person. Hence, it involves a notion of causal responsibility, but not moral responsibility (see Chapter 1).

A better argument may be that in Buddhist texts persons are often held morally responsible for their actions. For example, there are passages in which it is regarded as appropriate to praise and blame persons (see *AN* I 190). Moreover, in the *Vinaya Piṭaka,* the section of the Pali Canon that governs the monastic community, monks can be punished or expelled for violating the rules of the community (see Harvey 2000: 92–6). It might be argued that this juridical system involves some notion of moral responsibility that assumes that the monks are free to choose to observe or violate these rules. Against this, however, it may be objected that a juridical system need not be understood in retributivist terms that presuppose free will and responsibility. Rather, it may be justified on a consequentialist basis that is consistent with determinism. That is, its rules and sanctions (including praise and blame) may be warranted by what serves the good of the community without supposing that the persons involved are free and morally responsible for their actions. Hence, a rule along with sanctions for its violation may be justified on the ground that these have the best consequences in comparison with alternatives (for a defense of a Buddhist understanding of punishment along this line, see Goodman 2009: ch. 9).

Another consideration that might be thought to suggest a commitment to freedom is that the Buddha clearly rejected fatalism, the position of the Ājīvikas that we are fated or destined to do whatever it is we do. In response, the Buddha said:

> There is power, energy, manly strength, manly endurance. It is not the case that all beings, all living things, all creatures, all souls are without mastery, power, and energy, or that moulded by destiny *(niyati),* circumstance, and nature, they experience pleasure and pain in the six classes.
>
> *(MN* I 407)

One reason the Buddha rejected fatalism is that acceptance of it would undermine the motivation to seek enlightenment: if I believe that I am already fated to experience some measure of pain and pleasure, then I will not see any point in trying to overcome this by striving for enlightenment (see *DN* I 54). It might be argued that "mastery, power and energy" are suggestive of something akin to free will. Moreover, it might also be claimed that the concern not to undermine the motivation for enlightenment would apply equally well to causal determinism. Elsewhere the Buddha objected to the view that our actions are "due to God's creative activity" on the ground that this would destroy our "desire [to do] what should be done and [to avoid doing] what should not be done" *(AN* I 174). In general, it might be said, if you think that what you do is already determined by destiny, God or prior states of the universe and causal laws, then you might see no point in trying to live well or in undertaking the difficult path to enlightenment (see Repetti 2012b: 154). Hence, it might be supposed, our actions must be free in a sense that precludes them from being determined by something outside of us. Of course, this interpretation would need to take into account the Buddhist doctrines that suggest an acceptance of determinism that we will consider in the next section.

In any case, we now have before us the kinds of considerations that may be thought to imply that there is a commitment in Buddhist thought to some notion of free will and responsibility. In terms of the contemporary debate in Western philosophy, insofar as this is correct, Buddhism would need to be interpreted as a form of libertarianism or as a form of compatibilism. As we will see shortly, since many scholars have thought that Buddhism accepts some kind of determinism, compatibilist interpretations have been the most common. Libertarian interpretations face two significant and related obstacles: the determinism issue just noted and the problem observed earlier that many contemporary libertarians presuppose a conception of the self that Buddhism denies.

In response to the first obstacle, it has been claimed that Buddhist considerations that may appear to imply determinism leave room for some kind of free will. For example, against the claim that karma is a kind of determinism in which present actions are determined by past actions, it has been argued that past actions determine the parameters of choices, but we are still free to choose and act well or badly within these parameters (see Griffiths 1982: 286–7). Again, against the contention that the doctrine of dependent arising implies determinism, it has been maintained that this is a doctrine of causal conditioning rather than determinism: since human actions are conditioned, but not determined, they may be expressions of free will (see Jayatilleke 1974: 244–9; cf. L. de Silva 1991: 274). Insofar as these positions attribute to Buddhism an assertion of free will and a denial of strict determinism they may be considered libertarian interpretations. These interpretations appear to suppose, as contemporary libertarians suppose, that free will and determinism are incompatible with one another. We will consider other responses to the determinism interpretation in the next section.

Daniel Breyer has recently defended a qualified libertarian interpretation that takes into account the determinism objection (Breyer 2013). In his view, there is insufficient evidence to establish that Buddhism was committed to determinism or indeterminism. However, according to his Buddhist "perspectivalism," the best interpretation of the Buddhist tradition is that it is committed to the view that we should regard *ourselves* as genuinely free and responsible, but we should never regard *other persons* as free or responsible. That is, we should be libertarians with regard to ourselves, but not with regard to other persons. To simplify the argument, Breyer's central claim is that, for Buddhist teaching, embracing this dual attitude increases the likelihood of our attaining enlightenment since it is helpful both to believe enlightenment is up to us (the first part) and to overcome reactive attitudes such as anger towards other persons (the second part). Because there is no commitment to determinism, libertarian freedom is possible, and Buddhist followers should embrace this possibility with regard to themselves in view of the practical efficacy of doing so. Nonetheless, Buddhist views about causal conditioning and the absence of a genuine self make it unlikely that other persons have the freedom needed for us appropriately to react to them with anger and other reactive attitudes when they harm us (see the last chapter). So Buddhist followers should abandon these attitudes and their supporting beliefs with respect to other persons. In support of Breyer's argument, it may be said that some Buddhist texts do seem to exhibit the dual attitude he describes, assuming oneself is free and others are determined. It may be objected, however, that relying on the possibility of freedom for oneself and the probability of its absence for others is an unstable position for Buddhists insofar as, metaphysically, they emphasize the fact that all human beings are the same and, practically, they are committed to promoting the enlightenment of all human beings, not just their own (and so they would have reason to encourage each person to believe in his or her own freedom).

The second obstacle that libertarian interpretations face is that a free will, as often understood, presupposes that there is a self that is or includes this will. Since Buddhism denies that there is a self, there cannot be a free will. As Goodman (2009) puts it, "if you don't exist, then nothing is up to you" (149). If there is no fundamental distinction between oneself and other things, then there is no basis for distinguishing actions that come from the self and actions that come from other things. In addition, recall the argument for the no-self teaching discussed in Chapter 1 in which it was claimed that, for each aggregate, if the aggregate were the self, then it would have self-control in the sense that it could bring it about that it was in some condition or another. Since no aggregate has self-control, the argument concluded, no aggregate is a self (and there is nothing else that could be a self). This argument might be seen as implying a denial of free will in the sense of self-control (see Adam 2010: 243–8 and Federman 2010: 6–8).

Jonathan Gold has recently proposed a quasilibertarian interpretation that responds to this objection (Gold 2014: ch. 6). He grants that the no-self teaching precludes supposing that there is a self with a free will. However, in a reading of Vasubandhu, Gold proposes that he does not endorse strict determinism and he holds that a key class of the momentary dharmas that make up what we mistakenly call a self—volitions or intentions *(cetanā)*—are in some sense free and grounds of moral responsibility. Hence, there are, we might say, free willings even though there is no free will. These momentary volitions are conditioned by the past (in particular by our delusions) due to karma, but because they are free mental actions it is possible to gradually move in the direction of enlightenment—as the Buddhist liberation project requires. Gold's interpretation does not purport to explain the commonsense notion of a free will, but to provide an account of the freedom that Buddhism needs. It has the advantage of providing a basis for passages in Buddhist texts suggesting freedom and responsibility without supposing that there is a self. It may be objected, however, that volitions without an agent are incoherent. Of course, this is a version of the standard objection to the Buddhist no-self teaching that a variety of mental events require a subject (for example, the claim that thoughts require a thinker). In this case, the account would need to distinguish free volitions from random events without invoking the concept of an agent.

## Considerations Thought to Suggest Determinism

There are several elements of Buddhist thought that might be interpreted as implying a commitment to determinism. The main ones are the doctrines of karma, the twelvefold series of conditioning links, and dependent arising. Karma is usually understood to be the view that a person's morally good (bad) actions bring about an increase (decrease) in the person's well-being in the future. As we saw in Chapter 4, one way in which this may occur is by developing one's moral character. This would make sense if well-being includes virtue. In this reading, a person's kind acts now lead the person to perform kind acts in the future, and a person's cruel acts now lead the person to perform cruel acts in the future (see *MN* III 169–71 and 177–8). This might be thought to imply that our actions at a given point in time are determined by our past actions. However, the Buddha apparently rejected such a strong position: he denied that our actions are "due to past deeds" (*AN* I 174). Presumably, to the extent that karma was thought to involve character development, the understanding was that it does so by increasing the likelihood of future actions, not strictly determining them. In Buddhist teaching, karma is very much a causal concept: our actions in the present causally affect our well-being in the future. But the specific ways in which karma works are complex and difficult to understand, and the doctrine does not seem to be that our actions in the present strictly determine our actions in the future. Hence, karma as such would not seem to be a plausible basis for attributing to Buddhism the position that all our actions are causally determined by prior events (for a discussion of karma and free will in the Theravāda tradition, see Harvey 2007b: 47–61).

The twelvefold series of conditioning links may be seen as an elaboration of the Second Noble Truth that the origin of suffering is craving. According to the twelvefold series:

With ignorance as condition, formations [come to be]; with formations as condition, consciousness; with consciousness as condition, mentality-materiality; with mentality-materiality as condition, the sixfold base; with the sixfold base as condition, contact; with contact as condition, feeling; with feeling as condition, craving; with craving as condition, clinging; with clinging as condition, being; with being as condition, birth; with birth as condition, ageing and death, sorrow, lamentation, pain grief and despair come to be. Such is the origin of the whole mass of suffering.

(MN III 63–4)

Sometimes this series is accompanied by a reverse sequence depicted in terms of cessations rather than conditions. The "cessation of ignorance" is said to bring about the "cessation of formations," followed by the cessation of each of the same aforementioned elements until we reach the culmination, "the cessation of the whole mass of suffering" (*MN* III 64). This may be seen as an elaboration of the Third Noble Truth. It is not obvious how to understand these series, and they have been interpreted in different ways. But they might be interpreted as implying causal determinism: each element in the series causally determines the next element. However, if in the first series this is taken to mean that each element is a causally sufficient condition for the next element, then it would seem that once ignorance is in place, it would not be possible to overcome suffering. Yet the Buddha plainly taught that this is possible. For this reason, it has sometimes been argued that we should not suppose that it is always the case that each condition is sufficient for the next (see Potter 1972: 102). Moreover, the two series might be interpreted, not as expressions of causal determinism, but as guides to the sources of suffering and how to overcome these: for example, since clinging is typically brought on by craving you need to work on overcoming craving in order to eliminate clinging (for discussion of these issues, see Meyers 2010: 51–7).

The most prominent reason for interpreting Buddhist thought as committed to a form of causal determinism is the doctrine of dependent arising. According to the classic Pali Canon formulation of this doctrine: "When this exists, that comes to be; with the arising of this, that arises. When this does not exist, that does not come to be; with the cessation of this, that ceases" (*MN* II 32). This has often been interpreted as a statement of causal determinism (for example, see Federman 2010: 11 and Garfield 2014: 175) In fact, it might be thought that it could not be interpreted in any other way: taken at face value, it appears to be a general statement pertaining to the causal conditions of the existence, non-existence, arising and cessation of all events. However, as we have already seen, this reading has been challenged. The understanding of dependent arising raises complex issues of translation and interpretation. There are also variations between the statement of this doctrine in the Pali Canon and the elucidations of the statement in the different Abhidharma schools and beyond. Several grounds for a non-determinist reading have been proposed. As already noted, one is that dependent arising is more plausibly considered a doctrine of conditioning rather than of strict determination. Another is that, though dependent arising is a doctrine of universal causation, this may be interpreted in probabilistic rather than deterministic terms (see Breyer 2013: 363). A third is that a determinist interpretation may exhibit an unwarranted imposition of a mechanical model of causation presupposing strict determinism into a context in which causality was more likely to have been understood in terms of an organic model of causality that need not involve determinism (see Meyers 2010: 69–71). A fourth proposal is that dependent arising was originally intended, not as a general metaphysical theory, but as a basic practical presupposition in the Buddha's liberation project: since suffering has conditions (as explained in the twelvefold series), it is possible to change these conditions so as to overcome suffering. From this perspective, dependent arising is a forward-looking instrument of empowerment, drawing attention to the efficacy of our actions in improving our lives, and not a backward-looking statement that whatever we do is already determined by past events in the universe (see Repetti 2010b: 283–4). In this view, it might be supposed, the Buddha was not concerned to affirm or deny what contemporary philosophers call causal determinism (for discussion of some of these issues in connection with the free will debate, see Meyers 2010: 57 ff.).

Nonetheless, many scholars think that Buddhist thought is committed to determinism. Insofar as this is correct, from the standpoint of the contemporary debate in Western philosophy, Buddhism would need to be understood as a form of hard determinism or as a form of compatibilism. Though compatibilist approaches are more common, Buddhism has been interpreted as committed to hard determinism. In this view, defended by Goodman (2002 and 2009: ch. 8), Buddhism accepts determinism and rejects free will and moral responsibility insofar as it depends on free will. For Goodman, Buddhist teaching is incompatible with the ascription of free will and moral responsibility on account of the no-self doctrine and a kind of causal determinism that rules out the notion of agent causation commonly employed in libertarian accounts. This might seem to permit a compatibilist approach, but Goodman argues that a compatibilist interpretation cannot account for what Buddhist authors say about moral responsibility and reactive attitudes such as anger and resentment. In particular, he says, Buddhaghosa and Śāntideva oppose these attitudes on the ground that it does not make sense to regard beings who harm us as morally responsible for this harm because these beings are not selves but collections of momentary elements that are causally conditioned. Since compatibilists try to show that these reactive attitudes make sense, it is not plausible to interpret Buddhism as committed to a form of compatibilism. Goodman grants that Śāntideva employs other concepts such as desert and remorse that might be thought to presuppose that we are free and responsible. But he thinks that, since the dominant theme is that we should radically revise our reactive attitudes, hard determinism is a better interpretation. A common response to this argument is that, as seen earlier, there are many ways in which Buddhist texts speak as if our actions are up to us or we are responsible for them. Hence, Buddhism must be interpreted as either a libertarian or a compatibilist position (for critiques of Goodman, see Breyer 2013, Harvey 2007b, Meyers 2010, Repetti 2012b and Sridharan 2013). For those who make this point, but agree with Goodman that Buddhism is committed to determinism, compatibilism is the only option.

## Compatibilist Approaches

Compatibilism is the view that, despite appearances, determinism is compatible with freedom (and usually responsibility as well). There have been several interpretations of Buddhist thought as committed to some form of compatibilism, but these vary considerably in the specific form of compatibilism they have in mind. Some early discussions (for example, Gómez 1975) might be seen as roughly compatibilist in that they tried to develop a position that takes into account considerations suggesting determinism and considerations suggesting freedom or responsibility (for an examination of some of these discussions, see Repetti 2010b). In more recent years, there have been several more explicit defenses of compatibilist approaches, often with reference to the contemporary philosophical debate about free will and determinism (in addition to the works considered in the remainder of this chapter, see Adam 2010, Gier and Kjellberg 2004 and Harvey 2007b).

The most prominent and best-developed compatibilist approach is the "paleo-compatibilism" of Siderits (see Siderits 1987, 2008 and 2013). His position is based on the early Abhidharma Buddhist understanding of the distinction between conventional and ultimate truth. In this view, at the level of ultimate truth, there are no selves or persons: there are only causally related series of momentary physical and mental events. At this level, psychological determinism is true: each of these events is causally determined by prior events. At the level of conventional truth, by contrast, instead of complex series of momentary events, we speak of selves or persons as distinct entities with identity though time that are in charge of their life. We employ this "conceptual fiction" on pragmatic grounds: for various reasons, it is more useful to speak of a person rather than the series of events. One of these reasons is that we can better control human behavior by assuming that persons freely choose their actions and so may be held responsible for performing them through rewards and punishments. Hence, at the level of conventional truth, the whole ensemble of folk psychology concepts applies: evaluation, deliberation, choice, willing and action are things a person does freely without determination by prior causes outside the person. At the level of ultimate truth, however, there are no persons and so it is neither true nor false that persons act freely and are responsible for their actions.

Siderits maintains that early Buddhists were implicitly committed to this position even though they did not directly address the issue of free will and determinism (in the 2008 paper he extends this claim to Śāntideva). It is a compatibilist position insofar as it allows us to affirm determinism as well as freedom and responsibility. However, it differs from most compatibilist positions in that it does not identify a sense of freedom that is compatible with determinism when applied to the very same thing in the same respect (as in Federman's approach discussed later). Rather, it is a two-level compatibilist view in which determinism is true at the level of ultimate truth and freedom is true at the level of conventional truth. These are compatible because there is "semantic insulation" between the two levels of truth: freedom and determinism would be incompatible if they were applied to the same thing, but they are compatible because they are applied in two levels of discourse that are incommensurable with one another. In this regard, Siderits's position is similar to what might be considered Kant's compatibilism in which two levels of discourse are distinguished (for Kant the phenomenal and the noumenal), and determinism is attributed to one level and freedom is attributed to the other (see Siderits 2008: 42). A key difference, however, is that for Kant freedom is attributed to the more ultimate level whereas for Siderits determinism is attributed to the more ultimate level (the distinction of levels is not the same, of course, but each has something that may be considered ultimate).

Siderits's argument is an elegant statement of a Buddhist response to the problem of free will and determinism, but objections have been raised against it. First, ordinary elements of folk psychology such as actions and intentions are sometimes depicted as being conditioned. If conditioning were interpreted as causal determination, then we would seem to have determinism at the conventional level. Second, a good deal of Buddhist discourse does not appear to respect semantic insulation: for example, as we saw in the last chapter, there are appeals to the ultimate level of truth to enable us to overcome anger and other reactive attitudes. In response to both these points, it might be said that these passages are exercises in skillful means, not philosophical analyses (or perhaps that they are in contexts in which the distinction between ultimate and conventional truth was not yet articulated or was not being faithfully observed). Finally, it may be objected that entities affirmed in conventional truth are fictions and not ultimate realities. Hence, on this account, freedom has only been shown to be a useful fiction, and this is not sufficient to account for beliefs that we are responsible for our actions because they are up to us. It might be responded that the first part of this claim is correct, but the second part is misleading in that this account does explain something important—namely, why these beliefs have such a powerful hold on us insofar as we mistakenly think that we are selves (for critiques of Siderits's position, see Breyer 2013, Meyers 2010 and Repetti 2012a; an alternative compatibilist approach in terms of the two truths is developed in Meyers 2014).

Classical compatibilism understands freedom as the ability to do what we want where this is taken to mean that we are not constrained by internal or external factors. More recent forms of compatibilism have qualified this account in various ways, for example, by adding that freedom requires the ability to control actions on the basis of rational considerations. The contention is that freedom in this sense is consistent with determinism. Asaf Federman (2010) has argued that Pali Canon Buddhism is committed to a similar position. Specifically, he claims that Buddhism rejected freedom in the sense of having ultimate self-control or free will. He thinks that determinism and the no-self teaching rule this out. However, he claims that Buddhism accepted freedom in the sense of the will being able to control one's actions as long as there are no constraints preventing this. Moreover, he thinks that in Buddhism this control involves the conscious deliberation stressed by compatibilists such as Daniel Dennett. For Federman, freedom in this sense is a crucial feature of the Buddha's liberation project, both the path to liberation (which requires some measure of control) and ultimately liberation itself (in which all mental constraints are overcome). He thinks that freedom so understood is compatible with both no-self and determinism.

Karin Meyers (2010) has defended a partly similar view. She maintains that, though the Ābhidharmikas (in particular, Theravāda commentators and Vasubandhu) cannot be classified easily in terms of the options in the contemporary free will and determinism debate, their orientation is in some ways closest to that of compatibilists. For Meyers, these Buddhist thinkers held that actions are the product, not of agents, but of various causes (though she doubts that they endorsed determinism in the sense of denying alternative possibilities for action). However, they believed that there is an important sense in which we have an ability to control our actions. In this respect, they held that our actions are free and we are responsible for them. Self-control, on this view, involves responsiveness to reasons as in some recent compatibilist accounts. But it also involves a wider range of considerations including moral, affective and conative factors embodied in our habits. Moreover, there is a distinction between the self-control of ordinary persons and the self-control of persons who are on the path to enlightenment. Ordinary persons are impaired by the unwholesome roots of greed, hatred and delusion, and for this reason their measure of self-control is limited. By contrast, persons who have made significant progress to enlightenment have overcome greed, hatred and delusion in significant respects, and so they have achieved a greater measure of self-control (there is more about this in the next section).

A challenge for compatibilist approaches is to make sense of texts in which some form of determinism or the absence of an agent is appealed to in order to overcome reactive attitudes such as anger (see Breyer 2013 and Goodman 2002 and 2009: ch. 8). Since compatibilists typically defend the appropriateness of such attitudes, it may be said that Buddhism should not be assimilated to their position. In response, it may be argued that such considerations are a legitimate part of Buddhist practice insofar as it moves back and forth between the levels of ultimate and conventional truth. But this does not diminish the extent to which Buddhist thought bears a similarity to some forms of compatibilism. Another concern, of course, is a common libertarian objection to all forms of compatibilism, that they do not give us genuine freedom insofar as they do not affirm that agents are the first causes of actions. One response to this objection would be to concede that Buddhism, with its emphasis on causal conditioning and the absence of a self, cannot provide the ultimate control that some libertarians want. Another response, as we will see in the next section, would be to say that Buddhism can provide the only real freedom truly worth wanting, the liberation that is nirvana.

## Buddhist Freedom

The word 'freedom' has many different senses. In one sense, freedom is not something human beings have *by nature,* but something that human beings may or may not *achieve* in their lifetime. In a wide variety of discourses, we are told that human beings are ordinarily enslaved by their desires, passions, memories, ideologies and the like, but that through some process of transformation they may overcome these impediments and attain a life of liberation. Though the Western debate about free will and determinism is often presented as a debate about human nature (whether by nature human beings have a free will or are determined), in some discussions of compatibilism a sense of freedom as achievement is introduced. This is evident in Harry Frankfurt's well-known hierarchy account according to which having a free will is wholeheartedly endorsing one's desires (see Frankfurt 1971 and 1987). A person may have two conflicting desires without standing back and endorsing either of them. In Frankfort's account, such a person does not have a free will. But if the person stands back, decisively endorses one of these desires and repudiates the other, then the person has a free will in this respect. Freedom in this sense is willing what one wants. So understood, having a free will is an achievement that a human being may or may not attain (though on this view it is part of our nature to be capable of this achievement).

Buddhist thought might also be understood as employing an achievement sense of freedom. Hence, it may be said that oftentimes in Buddhism there is a kind of freedom that unenlightened persons lack, that persons on the Buddhist path gradually acquire, and that enlightened persons fully achieve. This model of freedom was evident in the compatibilist approaches of Federman and Meyers just considered, and it is a feature of several analyses of how Buddhism relates to the problem of freedom and determinism (see also Adam 2010, Gold 2014: ch. 6, Harvey 2007b, Repetti 2010a and Wallace 2008). In Buddhist teaching, unenlightened persons are often portrayed as enslaved by a variety of mental states, and enlightened persons are presented as freed from these impediments. For example, in the Pali Canon it is said that there are five hindrances to enlightenment: covetousness, ill will, sloth and torpor, restlessness and remorse and doubt. According to the Buddha:

> When these five hindrances are unabandoned in himself, a *bhikkhu* sees them respectively as a debt, a disease, a prisonhouse, slavery, and a road across a desert. But when these five hindrances have been abandoned in himself, he sees that as freedom from debt, healthiness, release from prison, freedom from slavery, and a land of safety.
>
> (*MN* I 276)

Likewise, various mental states such as craving, clinging, greed, hatred and the like are thought of as mental impairments that keep us trapped in the suffering of the cycle of rebirth while the progressive elimination of these impairments leads to the liberated state of enlightenment. On this model, the ethical and meditative disciplines outlined in programs such as the Eightfold Path and the Six Perfections are designed to enable us to overcome these afflictions. Enlightenment or nirvana is portrayed as the ultimate form of freedom. As we have seen, the highest state of enlightenment in Buddhism is always difficult to understand in recognizable human terms. But the stage just prior to this (the fourth stage in the earlier five-fold classification) may be seen as a condition in which we are no longer dominated by such mental states as craving and hatred that often dominate our lives.

Freedom so understood is something that Buddhist thought clearly embraces. Though this is something that we may or may not achieve, there is usually a tacit assumption that human beings have a nature that makes this achievement possible (as we have seen, this is sometimes called Buddha-nature). It has been suggested that there is a similarity between the Buddhist conception of enlightenment as freedom and Frankfurt's understanding of free will (see Repetti 2010b; cf. Adam 2010 and Tuske 2013: 426–8). According to Repetti, Buddhist mindfulness meditation involves a hierarchal model similar to Frankfurt's in that the meditator takes his or her mental states as objects of attention and thereby shifts control from these states to the metavolitional perspective of the meditator. In particular, the meditator observes the insubstantial and impersonal character of desires, becomes detached from them, and thereby diminishes their control while enhancing his or her own control though activities such as right intention and right action (aspects of the Eightfold Path). Buddhist freedom is both freedom from our desires and freedom to live in accord with understanding the way things really are. Though more inclusive than Frankfurt's analysis, Repetti argues, the Buddhist approach agrees with Frankfurt that freedom is attained at the meta-level (Repetti also thinks that Buddhism is committed to a form of compatibilism similar to Frankfurt's).

This analysis correctly draws attention to the fact that Buddhist liberation entails not being enslaved by our desires and (at least at the fourth level of the progress to enlightenment sequence) involves an integrated mental outlook similar to Frankfurt's wholeheartedness. It may be pointed out, however, that there are also some deep differences in the two enterprises. In Frankfurt's view, we are to constitute ourselves by decisively endorsing a desire and thereby making it our own. This process of self-constitution is not guided by any metaphysical understanding of the world, and it can take a wide variety of forms. Buddhist enlightenment, by contrast, is crucially underwritten by wisdom, by the realization of the selflessness or emptiness of all things, and it brings about compassion for all sentient beings. This is a kind of freedom in that it is liberation from the enslavement of craving that is the key cause of suffering. But in comparison with what most people would consider a freedom worth attaining, this is a rather radical conception of freedom, and establishing its possibility is not part of the agenda of the main compatibilist projects in Western philosophy.

# PART 3

# Practical Issues in Buddhist Moral Philosophy

CHAPTER **11**
# Socially Engaged Buddhism

In the last several chapters we have considered a number of rather theoretical issues pertaining to normative ethics, meta-ethics and moral psychology. In the remaining chapters we will discuss several more practical concerns, some issues that in Western philosophy are usually considered topics in applied ethics. As we saw in Chapter 3, applied ethics employs the resources of moral philosophy, especially normative ethics, to analyze specific moral topics about which, typically, there is some controversy. These topics may pertain to personal life, but they commonly involve broader social concerns with a political, legal or economic dimension. For example, analyses in applied ethics may pertain to human rights, war and terrorism, environmental problems and a host of other issues. In recent decades, there have also been numerous examinations of these same issues from the perspective of Buddhist ethics. Moreover, many of these accounts have a philosophical character (sometimes in a more interpretive mode and sometimes with a more constructive orientation). Hence, there is now a body of literature that might well be called Buddhist applied ethics, a literature that has some affinity with applied ethics in contemporary Western philosophy. As we will see, Buddhist applied ethics is closely connected with a broader movement in recent Buddhist thought and practice called socially engaged Buddhism (or sometimes simply engaged Buddhism). Before we consider the specific issues in applied Buddhist ethics in the chapters to come, it will be helpful to situate these discussions with respect to this movement.

After identifying some characteristic features of socially engaged Buddhism, we will consider its roots in the tradition and some representative manifestations of it in the world today.

## What Is Socially Engaged Buddhism?

The expression 'engaged Buddhism' was originally coined in 1963 by Thich Nhat Hanh, one of the most prominent figures in the movement (see Kraft 1992b: 18). As we will see, there is a debate about the extent to which engaged or socially engaged Buddhism is an extension of traditional Buddhist ideas and practices and the extent to which it is a modern phenomenon that draws on Western perspectives and ideas. In any case, what is usually called socially engaged Buddhism is a rather loosely organized group of activities and practices that began in the latter half of the 20th century in some Asian countries where Buddhism has been prominent as well as some Western countries such as the United States and those in the United Kingdom. There is tremendous diversity in the movement: it is animated by virtually all the different Buddhist traditions in the world today, and it includes activities ranging from the application of Buddhist ideas to ordinary affairs in life such as friendship, family and career, to volunteer work in hospitals, prisons and soup kitchens, to organized social and political activism aiming at fundamental institutional changes. In any form, socially engaged Buddhism is an application of Buddhist values to the contemporary world, but it may also be considered, more specifically, as itself a form of Buddhist practice in pursuit of enlightenment.

Socially engaged Buddhism has been characterized in a variety of ways. Sometimes it is claimed that there are necessary conditions of socially engaged Buddhism such as non-violence. For example, according to Sallie B. King, "engaged Buddhism is by definition nonviolent" (S. B. King 2009a: 3). This is meant to exclude from the fold Buddhist nationalists in Sri Lanka (who have sometimes engaged in violence). Though such claims are not uncommon (cf. K. Jones 2003: 181), they are more a kind of advocacy for a particular form of socially engaged Buddhism than they are impartial descriptions of ways in which contemporary Buddhists are engaged in the world. As we will see in Chapter 13, though not killing is certainly a fundamental Buddhist value, there are differences within the tradition about whether this value implies pacifism or something more akin to a just war theory that would permit—and perhaps even require—forms of violence in some circumstances. It is true that socially engaged Buddhists often draw on the pacifist rather than the just war strand, but they might well do the reverse, even if some Buddhists who have resorted to violence could not plausibly claim any justification in the tradition.

Rather than supposing that there is a set of essential features, a statement of necessary and sufficient conditions, that define socially engaged Buddhism, it is more illuminating to recognize that there are some general characteristics that are commonly, but not necessarily universally, associated with it. First, most obviously, socially engaged Buddhists confront ethical issues in the contemporary world on the basis of fundamental Buddhist moral values such as:

- The manifestly ethical parts of the Eightfold Path (right speech, right action and right livelihood) and/or the Six Perfections (generosity, morality and patience),
- Fundamental moral virtues, especially compassion and loving-kindness, and
- Standard ethical motifs, for example, the importance of overcoming greed, hatred and delusion, traditionally the three obstacles to enlightenment.

Second, engaged Buddhists also appeal to other aspects of Buddhist thought and practice such as wisdom (no-self, emptiness, impermanence and dependent arising) and mindfulness (both as a specific meditation practice and as a way of being in the world). In this connection, a prominent theme in engaged Buddhism is the Mahāyāna concept of the interdependence of all things, especially as conveyed by the metaphor of Indra's net, in which each jewel in the net reflects every other jewel. Engaged Buddhists appeal to interdependence and Indra's net in a wide variety of contexts (see K. Jones 2003: 16–18 and Macy 1979). Third, socially engaged Buddhists often maintain that spiritual development and social activism go hand-in-hand and should be combined: pursuit of enlightenment (for example, by following the Eightfold Path or the Six Perfections) without active compassion for others is misguided, but so is advocacy of social and political causes without the cultivation of wisdom and inner peace. In this view, both are essential. Fourth, a related but somewhat different point, though engaged Buddhists are committed to overcoming suffering in traditional Buddhist ways by changing our attitudes (eliminating craving, attachment and the like), they are often also committed to overcoming suffering in more conventional ways by eliminating poverty, illness, exploitation and so forth. Finally, especially in its more political forms, socially engaged Buddhists often appeal to ideas drawn from the modern Western tradition such as human rights, human dignity, democracy and gender equality (though they are often critical of other aspects of Western values such as consumerism).

## Socially Engaged Buddhism and the Tradition

Some of these characteristics relate to the question, noted earlier, about the extent to which socially engaged Buddhism is rooted in the tradition and the extent to which it is a modernist departure from the tradition. In the past, Buddhism has certainly had the reputation, especially in the West, of being more concerned with an other-worldly pursuit of individual salvation than a this-worldly engagement with social and political issues. This was the influential understanding of the social theorist Max Weber (for discussion, see Harvey 2000: 206–7 and K. Jones 2003: 213–14). There are, however, different interpretations of the Buddhist tradition in this regard (see Yarnall 2003). Some have argued that some form of social engagement has always been a feature of Buddhism. For example, according to Nhat Hanh, "Buddhism means to be awake" and:

> If you are awake you cannot do otherwise than act compassionately to help relieve suffering you see around you. So Buddhism must be engaged in the world. If it is not engaged it is not Buddhism.
>
> (cited in K. Jones 2003: 179)

Likewise, for Thurman, Buddhism is an "activism" in the service of both self-transformation and world-transformation. "It is squarely in the center of all Buddhist traditions," he says, "to bring basic principles to bear on actual contemporary problems to develop ethical, even political, guidelines for action" (Thurman, 1988a: 120). By contrast, according to Gombrich, echoing Weber, the Buddha's "concern was to reform individuals and help them to leave society forever, not to reform the world" (Gombrich 1988: 30; cf. W. L. King 1995: 73–6 and Lele 2013). Those who stress discontinuity with the tradition may grant that there are latent forms of social engagement in Buddhist traditions, but they maintain that socially engaged Buddhism is a modern innovation. According to Christopher S. Queen, a prominent Western scholar of engaged Buddhism:

> The general pattern of belief and practice that has come to be called "engaged Buddhism" is unprecedented, and thus tantamount to a new chapter in the history of the tradition. As a style of ethical practice, engaged Buddhism may be seen as a new paradigm of Buddhist liberation.
>
> (Queen 2000b: 1–2; cf. Queen 1996: 10)

Those who believe that there is a basis in the tradition for socially engaged Buddhism have pointed to a number of historical sources to show this (for overviews, see Harvey 2000: 112–18 and K. Jones 2003: ch. 5). Three of these sources are commonly referred to and are worth describing briefly here.

First, it has been argued that the Buddha himself, or at any rate Buddhist thought as represented in the Pali Canon, taught about a variety of social, political and economic issues (see Rahula 1974: ch. 8). For example, in the *Sigālaka Sutta* the Buddha articulated a set of reciprocal responsibilities for friends, sons and parents, students and teachers, husbands and wives, masters and servants and laypersons and ascetics (see *DN* III 189–91). Again, in the *Aggañña Sutta,* it is suggested in a story about the origins of human life that government began when people, confronted by social unrest (theft, retaliation and so forth), appointed a person to punish wrongdoers in exchange for rice (*DN* III 92–3). This has been interpreted as an anticipation of the social contract theory in Western philosophy (see Harvey 2000: 114 and 118). In the *Cakkavatti-Sīhanāda Sutta,* a contrast is drawn between two monarchs, one righteous and ruling according to the Dharma (for instance, by giving property to the needy) and the other the opposite. We are told that the people prospered under the first monarch, but under the second monarch the people declined morally and suffered greatly (see *DN* III 58 ff.). The concept of a morally ideal ruler, a "Wheel-turning King" *(cakkavatti/cakravartin),* was developed early in the tradition (see Halkias 2013). Elsewhere in the Pali Canon 10 moral virtues of a king are listed. These are charity, morality, self-sacrifice, honesty, gentleness, austerity, non-anger, non-violence, patience and non-offensiveness (see Collins 1998: 460–1 and Rahula 1974: 85). Discussions such as these are plausibly interpreted as showing that the Buddha, or at least some very early Buddhists, had some concern with social and political issues. However, there are questions about how to interpret these texts (for example, see Collins 1998: 448–96), and it may be disputed to what extent they have clear implications for understanding such issues in the contemporary world.

A second historical source for socially engaged Buddhism, this time in the Mahāyāna tradition, is Nāgārjuna's *Precious Garland of Advice* (Hopkins 1998). In this work, Nāgārjuna (generally thought to be the same person as the founder of the Madhyamaka school discussed in Chapter 2) explains the Bodhisattva path to a king. Much of the work expounds common Mahāyāna teaching, especially as it pertains to morality. Hence, a good deal of the text concerns the moral development of a king. For example, he should develop "the four goodnesses—truth, generosity, peace, and wisdom" (verse 139). Beyond this, the king is advised to benefit his subjects in numerous ways. For example, he should provide water-vessels and rest houses, build hostels and parks, nourish the poor, care for the sick, aid victims of disasters, keep taxes low and prices fair, and reduce tolls (see verses 241–54). Again, though the king should eliminate robbers and murderers by punishing them, he should do so with great compassion. In some cases law-breakers should be freed, and even when they are not "they should be made comfortable with barbers, baths, food, drink, medicine and clothing" (verse 335). In the case of "angry murderers," they should be "banished without killing or tormenting them" (verse 337).

On the basis of such claims, Thurman has argued that Nāgārjuna's *Garland* can be used to develop "guidelines for Buddhist Social action in our modern times" (Thurman 1988a: 130). In some respects, this text is certainly suggestive of what in contemporary terms might be considered a humane welfare state. In other respects, however, the state envisioned by Nāgārjuna is at odds with basic features of a modern liberal, democratic state. This is not only because he assumes that a king will rule the state, but also because he urges the king to construct "images of the Buddha, monuments, and temples" (verse 231). Neither democracy nor most of the basic liberties are in view. Nāgārjuna's state is more concerned with the promotion of Mahāyāna Buddhist virtue than with respect for individual freedom to live according to one's own conception of the good (often taken to be a key feature of the liberal state). For this reason, contemporary socially engaged Buddhists who embrace a liberal, democratic state, as they often do, are likely to supplement and modify Nāgārjuna's account in significant ways (for discussion of this, see Garfield 2002c). There is no question, though, that the *Garland* shows that there was a concern for political issues at the heart of the Mahāyāna tradition.

Finally, a third historical source often appealed to by socially engaged Buddhists is not a text, but a person: Aśoka, the third century BCE Indian king in the Mauryan dynasty who, having ruthlessly conquered the Kalinga region, became a lay Buddhist and ruled for many years according to Buddhist Dharma (for a sympathetic account of his life, see Akira 1990: ch. 7). We know this largely on the basis of numerous rock and pillar edicts (33 extant) Aśoka had carved throughout India and nearby vicinities (see Nikam and McKeon 1959). According to the edicts, Aśoka's state was devoted to promoting Buddhist morality. For example, people were urged to embrace moral virtues such as compassion, kindness, generosity, truthfulness, gentleness, non-violence and moderation. They were also encouraged to respect ascetics, honor their teachers and obey their parents. In addition to posting edicts to this effect, Aśoka assigned state officials to expound these virtues and responsibilities. However, though Aśoka was very much concerned to foster Buddhist morality and to directly support the Buddhist monastic community, he also advocated tolerance and understanding of other religions. He said that he "honors men of all faiths" and wishes them "to live everywhere in his kingdom" (Nikam and McKeon 1959: 51) He also said that persons of different faiths should know one another's doctrines and should not extoll their own faith or disparage the faith of others in an improper or immoderate manner. According to the edicts, Aśoka also undertook various actions in accordance with the Dharma to promote the welfare of his people such as providing medical treatment, planting orchards, digging wells and building rest houses. With respect to those who broke the law, he urged his officials to be impartial and to avoid unjust imprisonment and torture. Though he retained capital punishment, he granted those sentenced to death a three-day postponement so that they could appeal or at least prepare for the next life. The edicts also portray Aśoka as expressing concern for animals by restricting their slaughter, prohibiting cruel treatment and supplying medical care.

It is hard to know to what extent Aśoka's actual policies were in accord with what is reported in the edicts. Moreover, he has been criticized for being an unrealistic and ineffective king (see Basham 1982). However, whatever the history, Aśoka has certainly been a source of inspiration and guidance for many socially engaged Buddhists. According to Thurman, the edicts "provide the operative principles of the 'politics of enlightenment'" (Thurman 1988b: 111). In conjunction with the sources in the Pali Canon and Nāgārjuna's *Garland,* the edicts provide ample evidence that early in the Indian traditions of Buddhism there was significant Buddhist interest and involvement in social, political and even economic affairs. It is a further question, however, to what extent this history provides a precedent for the various forms that socially engaged Buddhism takes today. Many engaged Buddhists would be reluctant to endorse a state devoted to the promotion of Buddhist virtue, but most of them are more likely to approve of Aśoka's views about religious tolerance and understanding. On another issue, socially engaged Buddhists sometimes suggest that engagement in social and political issues is a way, perhaps even the way, of pursuing the Buddhist path to enlightenment (see Kraft 2000: 494–5). This is contrary to some traditional forms of Buddhism. For example, a dominant theme in the early Indian tradition of the Pali Canon is a basic distinction between monastics who are seeking enlightenment, but are withdrawn from the world in important ways, and laypersons who are involved in the world, but in this lifetime are only seeking a better rebirth (though there were exceptions such as laypersons who attained enlightenment). There is a related distinction, at the level of ideal figures, between a Buddha and a Wheel-turning king (see Collins 1998: 474–5). However, other traditions, especially in Mahāyāna Buddhism, provide a more promising precedent for combining the pursuit of enlightenment with engagement in the world. For instance, the *Vimalakīrti Sutra* features a layperson, Vilmalakīrti, who is involved in the world and yet possesses an extraordinary degree of wisdom (see Thurman 1976).

## Some Representative Proponents of Socially Engaged Buddhism

Socially engaged Buddhism encompasses a wide variety of persons, organizations, traditions, perspectives and issues. It is not a philosophical school of thought as such. However, engaged Buddhists are often informed by a philosophical outlook, and in this way their activities provide the social context for the discussions of applied Buddhist ethics that we will consider in the chapters ahead. In order to appreciate these discussions, it is important to have some understanding of this context. Though it is not possible to provide a full overview of socially engaged Buddhism here (for this, see Eppsteiner 1988, S. B. King 2005 and 2009a, Kotler 1996, Queen 2000a and Queen and S. B. King 1996), it will be helpful to gain some understanding of it by briefly looking at some important representative proponents: three Asian leaders—Sulak Sivaraksa, the Dalai Lama and Thich Nhat Hanh—and one organization in the United States—The Buddhist Peace Fellowship.

Sulak Sivaraksa is a lay Buddhist critic and activist in Thailand, born in 1933, who has worked for many years in support of a culture of peace and non-violence, economic justice, protection of the environment and other concerns on the basis of traditional Buddhist values. He has written extensively in both Thai and English (for examples of the latter, see Sivaraksa 1992 and 2005) and has established numerous publications and organizations, including the International Network of Engaged Buddhists (with others in 1989). In this work, Sulak has often been quite critical of the Thai government and has been arrested and imprisoned, as well as exiled, as a result. Though he draws on some aspects of Western thought such as human rights (he studied and worked for several years in the United Kingdom), he is critical of other Western values, especially capitalist models of economic development and the consumer lifestyle that this promotes. His activities and writings have had considerable influence in Thailand and beyond, making him a prominent figure in socially engaged Buddhism (for a discussion of Sulak, see Swearer 1996).

One important theme in Sulak's work, among many others, is his advocacy of small, indigenous and self-sustaining economic communities as an alternative to the global capitalist economic system that he sees dominating and damaging much of the world today, including in particular Thailand (he prefers the traditional term *Siam* as a way of expressing this). This theme nicely illustrates his appeal to traditional Buddhist values in confronting contemporary issues. For Sulak, global capitalism is driven by, and promotes, greed, hatred and delusion—what for Buddhism are the three primary obstacles to enlightenment, contrasting with the generosity, harmony and wisdom that we need. Sulak calls the dominant ethic of the global capitalist system, with its unending pursuit of the acquisition of material wealth, "the religion of consumerism." It has, he says, replaced the temple with the department store as the center of human life (see Sivaraksa 1992: ch. 1). As a way of developing this theme, Sulak has drawn attention to what he regards as the contemporary implications of the five traditional Buddhist moral precepts. For example: not killing implies not allowing people to die of starvation caused by unjust economic systems; not stealing implies using natural resources with moderation; not engaging in sexual misconduct implies opposing structures of male dominance that exploit women; not speaking falsely implies criticizing the transmission of false and misleading information in mass media forms of advertising, political propaganda and education; and not using intoxicants implies opposing economic systems that promote the production of heroin, tobacco and coffee over essential foods such as rice and vegetables (see Sivaraksa 1992: ch. 8; cf. Loy 2003: 34–9). In each case, a moral precept, which was traditionally employed in a more personal context, is taken to have broader implications for our responsibilities regarding social, political and economic institutions.

The Dalai Lama was born in 1935 as Tenzin Gyatso and identified two years later as the 14th Dalai Lama (meaning that he was the rebirth of the 13th Dalai Lama). As such, he has been a spiritual leader of the Geluk order of Tibetan Buddhism and the political leader of Tibet (in exile in Dharamsala, India since 1959 because of the occupation of Tibet by China beginning in 1950). On account of his tireless advocacy for the peaceful liberation of Tibet (for which he won a Noble Peace Prize in 1989), his extensive travels throughout the world, his congenial and persuasive manner and his prolific writing, the Dalai Lama is arguably the best-known Buddhist in the world today. In recent decades, he has gone beyond his specific roles as spiritual and political leader of the Tibetan people and has spoken and written to a broad audience on a wide range of topics including Buddhist philosophy, prominent figures such as Śāntideva, science and religion (as we saw in Chapter 4), happiness and numerous moral and political issues (for examples of the last, see Dalai Lama 1999 and 2011).

Though he is undeniably a Buddhist rooted in the Geluk school (hence specifically committed to a form of Madhyamaka Buddhism), he has often addressed ethical concerns in a language that resonates with many people irrespective of their religious affiliations (for accounts of the Dalai Lama's thought, see Puri 2006 and Vélez de Cea 2013).

An example of this is his signature concept of universal responsibility. As we will see in Chapter 12, the Dalai Lama is a strong advocate of human rights as articulated in documents such as the "Universal Declaration of Human Rights." However, he has also attempted to shift the rhetoric of human rights discourse in a direction more congenial to a Buddhist outlook. "When we demand the rights and freedoms we so cherish," he says, "we should also be aware of our responsibilities" (Dalai Lama 1998a: xviii). Conceptually rights and responsibilities are linked: to say that someone has a right is to say that others have a responsibility to respect that right. But oftentimes in political discussions of human rights it appears that people are more interested asserting their own rights than they are in respecting the rights of others. By emphasizing the importance of responsibility, the Dalai Lama is trying to counter this tendency. He writes:

> I believe that to meet the challenges of our times, human beings will have to develop a greater sense of universal responsibility. Each of us must learn to work not just for one self, one's own family or one's nation, but for the benefit of all humankind. Universal responsibility is the key to human survival. It is the best foundation for world peace.
>
> (Dalai Lama 1998a: xx)

If universal responsibility is the foundation, then there is less danger of making demands for one's own rights a priority. Though the Dalai Lama does not always emphasize its Buddhist origins, the concept of universal responsibility clearly captures the basic Buddhist value of striving impartially to improve the well-being of all people, not simply that of one's friends, family or nation (he says it translates the Tibetan expression *chi sem,* meaning literally universal consciousness; see Dalai Lama 1999: 162). The key Buddhist virtues of compassion and loving-kindness are both expressions of universal responsibility, and the repeated attention the Dalai Lama has given to universal responsibility is one way in which he has tried to influence contemporary moral and political affairs from a Buddhist perspective.

Thich Nhat Hanh was born in Vietnam in 1926 and became a Buddhist monk at age 16. His conception of engaged Buddhism was forged during the Vietnam War: Nhat Hanh was committed to a Buddhist meditative practice and was opposed to the war (siding with neither the communist North nor the American-allied South). This led him to suppose that Buddhist practice itself, though centered on mindfulness meditation, could involve aiding victims of the war and working actively, but non-violently, for its end. In 1966 Nhat Hanh sought to foster this outlook by founding the Order of Interbeing, a lay and monastic Buddhist community, including both men and women, in the Lin Chi (Ch'an) tradition committed to the "Fourteen Mindfulness Trainings" of the Order (there is more about these Trainings later). Shortly thereafter, Nhat Hanh was exiled from Vietnam, welcomed by neither of the opposing sides, and he settled in France where, in 1982, he established Plum Village, a meditation community that became the home of Nhat Hanh and the Order of Interbeing (he was not permitted to visit Vietnam again until 2005). Nhat Hanh is an extraordinarily prolific author, having published scores of books, in prose as well as poetry, on themes pertaining to Buddhist thought and practice (for example, see Hanh 1999 and 2005, and the selections by him in Kotler 1996). He has also travelled extensively throughout the world teaching his distinctive mindfulness-centered form of socially engaged Buddhism (for discussions of Nhat Hanh, see Hunt-Perry and Fine 2000 and S. B. King 1996).

A central motif in Nhat Hanh's approach is the interdependence of all things (recall Indra's net). Nhat Hanh's term 'interbeing' is meant to capture this: "I am, therefore you are. You are, therefore I am. This is the meaning of the word 'interbeing'. We interare" (Hanh 2005: 88). (The term *interbeing* comes from the *Avataṃsaka Sūtra,* a fundamental text in the Hua-yen school; *interbeing* is a substitute for Nhat Hanh's original Vietnamese expression, *Tiep Hien,* which he thought could not be easily translated into English.) For Nhat Hanh, interbeing has profound moral implications. These are expressed in his well-known poem "Please Call Me By My True Names" (Hanh 2005: 67–8). In the aftermath of a pirate's rape of a young girl trying to escape Vietnam by sea, and her subsequent suicide, he wrote this striking stanza:

> I am the twelve-year old girl,
> refugee on a small boat,
> who throws herself into the ocean
> after being raped by a sea pilot.
> And I am the pirate,
> my heart not yet capable
> of seeing and loving.

Nhat Hanh takes the realization of interbeing to compel us to identify with all other persons (indeed with all other things), oppressors as well as their victims, and he takes this identification to be a source of compassion. The poem concludes:

> Please call me by my true names,
> so I can hear all my cries and laughter at once,
> so I can see that my joy and pain are one.
> Please call me by my true names,
> so I can wake up
> and the door of my heart can be left open,
> the door of compassion.

As we have seen, it is a common theme in Buddhist thought that awareness of the way things really are—interdependence, emptiness and the like—is a source of moral insight (see Chapter 8).

Much of Nhat Hanh's moral outlook is contained in the "Fourteen Mindfulness Trainings" (see Hanh 2005: ch. 6). These Trainings are expressed as vows (commitments or determinations) made by those who join the Order of Interbeing. They draw on familiar ethical ideas in the Buddhist tradition (for example, the five precepts, the Eightfold Path, and the Six Perfections), but they are often shaped by contemporary concerns. A sample of key themes in these Trainings will give us a sense of Hanh's approach. First, realizing that happiness is available only in the present moment, there is a commitment to "practice mindful breathing" and to "learn the art of mindful living" (Seventh Training). The emphasis on the importance of bringing mindfulness to each feeling, experience and action in our lives—the calm, focused and alert mental attention first taught by the Buddha in the *Satipaṭṭhāna Sutta* (*MN* I 55–63)—is perhaps the most distinctive feature of Hanh's understanding of engaged Buddhism. For instance, we are mindfully to "acknowledge, embrace, and look deeply into our anger" (Sixth Training). Second, though the Buddhist community should not be turned into "a political instrument," there should be a commitment to "take a clear stand against oppression and injustice" and to "strive to change the situation without engaging in partisan conflicts" (Tenth Training). Third, a member of the community should be "determined to cultivate nonviolence." This includes the promotion of peace education and reconciliation as well as, most importantly, a determination "not to kill and not to let others kill" (Twelfth Training). Fourth, there are commitments to "not live with a vocation that is harmful to humans and nature," to not accumulating "wealth while millions are hungry and dying," and more broadly to "living simply" and consuming in a mindful and responsible manner, for example, by not using drugs or alcohol (Fifth and Eleventh Trainings). Finally, though clearly committed to a definite moral outlook, community members are "determined not to be idolatrous about or bound to any doctrine, theory or ideology, even Buddhist ones," and similarly they are determined "to practice nonattachment from views" in the awareness that "the knowledge we presently possess is not changeless, absolute truth" (First and Second Trainings).

The three figures we have just considered—Sulak Sivaraksa, the Dalai Lama and Thich Nhat Hanh—are all well-known Asian Buddhist leaders. But there are also prominent forms of socially engaged Buddhism in the Western world. An important example of this is The Buddhist Peace Fellowship (BPF), an organization founded in 1978 in Hawai'i by the American Zen Buddhist author Robert Aitken Rōshi and others specifically "to serve as a catalyst for socially engaged Buddhism." Early participants in BPF included influential American Buddhist figures such as Joanna Macy and the poet Gary Snyder. Though centered in the San Francisco Bay Area it now has chapters across the country. BPF presents itself has having an "ecumenical approach to the Dharma." But it is strongly influenced by Nhat Hanh and it is equally influenced by the tradition of American progressive political activism. Its mission is to "link Buddhist teachings of wisdom and compassion with progressive social change." Through activities such as training "radical Buddhist activists" and publishing the magazine *Turning Wheel* (now the online *Turning Wheel Media*) it has advocated a non-violent Buddhist approach to a wide variety of issues such as war, disarmament, nuclear weapons, human rights, social and economic justice, prisons, the environment, sex, gender and race. With its aim of helping "connect Buddhists to social movements and social movement activists to Buddhist practice for mutual deepening and grounding," BPF is a distinctive form of modern Western Buddhism (all quotations are from the BPD website www.buddhistpeacefellowship.org; for an account of BPF, see Simmer-Brown 2000).

There are many more forms of socially engaged Buddhism—many more persons, organizations and orientations—than those we have quite selectively and briefly reviewed here. Engaged Buddhism in all its manifestations, whether in Asian countries or in the Western world, applies a Buddhist moral perspective to an array of social, political and economic concerns in the contemporary world. Though socially engaged Buddhism is a form of Buddhist thought and practice, and is not in itself an academic moral philosophy, its proponents have a variety of philosophical commitments. These commitments will be an important part of the background in our discussion of applied Buddhist ethics in the chapters ahead. There are many topics we might consider, but we will restrict our attention to three topics that are important in themselves and have been central areas of debate: human rights, war and peace and environmental ethics. Our analysis of the interpretive and philosophical dimensions of these topics will often be informed by the activities of socially engaged Buddhists.

CHAPTER **12**

# Human Rights

The relationship between contemporary practices concerning human rights (discourse, advocacy, enforcement and so forth) and Buddhist thought and practice has been extensively debated in recent years (for an overview of the debate, see S.B. King 2005: ch. 5). It is widely acknowledged that human rights were not explicitly recognized or endorsed in traditional Buddhist texts. For example, according to Goodman, "premodern Buddhist ethics simply has no concept of rights" (Goodman 2009: 216). And yet human rights are endorsed and advocated by most (though not all) socially engaged Buddhists today—including each of the four proponents of engaged Buddhism discussed in the last chapter. These two phenomena—the absence of direct recognition of human rights in the tradition and their importance for socially engaged Buddhists today—are part of the background of a recent philosophical debate about whether Buddhism is compatible with human rights. Some scholars have argued that there is a basic affinity between Buddhism and human rights—and perhaps, more strongly, that Buddhism can provide a basis for human rights. Other scholars have argued against this and have maintained that there are important features of human rights—the concept of human rights and especially the role they play in contemporary political affairs—that conflict with or are in serious tension with Buddhist moral perspectives. Another part of the background of this debate is a broader discussion about whether human rights are compatible with "Asian values" (see Bauer and Bell 1999) and an even broader conversation about whether human rights have universal validity as opposed to having validity only in the Western world (see Renteln 1990). In this chapter, we will briefly review the concept, history and contemporary disputes about human rights, and we will then consider arguments first favoring, and then challenging, their compatibility with Buddhism. As we will see, this debate is one of the frontiers of Buddhist modernism, of reflections about the role Buddhist moral thought might play in the modern world.

## Human Rights in the Contemporary World

Much of the contemporary discussion of human rights centers on the "Universal Declaration of Human Rights" (hereafter Declaration) that was passed by the United Nations in 1948 (United Nations 1995b). According to Jack Donnelly, a well-known proponent and theorist of human rights:

> Internationally recognized human rights today provide a standard of political legitimacy. In the contemporary world—the world in which there is an overlapping consensus on the Universal Declaration model—states are legitimate largely to the extent that they respect, protect and implement the rights of their citizens.
>
> (Donnelly 2013: 62)

Donnelly employs Rawls's expression *overlapping consensus* (see Rawls 1993) to claim that throughout the world people with very different "comprehensive doctrines" (religions, philosophies, moralities and so forth) agree on the basic rights of the Declaration, even though their justification of these rights, based on their respective comprehensive doctrines, may well diverge sharply from one another. It is a large question to what extent this is true. But Donnelly's claim provides a useful way of framing the debate about human rights and Buddhism (see C. Taylor 1996). To what extent could Buddhists, with their comprehensive doctrines, participate in an overlapping consensus on the rights stated in the Declaration? There is no question that the Declaration (and subsequent elaborations in other international documents) has been enormously influential, and many discussions of human rights and Buddhism make reference to it. Hence, the Declaration is a natural focal point for our discussion and it will be helpful to begin with a brief account of its history and contents.

In the Declaration, the concept of human rights that is tacitly assumed has several components. First, human rights are *rights,* meaning that they are ways of being treated to which each individual person is entitled. The notion of entitlement is central to the concept of human rights (see Donnelly

2013: 7–8). Second, in the Declaration it was supposed that the primary bearers of human rights are *individual* human beings (though in recent decades there has been much discussion of whether there are other bearers of rights such as non-human animals or groups of persons). In addition, human rights are entitlements that persons have *equally simply in virtue of being human*. Hence, people have them, in the words of the Declaration, irrespective of "race, color, sex, language, religion, political or other opinion, national or social origin, property, birth or other status" (Article 2). Finally, human rights are *moral* rights, meaning that people have them irrespective of their recognition by legal authorities (though they can become legal rights through such recognition).

There is disagreement about whether, or to what extent, human rights may have been recognized in ancient cultures in the Western world or elsewhere. But it is widely agreed that the specific concept of human rights in the Declaration has its origin in Europe in the 17th and 18th centuries, specifically in philosophers such as John Locke and Immanuel Kant, and in Western political documents such as the American "Declaration of Independence" and the French "Declaration of the Rights of Man and the Citizen." The Universal Declaration itself was the product of a political process closely tied to the birth of the United Nations in the aftermath of the atrocities of World War II. The 1945 Charter of the United Nations made it clear that one of the central purposes of the organization was to promote respect for human rights (see United Nations 1995a), and the Declaration spelled out in in some detail what these rights were. The Declaration did not provide an explicit philosophical justification for human rights. However, it did refer to "the dignity and worth of the human person," and this might be thought to be suggestive of a justification. The phrase is certainly reminiscent of Kant's language in *The Metaphysics of Morals*. "Man regarded as a *person*," Kant wrote, "possesses a *dignity* (an absolute inner worth) by which he exacts *respect* for himself from all other rational beings in the world" (Kant 1991: 6:434–5). Donnelly maintains that the rights in the Declaration are grounded in the notion of human dignity, but he thinks that explanations of human dignity might be based on very different comprehensive doctrines (see Donnelly 2013: 131).

In any case, the list of rights delineated in the Declaration's 30 articles is quite extensive. Here is a brief overview of some of its main features. There is to begin with the fundamental "right to life, liberty and security of person" and the corresponding right not to "be held in slavery or servitude" (Articles 3 and 4). In addition, there is a right not to "be subjected to torture or to cruel, inhuman or degrading treatment or punishment" (Article 5). Many of the rights pertain to a person's relationship to the law and legal authorities. For example, all persons are entitled "to equal protection of the law," "no one shall be subjected to arbitrary arrest, detention or exile," and everyone charged with a crime shall have "a fair and public hearing by an independent and impartial tribunal" in which there is a "right to be presumed innocent until proved guilty according to law" (Articles 7, 9, 10 and 11). The Declaration also affirms a host of individual freedoms. Thus there is a "right to freedom of movement and residence," a "right to leave any country," a "right to marry and to found a family," a "right to own property," a "right to freedom of thought, conscience and religion" and a "right to freedom of opinion and expression" (Articles 13, 16, 17, 18 and 19). Several of the rights in the Declaration pertain to political participation. Hence, each person has a "right to freedom of peaceful assembly and association" and a "right to take part in the government of his country" (Articles 20 and 21). There is also a clear endorsement of democracy: "The will of the people shall be the basis of the authority of the government; this will shall be expressed in periodic and genuine elections which shall be by universal and equal suffrage" (Article 21). Many of the remaining rights pertain to material well-being. For example, there is a "right to social security," a "right to work" for a "just and favorable remuneration" and a "right to rest and leisure" (Articles 22, 23 and 24). In general, "everyone has the right to a standard of living adequate for the health and well-being of himself and of his family" (Article 25). Moreover, mothers and children "are entitled to special care and assistance" (Article 25). There is also a "right to education" and a right to participate in cultural life and to share in science and its benefits (Articles 26 and 27). Toward the end of the Declaration it states that "everyone has duties to the community" (Article 29). For the most part, however, the document is about rights rather than duties, about what individual persons are entitled to—though of course the implication is that there is a duty to respect these rights.

Statements of human rights are usually addressed to governments. Though respect for human rights could be part of a personal moral outlook, this is not ordinarily considered to be the whole of such an outlook. Many people would say that personal moral virtue goes well beyond such respect. As a code addressed to governments, it is sometimes said that human rights establish a minimal moral standard that aims to prevent the worst abuses of people, protecting their fundamental interests, rather than striving to bring about an ideal society. There is some truth to this. However, in the Declaration the standard is fairly extensive and the rights concerning material well-being are clearly dependent on resources that are not always immediately available. In any case, despite Donnelly's claim that there is an overlapping consensus on these rights, there have been and continue to be disputes about them. It is obvious that violations of human rights, indeed massive and egregious violations, have persisted throughout the world. Aside from this, there have been philosophical controversies about their significance and validity. Some of these controversies concern the comparative importance of kinds of rights such as rights to individual freedoms, political participation and economic security. But there have also been disagreements about the whole idea of human rights. MacIntyre famously declared that they are "fictions" similar to witches and unicorns (see MacIntyre 1984: 70). He is a proponent of a critique that has been made from several different traditions that questions the importance placed on individual entitlements in contrast to the common good (in recent years this has been pressed by communitarian philosophers in the West). There have also been challenges to the purported universality of human rights. The Declaration presents them "as a common standard of achievement for all peoples and all nations" (Preamble). But some have argued against this, claiming for instance that their individualism is a Western bias that is alien to many cultures outside the West. A well-known example of this dissent is the 1993 "Bangkok Declaration" of Asian states that emphasized the importance of regarding human rights in light of "national and regional particularities and various historical, cultural and religious backgrounds" (quoted in Cerna 1994: 743). Though this statement has been criticized as being a pretense that served the interests of oppressive Asian governments, there are important philosophical issues about whether there is an objective justification of human rights and whether they could be justified from the standpoint of various Asian traditions. This is an important part of the context in which the debate about the relationship between Buddhism and human rights has taken place.

## Arguments Favoring the Compatibility of Buddhism and Human Rights

Some Western philosophers think that there is an objective justification of human rights (for example, see Gewirth 1982). If there were an objective justification of human rights on the basis of a normative theory that Buddhists were committed to accepting (such as those discussed in Chapter 6), then that would show that Buddhism is not only compatible with human rights but provides a rationale for it. For example, there might be a deontological justification for human rights (as Kant might be thought to have provided) or a rule-utilitarian argument in favor of human rights. However, arguments of this kind have not played a central role in discussions of Buddhism and human rights. Rather, these discussions have focused on explicit features of traditional Buddhist morality, or other features of Buddhist thought, and have considered how these features might relate to the notion of human rights (Keown, Prebish and Husted 1998 is a helpful collection of papers).

In one respect, the most ambitious argument in support of the claim that there is a Buddhist basis for human rights was made by L.P.N. Perera in a Buddhist commentary on the entire Declaration (see Perera 1991). Perera examined each Article in the Declaration and tried to show that, at least for the most part, the Article was supported by the teaching of the Buddha (mainly as represented in the Pali Canon, with supplementary reference to later commentaries and to Aśoka). From one point of view, Perera's argument is a powerful one: If we ask the question "Would a follower of the teaching of the Buddha have any basis for violating people's human rights?" then it might plausibly be said that Perera has shown that to a very large extent the answer is "No." Insofar as this is true, it would establish a kind of compatibility between the Buddha's teaching and human rights. However, from another point of view, Perera's argument appears inconclusive. This can be seen in his claim, in the discussion of Article 3, that "the Buddhist concept of human rights is founded" on the belief that "all life has a desire to safeguard itself and to make itself comfortable and happy" (Perera 1991: 29). It is difficult to see why a desire of all living things would provide a basis for human rights as envisioned in the Declaration (see Keown 1995: 28). How does a *desire,* even if universal, become an *entitlement* that we ought to respect? This question brings into focus the basic difficulty in Perera's project: the concept of a human right as *an entitlement of individual persons* is not thematized. As a result, Perera makes a series of claims to the effect that, from a Buddhist standpoint, something is either good, valuable, important and so forth or else morally ought to be done, and he concludes straightaway from these claims that, from a Buddhist standpoint, there is a human right to whatever is under consideration. For example, in the discussion of the same article, he says that the first moral precept that we ought not to kill shows that Buddhism recognized "the right to life" (Perera 1991: 29). This only follows, however, if what we ought to do is based on the recognition of people's rights. Without showing that the Buddha thought people had rights, or was committed to thinking this, the fact that he thought something was good or ought to be done does not by itself provide a Buddhist basis for human rights.

This lacuna is recognized by Keown in one of the seminal discussions of Buddhism and human rights. He does thematize the concept of a right and he grants that Pali and Sanskrit, the traditional languages of Indian Buddhism, have no word for a right as an individual entitlement. But he argues that "the concept of rights is implicit in classical Buddhism" (Keown 1995: 22). Keown's argument for this claim is that there is a concept of duties in the Buddha's teaching and duties imply rights. Hence, by endorsing many duties, the Buddha implicitly endorsed many rights. In support of the claim that the Buddha had a concept of duties, Keown refers to texts such as the *Sigālaka Sutta* in which the Buddha describes the reciprocal responsibilities of various pairs of persons. For example, a husband should give authority to his wife and she should reciprocate by "being skillful and diligent in all she does" (*DN* III 190). It is not implausible to interpret these statements as depictions of duties (for discussion of whether the Buddha had a concept of duty or obligation, see Chapter 6). However, the claim that duties imply rights has been challenged. In a response to Keown, Craig Ihara argued that in cooperative activities in which there are role-based responsibilities there may be duties without corresponding rights. For example, a ballerina and her male partner may have responsibilities to come together at a certain point. But if the male fails to do so, he has not violated the rights of the ballerina by depriving her of something to which she is entitled as an individual. He has simply failed to fulfill his responsibility in their joint activity. And the same could be said of husbands and wives (see Ihara 1995). Moreover, in the philosophical literature on rights, the thesis that duties entail rights (that my having a duty to do X entails that another person has a right to my doing X) has been widely challenged (for discussion, see Feinberg 1980a). For instance, consider the duty of a citizen to vote or of a person to give to charity. It seems difficult to identify specific individuals who have a right to these actions. Of course, it is plausible to suppose that some duties do entail rights. For example, a teacher's duty to grade fairly would seem to entail a student's right to be graded fairly, and perhaps this is the kind of duty the Buddha had in mind in the *Sigālaka Sutta*.

In any case, even if the Buddha (or Buddhist traditions) had, or was committed to having, a concept of a right as an individual entitlement, the question remains whether he thought, or was committed to thinking, that there are human rights—rights which individual persons have simply in virtue of being human. Various arguments have been given for supposing that there is a Buddhist basis for human rights. One common argument is that human rights involve a doctrine of moral equality—the Declaration says that human beings have equal rights—and there is a clear affirmation of some form of moral equality in Buddhist teaching (for example, see Adam 2013, Dalai Lama 1998b: 101 and S. B. King 2005: 145). For instance, the Four Noble Truths apply equally to all human beings: all human beings suffer, but all are capable of attaining enlightenment and overcoming suffering. This is evident in the fact that the Buddha challenged the Indian caste system by declaring that members of any caste were capable of enlightenment (see *DN* III 83). Moreover, he said that both men and women could attain enlightenment (see *SN* I 70). Again, key Buddhist virtues such as loving-kindness and compassion require us to be concerned with the happiness and suffering of all human beings equally. For example, Buddhaghosa described meditation techniques in which we learn to extend loving-kindness and compassion to all beings (see *Vism.* ch. IX), and in Mahāyāna Buddhism the Bodhisattva seeks enlightenment so that all sentient beings may become enlightened.

There are, however, some qualifications that should be noted in the claim that Buddhist teaching is basically egalitarian in character. This is especially true with respect to gender. In the Pali Canon, the Buddha sometimes praised women for their spiritual accomplishments, and he established a monastic order for women as well as men because he recognized that both could attain enlightenment. Nonetheless, as we saw in Chapter 1, he established this order only after refusing to do so on three occasions. Moreover, he imposed eight rules on the order that rendered it institutionally subordinate to the male order. For example, women could be admitted only with the approval of both men and women whereas men could be admitted with the approval of men alone. Again, men could admonish women, but women could not admonish men. Hence, gender egalitarianism was tempered with elements of male domination (see Gowans 2003: 165–7). Perhaps on account of this domination, the monastic order of women established by the Buddha did not survive in the Theravāda tradition (in the last several decades there have been attempts to revive it). However, a record of the early history remains in the *Therīgāthā,* a Pali Canon text in which women of the ancient monastic community speak about their own spiritual aspirations and attainments (see Murcott 1991). In recent years, Buddhist thought and practice has been the subject of a number of feminist analyses and critiques (for an overview, see Wilson 2012). The *Therīgāthā* has been an invaluable resource for a feminist reconstruction of Buddhism. According to Rita M. Gross, a prominent feminist Buddhist scholar, though Buddhist institutions have been deeply patriarchal, there is nothing in fundamental Buddhist teaching that supports the oppression of women (see Gross 1993). Thus, it may be argued that, despite the institutional history, a central theme in various Buddhist traditions is that all human beings, men and women both, are equally worthy of our compassion and capable of enlightenment. This might be interpreted as providing a basis for equal human rights.

A possible difficulty with this argument is that it may establish too much because in Buddhism, not only all human beings, but all sentient beings, are worthy of compassion and are ultimately capable of enlightenment. If these features are a basis for assigning rights, then some beings besides human beings may have rights. However, the Declaration did not envision that any beings other than human beings have rights. Of course, in recent decades some people have argued that non-human animals have some rights as well as human beings, and from this perspective it might be considered an advantage of Buddhism that it extends moral concern to all sentient beings (see Chapter 14).

Another difficulty, or at least limitation, in the moral equality argument is that by itself it would seem to establish too little. Human rights presuppose a concept of moral equality, but moral equality alone is not sufficient to justify human rights. As was seen in Chapter 6, act-utilitarianism also presupposes a concept of moral equality, but it makes no reference to rights. It simply states that in assessing the consequences of our actions the well-being of each human (or sentient) being counts equally. In fact, act-utilitarianism could in principle justify torturing a person on the ground that in a particular situation this would bring about the best overall consequences. This would be a violation of the right not to be tortured in the Declaration (this is a standard objection to act-utilitarianism). This would mean that, if the best interpretation of Buddhist ethical thought is that it is committed to act-utilitarianism, then it would seem to preclude human rights. In any case, for those who think Buddhist ethics could provide a basis for human rights, something more needs to be said than that it has a concept of moral equality.

A central issue is why we should think that human beings, in virtue of being human, have rights such as those enunciated in the Declaration. As we saw earlier, the Declaration does not offer an explicit justification for human rights. But it does refer to "the dignity and worth of the human person," and it might be thought that human dignity provides a justification for human rights. Once again, though human dignity is not featured in the traditional moral vocabularies of Buddhism, it has been argued that there is a basis in Buddhism for a concept of human dignity. The most prominent candidate for this is the capability of human beings to attain enlightenment. For example, according to Keown, "the source of human dignity in Buddhism lies nowhere else than in the literally infinite capacity of human nature for participation in goodness" (Keown 1995: 29–30; cf. Adam 2013, Harvey 2000: 119–21, Sevilla 2010 and Shiotsu 1999). By this he means our capacity for enlightenment, what in in Mahāyāna Buddhism was sometimes referred to as our Tathāgata-garbha or Buddha-nature (see Chapter 2). If we think of enlightenment as the highest form of goodness, then it might seem plausible to suppose that a being with the capacity to attain this has a special kind of worth—dignity—in virtue of that capacity. This would be analogous to the way in which Kant supposed human beings possess dignity in virtue of their freedom and rationality (which could be seen as a capacity for a kind of enlightenment). In both cases, human beings ought to be respected on account of their dignity and this means respecting their rights.

An objection to this argument was raised in Chapter 8: if Buddha-nature (or other depictions of our capacity for enlightenment) is a metaphysical theory, then it looks like an attribution of an inherent nature that would conflict with the no-self and emptiness teachings, but if it is a mere soteriological device to encourage the pursuit of enlightenment, then it would not seem to provide a metaphysical basis for human dignity. As we saw, a possible response to this objection is that Buddha-nature could be considered a metaphysical theory at the level of conventional truth and could provide a justifying role for human rights at that level.

Another objection reprises a difficulty noted earlier: dignity-based defenses of human rights typically assume that dignity is a feature of all and only human beings, but in Buddhism the capacity for enlightenment is ordinarily a feature of all beings in the cycle of rebirth, not simply human beings. One response to this objection is that birth as a human being is distinctive in that it is an especially propitious stage in the cycle of rebirth to pursue and attain enlightenment (see S. B. King 2000: 300–1). This makes it possible to say that, even though all beings in the cycle of rebirth are worthy of moral concern, human beings deserve special consideration (something that, in various ways, is often supposed in Buddhist ethical thought in any case). It could then be claimed that rights such as those stated in the Declaration spell out the consideration that is needed. Hence, people have rights not to be harmed in ways that would prevent or impede the pursuit of enlightenment and they have rights to be benefited in ways that would facilitate this pursuit. On this approach, we could then say, for example, that the precept that we ought not to kill is based on a right to life, that the precept that we ought not to steal is based on a right to property and so forth.

There are other Buddhist arguments in favor of human rights that emphasize different aspects of Buddhist morality. For example, Garfield has claimed that compassion is the basic value in Buddhism and that from this standpoint human rights have an important, albeit subordinate, role to play. He criticizes a conception of human rights that he associates with liberal morality on the ground that it protects a right to private life in which compassion is morally optional. From a Buddhist perspective, compassion is not an option, but is the heart of morality. Moreover, the compassionate person seeks to benefit others irrespective of whether or not they have a right to this concern. Nonetheless, Garfield claims, a structure of rights may be valuable from a Buddhist perspective, for example as a supplement to compassion (to help extend the limited reach and failures of "natural compassion") or as "part of a rhetorical demonstration of the humanity" of people "so as to generate compassion" (Garfield 2002b: 199–201). On the critique of liberal defenses of human rights, it is not clear that people who regarded human rights as a moral minimum for governments to respect would need to think that in personal morality compassion is optional. However, the main point, that Buddhist compassion could provide a basis for human rights, might be considered an employment of Buddhist skillful means whereby a widely accepted moral vocabulary that is not native to Buddhism is used to facilitate the ends of Buddhist compassion.

In any event, Garfield presented this argument as a defense of the Dalai Lama's advocacy of human rights in light of his commitment to the primacy of Buddhist compassion. It is easy to see that this approach is in line with the importance the Dalai Lama assigns to universal responsibility in discussions of human rights (explained in the last chapter). The orientation of Garfield and the Dalai Lama is not to fully embrace human rights as they are often understood by Western proponents, but to show how Buddhists can find a real but qualified place for human rights in their overall ethical outlook (see also Hershock 2000). The objections we will consider in the next section will make it more evident why Buddhists might be attracted to such a "middle way" stance on human rights.

## Arguments Challenging the Compatibility of Buddhism and Human Rights

Many of the arguments that question the compatibility of Buddhism and human rights concern practices or outlooks commonly associated with human rights and not necessarily the basic concept of human rights. Hence, though these arguments are sometimes presented as flatly rejecting compatibility, in many cases they may be interpreted as suggesting that a Buddhist acceptance of human rights would need to be limited or qualified in some important way (the "middle way" stance). We have already seen some of these arguments. The contention that the capacity for enlightenment applies to all sentient beings and not just human beings need not undermine the claim that this capacity provides a basis for human rights, but it does imply that moral concern should extend beyond human beings. This is something that some proponents of human rights may deny, but this denial does not seem essential to human rights advocacy. Again, the contention that, from a Buddhist standpoint, we should be more concerned with compassion or universal responsibility than with rights need not preclude a concern with rights. But it may well mean a moral outlook with a different emphasis from that of many proponents of human rights.

One argument that might seem to preclude human rights altogether is the assertion that the no-self teaching means that there is no entity that could have rights (see Jeffreys 2003: 275–7). Proponents of compatibility sometimes dismiss this objection quickly, but there is a real issue here. Most advocates of human rights presuppose that the right-holder is a self that Buddhism denies. However, in this respect the no-self teaching raises a problem for many moral outlooks, not simply for human rights. Virtually any moral viewpoint presupposes that there are agents, but the no-self teaching denies this as well. Buddhaghosa said, "doing exists although there is no doer" (*Vism.* XVI 513). Hence, this problem is not peculiar to the human rights position. Moreover, as we have sense, there are Buddhist responses to the problem. The most prominent response is that, though we cannot speak of selves in ultimate truth, we can speak of them in conventional truth. This would mean that Buddhist human rights discourse would have to be situated at the level of conventional truth. No doubt this is not something most human rights advocates would accept, but it is not an unusual position for a Buddhist to take. This need not mean that human rights are unimportant in Buddhism any more than it would mean that virtues such as compassion are unimportant because it is only in conventional truth that there are agents with virtues.

A related objection is that human rights discourse emphasizes the importance of individuals in ways that are at odds with Buddhist teaching (see Ihara 1995: 49–51; cf. Shiotsu 1999). For example, emphasizing rights of individuals might encourage the illusion of the self or it might encourage us to think of society as a collection of atomic individuals rather than as interconnected beings. Such critiques echo many communitarian critiques of rights perspectives as being excessively individualistic (though communitarians do not typically deny that there is a self, they do often claim that liberal rights theories presuppose an atomic self that is a fiction). One Buddhist response to the individualism objection is to suggest that individualism is not entirely foreign to Buddhism. For example, as we have seen, at the end of his life the Buddha said to his disciple Ānanda, "you should live as islands unto yourselves, being your own refuge, with no one else as your refuge, with the Dharma as an island, with the Dharma as your refuge, with no other refuge" (*DN* II 100). The stress on self-reliance in early Buddhism could be seen as providing a basis for compatibility with individual human rights (see Perera 1991: 21). However, the emphasis in Mahāyāna Buddhism is rather different: we are often told that enlightenment is not entirely dependent on individuals because there are numerous Buddhas and

Bodhisattvas available, and perhaps needed, to help us attain enlightenment. Another more common response to the individualism objection is to try to show how human rights could be defended without being excessively individualistic (as some communitarians have tried to do). A Buddhist advocate of human rights cannot very well encourage attachment to self or discourage recognizing our interdependence with one another. But perhaps acceptance of human rights does not require this. As we will see, this is a common theme in responses to the remaining challenges to compatibility.

An example of the concern with the association of rights and individualism is the claim that Buddhists should be skeptical about the right to property because of the ideological connections between this right and the "emphasis on individuals blinding pursuing their own selfish interests" (Junger 1995: 83). It might be thought that advocating property rights would encourage greed. As we have seen, greed is one of the three obstacles to enlightenment and socially engaged Buddhists such as Sulak Sivaraksa and Thich Nhat Hanh have spoken against it. Hence, it might be supposed that Buddhists would have reason to reject human rights that center on the right to property. As noted earlier, the right to property is included in the Declaration, though it is one right among others and is not obviously given primacy. However, it is arguable that there is a close historical relationship between the assertion of the right to property, the development of capitalism and the encouragement of greed (Locke is often featured in accounts of this relationship). From this perspective, there is a point to this objection.

In response, it may be said that Buddhists can affirm the right to property as one right among many without endorsing whatever historical association it may have with greed. In fact, the moral precept that we ought not to steal, part of "right action" in the Eightfold Path, would seem to presuppose some conception of property ownership (see Perera 1991: 74). Moreover, in the *Aggañña Sutta* story of origins discussed in the last chapter, a ruler is appointed in order to protect people's property (see *DN* III 92–3). Hence, there is some basis for supposing that the Buddha affirmed both that people were entitled to their property and that they should strive to overcome greed. Nonetheless, attachment to property is a deep concern in Buddhism. This is why Buddhist monks and nuns have almost nothing in the way of personal possessions—in the Pali Canon only a robe, almsfood, a resting place and medicine (see *MN* I 10). Hence, a Buddhist affirmation of the right to property is likely to be accompanied by a stronger affirmation of the dangers of attachment to it.

Another expression of the concern about the connection between rights and individualism is the contention that human rights advocates commonly assume that the assertion of human rights implies that self-respect is an important character trait and that self-respect may require assertively demanding that one's rights be respected (see Gowans 2006). For example, Joel Feinberg says that to think that I have rights is to "have that minimal self-respect that is necessary to be worthy of the love and esteem of others" (Feinberg 1980b: 151), and Alan Gewirth maintains that for someone to have human rights "is for him to be in a position to make morally justified stringent, effective demands on other persons" (Gewirth 1982: 11). Moreover, in this view failure to make these demands is a kind of servility. For Feinberg, "not to claim in the appropriate circumstances that one has a right is to be spiritless or foolish" (Feinberg 1980b: 151). The apparent difficulty for a Buddhist advocate of human rights is clear enough: promoting self-esteem and standing up for one's own rights would seem to be ways of encouraging attachment to self and would seem to be contrary to virtues such as patience. For example, in the *Dhammapada* we are encouraged to be patient and to endure without anger "insult, assault, and binding" (Carter and Palihawadana 2000: 399), and Śāntideva says "even if people are extremely malignant, all that is skilful should be done for them" (*BCA* 6.120). These passages appear very much at odds with the advice to stand up for our rights.

One response to this objection is to argue that promoting self-respect and standing up for our rights are not essential features of accepting human rights. But many human rights advocates believe that these are extremely important. For example, according to Martin Luther King, Jr., freedom "must be demanded by the oppressed" (M. L. King 2000: 68). Another response is to say that, though a fully enlightened person would not be concerned to stand up for his or her own rights (in accordance with the aforementioned passages), it may well be appropriate for persons who are not yet enlightened to do so. In fact, making sure that one's rights are respected might be a pre-condition of pursuing enlightenment. Hence, on the assumption that most persons are not enlightened, there is no reason that Buddhists should not affirm to such persons the importance of standing up for their rights. The Dalai Lama, though stressing the importance of universal responsibility, might be interpreted as taking this position. He says "it is natural and just for nations, peoples and individuals to demand respect for their rights and freedoms" (Dalai Lama 1998b: 105).

There is a larger issue in the background of this discussion. Human rights advocacy often presupposes what might be called a confrontational or adversarial model of politics, but there is a good deal in Buddhist ethical thought that encourages something rather different, what might be called a reconciliation or consensus model of politics (see Gowans 2006 and S. B. King 2005: 133–7). The first model sees individuals as distinct from one another, each equal in inherent worth or dignity, but with competing interests. On this model, in the face of oppression, individuals are encouraged to confront their oppressors and demand that their rights be respected. The voices of anger, indignation and resentment are familiar modes of expression in this mode of political engagement. This adversarial approach is, of course, a familiar one that is taken for granted in much human rights advocacy in the world today. However, the main features of Buddhist moral teaching might be taken to suggest a rather different approach to politics. This second model also regards individuals as equal in inherent worth or dignity, but it sees them as interconnected and ultimately as having shared interests. On this model, there is an effort to overcome oppression, but people are encouraged to identify with both victims and their oppressors (recall Nhat Hanh's poem "Please Call Me By My True Names"), and to strive to improve their relations through compassion and loving-kindness for all persons on the basis of peaceful persuasion and encouragement rather than through the angry expression of demands. As we have seen, there is much in the human rights agenda that Buddhists have reason to agree with, and for this reason most socially engaged Buddhists have been willing to embrace the language of human rights even though it is not the natural language of Buddhist traditions. But the frequent association of the promotion of this agenda with a confrontational mode of politics may be a reason why Buddhists such as the Dalai Lama have tried to shift the moral discourse from individual rights to universal responsibilities. This is more in keeping with a reconciliation approach. We will see in the next chapter that this outlook is related to Buddhist attitudes to war and peace.

CHAPTER **13**

# Violence, War and Peace

In the Western world, Buddhism is widely regarded as a religion devoted to peace, non-violence, pacifism and opposition to war. There are obvious reasons for this reputation. Traditional Buddhist texts advocated the value of non-harming *(ahiṁsā/ahiṃsā)*. For example, in the *Dhammapada* we are told "one who is harmless toward all living beings is called a 'noble one'" (Carter and Palihawadana 2000: 270). In the Buddha's original teaching, "abandoning the killing of living beings" was said to be the first form of "bodily conduct in accordance with the Dharma" (*MN* I 287). Not killing has traditionally been regarded as the first of the five basic moral precepts in Buddhism. Moreover, all of the proponents of socially engaged Buddhism featured in Chapter 11 have expressed their strong opposition to violence and war. For example, as we have seen, Nhat Hanh stated his determination not to kill in the Twelfth Mindfulness Training. Moreover, the Dalai Lama has regularly spoken of his "firm commitment to nonviolence" (Dalai Lama 1996: 6). There is no question that opposition to violence and killing is a fundamental value in all Buddhist traditions.

However, this is not the whole story. Many Japanese Zen Buddhists were ardent supporters of Japanese militarism leading up to and during World War II (see Victoria 2006 and Ives 2009a), and more recently Sinhala Buddhists in Sri Lanka engaged in a long, violent struggle against the mostly Hindu Tamil people with whom they share the island (see Bartholomeusz 1999 and 2002, and Bond 2009). In both cases, ostensibly Buddhist reasons were offered in support of violence. Moreover, to complicate the picture further, during the Vietnam War some Vietnamese Buddhists immolated themselves to protest war, and in recent years some Tibetan Buddhists have done the same to protest the Chinese occupation of Tibet.

It might be argued that these events should be regarded as aberrations that are contrary to Buddhist teachings and show only that people do not always live up to the values of their own religion. This is no doubt true in some cases. But it is not the full explanation of Buddhist participation in violence. Recent scholarship has made it clear that there is more complexity in Buddhist positions concerning violence and war than its peaceful image would suggest (for example, see the essays in Jerryson and Juergensmeyer 2010 and Zimmermann 2006). As we will see, there are purported justifications for some forms of violence in some Buddhist texts and traditions ancient as well as modern. In fact, there is more variation in the positions of contemporary socially engaged Buddhists than their pacifist reputation might imply.

In contemporary Western thought about morality and war, it is common to distinguish pacifism, the view that war is never morally justified, from just war theory, the view that war is sometimes morally justified. These categories did not explicitly inform traditional Buddhist thinking about morality and war. Much Buddhist ethical thought looks to be opposed to violence and killing, but on occasion it suggests that these may be justified in some circumstances. In view of this, it might be argued that some Buddhists were implicitly committed to pacifism while others were implicitly committed to some form of just war theory. Or it might be argued that contemporary Buddhist positions could be constructed and defended in terms of these categories. In order to assess such possibilities, we will first briefly explain the Western debate about morality and war. We will then review some traditional Buddhist texts respectively opposing and supporting violence, and we will examine some of the more recent discussions referred to earlier pertaining to this issue.

## Western Moral Philosophies of War

There has been considerable reflection about morality and war in the Western world. In these discussions, war is usually understood as more or less organized violence between political communities as a means of resolving a disagreement about some issue of political control or governance. In contemporary thought, three broad philosophical approaches to thinking about the morality of war are commonly distinguished (for an overview, see Orend 2013). Each approach has a long history and each has numerous variations. The best-known and probably most widely accepted approach is *just war theory:* this claims that there is a set of conditions according to which, first, engaging in war is sometimes morally justified and sometimes not, and second, some ways of fighting war are morally justified and some are not. A second approach is *pacifism:* this contends that war is never morally justified (though we will see that there are some difficulties with this definition). Finally, there is a third approach that is often called *realism:* this claims, not that war is always morally justified, but that morality does not apply to the issue of fighting war (a descriptive form of realism says that as a matter of fact people do not consider morality when it comes to war, but it is the normative form, that they are correct in thinking this, that contrasts with the other two approaches). On occasion some Buddhists may have exhibited a realist approach to war: they may have supposed that war is basically outside the concerns of ordinary morality. But the dominant traditions of Buddhist ethical thought are more plausibly interpreted as implicitly debating the respective merits of positions more akin to pacifism and just war theory.

In Western traditions, just war theory has its roots in philosophers such as Aristotle and Augustine, and it has become more sophisticated over time as proponents of the theory have developed it in the face of new circumstances. In contemporary discussions, it is widely agreed that the theory consists of a set of conditions specifying when it is morally justified to enter war *(jus ad bellum)* and what forms of conducting war are morally justified *(jus in bello)*. (In some versions, there is a third category, *jus post bellum,* specifying morally just ways of terminating war.)

Six conditions for entering a war are commonly accepted by proponents of the just war theory. First and most important, the war must be fought for a just cause (Just Cause). Self-defense against an unjust attack is commonly regarded as the primary just cause, but there are other candidates such as helping others who have been unjustly attacked or liberating people from oppression by their own government (humanitarian intervention). From a human rights standpoint, establishing a just cause might be understood in terms of protecting human rights. Second, the motive for fighting the war must be (or at least include) the just cause and not some ulterior illicit motive such as ethnic hatred (Just Intention). Third, the war must be fought by an appropriate political authority on the basis of proper procedures such as those specified in a constitution (Appropriate Authority). Fourth, the war must be a last resort because diplomatic or other non-military efforts at resolution have failed and are likely to continue to fail (Last Resort). Fifth, there must be a reasonable likelihood that the war will achieve its end (Reasonable Chance of Success). Finally, it must be reasonable to expect that the war will produce proportionate results: overall more benefit than harm or at least not a great deal more harm than benefit (Proportionality).

With respect to fighting a war, a variety of conditions have been discussed. The most important of these is that military force may be intentionally directed only at combatants and not at civilians; that is, at those who are engaged in fighting and not others (Discrimination). Other conditions include using only as much force as is necessary to achieve an objective (Necessity) and using force that is proportionate to the importance of the objective (Proportionality).

In both cases, entering and conducting a war, the central contention of just war theorists is ordinarily that *each* of the conditions must be fulfilled for a country's participation in a war to be just. However, there is some disagreement among proponents of just war theories about which conditions should be included. For example, if there were a right to overthrow an unjust government, as Locke believed, then the Appropriate Authority condition would need to be modified. There are also disagreements about how the various conditions should be understood and interpreted (the formulations above are only approximations of commonly accepted ideas). But there is a central ethical thought animating all versions of just war theory: as bad as war is, it is sometimes morally justified and it is important to specify the conditions for determining when it is justified. There are also disagreements about the philosophical justification of the theory. It might be supported by a deontological or rule-consequentialist approach (see Chapter 6), but historically the just war theory was closely associated with the natural law tradition and in contemporary accounts justification often takes the form of elaborating intuitions such as the belief that, though it is ordinarily morally wrong to kill a person, there are exceptions to this rule such as self-defense.

Pacifism is often understood to be the view that war is never morally justified. There are, however, some difficulties with this definition. With respect to ordinary use of the term, this definition may be too strong because some people who are considered, or consider themselves, pacifists may accept a weaker position such as that contemporary wars involving modern weapons are always wrong or that actual wars have always been wrong (allowing in both cases that in principle a war could be justified). The definition may also be too weak in that pacifists may be opposed to all forms of violence or killing, not simply war, and they may embrace a doctrine of active non-violent resistance to injustice such as was advocated by Mahatma Gandhi and Martin Luther King, Jr. Stronger positions that object to *any* use of violence or the threat of violence might put into question the legitimacy of governments insofar as they typically depend on this in their law enforcement systems (Leo Tolstoy moved in this direction). Though many who consider themselves pacifists do not accept this position, it is clear that opposition to all violence and killing would have implications far beyond opposition to war. We will see that this point has some bearing on the interpretation of Buddhist thought.

In the Western world, pacifism has often been based on religious convictions, usually Christian beliefs rooted in texts such as the Sermon on the Mount. However, there are also Indian sources of religious pacifism—Hindu, Jain and of course Buddhist—that have now become influential in the West (conversely Gandhi drew on Western as well as Indian sources). In all these cases, pacifism is usually an important aspect of a broad program of spiritual discipline and transformation. But there are secular pacifists for whom the stance is basically an ethical or political position. The most obvious philosophical justification of pacifism is a strong deontological position according to which violence and killing are always wrong (perhaps based on some general moral principle such as Kant's Categorical Imperative, though Kant himself was not a pacifist). Rule-consequentialist justifications are also possible, but these are more likely to result in a more qualified outlook according to which violence, killing, war and the like are typically wrong, but could be justified in circumstances where they would bring about the best result. A virtue ethics justification is also possible, according to which a virtuous agent would never kill, though this was certainly not the position of Aristotle.

## Buddhist Opposition to Violence and Killing

From one point of view, it is obvious that Buddhism is opposed to violence and killing. Speaking about Buddhist monks, the Buddha said: "abandoning the killing of living beings, he abstains from killing living beings; with rod and weapon laid aside, gentle and kindly, he abides compassionate to all living beings" (*MN* I 345). This teaching was not directed only to monks and nuns. A passage in the opening paragraph of this chapter was addressed to laypersons and employed the exact same formulation, "abandoning the killing of living beings," to describe what is "in accordance with the Dharma" and so would have positive benefits on account of the doctrines of karma and rebirth (*MN* I 287). Not killing is commonly regarded as the first of the five basic moral precepts in the Buddha's teaching (for example, see *AN* III 212) and passages opposing killing are omnipresent in the Pali Canon. For example, in the *Dhammapada* we are told that enmity is to be quelled "by the absence of enmity" and that "one should neither slay nor cause to slay" (Carter and Palihawadana 2000: 5 and 129). Opposition to violence is expressed in a variety of ways. Right livelihood is an important aspect of the Eightfold Path and the Buddha makes it clear that "trading in weapons" is a form of wrong livelihood (see *AN* III 208). He also said that mercenaries who die in war would be reborn in "the 'Battle-Slain Hell'" (*SN* IV 309). There is opposition to violence and killing in Mahāyāna Buddhism as well. For example, Nāgārjuna makes it clear that not killing is one of "the ten gleaming paths of action" and that killing will have negative karmic consequences such as a short life (see Hopkins 1998: verses 8, 9 and 14). And Śāntideva vows "Let there never be harm to anyone on account of me" (*BCA* 3.14).

In addition, Buddhist texts focus much attention on analyzing the roots of violence and killing in mental states such as craving, attachment, greed, anger, hatred and ignorance, and explaining how to overcome these states by developing virtues such as compassion, loving-kindness, patience and wisdom (see Harvey 2000: 239–49). A good deal of Buddhist teaching is centered on the development of a non-violent state of character. There is much less concern, however, with analyzing why violence and killing are wrong and with exploring the various implications of this position.

In one respect, the rationale for the opposition to violence and killing is obvious: the primary aim in the Buddhist moral outlook is to overcome suffering, and violence and killing typically result in suffering. Nonetheless, this basic point leaves open important questions such as whether it would be wrong to kill one person if this was the only way to prevent that person from killing many others. The claim that this would not be wrong, and might in fact be morally required, is a key feature of the perspective that leads to just war theory. A straightforward application of the first precept, however, would seem to reject this claim and support some form of pacifism (see Schmithausen 1999: 45–9). This appears to be the dominant view in the Pali Canon. According to Rupert Gethin, in the Abhidharma tradition of Theravāda Buddhism, killing could not be justified on the basis of compassion (see Gethin 2004). However, as we have seen before and will see again in this chapter, numerous Buddhist texts suggest that there are exceptions to this precept. Whether there are such texts in the Pali Canon is not obvious, but it is certainly the case that there are such texts in Mahāyāna Buddhism. Suggestions that there are exceptions to the prohibition on killing might be thought to lend support to the interpretation that Buddhism, or at least some manifestations of it, is implicitly committed to something akin to just war theory.

It might be supposed that the interpretations of Buddhist ethics in Chapter 6 (as a deontological, consequentialist or virtue ethics normative theory) would help resolve the question whether Buddhist ethics is best interpreted in terms of pacifism or just war theory. For example, since pacifism is often understood as the strong deontological position that killing is always wrong without exception, if Buddhist ethics were interpreted as committed to a form of deontology, then this might be a reason to interpret it as committed to pacifism. For the most part, however, the help is likely to move in the other direction: the interpretation of passages pertaining to violence may provide a basis for determining which normative theory, if any, is the best interpretation of the commitments of Buddhist ethics as a whole. For instance, since exceptions to the first precept are recognized in some texts, so that killing is sometimes permissible or obligatory, then that would be a reason to think that Buddhist ethics, at least as represented in those texts, is not committed to a strong deontological theory in which there are exception-less moral rules stating our obligations.

Much Buddhist moral teaching was directed to individuals, usually monastics but sometimes lay followers, who were seeking enlightenment or at least a better rebirth. Many of the texts opposing violence and killing are found in this context: they appear to be primarily concerned to articulate a personal moral code for these persons. Most of the texts that suggest exceptions to non-violence have a rather different focus. They pertain to actions of Buddhas and Bodhisattvas or else to the actions of kings. The former may leave open questions about their implications for the lives of ordinary persons. The latter is a key arena in human life where pressure is likely to be put on the opposition to violence and killing. It is ordinarily assumed that a primary responsibility of a king, indeed of any government, is to provide for the security of its citizens, and this is commonly believed to require both a law enforcement system to ensure domestic tranquility and a military force to protect against foreign attack. Both of these—law enforcement and a military force—usually involve violence and killing (or at least the threat of these). As we saw in Chapter 11, issues of kingship were sometimes addressed in the Pali Canon. Some of these texts might be interpreted as supposing, perhaps in a utopian vein, that a king could rule without violence. For example, the 10 moral virtues of a king include gentleness, patience, non-anger and non-violence (see Collins 1998: 460–1 and Rahula 1974: 85). Moreover, another text depicts a king (the Buddha in a previous lifetime) who refuses to use violence to protect his kingdom. After being attacked and imprisoned, the king directs compassion to the attacker, who then experiences great pain, which leads to the liberation of both the king and his kingdom (see Jenkins 2010: 65–6). The message, perhaps, is that rule through the power of non-violent compassion is possible. However, by and large there is little indication in the Pali Canon that the Buddha thought that a king could rule without the use of violence. Moreover, as we will now see, there is some indication that he thought that political rule required violence—a position that is clearly affirmed in later Buddhist traditions.

## Buddhist Support for Violence and Killing

There are texts in the Pali Canon that seem to assume that kings need to employ violence in order to rule properly. In the *Aggañña Sutta,* discussed in Chapter 11, it is suggested that government was established because someone was needed "who would show anger where anger was due, censure those who deserved it, and banish those who deserved punishment" (*DN* III 92). Perhaps this is more an explanation than a justification of violence by kings. But there are several other texts in which the Buddha declines to condemn war when given the opportunity, for example, when a king asks the Buddha if an attack will be successful (see *DN* II 72–4). From this it might be concluded that the Buddha was not interested in applying his non-violent ethical principles to political affairs (see Schmithausen 1999: 49–51). It is, in any case, rather difficult to discern a clear position in the teaching of the Buddha on how to relate the first moral precept proscribing violence and killing to what are commonly assumed to be the necessities of political rule in enforcing the law and defending against external attack. The example of Aśoka, thought to be the first Buddhist ruler, does little to clarify this: he is portrayed as having abandoned violent conquest, but he retained his army and, though he warned against unjust imprisonment and torture, did not forego capital punishment.

In Mahāyāna Buddhism the situation is rather different. There are several texts that suggest that violence is sometimes justified. We have already seen two of these in the discussion of moral dilemmas in Chapter 7. In the *Upāyakauśalya Sūtra* we are told about a sea captain called "Great Compassionate" (the Buddha in a past life) who kills a robber "with great compassion and skill in means" in order to prevent him from killing many Bodhisattvas (thereby saving their lives, but also preventing negative karmic consequences for the robber's would-be action as well as for the Bodhisattva's would-be action of killing the robber if the Captain told them of the robber's plan). Though Great Compassionate is portrayed as himself being willing to accept immense negative karmic results for this action, he did not in fact suffer these results (see Tatz 1994: 73–4 and 107, n. 148). It seems clear that killing the robber out of compassion is being presented as a morally justified action (for diverse interpretations, see Gethin 2004: 188–9, Harvey 2000: 135–6 and Jenkins 2011: 315–8).

The second text is Asaṅga's *Chapter on Ethics.* In a scenario similar to that of Great Compassionate, Asaṅga says that, if a Bodhisattva kills a robber who is about to kill hundreds of Bodhisattvas and other extraordinary beings, as long as the Bodhisattva has a "virtuous or indeterminate" thought with "mercy for the consequence," he would act "with such skill in means that no fault ensues." Although this act "is reprehensible by nature," in this situation "there is a spread of much merit" (Tatz 1986: 70–1). Though the phrase "reprehensible by nature" introduces some ambiguity, it seems evident that Asaṅga thinks that killing is morally justified in this situation, even though it is somewhat problematic. This is why there is "no fault" and "much merit" as a result (similar defenses are offered for overthrowing a king, having sex, lying and speaking in divisive and harsh ways). According to Stephen Jenkins, this position is common among Indian Mahāyāna Buddhists: "Asaṅga, Vasubandhu, Śāntideva, Āryadeva, Bhāviveka, and Candrakīrti agree on the basic point that a bodhisattva may do what is normally forbidden or inauspicious, *akuśala*" (Jenkins 2011: 310; cf. Jenkins 2010: 68–70). Jenkins believes that these figures thought that killing on the basis of compassion could sometimes be justified, that in some circumstances such an action could be auspicious or skillful *(kuśala)* and hence a source of karmic merit.

It has been argued that Mahāyāna texts justifying violations of the precepts on the basis of compassion, as an exercise in skillful means, are intended to apply only to "the Buddhas and Great Bodhisattvas." As such, the actions of these figures "are located primarily in the domain of myth and symbol" and are not "to be taken as a model for imitation in everyday life" (Keown 1992: 162). Against this, it has been claimed that in the tradition these texts were in fact taken as providing actual guidelines for all those who had entered the bodhisattva path and not simply those who were at an advanced stage on it (see Kleine 2006: 82). Moreover, Jenkins has argued that another Mahāyāna text, the *Satyakaparivarta* (in its better known brief title), relied on the concept of compassionate violence to provide Buddhist kings with resources for defending the social order on the basis of "warfare, torture, and harsh punishments" (Jenkins 2010: 59). For example, in the text an ascetic warns the king not to confuse compassion with sentimentality and to "bind, imprison, terrorize [or hurt/whip], beat, and harm uncivilized people" when necessary (quoted in Jenkins 2010: 64; cf. Jenkins 2013: 473–4). Jenkins maintains that this text undermines the claim that Buddhist ethics is committed to an unqualified form of pacifism. Moreover, he points out that warfare was justified only under certain conditions (see Jenkins 2010: 66–7). Some of these resemble the Just Intention, Last Resort and Discrimination conditions of just war theory. Hence, this text might be interpreted as providing support for the contention that there was an implicit commitment to a just war theory in at least some aspects of Mahāyāna Buddhism.

In addition, there are a number of other texts in Mahāyāna traditions that appear to justify violence. Nāgārjuna offers the following analogy: "Just as it is said that it will help to cut off a finger bitten by a snake, so the Subduer says that if it helps others, one should even bring [temporary] discomfort" (Hopkins 1998, verse 264). This may be read in different ways, but it is easy to see how the image of cutting off a finger to save the body might be interpreted as justifying harming some for the good of others. Again, in the *Mahāparinirvāṇa Sūtra* we are told that violence may employed against those who oppose Mahāyāna Buddhism (see Kleine 2006: 91–2 and Schmithausen 1999: 57–8; cf. Demiéville 2010: 38). Finally, the doctrine of emptiness, the philosophical heart of Mahāyāna Buddhism, was also appealed to in defenses of killing. For example, the *Mahāprajñāpāramitopadeśa* states that:

> [S]ince the living being *(sattva)* does not exist, neither does the sin of murder. And since the sin of murder does not exist, there is no longer any reason to forbid it. . . . In killing then, given that the five aggregates are characteristically empty, similar to the visions of dreams or reflections in a mirror, one commits no wrongdoing.
>
> (cited in Demiéville 2010: 20)

This might well seem to abolish morality altogether, not simply to justify violence and killing in special circumstances. The same might be said of the use of the phrase "beyond good and evil" in some Mahāyāna contexts (see Kleine 2006: 86–7). In any case, though there are texts justifying violations of the precepts on the basis of emptiness and related ideas, there were also concerns expressed about the implications of this notion and its potential for abuse (for discussion, see Demiéville 2010: 42–4, Keown 1992: 160–2, Kleine 2006: 88–91 and Schmithausen 1999: 60–1).

## Violence and Killing in Some Recent Buddhist History

Non-violence is a pervasive Buddhist teaching, but it has been interpreted in very different ways. As we have seen, though there are strands of Buddhist ethical thought that interpret non-violence in rigorist fashion and appear to be committed to a form of pacifism, there are other strands that suppose that violence may sometimes be justified on the basis of compassion and, in at least in some places, appear to be committed to (or at least consistent with) some form of just war theory. The various Buddhist traditions do not speak with a single unambiguous voice on this issue. To some extent, there is greater support for the just war approach in Mahāyāna Buddhism than there is in Theravāda Buddhism. However, as we will see momentarily, this generalization requires qualification. It is possible, of course, for contemporary Buddhists to construct what purports to be the "correct" Buddhist position on violence—say, something favoring a pacifist approach, or a just war approach, or perhaps another approach that would justify violence in some circumstances without supposing that the conditions for this could be codified as they are in just war theory. However, any such construction would need to be defended by interpreting some Buddhist values as more fundamental than others and/or by reading some texts as more important or authentically Buddhist than others. In light of these considerations, let us return to the Buddhist controversies about violence referred to at the beginning of this chapter.

Robert Aitken Rōshi, a principal founder of The Buddhist Peace Fellowship (BPF; discussed in Chapter 11), was both a Zen Buddhist and a pacifist who opposed the Vietnam War. He and others associated with the establishment of the BPF saw Buddhism, especially Zen, and anti-war activism as natural allies. In view of this, some were surprised when Brian Daizen Victoria published the first edition of *Zen at War* in 1997 (see Victoria 2006). Victoria argued with considerable documentation that institutional Buddhism in Japan, in particular Zen Buddhism, was an avid supporter of Japanese militarism during the period from 1868 to 1945. Though Victoria is not without his critics, his main contention is now widely accepted. The backstory of his account is a long Buddhist association with the state and the military in East Asian countries. In Japan, according to Victoria, starting with the Meiji Restoration in 1868, Buddhists embraced unqualified loyalty to the nation and the emperor, and with Japan's military expansion that ended only with its defeat in 1945, Buddhists provided various kinds of support for war. In addition, Victoria says, they offered purportedly Buddhist justifications for war. For example, a 1937 book by Zen scholars Hayashiya Tomojirō and Shimakage Chikai entitled *The Buddhist View of War (Bukkyō no Sensō Kan)* endorsed the slogan "killing one in order that many may live" as approved by Mahāyāna Buddhism. Moreover, in defense of Japan's war with China, they claimed that Buddhism "vigorously supports" wars that are "in accord with its values" and have a "good purpose," meaning "to save sentient beings and guide them properly" (cited in Victoria 2006: 87–8). Victoria claims that these assertions justifying war are directly contrary to the Buddhist precept against killing and other expressions of non-violence (see Victoria 2010). However, as we have seen, this position requires him to dismiss, as not authentically Buddhist, Mahāyāna texts such those we discussed in the last section. This is not to say that these texts could justify Japan's war effort, only that they might justify war in some circumstances. Other arguments documented by

Victoria, such as efforts to link Buddhist selflessness and emptiness to identification with the Japanese emperor, are obviously departures from earlier Buddhist traditions.

In Sri Lanka, some Sinhala Buddhist monks supported the government in the 1983–2009 civil war with the Liberation Tigers of Tamil Eelam (LTTE), a rebel organization of the minority Tamil people on the island. The political involvement of the monks was not without controversy. In some respects it was an aspect of the Buddhist modernism associated with the Sri Lankan nationalism that led to independence from Great Britain in 1948 and continued into the post-colonial era. But the involvement also had deep roots in Sri Lankan history. Ancient chronicles such as the sixth century CE *Mahāvaṃsa* (Great Chronicle), written in Pali, portray Sri Lanka as a *dharmadwipa,* an island of Dharma, that the Buddha himself visited three times and foretold would become a sacred Buddhist nation. In modern times, this text has been appealed to in support of the contention that Buddhism is essential to the identity of Sri Lanka. Moreover, according to Tessa Bartholomeusz, this text has been a source of a just war defense of the war against the LTTE (see Bartholomeusz 1999 and 2002). Though she grants that there are pacifist narratives in Sri Lankan Buddhist history, there are also just war narratives. For example, monks who supported the war appealed to the *Mahāvaṃsa* account of the Buddhist King Dutugemunu who they claimed used violence to unite the island and ensure that Buddhism would be protected. Bartholomeusz points out that the text appeals to the Just Cause condition of just war theory (in this case, establishing a Buddhist order) as well as a Proportionality condition (see Bartholomeusz 1999: 8–10). Hence, though the Buddhism of Sri Lanka is in the Theravāda tradition, there was an implicit commitment to some form of just war theory in its early history as well as in the recent civil war. It may be objected that the *Mahāvaṃsa* is a post-canonical source that cannot override the Pali Canon. However, it may be said in response that, from the standpoint of many Buddhists in Sri Lanka, both the *Mahāvaṃsa* and the Pali Canon are important sources of their Buddhist convictions. Moreover, for these Buddhists there are Pali Canon texts such as the *Cakkavatti-Sīhanāda Sutta* (*DN* III 58–79) that justify a king's using violence to protect Buddhism (for this claim see Bartholomeusz 1999: 4; cf. Collins 1998: 480–96 for a very different reading of the *Sutta*).

The discussion of Japan and Sri Lanka raises questions about which aspects of Buddhist discourses on violence are most authentically Buddhist and about the extent to which Buddhist ethical thought can be distinguished from its manifestations in particular historical circumstances. These questions are no less relevant as we turn to two contemporary Buddhist monks who have drawn on the pacifist rather than the just war strands of Buddhist teaching: the Dalai Lama and Nhat Hanh. Each was deeply involved with a major war in the 20th century—the Chinese invasion of Tibet and the American Vietnam war—and each responded with a non-violent approach (for discussion of these and other recent nonviolent Buddhist strategies, see S. B. King 2009b and Swearer 1992).

As the political leader in exile of Tibet (and a spiritual leader of the Geluk order of Tibetan Buddhists), the Dalai Lama has long argued that Tibet should be an autonomous "zone of peace" that would preserve the Tibetan culture that has been threatened by the Chinese occupation since 1950. However, he has maintained that this should be achieved through dialogue and negotiation rather than violence. Not all Tibetans have agreed with this approach (see Puri 2006: 36–7). But the Dalai Lama has urged that there are compelling Buddhist reasons for a non-violent stance. First, echoing the first precept, he says that "violence is immoral" and is "unworthy of a human being" (quoted in Puri 2006: 36). Second, following the *Dhammapada* passage that enmity is not to be quelled by enmity (referred to earlier), he says:

> Of course it is true that violence can achieve certain short-term objectives, but it cannot obtain long-lasting ends. If we look at history, we find that in time, humanity's love of peace, justice, and freedom always triumphs over cruelty and oppression. This is why I am such a fervent believer in non-violence. Violence begets violence. And violence means only one thing: suffering.
>
> (Dalai Lama 1999: 201)

In addition, the Dalai Lama has argued, in typical Buddhist fashion, that compassion should be extended to the Chinese. In his 1959 "A Prayer of Words of Truth" he said: "The violent oppressors are also worthy of compassion. Crazed by demonic emotions, they do vicious deeds that bring total defeat to themselves as well as others" (quoted in Thurman 1992: 87). In fact, again expressing a common Buddhist theme (for example, in Śāntideva), the Dalai Lama has said that an "enemy" such as China provides the opportunity to develop the perfection of patience so as to overcome anger and hatred. For this, he says, he should be grateful (see S. B. King 2009a: 72). Though these reasons for a non-violent approach all have credentials within the Buddhist tradition, it is possible that another more recent influence is at work. The Dalai Lama has said, "I consider myself to be one of the followers of Mahatma Gandhi" (quoted in Puri 2006: 20). However, it is worth noting that the Dalai Lama is not opposed to violence in every imaginable circumstance. He has said that, hypothetically, if the death of one person "would cause the whole of Tibet to lose all hope of keeping its Buddhist way of life, then it is conceivable that in order to protect that one person it might be justified for one or 10 enemies to be eliminated" (quoted in Bartholomeusz 2002: 29; cf. Puri 2006: 24).

We have already discussed Nhat Hanh's understanding of non-violence in Chapter 11. During the Vietnam War, he did not take sides and he worked actively to promote peace and help the victims of the war (by contrast, there is an obvious sense in which the Dalai Lama is on one side of the dispute between China and Tibet). Hence, Nhat Hanh was not simply opposed to violence and killing: he was energetically, though peacefully, engaged in trying to end the suffering caused by the war. This was the origin of one of the signature themes in his understanding of engaged Buddhism. He observed that many persons in the American peace movement who opposed the Vietnam War were full of hatred and anger directed at the American government and military. Nhat Hahn maintained that this was misguided. "Without being peace," he said, "we cannot do anything for peace" (Hanh 2005: 82). This is closely related to aspects of the Dalai Lama's approach such as the importance of having compassion for all, including oppressors (recall Nhat Hanh's identification with the pirate), and developing the perfection of patience. For Nhat Hanh, a crucial element of "being peace" is bringing mindful meditation to each situation in order to calmly understand it, a unifying theme of the Mindfulness Trainings discussed earlier. In a commentary on the Twelfth Training opposing killing, Nhat Hanh emphasizes that this means not killing *any living beings*. Since this is virtually impossible because we often kill tiny living beings when we boil water or take a step, the training is an aspiration: it is a commitment "to make every effort to respect and protect life, to continuously move in the direction of peace and reconciliation" (Hanh 1998: 47) We do this by trying to live and consume in ways that do not bring harm and death to others (for example, by not eating meat or drinking alcohol). These are common Buddhist themes with clear roots in the Eightfold Path and the traditional five moral precepts. For Nhat Hanh, non-violence is an entire way of life, not simply disapproval of war.

There is, however, one striking exception to Nhat Hanh's opposition to killing. During the Vietnam War, a Buddhist monk named Thich Quang Duc publically burned himself to death to protest the government's repression of Buddhism. Other Vietnamese Buddhists did the same, including Nhat Chi Mai, a member of Nhat Hanh's Order of Interbeing. Nhat Hanh has defended these actions as morally courageous. He says that Quang Duc's act "awakened the world to the suffering of the war and the persecution of the Buddhists." It "expressed the unconditional willingness to suffer for the awakening of others." From this perspective, self-immolation may be seen as the compassionate sacrificial act of a person committed to the bodhisattva path. Nhat Hanh says that this is "not really suicide" and is consistent with his "commitment to nonviolence" (Hanh 1996: 60–1). Yet it is intentionally taking one's life and hence is surely contrary to the first precept on a straightforward reading. However, it has been pointed out that the practice has precedents in the Mahāyāna tradition in China and Vietnam, and it has a mythical antecedent in the very early *Lotus Sūtra* (from perhaps the 1st century BCE). Moreover, it may be compared to the theme of compassionately killing one to save many in the *Upāyakauśalya Sūtra* (for these points, see S.B. King 2013: 641–2). In recent years, several Tibetans have also burned themselves to death, in protest against China's occupation of Tibet, though the Dalai Lama has not encouraged these actions.

There are others associated with socially engaged Buddhism whose opposition to violence is not categorical. For example, Aung San Suu Kyi, the Buddhist opposition leader in Burma, has employed a non-violent approach as most suited to achieving her goals, but she refuses to condemn or disown those who employ violence (see S.B. King 2005: 187). It is evident that there is tremendous diversity in Buddhist positions on violence and killing. There is certainly a striking contrast between, on the one hand, the non-violent stances of the Dalai Lama and Nhat Hanh and, on the other hand, the Zen Buddhists who supported Japanese militarism and the Sinhala Buddhists who supported the war against the LTTE in Sri Lanka. To some extent, all of these perspectives might find some resources in some Buddhist tradition to support their position, and yet the overall disposition of the first two differs markedly from the overall outlook of the second two.

In one respect, the basic moral issue is contained in Nhat Hanh's twofold determination "not to kill and not to let others kill" in the Twelfth Mindfulness Training. What if killing a person is the only way to prevent him or her from killing others? If we give priority to *our not killing,* then we move in the direction of pacifism. But if we give priority to *our not letting others kill,* then we may move in the direction of a just war theory or at least a stance in which killing is sometimes justified. With respect to the normative outlooks discussed in Chapters 6 and 7, those who favor developing Buddhist ethical thought in a consequentialist framework are likely to think that killing could sometimes be justified so as to prevent worse consequences, even if it is allowed that we should usually follow a rule prohibiting killing. Likewise, those who think that Buddhist ethics should be understood in terms of pluralism or particularism would probably accept a more permissive posture in which killing could sometimes be justified. A strict pacifist stance is most naturally associated with a deontological theory in which there is an unqualified rule against killing. However, despite the prominence of pacifist understandings of Buddhism, it is not usually believed that deontology is a promising framework for developing Buddhist ethics. A virtue ethics approach is often thought to be much more promising as an interpretive perspective, but this could be taken in different directions on this issue. An Aristotelian virtue ethics has more kinship with a just war theory than with pacifism (recall that for Aristotle the courage of the soldier is the paradigmatic instance of courage). But a virtue ethics approach could be developed that features non-violence as fundamental to good moral character (in this connection, see Gier 2004).

The morality of violence and killing can arise at the level of personal morality, but it comes to a head most forcefully in the context of government insofar as government is commonly understood to have the responsibility to use force to provide for the security of its citizens. Sallie B. King has argued that socially engaged Buddhists, whom she understands as being deeply committed to non-violence, nonetheless face a difficulty: "the personal ethic of nonviolence," which she sees as the traditional strength of Buddhist ethical thought, "does not neatly translate into a social ethic of nonviolence," which she thinks was not fully developed in traditional Buddhism (S. B. King 2005: 199). In a world full of violence, most people find strict pacifism, in which intentionally killing a human being is never justified, a difficult position to defend. Moreover, as we have seen, even the Dalai Lama and Nhat Hanh allow that killing may sometimes be justified, albeit in different and very special circumstances. This might be taken to suggest that many Buddhists have reason to move in the direction of a just war theory. However, though this is one possibility, it is not the only one. There is a difference between arguing that war is morally justified under certain conditions that can be spelled out and arguing that violence and killing are morally unjustified except in very extreme and perhaps unpredictable circumstances. For the most part, when Buddhists have not been strict pacifists, they have opted for the latter position. They have not been attracted to an explicit just war theory any more than they have been attracted to other moral theories, even though on occasion they might appear to be implicitly committed to such a theory (in this connection, see Keown Forthcoming).

CHAPTER **14**

# Environmental Ethics

Buddhism is often presented, especially in more popular venues, as providing a moral outlook that is naturally sympathetic to environmental concerns. For example, Allan Hunt Badiner enthusiastically asserted, "Buddhism offers a clearly defined system of ethics, a guide to ecological living, right here, right now" (Badiner 1990b: xvii; see also the papers collected in Badiner 1990a, M. Batchelor and Brown 1994 and Kaza and Kraft 2000). Environmental ethics has been one of the fundamental concerns of socially engaged Buddhists and has been a central issue for each of the proponents of engaged Buddhism featured in Chapter 11. For instance, the Dalai Lama's "Five Point Peace Plan" includes a provision for the "restoration and protection of Tibet's natural environment" (Puri 2006: 192). In fact, there has probably been more written about Buddhism and environmental ethics than any other practical ethical issue. At the same time, in recent Western moral philosophy, environmental ethics has been among the most widely discussed topics in applied ethics. Obviously the Buddha and traditional Buddhist societies did not face the environmental problems that confront us today. Hence, they cannot be expected to have developed an explicit environmental ethic that addresses these problems in the way that those working in contemporary environmental ethics have done. Nonetheless, many contemporary Buddhists and scholars of Buddhism think that traditional Buddhist ethical thought has numerous and significant resources for the construction of such an ethic. According to

276

Sulak Sivaraksa, "Buddhism has been concerned with caring for the natural environment for over twenty-five hundred years" (Sivaraksa 2005: 71). There are, however, some skeptical voices that have questioned the extent to which traditional Buddhist values and ideas have been relevant to and supportive of an environmental ethical outlook that meets the concerns of contemporary proponents of environmental ethics. As a result, there has been a scholarly debate about the relationship between Buddhism and environmental ethics (Tucker and Williams 1997 is a valuable collection of papers; for overviews of the debate, see Harris 1995 and James 2013).

In this chapter, after surveying some of the main contours of work in environmental ethics in Western moral philosophy, we will consider how this work might relate to Buddhist ethical thought by examining some features of Buddhism that have been thought to suggest that it is environmentally friendly and in particular that it overcomes the anthropocentrism that is widely regarded as the source of many current environmental problems. We will also examine some recent attempts to develop a virtue ethics approach to constructing a Buddhist environmental ethic, and we will briefly discuss the specific issue of the ethical treatment of animals. Since the literature on Buddhist environmental ethics is vast, we can only touch on some of the central issues.

## Environmental Ethics in Western Moral Philosophy

Environmental ethics, as a specific academic discipline within applied ethics, developed in the 1970s in response to the growing realization in the previous decade that human beings had created an environmental crisis by polluting land, water and air, depleting natural resources, and threatening the well-being of all living creatures, among other problems. Though this crisis was obviously made possible by modern technology and facilitated by economic development and population growth, many people believed that the deeper source of it was a set of attitudes rooted in Western philosophies and religions that assumed that human beings were superior to other living things and that the value of the natural world was simply to serve human purposes. This led some philosophers to develop alternative perspectives on these issues and the debates about these alternatives gave rise to the field of environmental ethics, the philosophical discipline that examines ethical issues pertaining to the natural environment and the interactions of human beings with it. In the decades that have followed, numerous philosophical approaches have been developed and additional issues have come to the forefront of attention such as species preservation, the importance of ecosystems and the dangers of climate change.

Much of the early debate in environmental ethics concerned foundational issues about what has moral standing and why. In this debate, to say that something has moral standing is to say that it is worthy of moral consideration and so should be taken into account in moral deliberation. Something has extrinsic moral standing when its moral standing depends on its relationship to something else. For example, most people would say that an iPod has extrinsic moral standing when someone owns it: this means that we have a moral reason not to destroy it because it belongs to someone else. By contrast, something has intrinsic moral standing when its moral standing depends on its own non-relational properties and not on its relationship to anything else. It is commonly believed that human beings have intrinsic moral standing: this means that we have a moral reason not to harm a person because he or she is a human being and not simply because of the person's relationship to something else. That human beings have intrinsic moral standing is a common assumption in human rights discourse and in many other moral outlooks. One of the central concerns in environmental ethics is whether anything other than human beings has intrinsic moral standing (sometimes this is expressed in the language of what has intrinsic value).

Anthropocentrism is the position that only human beings have intrinsic moral standing. This means that features of the natural environment such as non-human animals, plants, ecosystems and the like have at most extrinsic moral standing and could be morally important only insofar as they serve human interests. Some people believe that an enlightened anthropocentrism (for example, that focuses on human interests in the long run) is a sufficient philosophical basis for addressing environmental problems. But most philosophers in environmental ethics think that the acceptance of anthropocentrism is an important source of our environmental problems. Hence, they have proposed a variety of non-anthropocentric theories that maintain that some things other than human beings have intrinsic moral standing. Non-anthropocentric philosophers do not typically deny that human beings have intrinsic moral standing; their claim is that intrinsic moral standing extends beyond human beings to other things. However, they disagree about what these other things are (and about their comparative moral importance in relationship to human beings). A view that is commonly called sentientism says that all beings capable of experiencing pleasure and pain have intrinsic moral standing. This would mean that at least many non-human animals would have intrinsic moral standing. Another view that is often called biocentrism states that all living beings have intrinsic moral standing. This would mean that all plants and animals have this moral status.

A rather different position that is usually called ecocentrism holds that ecosystems have intrinsic moral standing. There is an important difference between ecocentrism and all the positions defined in the previous paragraph. Anthropocentrism, sentientism and biocentrism each maintain that it is individuals that have intrinsic moral standing. Ecocentrism supposes that it is a whole—an ecosystem that includes individuals—that has intrinsic moral standing (see Callicott 1980). The distinction between individualism and holism is an important one in environmental ethics (the view that species have intrinsic moral standing is another holist position). For example, preservation of an ecosystem might require the elimination of individuals that threaten it such as the members of an invasive species. Ecocentrism might favor this elimination, but biocentrism might oppose it. Of course, someone could hold both positions and would then have a moral conflict. But there are philosophers who hold one, but not the other, position and they might disagree about this issue. This is one of many instances in which there are significant tensions and sometimes disagreements among environmental ethicists (in fact, there have been disputes about whether positions that focus on the treatment of individual animals are forms of environmental ethics).

Non-anthropocentric views may have radical implications. For instance, if biocentrism were correct, then it would seem that bacteria that threaten human life have intrinsic moral standing. Most people would resist such claims, but some environmental ethicists have argued that we need a radically different orientation to the world. For example, Arne Naess proposed a "deep ecology" that embraces biocentrism and requires significant changes in our way of life. Though Naess thought that the basic principles of deep ecology could be supported in different ways (including Buddhist approaches), he himself justified them on the basis of a philosophy of self-realization that involves fulfilling our "ecological self" by identifying with and living "in community with all living beings" (Naess 2008a: 96). Another quite different but still radical approach that emphasizes our connections with nature is Murray Bookchin's "social ecology" that relates environmental problems to other social problems rooted in hierarchy and domination (see Bookchin 2005). There is also an array of feminist perspectives that associate environmental concerns with patriarchy as well as, more recently, panpsychist or animist theories that propose re-enchanting the disenchanted natural world of modern science and technology.

Overall there is enormous diversity in philosophical approaches to environmental ethics. Some of these approaches are more conventional in that they are closely related to standard normative ethical theories such as those that were discussed in Chapter 6. Consequentialist theories such as classical utilitarianism define morally right actions in terms of what maximizes happiness where this is understood as the overall balance of pleasure and pain. This is naturally associated with sentientism, and both classical utilitarians such as Bentham and more recent utilitarians such as Singer have maintained that all sentient beings have intrinsic moral standing. Singer has argued on this basis that many common practices regarding animals, such as eating them, are ordinarily unjustified (see Singer 2000). However, on this view, non-sentient individual beings such as plants as well as wholes such as species and ecosystems do not have intrinsic moral standing. There are also deontological theories that bear on environmental issues. For example, Tom Regan has argued that we have a *prima facie* duty to not harm animals because they have inherent value insofar as they are the subject of a life (see Regan 1983), and Paul W. Taylor has maintained, more strongly, that we have *prima facie* duties to respect all living things since each of these has inherent worth because it is a "teleological-center-of-life" with its own well-being (see P. Taylor 1986). Once again, both of these theories focus on individuals rather than ecological wholes as the bearers of intrinsic moral standing.

In addition, in recent years more attention has been given to discussing environmental concerns in connection with virtue ethics. To some extent this has taken the form of suggesting that virtuous character traits such as humility, temperance and wonder are important for being properly morally responsive to environmental concerns (see Hill 1983). Beyond this, it has also been proposed that virtue ethics could provide the foundation for environmental ethics (see Sandler 2007). It might be supposed that a eudaimonistic environmental virtue ethics that justifies the virtues on the basis of human flourishing would be an anthropocentric account. But it may be responded that, just as Aristotle supposed that a virtuous person is concerned with the well-being of his friends for their own sake (see Aristotle 2002: 1155b31–34), so a proponent of this approach could say that a virtuous person cares about animals, plants or even ecosystems for their own sake (a virtue approach as such would seem to be neutral in the debate between individualism and holism).

## Some Early Buddhist Resources for Environmental Ethics

It is often claimed that Buddhist ethical thought possesses significant resources for the construction of a contemporary environmental ethic. Upon examination, though, the traditional Buddhist sources turn out to be quite diverse: in some respects they seem support this contention, while in other respects they appear to challenge it, and on some issues it is not clear that they have much to say that is relevant (for a critique of this textual approach, see Clippard 2011). Overall, if we employ two distinctions that have been central in the contemporary Western debate (anthropocentrism vs. non-anthropocentrism and individualism vs. holism), then it may be said as a very rough generalization that in early pre-Mahāyāna forms of Buddhism, especially in the Pali Canon, there are greater resources for developing an environmental ethic in which anthropocentric and individualistic themes are more dominant, while in Mahāyāna Buddhism, especially as it developed in East Asia, there are greater resources for developing an environmental ethic in which non-anthropocentric and holistic outlooks are central. Let us begin with early Buddhism, starting with three preliminary considerations that have been thought to be relevant to the development of a Buddhist environmental ethics.

First, the origin story in the *Aggañña Sutta* (*DN* III 80–116) has been interpreted as teaching the message that our immoral actions can have an adverse impact on the environment. The first part of the story depicts a descent of beings from a "self-luminous" state to increasingly coarse and differentiated bodily forms in which theft and revenge prevail. The descent is driven by craving, greed and laziness, and the results of these vices are the successive loss or deterioration of the savory earth and tasty foods such as fungi, creepers and rice. Similar accounts are not uncommon in the Pali Canon. For example, lust and greed are said to result in drought, famine and death (see *AN* I 160). Though such texts are evidently intended as illustrations of karma, the specific emphasis on environmental effects may be read as a Buddhist realization of the "close relationship between human morality and the natural environment" (L. de Silva 1994: 20). But these texts might be interpreted in a rather different way. For instance, it has been suggested that the message of the *Aggañña Sutta* is that the natural world is impermanent and that liberation comes form escaping it (see I. Harris 2000: 123).

Second, it has also been proposed that some of the *Jātaka* stories in the Pali Canon convey "an inherently ecological message" (Chapple 1997: 135). In these stories, which are presented as portraying the past lives of the Buddha, animals and sometimes plants are often personified so as to teach a moral lesson. For example, in one story some trees chose to stand by themselves in the open and they were destroyed by a storm while other trees remained together in the forest connected with one another and they were safe in the storm. This was intended to teach the lesson that people should stand together, but it could be interpreted as teaching a lesson about "the interconnectedness of life" (see Chapple 1997: 140). Such interpretations are possible and some *Jātaka* stories oppose killing animals and encourage helping them, in line with common Buddhist teaching. The main perspective of many these stories, however, is basically anthropocentric: they are not primarily about how we human beings should treat plants, animals and other features of nature as such, but about how we should live our lives in general, using the familiar device of depicting various living beings as proxies for human beings. For example, in these stories some animals are represented as wise and virtuous while others are portrayed as foolish and vicious. These are mainly morality tales about human beings and they are often accompanied by a karmic message about the advantages and disadvantages of these all-too-human orientations (see Sahni 2008: ch. 6 for a balanced discussion of the relevance of the *Jātaka* stories for environmental ethics).

Finally, it has also been pointed out that the natural world is often represented in positive ways in Buddhist texts in the Pali Canon. For example, the major events of the Buddha's life (birth, enlightenment, first sermon and death) are said to have taken place in a natural setting. Moreover, some monks regarded the wilderness as an ideal environment to pursue enlightenment. However, there are contrary indications as well. The Buddha spent a good deal of time in cities, and in early Buddhism nature is often represented as a dangerous place while more cultivated and urban environments are praised. Moreover, portrayals of nature as conducive to the pursuit of enlightenment may be interpreted as exhibiting an anthropocentric view of nature (it is valuable simply because it promotes our ends). On the whole, in early Buddhism rather diverse attitudes towards nature may be found, both a pro-nature "hermit strand" and a "pro civilization strand" (for discussion of these issues, see I. Harris 2000: 125–8 and Schmithausen 1997: 24–8).

Let us now turn to more directly philosophical considerations that have been regarded as relevant to the construction of a Buddhist environmental ethic. A prominent theme is the contention that human beings are part of a cycle of rebirth that also involves non-human animals (henceforth, simply animals). Hence, each of us may well have been an animal in a previous lifetime and may be reborn as an animal in the future. In this framework, there is no sharp dichotomy between human beings and animals: we are all part of a set of natural processes of change and conditioning (see Holder 2007). This would seem to encourage kinship with other animals, a sense that they are not radically different from us, and so it is not surprising that the prohibition on killing in the first precept is commonly understood to refer to animals as well as human beings (there is more about this later).

Still, there are important complexities in this picture. First, the cycle of rebirth is governed by the law of karma (the moral quality of a being's actions causally condition its future well-being). In this respect, it is not a natural process that would be acknowledged by contemporary science.

The "natural world" of the Buddha is a thoroughly moralized world, and it is situated in a larger cosmological scheme that includes supernatural elements such as gods and realms of hell (see Chapter 1). Moreover, in this hierarchal cosmology, animals are at a low level in the cycle of rebirth because they have lived morally badly in past lives. Hence, as a group animals are morally inferior to human beings and because of this they suffer more than human beings (see Schmithausen 1997: 28–9). Rebirth as an animal is something we all have reason to avoid. Nonetheless, everything in the cycle of rebirth at whatever level has the capacity to attain enlightenment. Insofar as having this capacity is thought to be a source of value, animals as well as human beings have this value. In short, human beings are on a par with animals in their capacity to attain enlightenment, but are superior to animals in their level of moral accomplishment—and for this reason, it is often said, human beings are in a much better position to attain enlightenment than animals.

For Buddhist naturalists who are skeptical about karma and rebirth none of this would have much significance. Though they might embrace the humane treatment of animals, the reason for this would not be rooted in the conviction that they are in the same cycle of rebirth as animals and so may have been or might yet be an animal (but it could be that human beings and animals both suffer, as Singer maintains). For those who embrace the traditional understanding of karma and rebirth, by contrast, this account does suggest a much more intimate relationship between human beings and animals than has been commonly accepted in Western traditions. From this Buddhist standpoint, we—humans and animals—are all in it together, and this might be taken to support a more positive environmental outlook, at least with respect to the treatment of individual animals.

There is, however, another aspect to this picture. In early pre-Mahāyāna Buddhism, what is stressed is that the entire cycle of rebirth is inherently flawed because it is permeated by suffering, and the aim is to escape this cycle by attaining nirvana. Taken as a whole, the cycle of rebirth extends well beyond what we might consider the natural world (since it encompasses divine beings at the top and realms of hell at the bottom). Still, part of the cycle of rebirth (that which pertains to human and animal life) takes place in the natural world more or less as we ordinarily understand it. Moreover, many of the depictions of the cycle of rebirth as a scene of suffering—as a place of impermanence and decay, of birth, sickness, dying and death and so forth—would seem to apply first and foremost to the natural world. If enlightenment means in some sense escaping the cycle of rebirth and attaining nirvana, then it is hard to see that this outlook could provide a basis for an environmental philosophy that, for example, emphasizes the importance of preserving nature (see I. Harris 2000: 122–3 and Schmithausen 1997: 10–13 and 33).

It may be said, in response, that in early Buddhism suffering is not an essential feature of the natural world as such, but of our unenlightened way of experiencing the world. Moreover, enlightenment is not an escape from the natural world, but a non-attached way of living in it (as exemplified by the life of the Buddha). Hence, there is no reason to deny that early Buddhism would have a basis for preserving nature, and some reason for thinking it valued the natural world as a favorable context in which we seek enlightenment (see Holder 2007: 121–3). Here, however, it is important to distinguish nirvana as the state of an enlightened person who is still alive and nirvana as the state of an enlightened person who has died (see Chapter 1). Nirvana-in-life is a way of living in this world in which we still experience pleasure and pain, but are no longer afflicted by greed, hatred and delusion. But nirvana-after-death is another story. As we have seen, the Buddha said little about this state and it is portrayed in rather elusive ways in the Pali Canon. But it is sometimes depicted as a blissful state in which one is no longer reborn and as an unconditioned state in which "there is no earth, no water, no fire, no air" (Ireland 1997: 102). This strand of the Buddha's teaching would seem to suggest that the ultimate aim of Buddhist enlightenment is very much to escape the natural world of impermanence and conditioning, and this would seem to undermine any basis for preserving the natural world except perhaps as something that has instrumental value in our pursuit of enlightenment (thus providing only an anthropocentric basis for an environmental ethic).

Of course, some Buddhist naturalists may be skeptical about nirvana as a state after death and they may conceive of enlightenment only as a state that is found within this life. This would mean that the primary goal is living in the world selflessly, without attachment, and having compassion for all sentient beings. Such an orientation might provide a basis for much that many concerned about the environment want. For example, it would ensure concern for the suffering of sentient beings and it would challenge the consumer way of life that is thought to be a source of destruction of the environment (though the reasons for the challenge might not be direct concern for the environment). But this is not a traditional Buddhist outlook.

In sum, if we consider early Buddhism in traditional terms, without the modifications proposed by some Buddhist naturalists regarding karma, rebirth and nirvana, then we have a rather mixed set of resources for an environmental ethic. The most obvious point is the opposition to harming and killing animals. In this respect, there is a clear non-anthropocentric dimension in early Buddhist thought. Appreciation of the well-being of other living things such as plants is more mixed (see I. Harris 2000: 116–17 and Harvey 2000: 174–6), and the concern for animals is tempered by the belief that they are morally below us in the hierarchy of Buddhist karmic cosmology. This concern is also an individualist concern: there is little basis for the preservation of animal species (see Harvey 2007a: 23–5 and Schmithausen 1997: 19–20). More generally, it is hard to see that there is any direct concern for other environmental wholes such as ecosystems or nature itself. For the most part, to the extent that these are appreciated in early Buddhism, it is for anthropocentric reasons (for example, when natural surroundings are thought to be conducive to meditation). And the ultimate aim of liberation from the cycle of rebirth does not sit well with the outlook of many in environmental ethics, such as deep ecologists, who encourage us to identify with the natural world.

## Some Mahāyāna Buddhist Resources for Environmental Ethics

Mahāyāna Buddhist traditions inherit many features of earlier forms of Buddhism, but they include several additional themes that might be considered more favorable to the construction of an environmental ethic—in particular one that is non-anthropocentric and holistic. This is especially true with respect to the development of these ideas in East Asian Buddhist traditions, often under the influence of native religious outlooks such as Daoism in China and Shintō in Japan.

The first of these is the critique of the ultimate reality of distinctions and the emphasis on the fundamental non-duality of all things. This is a consequence of the teaching about emptiness: if in ultimate truth nothing has a nature that is independent, inherent or intrinsic, then it was supposed that in ultimate truth there are no real distinctions between things. Everything is fundamentally non-dual. The employment of distinctions and dualities in everyday thought and discourse may have a place in conventional truth, as practices that are pragmatically useful in negotiating our way in the world, but they have no ultimate reality. Expressions of non-duality are pervasive in Mahāyāna Buddhism. In a chapter of the *Vimalakīrti Sutra* entitled "The Dharma-Door of Nonduality" we are told of "one who, attaining equanimity, forms no conception of impurity or immaculateness, yet is not utterly without conception" and thereby "enters into nonduality" (Thurman 1976: 74). Perhaps the most famous example of non-duality is the claim of Nāgārjuna that "there is not the slightest difference between cyclic existence and nirvāṇa" (Garfield 1995: 25:19).

Non-duality is frequently emphasized in discussions of environmental ethics from a Mahāyāna perspective. For instance, Nhat Hanh says that "the non-dualistic way of seeing" enables us "to be the river" and "to be the forest" (Hanh 2005: 72). This emphasis is important for the development of environmental ethics for several reasons. First, for many Western philosophers in environmental ethics, especially proponents of more radical positions associated with deep ecology and some feminist theories, dualist ways of thinking have been regarded as a central source of environmental problems. The Mahāyāna critique of dualism may be interpreted as having a natural affinity with these positions. Second, in Mahāyāna Buddhism the subject-object dualism is considered one of the most fundamental forms of delusion (for example, as seen in Yogācāra Buddhism in Chapter 2). Dualism in this specific sense may be regarded as encouraging a sense of separation between us human beings and nature that is likely to have problematic environmental consequences, and realizing that this dualism is a delusion may help us to overcome these problems. Finally, Nāgārjuna's statement that there is no difference between the cycle of rebirth and nirvana was sometimes taken to mean that enlightenment is not liberation from cyclic existence, in the sense of transcending it, but is a different way of orienting ourselves to cyclic existence. This outlook might be thought to alleviate the earlier concern that Buddhism is primarily about transcending nature.

There are, however, objections to the Mahāyāna emphasis on non-dualism as an ethical resource in environmental ethics (and elsewhere in ethics). This stance is the source of a good deal of paradoxical discourse in Mahāyāna Buddhism, as in Nāgārjuna's statement, and some may find this unhelpful and perhaps even counter-productive in ethical reflection. More specifically, if all distinctions are ultimately unreal, then it would seem that there is no real difference between a polluted environment and a non-polluted one or between the destruction of an ecosystem and its continuation (remember the "no conception of impurity or immaculateness" passage in the *Vimalakīrti Sutra*). It might be argued that a viable environmental ethic needs to insist on the reality of these differences and on the superiority of the second over the first member of such distinctions (see Ives 2009b: 169–71 and 175). From this perspective, Buddhist non-dualism might be regarded as dangerous (recall the appeal to emptiness to justify killing referred to in the last chapter). In response, it may be said that the realization of the delusory nature of all distinctions goes hand-in-hand with the attainment of universal compassion, and that a person with universal compassion can be expected to act in an environmentally responsible way by employing—but only as important conventional truths—the distinctions just noted (not being "utterly without conception").

A closely related theme, but with a somewhat different emphasis, is the Mahāyāna Buddhist idea of interdependence, especially as it is expressed in the metaphor of Indra's net (see Chapter 2). Many scholars or proponents of Buddhism have suggested that this idea supports an environmental ethical outlook (see Barnhill 1997 and Ingram 1997; cf. Cook 1989). As we have seen, in Indra's net, there are an infinite number of nodes, and at each node there is a jewel that reflects every other jewel. This is meant to express the idea that each thing is dependent on or penetrated by all other things. Interdependence in this sense is a development of the Buddha's teaching that all things are dependently arisen, but as we have noted to say that each thing is dependent on all other things is to say something much stronger than to say that each thing is dependent on some other things (see Chapter 8). Interdependence is a feature of Mahāyāna Buddhism that was especially influential in East Asia. The image of Indra's net was featured in the Chinese Hua-yen school, and it is commonly appealed to by socially engaged Buddhists today. It is a striking image, one that comports well with holist ways of thinking, but care is required in considering its implications for environmental ethics.

Indra's net does bear some resemblance to a basic theme in the science of ecology that living things interact with one another and their environment in complex ways—a theme that is often appealed to in discussions of environmental ethics. Nonetheless, Hua-yen philosophy and contemporary scientific ecology differ in many respects. For example, the complex interactions asserted by ecology are said to be supported by empirical evidence, but the interdependence affirmed by Hua-yen philosophy requires the meditative disciplines to be fully comprehended (it is certainly difficult to accept from a commonsense standpoint; see Ives 2009b: 166–7). Moreover, the Hua-yen school suggested that all things exist in "one mind," and this is not ordinarily claimed by ecology (though to some extent this may resemble the controversial "Gaia hypothesis" put forward by James Lovelock that the earth as a whole is a living organism, an idea often appealed to in discussions of Buddhist environmental ethics). The more important issue for environmental ethics, however, is the relationship between the recognition of interdependence and ethical concern for the environment (see Chapter 8). For example, why should the realization that we human beings are interdependent parts of the natural world give us reason to value other parts of that world? That all things are interdependent would not seem to establish, all by itself, that these things have some kind of value that we should care about, appreciate or respect. There might be a plausible argument that the realization of interdependence gives us a self-interested reason to value things in nature: we should value them because we are dependent on them. But this would be an anthropocentric perspective (things in nature are instrumentally valuable because our well-being depends on them), and proponents of an environmental ethic based on interdependence usually see themselves as challenging anthropocentrism. Another argument that is more in tune with Buddhism is that interdependence undermines the idea that human beings are distinct substances and thereby undermines the idea that we should think from a self-interested perspective. This perspective might reasonably be thought to be an important source of environmental problems. Yet, as we saw in Chapter 8, it is not clear that the realization of selflessness or emptiness by themselves provide a basis for compassion and other Buddhist values (though it is clear that in Buddhist teaching this realization is commonly thought to bring about compassion).

Another idea in Mahāyāna Buddhism that has been thought to lend itself to an environmental ethic is the notion that all sentient beings have Buddha-nature *(buddha-dhātu)* or the embryo of the Buddha (Tathāgata-garbha), meaning that all sentient beings have the capacity for—in fact, in some sense already have—enlightenment or Buddhahood (see Chapter 2). This idea originated in India and in East Asian Buddhism it was explicitly extended to all living beings. In fact, it was sometimes extended to all beings, animate and inanimate, as in the case of the Japanese Zen philosopher Dōgen (see James 2004: 22 and 65–6). If we suppose that all things have Buddha-nature and that having Buddha-nature confers value on things, then we have a basis for saying that everything in the world has value. When combined with the earlier themes of non-dualism and interdependence, we have a picture of the world as an integrated and valued whole in which human beings are but one aspect. It is not difficult to see how this could support a non-anthropocentric and holist environmental ethic. In this account, nature as a whole and all its interconnected aspects may be equally valued in virtue of having Buddha-nature. From this perspective, there is no basis for privileging human beings and there is no ground for focusing only on individuals (in ultimate truth, there are no distinct individuals). This viewpoint bears a similarity to some expressions of deep ecology (see Naess 2008b and Parkes 1997).

Of course, objections may be raised against this outlook. First, as we saw earlier, there may be objections to the ideas of Buddha-nature and the embryo of the Buddha on the ground that these seem to attribute an inherent nature to things. Beyond this, it is unclear what moral significance follows from the claim that inanimate objects have value as aspects of the whole. For the most part, no clear sense can be attached to the idea of harming inanimate objects because it is not evident what it would mean for them to do well or badly (whereas we do have some sense of what this would mean for many living beings). If I smash a rock, have I harmed it or even the environment of which it is a part? It is not obvious that I have unless an anthropocentric value is assigned to it (such as that it is a feature of my garden). In addition, if all things have Buddha-nature, then it would seem that in this respect they all have equal value, and we may wonder once again if there is any evaluative difference between, say, a polluted and a clean environment. It seems clear that a viable environmental ethic needs to be able to establish such differences, and a non-anthropocentric environmental ethic needs to do this in a way that does not simply appeal to what serves the interests of human beings. A challenge for such a view is to establish a meaningful and plausible program of ethical environmental action that does not tacitly reinstate traditional anthropocentric hierarchies such as the commonly assumed "progression" from the inanimate to the animate to the sentient to the rational. Finally, and relatedly, it may be unclear how this approach would address traditional disagreements within environmental ethics such as whether it would be justified to kill or harm some individual living beings in order to preserve a species or an ecosystem. There is no clear recognition of the modern concepts of species or ecosystems in traditional forms of Buddhism. Hence, even if all things have Buddha-nature, it is not obvious that a species or an ecosystem as such has Buddha-nature (even though members of a species or aspects of an ecosystem do). This might be taken to mean that wholes such as species and ecosystems have no moral standing beyond that of their parts. But the holism of this approach, combined with the recognition that all such categories apply only in conventional truth, might be interpreted as meaning that such wholes within *the* whole, as it were, do have moral standing (after all, what we ordinarily call individuals are themselves wholes on this view). However, this would still leave open the question of whether and by what means we should try to preserve species and ecosystems.

There is much more that might be said about environmental ethics from a Mahāyāna perspective. For example, east Asian forms of Buddhism, especially in the Ch'an and Zen traditions, often emphasize reverence for, and living harmoniously with, the natural world (a dominant theme in artistic works associated with these traditions). But there are also indications of rather different attitudes towards nature in Mahāyāna Buddhism. In Tantric Buddhism, for instance, a central concern is to gain power over nature (see P. Williams *et al.* 2012: 146). This might be interpreted as expressing a "dominion ideal" that is the source of environmental problems (see I. Harris 1997: 385). Moreover, even Japanese Zen gardens, though they may be seen as expressions of appreciation of nature, are nonetheless highly developed products of culture. This too might be seen as expressing a "possessive" attitude towards nature (see Eckel 1997: 334).

## Buddhist Environmental Virtue Ethics

Much of the debate about foundational issues in environmental ethics, and of our discussion so far of Buddhist environmental ethics, has focused on the moral standing of individual human beings, animals and plants as well as that of wholes such as species and ecosystems. Resolution of these issues would seem to be important in a variety of normative moral theories such as a consequentialist approach (showing which consequences matter), a deontological approach (establishing that to which we have duties) and a rights approach (making clear which things have rights). However, though consideration of these three approaches has played a role in environmental ethics in Western philosophy (alongside debates about more radical theories such as deep ecology), it has not played a very significant role in discussions of Buddhist environmental ethics. In any case, as we have seen, a prominent alternative to these approaches is virtue ethics. In recent years, environmental virtue ethics has come to the forefront of both Western philosophical analyses of environmental ethics and Buddhist inquiries into environmental ethics. It is sometimes claimed that environmental virtue ethics is superior to other approaches because it shifts the emphasis from questions of moral standing to what it means to live a virtuous life in the context of environmental concerns. There have been several defenses of a Buddhist environmental virtue ethics (for an early suggestion of this approach, see Sponberg 1997: 370).

A good example is David E. Cooper and Simon P. James's (2005) text *Buddhism, Virtue and Environment*. They argue that Buddhist ethics is best interpreted as similar to a eudaimonistic virtue ethics in which the final end is a life of "nirvanic felicity" that they think is constituted by Buddhist wisdom and a set of moral virtues (a position they believe is closer to Epicurus and the Stoics than to Aristotle). These virtues include the "foundational" virtue mindfulness as well as three "self-regarding" virtues: humility (overcoming self-centered thoughts such as "I am" and "This is mine"), self-mastery (encompassing such things as right effort, temperance and a capacity for solitude) and equanimity (the ability to judge in a discriminating and appropriate way). These virtues also include three "other-regarding" virtues: solicitude (loving-kindness, compassion and empathetic joy), non-violence (not harming sentient beings and gentleness both of the intellect and in the treatment of non-sentient beings) and responsibleness (readiness to accept moral responsibilities). Cooper and James maintain that "Buddhism is 'green'" since these virtues "may and should be exercised with respect to non-human life and the wider world which sustains life" (Cooper and James 2005: 106). This is partly because in Buddhism nature is a "moral resource" that evokes the impermanence and suffering of the world and so provides an opportunity for the development of the aforementioned virtues. But it is also because these virtues enable us to overcome such vices as acquisitiveness, anthropocentrism, ignorance, cruelty, violence and passivity that are sources of environmental problems. For example, humility and self-mastery both counter acquisitiveness, and solicitude and non-violence oppose cruelty.

Other proponents of a virtue ethics approach to Buddhist environmental concerns have highlighted virtues similar to those featured in Cooper and James. For example, Keown (2007), who is well known for his interpretation of Buddhist ethics as similar to an Aristotelian eudaimonistic ethical theory (see Chapter 6), suggests that this approach is also fruitful in the environmental context. He appeals to Buddhist virtues such as love, compassion, gladness, equanimity, non-greed, contentment with what one has and non-violence as fostering attitudes that are favorable to the environment. Likewise, Pragati Sahni (2008), focusing on early Buddhism, has emphasized the environmental importance of the virtues of respecting life, simple living and contentment, generosity, responsibility and wisdom among others. It is also worth noting that James (2004), writing on his own, develops a virtue ethics approach specifically with respect to Japanese Zen Buddhism. He argues that Zen can be interpreted as a form of virtue ethics in which wisdom and compassion are central virtues. Moreover, in light of Dōgen's view that all things are Buddha-nature, Zen can extend the moral circle to animals and plants as well as to mountains and rivers (an outlook which James thinks is partly similar to the "extreme holism" of deep ecologists such as Naess, but also partly different, for instance, on account of Naess's understanding of self-realization).

There is no question that the way of life implied by various Buddhist virtues would be environmentally friendly in many respects. To this extent the virtue ethics approach to Buddhist environmental ethics is clearly valuable. Still, there are objections that may be raised against this approach. Aside from the questions that confront any virtue ethics interpretation of Buddhist ethics (see Chapter 6), there is the specific concern, noted earlier, that a eudaimonistic virtue ethics that construes the virtues as what is necessary for human flourishing will be too anthropocentric to be an adequate environmental ethic. In response to this objection, James says that valuing nature for its own sake may be a virtue that is a constitutive feature of well-being (James 2004: 60; cf. Keown 2007: 106–7). In this view, the virtuous person values nature for its own sake, and not because doing so promotes his own well-being, even though it does promote this. Against this, it may be said that if the basic justifying framework is eudaimonistic (meaning that something is a virtue only insofar as it contributes to human well-being), then the approach is still anthropocentric. It might be countered, however, that anthropocentrism in this sense would be harmless. Another objection is that the virtue ethics approach cannot avoid confronting the issues of moral standing discussed earlier. For example, Cooper and James maintain that species have no moral standing on their understanding of Buddhism (see 2005: 141–3) and, as we have just seen, James appeals to Dōgen's views about Buddha-nature to support his Zen environmental ethics. In response, it may be claimed that though it is true that issues concerning moral standing still need to be considered, the virtue ethics approach is nonetheless important in drawing attention to the way in which pursuing the Buddhist path to enlightenment, or being enlightened, has significant positive moral implications for how we deal with the environment (see Ives 2013).

**Animals**
The treatment of individual animals deserves special consideration because it is a very important issue in Buddhist traditions. It is also a central topic in contemporary environmental ethics, though it is sometimes in tension with other aspects of environmental ethics as in disputes about whether priority should be given to preventing the suffering of individual animals or to preserving ecological wholes such as species and ecosystems (an issue that does not arise traditionally in Buddhism insofar as these wholes were not recognized). We have already touched on two of the main Buddhist perspectives that bear on the treatment of animals. First, animals are part of the cycle of rebirth. This means that they are both susceptible to suffering and capable of enlightenment (meaning, in many Mahāyāna traditions, that they have Buddha-nature). Second, the first moral precept prohibits killing or harming (at least) all sentient beings including animals. There is thus a very prominent strand within Buddhist teaching that says that we have a strong kinship with animals and should not harm them (see Stewart 2010).

There are many indications of this strand in a variety of contexts. For example, it is often said that we should not kill any beings because at some point in the cycle of rebirth they all have been our mother or father (see Harvey 2000: 163 and Waldau 2000: 87). Among the forms of wrong livelihood is "trading in meat" (see *AN* III 208). In addition, Aśoka, according to the rock edicts, gave up hunting, promoted abstention from killing animals, banned animal sacrifice in his capital and prohibited killing a number of specific animals altogether or at least on certain days. In addition, he established medical treatment for animals (for summaries, see Chapple 1992: 57–8 and Harvey 2000: 158). There are, however, some complications and contrary indications. As noted earlier, animals as a group are lower in the hierarchy of the cycle of rebirth than human beings: they are morally inferior and suffer more. Moreover, perhaps for this reason, it is often said to be worse to kill a human being than to kill an animal (see Waldau 2000: 96–7). In addition, it has been claimed that there is evidence that in the Pali Canon animals such as elephants were treated in instrumental ways to serve human purposes without consideration of their own interests (see Waldau 2000: 101–3).

In view of the opposition to killing animals, one might expect that Buddhist teaching would ordinarily be that we should not eat meat. But in fact, this has not always been the case. Indeed, the Buddha himself may have died from eating meat (see *DN* II 127–8). At any rate, he instructed the monks that "there are three instances in which meat may be eaten: when it is not seen, not heard and not suspected [that the living being has been slaughtered for the bhikkhu]." Hence, the monks were not strictly prohibited from eating meat. Nonetheless, the Buddha emphasized that a layperson who slaughtered an animal for a monk "lays up much demerit" (*MN* I 369–71). Hence, this instruction is clearly not a permission to kill animals for food. Moreover, monks were not to encourage this: if they did see, hear or suspect that an animal was killed for them, they were not permitted to eat it. In Mahāyāna Buddhism, however, there are texts that proscribe eating meat. For example, *The Laṅkāvatāra Sūtra* represents the Buddha as stating:

> Wherever there is the evolution of living beings, let people cherish the thought of kinship with them, and, thinking that all beings are [to be loved as if they were] an only child, let them refrain from eating meat. So with Bodhisattvas whose nature is compassion, [the eating of] meat is to be avoided by him. Even in exceptional cases, it is not [compassionate] of a Bodhisattva of good standing to eat meat.
> (Suzuki 1999: 212)

The text goes on to give a number of reasons for not eating meat such as to avoid "causing terror to living beings" and it explicitly repudiates the earlier teaching that eating meat is sometimes permissible (Suzuki 1999: 213–8).

As we have seen, there is often more flexibility in applying the moral precepts in Mahāyāna Buddhism than in earlier forms of Buddhism, but here the opposite is the case: this prohibition admits no exceptions. Beyond such textual resources from the tradition, if we consider what followers of Buddhist teachings have actually done in this regard, we find a diversity of perspectives: vegetarianism is sometimes practiced, but often it is not (for a survey, see Harvey 2000: 161–5).

# Bibliography

**Traditional Buddhist Texts**

Bendall, Cecil and Rouse, W.H.D. (trs.) (1971) *Śikṣā-Samuccaya: A Compendium of Buddhist Doctrine, Compiled by Śāntideva Chiefly from the Earlier Mahāyāna Sūtras,* Delhi: Motilal Banarsidass.

Bodhi, Bhikkhu (tr.) (2000) *The Connected Discourses of the Buddha: A New Translation of the Saṃyutta Nikāya,* 2 volumes, Boston: Wisdom Publications.

———— (tr.) (2012) *The Numerical Discourses of the Buddha: A Translation of the Aṅguttara Nikāya,* Boston: Wisdom Publications.

Carter, John Ross and Palihawadana, Mahinda (trs.) (2000) *The Dhammapada,* Oxford: Oxford University Press.

Conze, Edward (tr.) (1975) *The Large Sutra on Perfect Wisdom with the Divisions of the Abhisamayālaṅkāra,* Berkeley: University of California Press.

———— (tr.) (2006) *The Perfection of Wisdom in Eight Thousand Lines and Its Verse Summary,* San Francisco: City Lights.

Crosby, Kate and Skilton, Andrew (trs.) (1995) *Śāntideva: The Bodhicaryāvatāra,* Oxford: Oxford University Press.

Davids, Rhys, and A. F., Carolyn (tr. and ed.) (1900) *A Buddhist Manual of Buddhist Psychological Ethics (Dhamma-Saṅgaṇi),* London: Royal Asiatic Society.

Garfield, Jay L. (tr.) (1995) *The Fundamental Wisdom of the Middle Way: Nāgārjuna's The Mūlamadhyamakakārikā,* New York: Oxford University Press.

Hopkins, Jeffrey (tr.) (1998) *Buddhist Advice for Living and Liberation: Nāgārjuna's Precious Garland,* Ithaca, NY: Snow Lion Publications.

Ireland, John D. (tr.) (1997) *The Udāna: Inspired Utterances of the Buddha and The Itivuttaka: The Buddha's Sayings,* Kandy, Sri Lanka: Buddhist Publication Society.

Lang, Karen C. (tr.) (1986) *Āryadeva's Catuḥśataka: On the Bodhisattva's Cultivation of Merit and Knowledge,* Copenhagen: Akademisk Forlag.

————— (tr.) (2003) *Four Illusions: Candrakīrti's Advice for Travelers on the Bodhisattva Path,* New York: Oxford University Press.

Meadows, Carol (tr. and ed.) (1986) *Ārya-Śūra's Compendium of the Perfections: Text, Translation and Analysis of the Pāramitāsamāsa,* Bonn: Indica et Tibetica Verlag.

Mendis, N.K.G. (ed.) (1993) *The Questions of King Milinda: An Abridgement of the Milindapañha,* Kandy, Sri Lanka: Buddhist Publication Society.

Murcott, Susan (tr.) (1991) *The First Buddhist Women: Translations and Commentary on the Therigatha,* Berkeley, CA: Parallax Press.

Ñāṇamoli, Bhikkhu (tr.) (1999) *The Path of Purification (Visuddhimagga)* by Buddhaghosa, Seattle: Buddhist Publication Society Pariyatta Editions.

Ñāṇamoli, Bhikkhu and Bodhi, Bhikkhu (trs. and eds.) (1995) *The Middle Length Discourses of the Buddha: A New Translation of the Majjhima Nikāya,* Boston: Wisdom Publications.

Pruden, Leo M. (tr.) (1988–90) *Treasury of Abhidharma (Abhidharmakośa) by Vasubandhu,* 4 Volumes, Berkeley, CA: Asian Humanities Press.

Suzuki, Daisetz Teitaro (tr.) (1999) *The Laṅkāvatāra Sūtra: A Mahāyāna Text,* New Delhi: Munshiram Manoharlal Publishers.

Tatz, Mark (tr.) (1986) *Asanga's Chapter on Ethics with the Commentary of Tsong-Kha-Pa, The Basic Path to Awakening, The Complete Bodhisattva,* Studies in Asian Thought and Religion, Volume 4, Lewiston, NY: Edwin Mellen Press.

————— (tr.) (1994) *The Skill in Means (Upāyakauśalya) Sūtra,* Delhi: Motilal Banarsidass.

Thurman, Robert A.F. (tr.) (1976) *The Holy Teaching of Vimalakīrti: A Mahāyāna Scripture,* University Park: The Pennsylvania State University Press.

Tsongkhapa (2004) *The Great Treatise on the Stages of the Path to Enlightenment,* Vol. 2, The Lamrim Chenmo Translation Committee (tr.), Ithaca, NY: Snow Lion Publications.

Walshe, Maurice (tr.) (1987) *The Long Discourses of the Buddha: A Translation of the Dīgha Nikāya,* Boston: Wisdom Publications.

## Secondary Sources

Adam, Martin T. (2005) "Groundwork for a Metaphysic of Buddhist Morals: A New Analysis of Punna and Kusala, in Light of Sukka," *Journal of Buddhist Ethics* 12: 62–85.

————— (2010) "No Self, No Free Will, No Problem—Implications of the *Anattalakkhaṇa Sutta* for a Perennial Philosophical Issue," *Journal of the International Association of Buddhist Studies* 33: 239–65.

————— (2013) "Buddhism, Equality, Rights," *Journal of Buddhist Ethics* 20: 421–43.

Akira, Hirakawa (1990) *A History of Indian Buddhism: From Śākyamuni to Early Mahāyāna,* Pauk Groner (tr.), Honolulu: University of Hawai'i Press.

Annas, Julia (2006) "Virtue Ethics," in David Copp (ed.) *The Oxford Handbook of Ethical Theory,* Oxford: Oxford University Press, 515–36.

Anscombe, G.E.M. (1958) "Modern Moral Philosophy," *Philosophy* 33: 1–19.

Aristotle (2002) *Nicomachean Ethics,* Christopher Rowe (tr.), Oxford: Oxford University Press.

Arnold, Dan (2008) "Dharmakīrti's Dualism: Critical Reflections on a Buddhist Proof of Rebirth," *Philosophy Compass* 3: 1079–96.

Aronson, Harvey B. (1980) *Love and Sympathy in Theravāda Buddhism,* Delhi: Motilal Banarsidass.

—— (2004) *Buddhist Practice on Western Ground: Reconciling Eastern Ideals and Western Psychology,* Boston: Shambhala.

Augustine (1993) *On Free Choice of the Will,* Thomas Williams (tr.), Indianapolis, IN: Hackett Publishing Company.

Badiner, Allan Hunt (ed.) (1990a) *Dharma Gaia: A Harvest of Essays in Buddhism and Ecology,* Berkeley, CA: Parallax Press.

—— (1990b) "Introduction," in Allan Hunt Badiner (ed.) *Dharma Gaia: A Harvest of Essays in Buddhism and Ecology,* Berkeley, CA: Parallax Press, xiii–xviii.

Barnhart, Michael G. (2012) "Theory and Comparison in the Discussion of Buddhist Ethics," *Philosophy East and West* 62: 16–43.

—— (2013) "Impermanence, Anattā, and the Stability of Egocentrism; or How Ethically Unstable is Egocentrism?" *Journal of Buddhist Ethics* 20: 591–611.

Barnhill, David Landis (1997) "Great Earth *Saṅgha:* Gary Snyder's View of Nature as Community," in Mary Evelyn Tucker and Duncan Ryūken Williams (eds.) *Buddhism and Ecology: The Interconnection of Dharma and Deeds,* Cambridge, MA: Harvard University Press, 187–217.

Bartholomeusz, Tessa (1999) "In Defense of Dharma: Just-War Ideology in Buddhist Sri Lanka," *Journal of Buddhist Ethics* 6: 1–16.

—— (2002) *In Defense of Dharma: Just-War Ideology in Buddhist Sri Lanka,* London: RoutledgeCurzon.

Basham, A.L. (1982) "Asoka and Buddhism: A Re-Examination," *Journal of the International Association of Buddhist Studies* 5: 131–43.

Batchelor, Martine and Brown, Kerry (eds.) (1994) *Buddhism and Ecology,* Delhi: Motilal Banarsidass Publishers.

Batchelor, Stephen (1997) *Buddhism without Beliefs: A Contemporary Guide to Awakening,* New York: Riverhead Books.

Batchelor, Stephen and Thurman, Robert (1997) "Reincarnation: A Debate," *Tricycle* 6: 24–7 and 109–16.

Bauer, Joanne R. and Bell, Daniel A. (eds.) (1999) *The East Asian Challenge for Human Rights,* Cambridge: Cambridge University Press.

Bechert, Heinz (1984) "Buddhist Revival in East and West," in Heinz Bechert and Richard Gombrich (eds.) *The World of Buddhism: Buddhist Monks and Nuns in Society and Culture,* London: Thames and Hudson, 273–85.

—— (1994) "Buddhist Modernism: Present Situation and Current Trends," in *Buddhism into the Year 2000: International Conference Proceedings,* Bangkok: Dhammakaya Foundation, 251–60.

Bommarito, Nicolas (2011) "Bile and Bodhisattvas: Śāntideva on Justified Anger," *Journal of Buddhist Ethics* 18: 356–74.

Bond, George D. (2009) "Buddhism, War and Peace in Sri Lanka," in John Powers and Charles S. Prebish (eds.) *Destroying Māra Forever: Buddhist Ethics Essays in Honor of Damien Keown,* Ithaca, NY: Snow Lion Publications, 141–9.

Bookchin, Murray (2005) *The Ecology of Freedom: The Emergence and Dissolution of Hierarchy,* Oakland, CA: AK Press.

Brear, A. D. (1974) "The Nature and Status of Moral Behavior in Zen Buddhist Tradition," *Philosophy East and West* 24: 429–41.

Breyer, Daniel (2013) "Freedom with a Buddhist Face," *Sophia* 52: 359–79.

Brink, David O. (2006) "Some Forms and Limits of Consequentialism," in David Copp (ed.) *The Oxford Handbook of Ethical Theory,* Oxford: Oxford University Press, 380–423.

Buckle, Stephen (1991) "Natural Law," in Peter Singer (ed.) *A Companion to Ethics,* Oxford: Blackwell Publishers, 161–74.

Buddhadāsa Bhikkhu (1989) *Me and Mine: Selected Essays of Bhikkhu Buddhadāsa,* Donald K. Swearer (ed.) Albany: State University of New York Press.

Burton, David (2004) *Buddhism, Knowledge and Liberation: A Philosophical Study,* Burlington, VT: Ashgate.

———— (2010) "Curing Diseases of Belief and Desire: Buddhist Philosophical Therapy," in Clare Carlisle and Jonardon Ganeri (eds.) *Philosophy as Therapeia,* Royal Institute of Philosophy Supplement 66, Cambridge: Cambridge University Press, 187–217.

Callicott, J. Baird (1980) "Animal Liberation: A Triangular Affair," *Environmental Ethics* 2: 311–38.

Carrithers, Michael (1983) *The Buddha,* Oxford: Oxford University Press.

Cerna, C. M. (1994) "Universality of Human Rights and Cultural Diversity: Implementation of Human Rights in Different Socio-Cultural Contexts," *Human Rights Quarterly* 16: 740–52.

Chapple, Christopher (1992) "Nonviolence to Animals in Buddhism and Jainism," in Kenneth Kraft (ed.) *Inner Peace, World Peace: Essays on Buddhism and Nonviolence,* Albany: State University of New York Press, 49–62.

———— (1997) "Animals and Environment in the Buddhist Birth Stories," in Mary Evelyn Tucker and Duncan Ryūken Williams (eds.) *Buddhism and Ecology: The Interconnection of Dharma and Deeds,* Cambridge, MA: Harvard University Press, 131–48.

Chisholm, Roderick M. (1982) "The Problem of the Criterion," in *The Foundations of Knowing,* Minneapolis: University of Minnesota Press, 61–75.

Clayton, Barbra R. (2001) "Compassion as a Matter of Fact: The Argument from No-Self to Selflessness in Śāntideva's *Śikṣāssamuccaya*," *Contemporary Buddhism* 2: 83–97.

———— (2006) *Moral Theory in Śāntideva's Śikṣāssamuccaya: Cultivating the Fruits of Virtue,* New York: Routledge.

———— (2009) "Śāntideva, Virtue, and Consequentialism," in John Powers and Charles S. Prebish (eds.) *Destroying Māra Forever: Buddhist Ethics Essays in Honor of Damien Keown,* Ithaca, NY: Snow Lion Publications, 15–29.

Clippard, Seth Devere (2011) "The Lorax Wears Saffron: Toward a Buddhist Environmentalism," *Journal of Buddhist Ethics* 18: 212–48.

Collins, Steven (1998) *Nirvana and Other Buddhist Felicities: Utopias of the Pali Imaginaire.* Cambridge: Cambridge University Press.

Condon, Paul, et al. (2013) "Meditation Increases Compassionate Responses to Suffering," *Psychological Science* 24: 2125–7.

Cook, Francis H. (1977) *Hua-yen Buddhism: The Jewel Net of Indra,* University Park: Pennsylvania State University Press.

——— (1989) "The Jewel Net of Indra," in J. Baird Callicott and Roger T. Ames (eds.) *Nature in Asian Traditions of Thought: Essays in Environmental Philosophy,* Albany: State University of New York Press, 213–29.

Cooper, David E. (1978) "Moral Relativism," *Midwest Studies in Philosophy* 3: 97–108.

Cooper, David E. and James, Simon P. (2005) *Buddhism, Virtue and Environment,* Burlington, VT: Ashgate.

Cooper, John M. (2012) *Pursuits of Wisdom: Six Ways of Life in Ancient Philosophy from Socrates to Plotinus,* Princeton, NJ: Princeton University Press.

Cowherds, The (2011) *Moonshadows: Conventional Truth in Buddhist Philosophy,* Oxford: Oxford University Press.

Crisp, Roger (Summer 2013) "Well-Being," *The Stanford Encyclopedia of Philosophy,* Edward N. Zalta (ed.), Retrieved from http://plato.stanford.edu/archives/sum2013/entries/well-being/

Crosby, Kate (2008) "Kamma, Social Collapse or Geophysics? Interpretations of Suffering among Sri Lankan Buddhists in the Immediate Aftermath of the 2004 Asian Tsunami," *Contemporary Buddhism* 9: 53–76.

Dalai Lama (1995) *The World of Tibetan Buddhism: An Overview of its Philosophy and Practice,* Geshe Thupten Jinpa (tr.), Boston: Wisdom Publications.

——— (1996) "Cultivating Altruism," in Arnold Kotler (ed.) *Engaged Buddhist Reader: Ten Years of Engaged Buddhist Publishing,* Berkeley, CA: Parallax Press, 3–6.

——— (1997) *Healing Anger: The Power of Patience from a Buddhist Perspective,* Geshe Thupten Jinpa (tr.), Ithaca, NY: Snow Lion Publications.

——— (1998a) " Human Rights and Universal Responsibility," in Damien Keown, Charles S. Prebish and Wayne R. Husted (eds.) *Buddhism and Human Rights,* Richmond, Surrey: Curzon Press, xvii–xxi.

——— (1998b) "Humanity's Concern for Human Rights," in Barend van der Heijden and Bahia Tahzib-Lie (eds.) *Reflections on the Universal Declaration of Human Rights: A Fiftieth Anniversary Anthology,* The Hague: Martinus Nijhoff Publishers, 101–6.

——— (1999) *Ethics for the New Millennium,* New York: Riverhead Books.

——— (2005) *The Universe in a Single Atom: The Convergence of Science and Spirituality,* New York: Broadway Books.

——— (2011) *Beyond Religion: Ethics for a Whole World,* Boston: Houghton Mifflin Harcourt.

Dancy, Jonathan (2004) *Ethics without Principles,* Oxford: Clarendon Press.

Darwall, Stephen (2006) *The Second-Person Standpoint: Morality, Respect, and Accountability,* Cambridge, MA: Harvard University Press.

Davis, Daphne M. and Hayes, Jeffrey A. (2011) "What Are the Benefits of Mindfulness? A Practice Review of Psychotherapy-Related Research," *Psychotherapy* 48: 198–208.

Davis, Gordon F. (2013a) "Traces of Consequentialism and Non-Consequentialism in Buddhist Ethics," *Philosophy East and West* 63: 275–305.

———— (2013b) "Moral Realism and Anti-Realism Outside the West: A Meta-Ethical Turn in Buddhist Ethics, *Comparative Philosophy* 4: 24–53.

Demiéville, Paul (2010) "Buddhism and War," Michelle Kendall (tr.) in Michael K. Jerryson and Mark Juergensmeyer (eds.) *Buddhist Warfare,* Oxford: Oxford University Press, 17–57.

de Silva, Lily (1991) "Freedom," in G. P. Malalasekera (ed.) *Encyclopedia of Buddhism,* Vol. 5, Colombo: Department of Government Printing, 272–77.

———— (1994) "The Hills Wherein my Soul Delights," in Martine Batchelor and Kerry Brown (eds.) *Buddhism and Ecology,* Delhi: Motilal Banarsidass, 18–30.

de Silva, Padmasiri (1995) "Theoretical Perspectives on Emotions in Early Buddhism," in Joel Marks and Roger T. Ames (eds.) *Emotions in Asian Thought: A Dialogue in Comparative Philosophy,* Albany: State University of New York Press, 109–21.

Donnelly, Jack (2013) *Universal Human Rights in Theory and Practice,* Third Edition, Ithaca, NY: Cornell University Press.

Dreyfus, Georges (1995) "Meditation as Ethical Activity," *Journal of Buddhist Ethics* 2: 28–54.

———— (2001) "Is Compassion an Emotion? A Cross-Cultural Exploration of Mental Typologies," in Richard J. Davidson and Anne Harrington (eds.) *Visions of Compassion: Western Scientists and Tibetan Buddhists Examine Human Nature,* New York: Oxford University Press, 31–45.

———— (2011) "Can a Mādhyamika Be a Skeptic? The Case of Patsab Nyimadrak," in The Cowherds, *Moonshadows: Conventional Truth in Buddhist Philosophy,* New York: Oxford University Press, 89–113.

Eckel, Malcolm David (1997) "Is There a Buddhist Philosophy of Nature?" in Mary Evelyn Tucker and Duncan Ryūken Williams (eds.) *Buddhism and Ecology: The Interconnection of Dharma and Deeds,* Cambridge, MA: Harvard University Press, 327–49.

Edelglass, William (2013) "Buddhist Ethics and Western Moral Philosophy," in Steven M. Emmanuel (ed.) *A Companion to Buddhist Philosophy,* West Sussex: John Wiley & Sons, 476–90.

Edwards, Paul (1996) *Reincarnation: A Critical Examination,* Amherst, NY: Prometheus Books.

Eppsteiner, Fred (ed.) (1988) *The Path of Compassion: Writings on Socially Engaged Buddhism,* Revised Second Edition, Berkeley, CA: Parallax Press.

Faure, Bernard (2009) *Unmasking Buddhism,* Malden, MA: Wiley-Blackwell.

———— (2010) "Afterthoughts," in Michael K. Jerryson and Mark Juergensmeyer (eds.) *Buddhist Warfare,* Oxford: Oxford University Press, 211–25.

Federman, Asaf (2010) "What Kind of Free Will Did the Buddha Teach?" *Philosophy East and West* 60: 1–19.

Feinberg, Joel (1980a) "Duties, Rights and Claims," in *Rights, Justice, and the Bounds of Liberty: Essays in Social Philosophy,* Princeton, NJ: Princeton University Press, 130–42.

———— (1980b) "The Nature and Value of Rights," in *Rights, Justice, and the Bounds of Liberty: Essays in Social Philosophy,* Princeton, NJ: Princeton University Press, 143–55.

Fink, Charles K. (2013) "The Cultivation of Virtue in Buddhist Ethics," *Journal of Buddhist Ethics* 20: 668–701.

Finnigan, Bronwyn (2010) "Buddhist Metaethics," *Journal of the International Association of Buddhist Studies* 33: 267–97.

———— (2011a) "How Can a Buddha Come to Act? The Possibility of a Buddhist Account of Ethical Agency," *Philosophy East and West* 61: 134–60.

———— (2011b) "The Possibility of a Buddhist Account of Ethical Agency Revisited: A Reply to Jay Garfield and Chad Hansen," *Philosophy East and West* 61: 183–94.

———— (Forthcoming) "Meta-ethics for Madhyamaka: Investigating the Justificatory Grounds of Moral Judgments," *Philosophy East and West.*

Finnigan, Bronwyn and Tanaka, Koji (2011) "Ethics for Madhyamikas," in The Cowherds, *Moonshadows: Conventional Truth in Buddhist Philosophy,* New York: Oxford University Press, 221–31.

Fitzgerald, Patrick (1998) "Gratitude and Justice" *Ethics* 109: 119–53.

Flanagan, Owen (2011) *The Bodhisattva's Brain: Buddhism Naturalized,* Cambridge, MA: The MIT Press.

Foot, Philippa (1978) *Virtues and Vices and Other Essays in Moral Philosophy,* Oxford: Basil Blackwell.

Frakes, Chris (2007) "Do the Compassionate Flourish? Overcoming Anguish and the Impulse Towards Violence," *Journal of Buddhist Ethics* 14: 99–128.

Frankfurt, Harry (1971) "Freedom of the Will and the Concept of a Person," *Journal of Philosophy* 68: 5–20.

———— (1987) "Identification and Wholeheartedness," in Ferdinand Schoeman (ed.) *Responsibility, Character, and the Emotions: New Essays in Moral Psychology,* Cambridge: Cambridge University Press, 27–45.

Gadamer, Hans-Georg (2000) *Truth and Method,* Second Revised Edition, Joel Weinsheimer and Donald G. Marshall (trs.), New York: Continuum.

Garfield, Jay L. (2002a) "Dependent Arising and the Emptiness of Emptiness: Why Did Nāgārjuna Start with Causation?" in *Empty Words: Buddhist Philosophy and Cross-Cultural Interpretation,* Oxford: Oxford University Press, 24–45.

———— (2002b) "Human Rights and Compassion: Towards a Unified Moral Framework," in *Empty Words: Buddhist Philosophy and Cross-Cultural Interpretation,* Oxford: Oxford University Press, 187–219.

———— (2002c) "Buddhism and Democracy," in *Empty Words: Buddhist Philosophy and Cross-Cultural Interpretation,* Oxford: Oxford University Press, 206–19.

———— (2006) "Why did Bodhidharma Go to the East? Buddhism's Struggle with Mind in the World," *Sophia* 45: 61–80.

———— (2010) "What Is it Like to Be a Bodhisattva? Moral Phenomenology in Śāntideva's *Bodhicaryāvatāra*," *Journal of the International Association of Buddhist Studies* 33: 333–57.

———— (2011a) "Taking Conventional Truth Seriously: Authority Regarding Deceptive Reality," in The Cowherds, *Moonshadows: Conventional Truth in Buddhist Philosophy,* New York: Oxford University Press, 23–38.

———— (2011b) "Hey, Buddha! Don't Think! Just Act!—A Response to Bronwyn Finnigan," *Philosophy East and West* 61: 174–83.

———— (2012) "Mindfulness and Ethics: Attention, Virtue and Perfection," *Thai International Journal of Buddhist Studies* 3: 1–24.

———— (2014) "Just Another Word for Nothing Left to Lose: Freedom, Agency and Ethics for Mādhyamikas" in M.R. Dasti and E.F. Bryant (eds.) *Free Will, Agency, and Selfhood in Indian Philosophy,* Oxford: Oxford University Press, 164–185.

———— (Forthcoming) "Buddhism and Modernity" in John Powers (ed.) *The Buddhist World,* London: Routledge.

———— (Unpublished) Buddhist Ethics.

Gethin, Rupert (1998) *The Foundations of Buddhism,* Oxford: Oxford University Press.

———— (2004) "Can Killing a Living Being Ever Be an Act of Compassion? The Analysis of the Act of Killing in the *Abhidhamma* and Pāli Commentaries," *Journal of Buddhist Ethics* 11: 167–202.

Gewirth, Alan (1982) *Human Rights: Essays on Justification and Applications,* Chicago: University of Chicago Press.

Ghose, Lynken (2007) "*Karma* and the Possibility of Purification: An Ethical and Psychological Analysis of the Doctrine of *Karma* in Buddhism," *Journal of Religious Ethics* 35: 259–89.

Gier, Nicholas F. (2004) *The Virtue of Nonviolence: From Gautama to Gandhi,* Albany: State University of New York Press.

Gier, Nicholas F. and Kjellberg, Paul (2004) "Buddhism and Freedom of the Will: Pali and Mahayanist Responses," in Joseph Keim Campbell, Michael O'Rourke and David Shier (eds.) *Freedom and Determinism,* Cambridge, MA: MIT Press, 277–304.

Gold, Jonathan C. (Winter 2012) "Vasubandhu," *The Stanford Encyclopedia of Philosophy,* Edward N. Zalta (ed.), Retrieved from http://plato.stanford.edu/archives/win2012/entries/vasubandhu/

———— (2014) *Paving the Great Way: Vasubandhu's Unifying Buddhist Philosophy,* New York: Columbia University Press.

Gombrich, Richard F. (1971) *Precept and Practice: Traditional Buddhism in the Rural Highlands of Ceylon,* Oxford: Clarendon Press.

———— (1988) *Theravāda Buddhism: A Social History from Ancient Benares to Modern Colombo,* London: Routledge & Kegan Paul.

———— (2009) *What the Buddha Thought,* London: Equinox Publishing.

Gómez, Luis O. (1973) "Emptiness and Moral Perfection," *Philosophy East and West* 23: 361–73.

———— (1975) "Some Aspects of the Free-Will Question in the Nikāyas," *Philosophy East and West* 25: 81–90.

———— (1992) "Nonviolence and the Self in Early Buddhism," in Kenneth Kraft (ed.) *Inner Peace, World Peace: Essays on Buddhism and Nonviolence,* Albany: State University of New York Press, 31–48.

Goodman, Charles (2002) "Resentment and Reality: Buddhism on Moral Responsibility," *American Philosophical Quarterly* 39: 359–72.

———— (2008) "Consequentialism, Agent-Neutrality, and Mahāyāna Ethics," *Philosophy East and West* 58: 17–35.

———— (2009) *Consequences of Compassion: An Interpretation and Defense of Buddhist Ethics,* New York: Oxford University Press.

———— (2013) "Buddhist Meditation: Theory and Practice," in Steven M. Emmanuel (ed.) *A Companion to Buddhist Philosophy,* West Sussex: John Wiley & Sons, 555–71.

Gowans, Christopher W. (1994) *Innocence Lost: An Examination of Inescapable Moral Wrongdoing,* New York: Oxford University Press.

———— (2003) *Philosophy of the Buddha,* London: Routledge.

———— (2006) "Standing Up to Terrorists: Buddhism, Human Rights, and Self-Respect," in Douglas Allen (ed.) *Philosophy and Religion in Times of Terror,* Lanham, MD: Lexington Books, 101–21.

———— (2010) "Medical Analogies in Buddhist and Hellenistic Thought: Tranquility and Anger," in Clare Carlisle and Jonardon Ganeri (eds.) *Philosophy as Therapeia,* Royal Institute of Philosophy Supplement 66, Cambridge: Cambridge University Press, 11–33.

Griffiths, Paul J. (1982) "Notes Towards a Critique of Buddhist Karmic Theory," *Religious Studies* 18: 277–91.

Griswold, Charles L., Jr. (1996) "Happiness, Tranquillity, and Philosophy," *Critical Review* 10: 1–32.

Gross, R. M. (1993) *Buddhism after Patriarchy: A Feminist History, Analysis, and Reconstruction of Buddhism,* Albany: State University of New York Press.

Gunaratna, V. F. (1980) *Rebirth Explained,* Kandy, Sri Lanka: Buddhist Publication Society.

Hadot, Pierre (1995) *Philosophy as a Way of Life: Spiritual Exercises from Socrates to Foucault,* Michael Chase (tr.), Cambridge, MA: Blackwell.

———— (2002) *What Is Ancient Philosophy?* Michael Chase (tr.), Cambridge, MA: Belknap Press of Harvard University Press.

Halkias, Georgios T. (2013) "The Enlightened Sovereign: Buddhism and Kingship in India and Tibet," in Steven M. Emmanuel (ed.) *A Companion to Buddhist Philosophy,* West Sussex: John Wiley & Sons, 491–511.

Hallisey, Charles. (1996) "Ethical Particularism in Theravada Buddhism," *Journal of Buddhist Ethics* 3: 32–43.

———— (1997) "A Response to Kevin Schilbrack," *Journal of Buddhist Ethics* 4: 184–8.

Hanh, Thich Nhat (1996) "Love in Action" in Arnold Kotler (ed.) *Engaged Buddhist Reader: Ten Years of Engaged Buddhist Publishing,* Berkeley, CA: Parallax Press, 57–63.

———— (1998) *Interbeing: Fourteen Guidelines for Engaged Buddhism,* Third Edition, Berkeley, CA: Parallax Press.

———— (1999) *The Heart of the Buddha's Teaching: Transforming Suffering into Peace, Joy and Liberation,* New York: Broadway Books.

———— (2005) *Being Peace,* Berkeley, CA: Parallax Press.

Hansen, Chad (2011) "Washing the Dust from My Mirror: The Deconstruction of Buddhism—A Response to Bronwyn Finnigan," *Philosophy East and West* 61: 160–74.

Hare, R.M. (1981) *Moral Thinking: Its Levels, Method, and Point,* Oxford: Clarendon Press.

Harris, Ian (1994) "Causation and Telos: The Problem of Buddhist Environmental Ethics," *Journal of Buddhist Ethics* 1: 45–56.

———— (1995) "Getting to Grips with Buddhist Environmentalism: A Provisional Typology," *Journal of Buddhist Ethics* 2: 173–90.

———— (1997) "Buddhism and the Discourse of Environmental Concern: Some Methodological Problems Considered" in Mary Evelyn Tucker and Duncan Ryūken Williams (eds.) *Buddhism and Ecology: The Interconnection of Dharma and Deeds,* Cambridge, MA: Harvard University Press, 377–402.

———— (2000) "Buddhism and Ecology" in Damien Keown (ed.) *Contemporary Buddhist Ethics,* Richmond, Surrey: Curzon Press, 113–35.

Harris, Stephen (2011) "Does *Anātman* Rationally Entail Altruism? On *Bodhicaryāvatāra* 8:101–103," *Journal of Buddhist Ethics* 18: 93–123.

Harvey, Peter (1990) *An Introduction to Buddhism: Its Teachings, History and Practices,* Cambridge: Cambridge University Press.

———— (1995) "Criteria for Judging the Unwholesomeness of Actions in the Texts of Theravada Buddhism," *Journal of Buddhist Ethics* 2: 140–51.

———— (2000) *An Introduction to Buddhist Ethics: Foundations, Values and Issues,* Cambridge: Cambridge University Press.

———— (2007a) "Avoiding Unintended Harm to the Environment and the Buddhist Ethic of Intention," *Journal of Buddhist Ethics* 14: 1–34.

———— (2007b) "'Freedom of the Will' in the Light of Theravāda Buddhist Teachings," *Journal of Buddhist Ethics* 14: 35–98.

———— (2010) "An Analysis of Factors Related to the *Kusula/Akusula* Quality of Actions in the Pāli Tradition," *Journal of the International Association of Buddhist Studies* 33: 175–209.

Haybron, Daniel M. (2008) *The Pursuit of Unhappiness: The Elusive Psychology of Well-Being*, Oxford: Oxford University Press.

Heim, Maria (2008) "Buddhism" in John Corrigan (ed.) *Religion and Emotion,* New York: Oxford University Press, 17–34.

———— (2013) "Mind in Theravāda Buddhism," in Steven M. Emmanuel (ed.) *A Companion to Buddhist Philosophy,* West Sussex: John Wiley & Sons, 377–94.

———— (2014) *The Forerunner of All Things: Buddhaghosa on Mind, Intention, and Agency,* New York: Oxford University Press.

Hershock, Peter D. (2000) "Dramatic Intervention: Human Rights from a Buddhist Perspective," *Philosophy East and West* 50: 9–33.

———— (2005) "Valuing Karma: A Critical Concept for Orienting Interdependence toward Personal and Public Good," *Journal of Buddhist Ethics* 12.

Hill, Thomas E., Jr. (1983) "Ideals of Human Excellence and Preserving Natural Environments," *Environmental Ethics* 5: 211–24.

———— (2006) "Kantian Normative Ethics," in David Copp (ed.) *The Oxford Handbook of Ethical Theory,* Oxford: Oxford University Press, 480–514.

Holder, John J. (2007) "A Suffering (But Not Irreparable) Nature: Environmental Ethics from the Perspective of Early Buddhism," *Contemporary Buddhism* 8: 113–30.

Hubbard, Jamie and Swanson, Paul L. (eds.) (1997) *Pruning the Bodhi Tree: The Storm over Critical Buddhism,* Honolulu: University of Hawai'i Press.

Hunt-Perry, Patricia and Fine, Lyn (2000) "All Buddhism Is Engaged: Thich Nhat Hanh and the Order of Interbeing," in Christopher S. Queen (ed.) *Engaged Buddhism in the West,* Boston: Wisdom Publications, 35–66.

Hursthouse, Rosalind (1999) *On Virtue Ethics,* Oxford: Oxford University Press.

Ihara, Craig K. (1995) "Why There Are No Rights in Buddhism: A Reply to Damien Keown," in Damien Keown, Charles S. Prebish and Wayne R. Husted (eds.) *Buddhism and Human Rights,* Richmond, Surrey: Curzon Press, 43–51.

Ingram, Paul O. (1997) "The Jeweled Net of Nature," in Mary Evelyn Tucker and Duncan Ryūken Williams (eds.) *Buddhism and Ecology: The Interconnection of Dharma and Deeds,* Cambridge, MA: Harvard University Press, 71–85.

Ives, Christopher (1992) *Zen Awakening and Society,* Honolulu: University of Hawai'i Press.

———— (2008) "Deploying the Dharma: Reflections on the Methodology of Constructive Buddhist Ethics," *Journal of Buddhist Ethics* 15: 22–44.

———— (2009a) *Imperial-Way Zen: Ichikawa Hakugen's Critique and Lingering Questions for Buddhist Ethics,* Honolulu: University of Hawai'i Press.

———— (2009b) "In Search of a Green Dharma: Philosophical Issues in Buddhist Environmental Ethics," in John Powers and Charles S. Prebish (eds.) *Destroying Māra Forever: Buddhist Ethics Essays in Honor of Damien Keown,* Ithaca, NY: Snow Lion Publications, 165–85.

———— (2013) "Resources for Buddhist Environmental Ethics," *Journal of Buddhist Ethics* 20: 539–71.

James, Simon P. (2004) *Zen Buddhism and Environmental Ethics,* Hampshire, UK: Ashgate.

———— (2013) "Buddhism and Environmental Ethics," in Steven M. Emmanuel (ed.) *A Companion to Buddhist Philosophy,* West Sussex: John Wiley & Sons, 601–12.

Jayatilleke, K. N. (1974) *The Message of the Buddha,* New York: The Free Press.

Jeffreys, Derek S. (2003) "Does Buddhism Need Human Rights?" in Christopher Queen, Charles Prebish and Damien Keown (eds.) *Action Dharma: New Studies in Engaged Buddhism,* London: RoutledgeCurzon, 270–85.

Jenkins, Stephen (2010) "Making Merit Through Warfare and Torture According to the *Ārya-Bodhisattva-gocara-upāyaviṣaya-vikurvaṇa-nirdeśa Sūtra,*" in Michael K. Jerryson and Mark Juergensmeyer (eds.) *Buddhist Warfare,* Oxford: Oxford University Press, 59–75.

—— (2011) "On the Auspiciousness of Compassionate Violence," *Journal of the International Association of Buddhist Studies* 33: 299–331.

—— (2013) "Compassion and the Ethics of Violence," in Steven M. Emmanuel (ed.) *A Companion to Buddhist Philosophy,* West Sussex: John Wiley & Sons, 466–75.

Jerryson, Michael K. and Juergensmeyer, Mark (eds.) (2010) *Buddhist Warfare,* Oxford: Oxford University Press.

Jinpa, Thupten (2003) "Science as an Ally or a Rival Philosophy? Tibetan Buddhist Thinkers' Engagement with Modern Science," in B. Alan Wallace (ed.) *Buddhism and Science: Breaking New Ground,* New York: Columbia University Press.

Jones, Ken (2003) *The New Social Face of Buddhism: A Call to Action,* Boston: Wisdom Publications.

Jones, Dhivan Thomas (2012) "The Five *Niyāmas* as Laws of Nature: An Assessment of Modern Western Interpretations of Theravāda Buddhist Doctrine," *Journal of Buddhist Ethics* 19: 545–82.

Junger, Peter D. (1995) "Why the Buddha Has No Rights," in Damien Keown, Charles S. Prebish and Wayne R. Husted (eds.) *Buddhism and Human Rights,* Richmond, Surrey: Curzon Press, 53–96.

Kalupahana, David J. (1995) *Ethics in Early Buddhism,* Honolulu: University of Hawai'i Press.

Kane, Robert (ed.) (2011) *The Oxford Handbook of Free Will,* Second Edition, New York: Oxford University Press.

Kant, Immanuel (1991) *The Metaphysics of Morals,* Mary Gregor (tr.), Cambridge: Cambridge University Press.

—— (1998) *Groundwork of the Metaphysics of Morals,* Mary Gregor (tr.), Cambridge: Cambridge University Press.

Kapstein, Matthew T. (2001) *Reason's Traces: Identity and Interpretation in Indian and Tibetan Buddhist Thought,* Boston: Wisdom Publications.

Kasulis, Thomas P. (1981) *Zen Action Zen Person,* Honolulu: University of Hawai'i Press.

Kaza, Stephanie and Kraft, Kenneth (eds.) (2000) *Dharma Rain: Sources of Buddhist Environmentalism,* Boston: Shambhala Publications.

Keown, Damien (1992) *The Nature of Buddhist Ethics,* New York: St. Martin's Press.

——— (1995) "Are There Human Rights in Buddhism?" in Damien Keown, Charles S. Prebish and Wayne R. Husted (eds.) *Buddhism and Human Rights,* Richmond, Surrey: Curzon Press, 15–41.

——— (1996) "Karma, Character, and Consequentialism," *Journal of Religious Ethics* 24: 329–50.

——— (ed.) (2000) *Contemporary Buddhist Ethics,* Richmond, Surrey: Curzon Press.

——— (2001) *Buddhism and Bioethics,* New York: Palgrave.

——— (2006) "Buddhism: Morality without Ethics?" in Damien Keown (ed.) *Buddhist Studies from India to America: Essays in Honor of Charles S. Prebish,* London: Routledge, 40–8.

——— (2007) "Buddhism and Ecology: A Virtue Ethics Approach," *Contemporary Buddhism* 8: 97–112.

——— (2013a) "Buddhist Ethics," in Hugh LaFollette (ed.) *The International Encyclopedia of Ethics,* Malden, MA: Blackwell Publishing, 636–47.

——— (2013b) "Some Problems with Particularism," *Journal of Buddhist Ethics* 20: 447–60.

——— (Forthcoming) "Towards a Buddhist Theory of the 'Just War'," in John Powers (ed.) *The Buddhist World,* New York: Routledge.

Keown, Damien, Prebish, Charles S. and Husted, Wayne R. (eds.) (1998) *Buddhism and Human Rights,* Richmond, Surrey: Curzon Press.

King, Martin Luther, Jr. (2000) "Letter from Birmingham Jail," in *Why We Can't Wait,* New York: Signet Classic/New American Library, 64–84.

King, Sallie B. (1991) *Buddha Nature,* Albany: State University of New York Press.

——— (1996) "Thich Nhat Hanh and the Unified Buddhist Church of Vietnam: Nondualism in Action," in Christopher S. Queen and Sallie B. King (eds.) *Engaged Buddhism: Buddhist Liberation Movements in Asia,* Albany: State University of New York Press, 321–63.

——— (1997) "The Doctrine of Buddha-Nature is Impeccably Buddhist," in Jamie Hubbard and Paul L. Swanson (eds.) *Pruning the Bodhi Tree: The Storm over Critical Buddhism,* Honolulu: University of Hawai'i Press, 174–92.

——— (2000) "Human Rights in Contemporary Engaged Buddhism," in Roger R. Jackson and John J. Makransky (eds.) *Buddhist Theology: Critical Reflections by Contemporary Buddhist Scholars,* Richmond, Surrey: Curzon Press, 293–311.

——— (2005) *Being Benevolence: The Social Ethics of Engaged Buddhism,* Honolulu: University of Hawai'i Press.

——— (2009a) *Socially Engaged Buddhism,* Honolulu: University of Hawai'i Press.

——— (2009b) "Buddhism, Nonviolence, and Power," *Journal of Buddhist Ethics* 16: 103–35.

——— (2009c) "Elements of Engaged Buddhist Ethics Theory," in John Powers and Charles S. Prebish (eds.) *Destroying Māra Forever: Buddhist Ethics Essays in Honor of Damien Keown,* Ithaca, NY: Snow Lion Publications, 187–203.

———— (2013) "War and Peace in Buddhist Philosophy," in Steven M. Emmanuel (ed.) *A Companion to Buddhist Philosophy*, West Sussex: John Wiley & Sons, 631–50.

King, Winston L. (1994) "A Buddhist Ethic without Karmic Rebirth?" *Journal of Buddhist Ethics* 1: 33–44.

———— (1995) "Judeo-Christian and Buddhist Justice," *Journal of Buddhist Ethics* 2: 67–82.

———— (2001) *In the Hope of Nibbāna: The Ethics of Theravāda Buddhism,* Second Edition, Seattle: Pariyatti Press.

Kleine, Christoph (2006) "Evil Monks with Good Intentions? Remarks on Buddhist Monastic Violence and Its Doctrinal Background," in Michael Zimmermann, with the assistance of Chiew Hui Ho and Philip Pierce (eds.) *Buddhism and Violence,* Lumbini: Lumbini International Research Institute, 65–98.

Kotler, Arnold (ed.) (1996) *Engaged Buddhist Reader: Ten Years of Engaged Buddhist Publishing,* Berkeley, CA: Parallax Press.

Kraft, Kenneth (ed.) (1992a) *Inner Peace, World Peace: Essays on Buddhism and Nonviolence,* Albany: State University of New York Press.

———— (1992b) "Prospects of a Socially Engaged Buddhism," in Kenneth Kraft (ed.) *Inner Peace, World Peace: Essays on Buddhism and Nonviolence,* Albany: State University of New York Press, 11–30.

———— (2000) "New Voices in Engaged Buddhist Studies," in Christopher S. Queen (ed.) *Engaged Buddhism in the West,* Boston: Wisdom Publications, 485–511.

Kuzminski, Adrian (2008) *Pyrrhonism: How the Ancient Greeks Reinvented Buddhism,* Lanham, MD: Lexington Books.

Lance, Mark and Little, Margaret (2006) "Particularism and Antitheory," in David Copp (ed.) *The Oxford Handbook of Ethical Theory,* Oxford: Oxford University Press, 567–94.

Lele, Amod (2013) "The Compassionate Gift of Vice: Śāntideva on Gifts, Altruism, and Poverty," *Journal of Buddhist Ethics* 20: 702–34.

Long, A.A. and Sedley, D.N. (eds.) (1987) *The Hellenistic Philosophers, Vol. 1: Translations of the Principal Sources, with Philosophical Commentary,* Cambridge: Cambridge University Press.

Lopez, Donald S. Jr. (2002) "Introduction" in Donald S. Lopez, Jr. (ed.) *A Modern Buddhist Bible: Essential Readings from East and West,* Boston: Beacon Press, vii–xli.

Louden, Robert B. (1992) *Morality and Moral Theory: A Reappraisal and Reaffirmation,* New York: Oxford University Press.

Loy David R. (2003) *The Great Awakening: A Buddhist Social Theory,* Boston: Wisdom Publications.

MacIntyre, Alasdair (1984) *After Virtue: A Study in Moral Theory,* Second Edition, Notre Dame, IN: University of Notre Dame Press.

MacKenzie, Matthew (2013) "Enacting Selves, Enacting Worlds: On the Buddhist Theory of Karma," *Philosophy East and West* 63: 194–212.

MacMillan, Thomas F. (2002) "Virtue-Based Ethics: A Comparison of Aristotelian-Thomistic and Buddhist Approaches," *Religion East and West* 2: 37–50.

Macy, J.R. (1979) "Dependent Co-arising: The Distinctiveness of Buddhist Ethics," *Journal of Religious Ethics* 7: 38–52.

Mason, Elinor (Fall 2011) "Value Pluralism," *The Stanford Encyclopedia of Philosophy,* Edward N. Zalta (ed.), Retrieved from http://plato.stanford.edu/archives/fall2011/entries/value-pluralism

McDermott, James P. (1980) "Karma and Rebirth in Early Buddhism," in Wendy Doniger O'Flaherty (ed.) *Karma and Rebirth in Classical Indian Traditions,* Berkeley: University of California Press, 165–92.

McEvilley, Thomas (2002) *The Shape of Ancient Thought: Comparative Studies in Greek and Indian Philosophies,* New York: Allsworth Press.

McMahan, David L. (2008) *The Making of Buddhist Modernism,* Oxford: Oxford University Press.

——— (2012) "Buddhist Modernism" in David L. McMahan (ed.) *Buddhism in the Modern World,* London: Routledge, 159–76.

McNaughton, David (2000) "Intuitionism," in Hugh LaFollette (ed.) *The Blackwell Guide to Ethical Theory,* Malden, MA: Blackwell Publishing, 268–87.

McNaughton, David and Rawling, Piers (2006) "Deontology," in David Copp (ed.) *The Oxford Handbook of Ethical Theory,* Oxford: Oxford University Press, 424–58.

McRae, Emily (2012a) "A Passionate Buddhist Life," *Journal of Religious Ethics* 40: 99–121.

——— (2012b) "Emotions, Ethics, and Choice: Lessons from Tsongkhapa," *Journal of Buddhist Ethics* 19: 344–69.

——— (2013) "Equanimity and Intimacy: A Buddhist-Feminist Approach to the Elimination of Bias," *Sophia* 52: 447–62.

Meyers, Karin L. (2010) *Freedom and Self-Control: Free Will in South Asian Buddhism,* PhD Dissertation, University of Chicago Divinity School.

——— (2014) "Free Persons, Empty Selves: Freedom and Agency in Light of the Two Truths" in Matthew R. Dasti and Edwin F. Bryant (eds.) *Free Will, Agency, and Selfhood in Indian Philosophy*, Oxford: Oxford University Press, 41–67.

Mikulincer, Mario and Shaver, Phillip R. (2007) *Attachment in Adulthood: Structure, Dynamics, and Change,* New York: The Guilford Press.

Mill, John Stuart (1957) *Utilitarianism,* Indianapolis, IN: The Bobbs-Merrill Company.

Naess, Arne (2008a) "Self-Realization: An Ecological Approach to Being in the World," in Alan Drengson and Bill Devall (eds.) *Ecology of Wisdom: Writings by Arne Naess,* Berkeley, CA: Counterpoint, 81–96.

——— (2008b) "Gestalt Thinking and Buddhism," in Alan Drengson and Bill Devall (eds.) *Ecology of Wisdom: Writings by Arne Naess,* Berkeley, CA: Counterpoint, 193–203.

Nagel, Thomas (1979) "The Fragmentation of Value," in *Mortal Questions,* Cambridge: Cambridge University Press, 128–41.

Nanayakkara, S.K. (1979) "Free Will," in G.P. Malalasekera (ed.) *Encyclopedia of Buddhism,* Vol. 5, Colombo: Department of Government Printing, 277–80.

Neeman, Or (2010) "Theravāda Buddhism and John Dewey's Metaethics," *Journal of Buddhist Ethics* 17: 141–65.

Nikam, N.A. and McKeon, Richard (eds. and trs.) (1959) *The Edicts of Asoka,* Chicago: The University of Chicago Press.

Nussbaum, Martha C. (1993) "Non-Relative Virtues: An Aristotelian Approach," in Martha Nussbaum and Amartya Sen (eds.) *The Quality of Life,* Oxford: Clarendon Press, 242–69.

———— (1994) *The Therapy of Desire: Theory and Practice in Hellenistic Ethics,* Princeton, NJ: Princeton University Press.

———— (2001) *Upheavals of Thought: The Intelligence of Emotions,* Cambridge: Cambridge University Press.

Olson, Phillip (1993) *The Discipline of Freedom: A Kantian View of the Role of Moral Precepts in Zen Practice,* Albany: State University of New York Press.

Orend, Brian (2013) *The Morality of War,* Second Edition, Toronto: Broadview Press.

Park, Jin Y. (2008) *Buddhism and Postmodernity: Zen, Huayan, and the Possibility of Buddhist Postmodern Ethics,* Lanham, MD: Lexington Books.

Parkes, Graham (1997) "Voices of Mountains, Trees, and Rivers: Kūkai, Dōgen, and a Deeper Ecology" in Mary Evelyn Tucker and Duncan Ryūken Williams (eds.) *Buddhism and Ecology: The Interconnection of Dharma and Deeds,* Cambridge, MA: Harvard University Press, 111–28.

Payutto, Phra Prayudh (1995) *Buddhadhamma: Natural Laws and Values for Life,* Grant A. Olson (tr.), Albany: State University of New York Press.

Perera, L.P.N. (1991) *Buddhism and Human Rights: A Buddhist Commentary on the Universal Declaration of Human Rights,* Colombo, Sri Lanka: Karunaratne & Sons.

Perrett, Roy W. (1987) "Egoism, Altruism and Intentionalism in Buddhist Ethics," *Journal of Indian Philosophy* 15: 71–85.

Pettit, John W. (1999) "Review of Paul Williams' *Altruism and Reality,*" *Journal of Buddhist Ethics* 6: 120–37.

Pincoffs, Edmund L. (1986) *Quandaries and Virtues: Against Reductionism in Ethics,* Lawrence: University Press of Kansas.

Potter, Karl H. (1972) *Presuppositions of India's Philosophies*, Westport, CT: Greenwood Press.

Powers, John and Prebish, Charles S. (eds.) (2009) *Destroying Māra Forever: Buddhist Ethics Essays in Honor of Damien Keown,* Ithaca, NY: Snow Lion Publications.

Puri, Bharati (2006) *Engaged Buddhism: The Dalai Lama's Worldview,* New Delhi: Oxford University Press.

Queen, Christopher S. (1996) "Introduction: The Shapes and Sources of Engaged Buddhism," in Christopher S. Queen and Sallie B. King (eds.) *Engaged*

*Buddhism: Buddhist Liberation Movements in Asia,* Albany: State University of New York Press, 1–44.

——— (ed.) (2000a) *Engaged Buddhism in the West,* Boston: Wisdom Publications.

——— (2000b) "Introduction: A New Buddhism," in Christopher S. Queen (ed.) *Engaged Buddhism in the West,* Boston: Wisdom Publications, 1–31.

Queen, Christopher S. and King, Sallie B. (eds.) (1996) *Engaged Buddhism: Buddhist Liberation Movements in Asia,* Albany: State University of New York Press.

Rahula, Walpola Sri (1974) *What the Buddha Taught,* Revised Edition, New York: Grove Press.

Rawls, John (1971) *A Theory of Justice,* Cambridge, MA: Harvard University Press.

——— (1993) *Political Liberalism,* New York: Columbia University Press.

Regan, Tom (1983) *The Case for Animal Rights,* Berkeley: University of California Press.

Reichenbach, Bruce R. (1990) *The Law of Karma: A Philosophical Study,* Honolulu: University of Hawai'i Press.

Renteln, Alison Dundes (1990) *International Human Rights: Universalism versus Relativism,* Newbury Park, CA: Sage Publications.

Repetti, Riccardo (2010a) "Meditation and Mental Freedom: A Buddhist Theory of Free Will," *Journal of Buddhist Ethics* 17: 165–212.

——— (2010b) "Earlier Buddhist Theories of Free Will: Compatibilism," *Journal of Buddhist Ethics* 17: 279–310.

——— (2012a) "Buddhist Reductionism and Free Will: Paleo-Compatibilism," *Journal of Buddhist Ethics* 19: 33–95.

——— (2012b) "Buddhist Hard Determinism," *Journal of Buddhist Ethics* 19: 130–97.

——— (2014) "Recent Buddhist Theories of Free Will: Compatibilism, Incompatibilism, and Beyond," *Journal of Buddhist Ethics* 21: 272–345.

Ross, W. D. (1988) *The Right and the Good,* Indianapolis, IN: Hackett Publishing Company.

Sahni, Pragati (2008) *Environmental Ethics in Buddhism: A Virtues Approach,* Abingdon, UK: Routledge.

Sandler, Ronald L. (2007) *Character and Environment: A Virtue-Oriented Approach to Environmental Ethics,* New York: Columbia University Press.

Sayre-McCord, Geoff (Spring 2012) "Metaethics," *The Stanford Encyclopedia of Philosophy,* Edward N. Zalta (ed.), Retrieved from http://plato.stanford.edu/archives/spr2012/entries/metaethics

Schilbrack, Kevin (1997) "The General and the Particular in Theravada Ethics: A Response to Charles Hallisey," *Journal of Buddhist Ethics* 4: 98–111.

Schmithausen, Lambert (1997) "The Early Buddhist Tradition and Ecological Ethics," *Journal of Buddhist Ethics* 4: 1–74.

——— (1999) "Aspects of the Buddhist Attitude Towards War," in Jan E. M. Houben and Karel R. van Kooij (eds.) *Violence Denied: Violence, Non-Violence and the Rationalization of Violence in South Asian Cultural History,* Leiden: Brill, 45–67.

Schroeder, John W. (2001) *Skillful Means: The Heart of Buddhist Compassion,* Honolulu: University of Hawai'i Press.

Seneca (1995) "On Anger" in John M. Cooper and J.F. Procopé (eds. and trs.) *Seneca: Moral and Political Essays,* Cambridge: Cambridge University Press, 3–116.

Sevilla, Anton Luis (2010) "Founding Human Rights within Buddhism" Exploring Buddha-Nature as an Ethical Foundation," *Journal of Buddhist Ethics* 17: 213–52.

Shiotsu, Toru (1999) "Buddhism and Human Rights: Points of Convergence. How Can Buddhism Clarify the Modern View of Human Rights?" *The Journal of Oriental Studies* 9.

Shulman, Eviatar (2010) "Mindful Wisdom: The *Sati-paṭṭhāna Sutta* on Mindfulness, Memory, and Liberation," *History of Religions* 49: 393–420.

Siderits, Mark (1987) "Beyond Compatibilism: A Buddhist Approach to Freedom and Determinism," *American Philosophical Quarterly* 24: 149–59.

———— (2000a) "The Reality of Altruism: Reconstructing Śāntideva," *Philosophy East and West* 50: 412–24.

———— (2000b) "Reply to Paul Williams," *Philosophy East and West* 50: 453-59.

———— (2001) "Buddhism and Techno-Physicalism: Is the Eightfold Path a Program?" *Philosophy East and West* 51: 307–14.

———— (2003) *Personal Identity and Buddhist Philosophy: Empty Persons,* Burlington, VT: Ashgate.

———— (2007a) *Buddhism as Philosophy: An Introduction,* Indianapolis, IN: Hackett Publishing Company.

———— (2007b) "Buddhist Reductionism and the Structure of Buddhist Ethics," in Purushottama Bilimoria, Joseph Prabhu and Renuka Sharma (eds.) *Indian Ethics: Classical Traditions and Contemporary Challenges,* Vol. 1, Burlington, VT: Ashgate, 283–95.

———— (2008) "Paleo-Compatibilism and Buddhist Reductionism," *Sophia* 47: 29–42.

———— (2013) "Buddhist Paleocompatibilism," *Philosophy East and West* 63: 73–87.

Simmer-Brown, Judith (2000) "Speaking Truth to Power: The Buddhist Peace Fellowship," in Christopher S. Queen (ed.) *Engaged Buddhism in the West*, Boston: Wisdom Publications, 67–94.

Singer, Peter (2000) *Writings on an Ethical Life,* New York: The Ecco Press (HarperCollins).

Sivaraksa, Sulak (1992) *Seeds of Peace: A Buddhist Vision for Renewing Society,* Tom Ginsburg (ed.), Berkeley, CA: Parallax Press.

———— (2005) *Conflict, Culture, Change: Engaged Buddhism in a Globalizing World,* Boston: Wisdom Publications.

Sorabji, Richard (2000) *Emotion and Peace of Mind: From Stoic Agitation to Christian Temptation,* New York: Oxford University Press.

Sponberg, Alan (1997) "Green Buddhism and the Hierarchy of Compassion," in Mary Evelyn Tucker and Duncan Ryūken Williams (eds.) *Buddhism and Ecology: The Interconnection of Dharma and Deeds,* Cambridge, MA: Harvard University Press, 351–76.

Sridharan, Vishnu (2013) "The Metaphysics of No-Self: A Determinist Deflation of the Free Will Problem," *Journal of Buddhist Ethics* 20: 287–305.

Stalnaker, Aaron (2013) "Comparative Religious Ethics," in Hugh LaFollette (ed.) *The International Encyclopedia of Ethics,* Malden, MA: Blackwell Publishing, 944–53.

Statman, Daniel (1997) "Introduction to Virtue Ethics," in Daniel Statman (ed.) *Virtue Ethics: A Critical Reader,* Washington, DC: Georgetown University Press, 1–41.

Stewart, James J. (2010) "The Question of Vegetarianism and Diet in Pāli Buddhism," *Journal of Buddhist Ethics* 17: 100–40.

Stevenson, I. (1987) *Children Who Remember Previous Lives,* Charlottesville: The University Press of Virginia.

Stocker, Michael (1976) "The Schizophrenia of Modern Ethical Theories," *The Journal of Philosophy* 73: 453–66.

Strawson, Galen (1993) "On 'Freedom and Resentment'," in John Martin Fischer and Mark Ravizza (eds.) *Perspectives on Moral Responsibility,* Ithaca, NY: Cornell University Press, 67–100.

Strawson, P.F. (1974) "Freedom and Resentment," in *Freedom and Resentment,* London: Methuen, 1–25.

Swearer, Donald K. (1992) "Exemplars of Nonviolence in Theravada Buddhism," in Kenneth Kraft (ed.) *Inner Peace, World Peace: Essays on Buddhism and Nonviolence,* Albany: State University of New York Press, 63–76.

——— (1996) "Sulak Sivaraksa's Buddhist Vision for Renewing Society," in Christopher S. Queen and Sallie B. King (eds.) *Engaged Buddhism: Buddhist Liberation Movements in Asia,* Albany: State University of New York Press, 195–235.

Taylor, Charles (1996) "A World Consensus on Human Rights?" *Dissent* 43: 15–21.

Taylor, Paul W. (1986) *Respect for Nature: A Theory of Environmental Ethics,* Princeton, NJ: Princeton University Press.

Thurman, Robert A.F. (1988a) "Nagarjuna's Guidelines for Buddhist Social Action," in Fred Eppsteiner (ed.) *The Path of Compassion: Writings on Socially Engaged Buddhism,* Revised Second Edition, Berkeley, CA: Parallax Press, 120–44.

——— (1988b) "Edicts of Asoka," in Fred Eppsteiner (ed.) *The Path of Compassion: Writings on Socially Engaged Buddhism,* Revised Second Edition, Berkeley, CA: Parallax Press, 111–19.

——— (1992) "Tibet and the Monastic Army of Peace," in Kenneth Kraft (ed.) *Inner Peace, World Peace: Essays on Buddhism and Nonviolence,* Albany: State University of New York Press, 77–90.

Tillemans, Tom J.F. (2011) "Madhyamaka Buddhist Ethics," *Journal of the International Association of Buddhist Studies* 33: 353–72.

———— (2013) "Yogic Perception, Meditation, and Enlightenment: The Epistemological Issues in a Key Debate," in Steven M. Emmanuel (ed.) *A Companion to Buddhist Philosophy,* West Sussex: John Wiley & Sons, 290–306.

Tucker, Mary Evelyn and Williams, Duncan Ryūken (eds.) (1997) *Buddhism and Ecology: The Interconnection of Dharma and Deeds,* Cambridge, MA: Harvard University Press.

Tuske, Joerg (2013) "The Non-Self Theory and Problems in the Philosophy of Mind," in Steven M. Emmanuel (ed.) *A Companion to Buddhist Philosophy*, West Sussex: John Wiley & Sons, 419–28.

United Nations (1995a) "Charter of the United Nations," in United Nations Department of Public Information (ed.) *The United Nations and Human Rights 1945–1995,* New York: United Nations Reproduction Section, 143–6.

———— (1995b) "Universal Declaration of Human Rights," in United Nations Department of Public Information (ed.) *The United Nations and Human Rights 1945–1995,* New York: United Nations Reproduction Section, 153–5.

Vélez de Cea, Abraham (2004) "Criteria of Goodness in the Pāli Nikāyas," *Journal of Buddhist Ethics* 11: 123–42.

———— (2005) "Dark and Bright Karma: A New Reading," *Journal of Buddhist Ethics* 12.

———— (2010) "Value Pluralism in Early Buddhism," *Journal of the International Association of Buddhist Studies* 33: 211–37.

———— (2013) "The Dalai Lama and the Nature of Buddhist Ethics," *Journal of Buddhist Ethics* 20: 499–540.

Vernezze, Peter J. (2008) "Moderation or the Middle Way: Two Approaches to Anger," *Philosophy East and West* 58: 2–16.

Victoria, Brian Daizen (2006) *Zen at War,* Second Edition, Lanham, MD: Rowman & Littlefield Publishers.

———— (2010) "A Buddhological Critique of 'Soldier-Zen' in Wartime Japan," in Michael K. Jerryson and Mark Juergensmeyer (eds.) *Buddhist Warfare,* Oxford: Oxford University Press, 105–30.

Waldau, Paul (2000) "Buddhism and Animal Rights" in Damien Keown (ed.) *Contemporary Buddhist Ethics,* Richmond, Surrey: Curzon Press, 81–112.

Wallace, B. Alan (2008) "A Buddhist View of Free Will: Beyond Determinism and Indeterminism," in Robert Pollack (ed.) *Neurosciences and Free Will,* New York: The Earth Institute at Columbia University, 59–69.

Watts, Jonathan S. (ed.) (2009a) *Rethinking Karma: The Dharma of Social Justice,* Chiang Mai, Thailand: Silkworm Books.

———— (2009b) "Karma for Everyone: Social Justice and the Problem of Re-ethicizing Karma in Theravada Buddhist Societies," in Jonathan S. Watts (ed.) *Rethinking Karma: The Dharma of Social Justice,* Chiang Mai, Thailand: Silkworm Books, 13–36.

Webster, David (2005) *The Philosophy of Desire in the Buddhist Pāli Canon*, London: RoutledgeCurzon.

Weng, Helen Y. *et al.* (2013) "Compassion Training Alters Altruism and Neural Responses to Suffering," *Psychological Science* 24: 1171–80.

Westerhoff, Jan Christoph (Fall 2010) "Nāgārjuna," *The Stanford Encyclopedia of Philosophy,* Edward N. Zalta (ed.), Retrieved from http://plato.stanford.edu/archives/fall2010/entries/nagarjuna/

——— (2011) "Abhidharma Philosophy," in Jay L. Garfield and William Edelglass (eds.) *The Oxford Handbook of World Philosophy,* London: Oxford University Press, 193–204.

Wetlesen, Jon (2002) "Did Śāntideva Destroy the Bodhisattva Path?" *Journal of Buddhist Ethics* 9: 34–88.

Whitehill, James (1987) "Is There a Zen Ethic?" *Eastern Buddhist* 20: 9–33.

——— (1994) "Buddhist Ethics in Western Context: The 'Virtues' Approach," *Journal of Buddhist Ethics* 1: 1–22.

Williams, Bernard (1985) *Ethics and the Limits of Philosophy,* Cambridge, MA: Harvard University Press.

Williams, Paul (1998) "The Absence of Self and the Removal of Pain: How Śāntideva Destroyed the Bodhisattva Path," in *Altruism and Reality: Studies in the Philosophy of the Bodhicaryāvatāra,* Richmond, Surrey: Curzon Press, 104–76.

——— (2000) "Response to Mark Siderits' Review," *Philosophy East and West* 50: 424–53.

——— (2009a) *Mahāyāna Buddhism: The Doctrinal Foundations,* Second Edition, London: Routledge.

——— (2009b) "Is Buddhist Ethics Virtue Ethics? Toward a Dialogue with Santideva and a Footnote to Keown," in John Powers and Charles S. Prebish (eds.) *Destroying Māra Forever: Buddhist Ethics Essays in Honor of Damien Keown,* Ithaca, NY: Snow Lion Publications. 113–37.

Williams, Paul, Tribe, Anthony and Wynne, Alexander (2012) *Buddhist Thought: A Complete Introduction to the Indian Tradition,* Second Edition, London: Routledge.

Wilson, Liz (2012) "Buddhism and Gender," in David L. McMahan (ed.) *Buddhism in the Modern World,* London: Routledge, 257–72.

Wong, David B. (2006) "The Meaning of Detachment in Daoism, Buddhism, and Stoicism," *Dao: A Journal of Comparative Philosophy* 5: 207–19.

——— (Fall 2011) "Comparative Philosophy: Chinese and Western," *The Stanford Encyclopedia of Philosophy,* Edward N. Zalta (ed.), Retrieved from http://plato.stanford.edu/entries/comparphil-chiwes/

Wright, Dale S. (2005) "Critical Questions Towards a Naturalized Concept of Karma in Buddhism," *Journal of Buddhist Ethics* 12: 78–93.

——— (2009) *The Six Perfections: Buddhism and the Cultivation of Character,* New York: Oxford University Press.

Yamamoto, Shuichi (2002) "Mahayana Buddhism and Environmental Ethics: From the Perspective of the Consciousness-Only Doctrine," *Journal of Oriental Studies* 11: 167–80.

Yarnall, Thomas Freeman (2003) "Engaged Buddhism: New and Improved? Made in the USA of Asian Materials," in Christopher Queen, Charles Prebish and Damien Keown (eds.) *Action Dharma: New Studies in Engaged Buddhism,* London: RoutledgeCurzon, 286–344.

Zimmermann, Michael (ed.) (2006) With the Assistance of Chiew Hui Ho and Philip Pierce, *Buddhism and Violence,* Lumbini: Lumbini International Research Institute.

# Index

Made in the USA
Middletown, DE
30 December 2020